iOS 6 Application Development

FOR

DUMMIES®

by Neal Goldstein
and Dave Wilson

WILEY

John Wiley & Sons, Inc.

iOS 6 Application Development For Dummies®

Published by
John Wiley & Sons, Inc.
111 River Street
Hoboken, NJ 07030-5774

www.wiley.com

Copyright © 2013 by John Wiley & Sons, Inc., Hoboken, New Jersey

Published by John Wiley & Sons, Inc., Hoboken, New Jersey

Published simultaneously in Canada

For general information on our other products and services, please contact our Customer Care Department within the U.S. at 877-762-2974, outside the U.S. at 317-572-3993, or fax 317-572-4002.

For technical support, please visit www.wiley.com/techsupport.

Wiley also publishes its books in a variety of electronic formats and by print-on-demand. Not all content that is available in standard print versions of this book may appear or be packaged in all book formats. If you have purchased a version of this book that did not include media that is referenced by or accompanies a standard print version, you may request this media by visiting http://booksupport.wiley.com. For more information about Wiley products, visit us www.wiley.com.

Library of Congress Control Number: 2012955762

ISBN 978-1-118-50880-0 (pbk); ISBN 978-1-118-55006-9 (ebk); ISBN 978-1-118-55013-7 (ebk); ISBN 978-1-118-55095-3 (ebk)

Manufactured in the United States of America

10 9 8 7 6 5 4 3 2 1

WILEY

About the Authors

Neal Goldstein is a recognized leader in making state-of-the-art and cutting-edge technologies practical for commercial and enterprise development. He was one of the first technologists to work with commercial developers at firms such as Apple Computer, Lucasfilm, and Mircrosoft to develop commercial applications using object-based programming technologies. He was a pioneer in moving that approach into the corporate world for developers at Liberty Mutual Insurance, USWest (now Verizon), National Car Rental, EDS, and Continental Airlines, showing them how object-oriented programming could solve enterprise-wide problems. His book (with Jeff Alger) on object-oriented development, *Developing Object-Oriented Software for the Macintosh* (Addison Wesley, 1992), introduced the idea of scenarios and patterns to developers. He was an early advocate of the Microsoft .NET framework, and he successfully introduced it into many enterprises, including Charles Schwab. He was one of the earliest developers of Service Oriented Architecture (SOA), and as Senior Vice President of Advanced Technology and the Chief Architect at Charles Schwab, he built an integrated SOA solution that spanned the enterprise, from desktop PCs to servers to complex network mainframes. (He holds six patents as a result.) As one of IBM's largest customers, he introduced the folks at IBM to SOA at the enterprise level and encouraged them to head in that direction.

Since the release of the iPhone SDK in March 2008, he has been focusing on mobile applications and has had eight applications in the App Store, including a series of Travel Photo Guides (developed with his partners at mobile fortytwo), and a Digital Field Guides series (`http://lp.wileypub.com/ DestinationDFGiPhoneApp`), developed in partnership with Wiley. He also has a free app called Expense Diary that allows you to keep track of things like expenses, mileage, and time by adding them to your calendar.

He has developed mobile strategies for a number of businesses, ranging from National Cinemedia to the American Automobile Association (AAA). His strategies focus on Mobile 2.0 — integrating mobile across the enterprise, creating a consistent user experience across devices and applications in an application ecosystem, and developing a user experience architecture that both leverages — and is constrained by — the device. He has spent the last three years working with mobile device users and developers to determine what makes mobile devices so appealing, what users want from an application on a phone or tablet, and what makes an app compelling. These efforts have resulted in the Application Ecosystem model for mobile applications and an underlying Model Application Controller Architecture based on web services, that has become a key element in his client work and his books.

In his copious spare time, he also teaches introductory and advanced classes on iPhone and iPad development (for clients as well as some public classes) and does expert witness work.

He has also written several books on iPhone programming: *iPhone Application Development For Dummies* (multiple editions all published by Wiley), *Objective-C For Dummies* (multiple editions all published by Wiley), and he co-authored (with Tony Bove) *iPad Application Development For Dummies* (multiple editions published by Wiley) and *iPhone Application Development All-in-One For Dummies* (Wiley). He is also the primary author (with Jon Manning and Paris Buttfield-Addison) of *iPhone & iPad Game Development For Dummies*.

Dave Wilson is the sole proprietor of Personal Concepts and an independent software consultant and software developer living in San Jose, California. Although Dave has a Bachelor's degree in Engineering Physics from Cornell University, and a Masters and Ph.D. in Applied Physics from Stanford University, he doesn't do physics research anymore — other than occasionally looking under the bed for Dark Energy, and collecting Higgs bosons for fun and profit.

Dave's areas of software expertise include graphical user interfaces, object-oriented programming, frameworks, and developing iOS apps.

Dave developed and taught the first regularly scheduled classes on Macintosh programming for Apple starting in 1984 and taught Apple's first regularly scheduled classes on object-oriented programming starting in 1987. He also taught Smalltalk-80 programming classes for Xerox PARC (and then ParcPlace) — the inventors of Smalltalk. Dave also taught advanced Java programming classes for Sun Microsystems — the inventors of Java and still teaches iOS programming classes when he has time.

Dave has presented programming seminars for IBM, Boeing, Visa International, and many other clients in lots of interesting places, such as London; Tokyo; Hamburg, Germany; Melbourne, Australia; and even Infinite Loop in Cupertino, California.

Dave was the lead author on a number of quick-reference guides and programming books, including the *IBM PC Diskguide*, *Programming with MacApp*, and *C++ Programming with MacApp*.

Dave's iPhone and iPad apps include *Deadlines*, *Rick Sammon's 24/7 Photo Buffet*, *Rick Sammon's 24/7 Photo Buffet for iPad*, and *Rick Sammon's iHDR*.

Dave also does expert witness work, which has included at least ten visits to the U.S. Patent and Trademark office. He has twice testified at trial, which is much less fun, and much more stressful, than writing iOS apps.

Dedication

To my friends and family, and especially my children Sarah and Evan and my wife, Linda. She deserves special recognition for her support and patience and for maintaining her (and my) sense of humor. Without her support, I never would have been able to write 12 books in 3.5 years. Thank you so much.

This is for you
As day follows night
The tunnel ends in the light
Finally time to play

— Neal Goldstein

To my wife, Cheryl, for being tolerant of all the time I spend in front of a Macintosh.

— Dave Wilson

Authors' Acknowledgments

Or thanks to Sr. Project Editor, Mark Enochs; Sr. Acquisitions Editor, Kyle Looper; Copy Editor, John Edwards; and Technical Editor, Jesse Feiler.

Publisher's Acknowledgments

We're proud of this book; please send us your comments at http://dummies.custhelp.com. For other comments, please contact our Customer Care Department within the U.S. at 877-762-2974, outside the U.S. at 317-572-3993, or fax 317-572-4002.

Some of the people who helped bring this book to market include the following:

Acquisitions and Editorial

Sr. Project Editor: Mark Enochs

Sr. Acquisitions Editor: Kyle Looper

Copy Editor: John Edwards

Technical Editor: Jesse Feiler

Editorial Manager: Leah Michael

Editorial Assistant: Anne Sullivan

Sr. Editorial Assistant: Cherie Case

Cover Photo: Cardboard box © 123render/iStockphoto.com; toolbox, wrench, hammer, gears, and calendar icons © PhotoHamster/iStockphoto.com; apple icon © Paul Pantazescu/iStockphoto.com

Cartoons: Rich Tennant (www.the5thwave.com)

Composition Services

Project Coordinator: Patrick Redmond

Layout and Graphics: Christin Swinford

Proofreaders: John Greenough, Evelyn Wellborn

Indexer: Broccoli Information Mgt.

Publishing and Editorial for Technology Dummies

    Richard Swadley, Vice President and Executive Group Publisher

    Andy Cummings, Vice President and Publisher

    Mary Bednarek, Executive Acquisitions Director

    Mary C. Corder, Editorial Director

Publishing for Consumer Dummies

    Kathy Nebenhaus, Vice President and Executive Publisher

Composition Services

    Debbie Stailey, Director of Composition Services

Table of Contents

Part III: Getting Your Feet Wet — Basic Functionality 203

Chapter 8: It's (Finally) Time to Code 205

Chapter 9: Adding Outlets and Actions to Your RoadTrip Code 235

Introduction

*i*OS 6 Application Development For Dummies* is a beginner's guide to developing iOS applications. And not only do you *not* need any iOS development experience to get started, but you also don't need any Macintosh development experience, either. We've written this book as though you are coming to iPhone and iPad application development as a blank slate, ready to be filled with useful information and new ways to do things. Well, almost a blank slate, anyway; see the upcoming "Foolish Assumptions" section for details on what you need to know before using this book.

Because of the nature of the iPhone and iPad, you can create small, bite-sized applications that can be quite powerful. Also, because you can start small and create real applications that do something important for a user, it's relatively easy to transform yourself from an "I know nothing" person into a developer who, though not (yet) a superstar, can still crank out quite a respectable application.

But the iPhone and iPad can be home to some pretty fancy software as well — so we'll take you on a journey through building an industrial-strength application and show you the ropes for developing one on your own.

A Bit of History

It's 6:00 a.m. PST on January 9, 2007. One of us (Dave) is walking through a cold mist to join the end of a distressingly long line of nerds wrapped all the way around San Francisco's Moscone Center. Why? To hear Steve Jobs give his MacWorld Expo keynote address. It was nuts to get up so early on a cold morning, but Steve Jobs was rumored to be introducing an Apple phone.

No one knew whether an Apple phone would be any good, but perhaps Steve would show us magic — something that would revolutionize an industry. Perhaps it would be as cool and important as the iPod! Probably not, but I wanted to be there, just in case.

A few hours later, Steve told us that "Apple is going to reinvent the phone." Steve was never modest, but he was certainly correct — Apple completely blew away the phone industry that day. The damage was not yet visible to the current phone vendors (Palm, Motorola, Nokia, Sony, Ericsson, RIM, and Microsoft), but they were suddenly left back in the twentieth century. The future had arrived.

The iPhone Stands Alone

The first iPhone shipped in late June 2007. It came with a bunch of Apple's native apps such as Contacts, Maps, Stocks, Safari, and so on. The problem was that only Apple could develop these native apps. The Apple developer "evangelists" told us developers that we should be happy writing web apps. This did not make us happy — we wanted to write native Objective-C apps.

Steve Jobs and Apple eventually saw the light. Apple released a beta version of the iPhone Software Development Kit (SDK) in the spring of 2008, and it opened the App Store for business in July 2008. At this point, you could develop apps — but only for the iPhone, because the iPad did not yet exist.

The iPad Joins the Party

Apple released the first iPad in April 2010, so now you could write apps for either the iPhone or the iPad.

Many developers then developed two different versions of each application — one for the iPhone and a different one (often called the "HD" version back in 2010) optimized for the larger iPad screen. The problem was that you would then have two separate Xcode projects to maintain. Some of the project code would be shared between the iPhone and iPad versions, but many of the files would be slightly different. Code maintenance became a nightmare.

It gradually became clear that it would be better to have a single Xcode project that could be used to build a universal app — a single app that runs with the iPhone user interface on the iPhone, but uses a different iPad user interface on the iPad.

A Universal App

"So," you say, "What are the benefits of merging the iPhone and iPad apps into a single universal app?" The benefits include the following:

- ✔ You can add a new feature in the one Xcode project that can appear in both the iPhone and iPad versions.
- ✔ You can fix a bug in one project rather than two.
- ✔ You only have to make changes for a new version of iOS in one project.
- ✔ You only have to make changes for new versions of Objective-C or the compiler in one place.

Serial or Parallel Development?

This book shows you how to build a universal version of our RoadTrip project. The compiled native app will run on the iPhone with a user interface designed for the iPhone. The same app will run on the iPad with a different user interface, optimized for the iPad's larger screen. The obvious question involves the order in which the different versions are developed. Your choices are diagrammed in the following figure, where time flows to the right. (Einstein's special theory of relativity proved that time always flows to the right, unless you are in the southern hemisphere.)

Strategies you can use include the following:

A. (Serial) Develop and test the iPhone version first, and later add the iPad version to the universal Xcode project.

B. (Serial) Develop and test the iPad version first, and later add the iPhone version to the universal Xcode project.

C. (Parallel) Incrementally develop both versions, more or less in parallel. Get the basic iPhone and iPad versions each working. Then add features to each version until time runs out. This is the approach we recommend, and the approach we use in this book.

Our Plan for This Book

You will build this book's RoadTrip app using the following steps:

1. Create the initial storyboards for both the iPad and iPhone versions, starting with Xcode's Master-Detail project template.

   The template's iPad storyboard is based on using UIKit's `UISplitView Controller`, which uses the same custom `MasterViewController` and custom `DetailViewController` used in the iPhone version. The Master View controller will appear on the left when the iPad is held in landscape orientation, while the Detail View controller appears on the right.

2. Build and test the iPad version in the iPad simulator. You should see a Table view embedded in a Navigation controller in the Master view.

   The template's initial iPhone storyboard design begins with a custom `MasterViewController` (a Table view) embedded in a Navigation view. Selecting an item in the Table view displays data managed by a custom `DetailViewController`.

3. Build and test the iPhone version in the iPhone simulator. It should also work perfectly, because you haven't had a chance to make any mistakes yet.

   The opening screens of the iPhone and iPad versions are compared in the following figure, as created by the Master-Detail template.

4. Add a `TestDriveController` to the iPhone storyboard. Build and test. Add it to the iPad storyboard. Build and test.

5. Add animation and sound to the Test Drive controller. Build and test both (BATB) the iPhone and iPad versions.

6. Add additional features to each version until done.

The final screens of the iPhone and iPad versions of RoadTrip are compared in the following figure.

iOS and Xcode Game Changers

With iOS 6 and — more importantly — with Xcode 4.5 (and later versions), the nuts and bolts of iOS application development have changed dramatically. Xcode 4.5 has added much more functionality to the Integrated Development Environment (IDE) with which you develop iOS applications, especially when it comes to writing syntactically correct (and bug-free) code that's better able to manage memory. Storyboards, one of our all-time favorite new features, allow you to develop applications in a new way, with much less code and a better idea of what the flow of the application (and subsequent user experience) will be. Of course, for all this new functionality, you pay a price: more complexity. But after you get the hang of working with Xcode 4.5, writing applications becomes much easier than it has ever been.

Of course, the rub is getting the hang of Xcode 4.5. That's where we come in. We carefully take you through Xcode 4.5, pointing out its features and describing how to best use them. When you set this book aside, you'll have a great understanding of how to take advantage of all those features that will make your life easier.

You find out how to develop a single application that includes features that readers and students of earlier books have been asking for — including more animation and sound — as well as an infrastructure that people can use to develop more robust applications. The resulting example is an app we call RoadTrip, which can send you on your way to developing apps that you can be proud of and that other people will want to have.

This new edition is based on iOS 6 *and* Xcode 4.5. If you want to find out how to develop applications, the tools discussed in this book are the tools you absolutely need to use to do it the right way.

But what's more, storyboards all of a sudden make it easier to develop universal applications — applications that run with equal aplomb on the iPad or iPhone — using the same code base!

This is great stuff!

About This Book

iOS 6 Application Development For Dummies distills the hundreds (or even thousands) of pages of Apple documentation (not to mention our own development experience) into only what's necessary to start you developing real applications. But this is no recipe book that leaves it up to you to put it all together. Rather, it takes you through the frameworks (the code supplied in the SDK) and iOS architecture in a way that gives you a solid foundation in how applications really work, and also acts as a road map to expand your knowledge as you need to.

We assume that you're in this for the long haul and that you want to master the whole application-development ball of wax. We use real-world applications to show the concepts and give you the background on how things actually work on iOS — the in-depth knowledge you need to go beyond the simple "Hello World" apps and create those killer iOS applications. So be prepared! You may find some places where you might want to say, "Get on with it," but — based on our experience (including more than ten apps in the App Store, 12 books (and counting), and untold hours expended on in-person classes and technical talks — you'll find what you need to move from following recipes in a cookbook by rote to modifying and even creating your own recipes.

It's a multicourse banquet, intended to make you feel satisfied (and really full) at the end.

Conventions Used in This Book

This book guides you through the process of building iOS applications. Throughout the book, you use the classes provided by Apple's iOS frameworks (and create new classes of your own, of course). You code them using the Objective-C programming language.

Code examples in this book appear in a monospaced font so that they stand out a bit better. That means that the code you see will look like this:

```
#import <UIKit/ UIKit.h>
```

Objective-C is based on C, which *is* case sensitive, so please enter the code that appears in this book *exactly* as it appears in the text. We also use the standard Objective-C naming conventions — for example, class names always start with a capital letter, and the names of methods and instance variables always start with a lowercase letter.

Note that all URLs in this book appear in a monospaced font as well, like this:

```
www.nealgoldstein.com
```

When we ask you to add code to a program, it will be in bold like this:

```
#import <UIKit/ UIKit.h>
```

You'll notice — starting around Chapter 8 — that you will sometimes be asked to delete some of the code you have in place for your project to make room for some new stuff. When that happens, we'll comment out the code (to make things really clear). We refer to code we want you to delete as commented out, bold, underline, and italic code, because said code will show up as commented out, bold, underlined, and italic. Simple enough, as shown in the following example:

```
// Delete this
```

If you're ever uncertain about anything in the code, you can always look at the source code on Neal's website at `www.nealgoldstein.com` or the For Dummies website at `www.dummies.com/go/ios6application development`. From time to time, we'll provide updates for the code there and post other things you might find useful.

Foolish Assumptions

To begin programming your iOS applications, you need an Intel-based Macintosh computer with the latest version of OS X on it. (No, you can't develop iOS applications directly on the iPhone or iPad.) You also need to download the iOS Software Development Kit (SDK) — which is free. And, oh yeah, you need an iPhone and/or iPad. You won't start running your application on it right away — you'll use the iOS Simulator that Apple provides with the iOS SDK during the initial stages of development — but at some point, you'll want to test your application on a real, live iOS device.

This book assumes that you have some programming knowledge and that you have at least a passing acquaintance with object-oriented programming, using some variant of the C language (such as C++, C#, or maybe even Objective-C). In case you don't, we point out some resources that can help you get up to speed. The application example in this book is based on the frameworks that come with the SDK; the code is pretty simple (usually) and straightforward. (We don't use this book as a platform to dazzle you with fancy coding techniques.)

We also assume that you're familiar with the iPhone and iPad themselves and that you've at least explored Apple's included applications to get a good working sense of an iOS app's look and feel. It might also help to browse the App Store to see the kinds of applications available there and maybe even download a few free ones (as if we could stop you).

How This Book Is Organized

iOS 6 Application Development For Dummies has six main parts, which are described in the following sections.

Part 1: Getting Started

Part I introduces you to the iOS world. You find out what makes a great iOS application and see how an iOS application is structured. In Chapter 2, we give an overview of how Xcode 4.5 works that gets you up to speed on all its features; you can use this chapter as a reference and return to it as needed. You also create your Xcode project in this part — a universal application that can run equally well on an iPad or iPhone — and we take you on a guided tour of what makes up the Xcode project that will become your home away from home.

Part II: Building RoadTrip

In this part of the book, you find out how to create the kind of user interface that will capture someone's imagination. We explain the Interface Builder editor, which is much more than your run-of-the-mill program for building graphical user interfaces. You also discover storyboards, which are the icing on the Interface Builder cake that let you lay out the entire user experience and application flow — saving you a lot of coding, to boot.

We also take you on a brief tour of the RoadTrip app, the app that you build along with us in this book. We show you not only what the app can do but also how it uses the frameworks and SDK to do that.

We also explain how the main components of an iOS application go together. We describe how the iOS applications work from a viewpoint of classes and design patterns, as well as show how the app works at runtime. We spend some time on three very important ideas: how to extend the framework classes to do what you want them to, how to manage memory, and how to take advantage of declared properties. We also explain how everything works together at runtime, which should give you a real feel for how an iOS application works.

Parts I and II give you the fundamental background that you need to develop iOS applications.

Part III: Getting Your Feet Wet — Basic Functionality

Now that you have the foundation in place, Part III starts you on the process of having your application actually *do* something. You start off by determining whether a network is available to support the application functionality that requires Internet access. You find out how to customize the appearance of the controls provided by the framework to make your application a thing of beauty. You finish off by adding animation and sound just to get going. You also see how to connect the elements on your storyboard to your application code to make them do things — such as have a '59 pink Cadillac Eldorado Biarritz convertible drive up and down the screen.

Part IV: The Model and Application Structure

Now you begin to get down to the real work. You find out about the iPad's popovers and Split View controllers, and you also add navigation to the application. Along the way, we really get into showing you how to account for the differences between an iPad and an iPhone, and make sure that the app can run flawlessly on whatever device the user has handy. You also add the application model, which provides both the data and the logic you need to create an application that delivers real value to the user. Finally, you finish the storyboard so that you can see your basic application flow.

Part V: Adding the Application Content

Now that you have the application foundation and the user experience architecture in place, Part V takes you into the world of applications that contain major functionality. We show you how to display the weather using a web page right off the Internet, how to allow the user to page through local events as if he were reading a book, how to display a map of where the user is going and where he is right now, how to find a location that he has always wanted to visit and display it on a map, and even how to change where he is going (limited in the RoadTrip app to New York and San Francisco, but it's incredibly easy to add other destinations). We don't go slogging through every detail of every detail, but we demonstrate almost all the technology you need to master if you intend to create a compelling application like this on your own.

Part VI: The Part of Tens

Part VI consists of some tips to help you avoid having to discover everything the hard way. It talks about approaching application development in an "adult" way right from the beginning (without taking the fun out of it). We also revisit the app and explain what else you would need to do to make this app a commercial and critical success.

Icons Used in This Book

This icon indicates a useful pointer that you shouldn't skip.

This icon represents a friendly reminder. It describes a vital point that you should keep in mind while proceeding through a particular section of the chapter.

This icon signifies that the accompanying explanation may be informative (dare we say interesting?), but it isn't essential to understanding iPad application development. Feel free to skip past these tidbits if you like (though skipping while learning may be tricky).

This icon alerts you to potential problems that you may encounter along the way. Read and obey these blurbs to avoid trouble.

This icon indicates how to use an important part of Xcode functionality. This helps you wade through Xcode's complexity and focus on how to get specific things done.

Where to Go from Here

It's time to explore iOS application development! If you're nervous, take heart: We've received lots of e-mails (and an occasional card or letter) from readers ranging in age from 12 to 67 who tell us how they're doing (and yes, we do respond to them all).

Also, be sure to visit the companion website for this book at `www.dummies.com/go/ios6applicationdevelopmentfd` for source code, all the figures from the book, and other information. For updates to this edition, check out `http://www.dummies.com/go/ios6applicationdevelopmentfd updates`. For helpful tables and tips, check out the book's cheat sheet at `www.dummies.com/cheatsheet/ios6applicationdevelopment`.

Go have some fun!

Part I
Getting Started

The 5th Wave   By Rich Tennant

In this part . . .

So, you've decided you want to develop some software for the iPhone, iPod touch, and/or iPad. You have a good idea for an app — one that displays information about interesting places, with maps showing how to get there. Now what?

This part of the book lays out what you need to know to get started on the development journey. First, what makes a great iOS application? Knowing that, you can evaluate your idea, see how it ranks, and maybe figure out what you have to do to transform it into something that knocks your users' socks off.

This part shows you how to use the iOS Software Development Kit (SDK), which includes Xcode — your home away from home when you are developing your app. You also find out how to create an Xcode project, within which you code and then build and run your app.

What's more, you see how to create a *universal app* — one that will run with equal aplomb on an iPhone as well as an iPad.

Chapter 1

What Makes a Killer iOS App

Douglas Adams, in the bestseller *The Hitchhiker's Guide to the Galaxy* (conceived in 1971 and published in 1979), introduced the idea of a handy travel guide that looked "rather like a largish electronic calculator," with a hundred tiny flat-press buttons and a screen "on which any one of a million 'pages' could be summoned at a moment's notice." It looked insanely complicated, and this is one of the reasons why the snug plastic cover it fitted into had the words DON'T PANIC printed on it in large friendly letters. According to Adams, this guide was published in this form because "if it were printed in normal book form, an interstellar hitchhiker would require several inconveniently large buildings to carry it around in."

The iPhone and iPad are different sizes of a hitchhiker's dream come true, and their users don't even have any reason to panic. The only "insanely complicated" part of the iOS experience may be trying to develop a killer app that best exemplifies iPhone and iPad features, but that's why I think this book should have DON'T PANIC printed on its cover — it takes you through the entire process of imagining, creating, developing, testing, and distributing your iOS app. And in this chapter, I talk about what would make that app a killer app.

The App Store is loaded with travel and digital media apps, so you already know that the iPhone and iPad as "Hitchhiker's Guides" aren't a fantasy. You may think it a fantasy that you could develop an iOS app in less than two months, starting from where you are now, with no iOS programming experience. But you *can* — the only question is whether you can make a *great* app, or even a *killer* app. To do that, you need to look at what it takes for an iOS app to be truly great.

Figuring Out What Makes a Great iOS Application

You use the same Software Development Kit and much of the same code to develop iPad, iPhone, and iPod touch applications. The iPad runs the same operating system as the iPhone and iPod touch. However, the iPad is a bigger device with more horsepower and a larger display, as shown in Figure 1-1.

For many iPhone/iPod touch app developers, the iPad's larger display alone changes everything. Apple demonstrated exactly how *much* things have changed when the company demonstrated the iWork suite of productivity tools (Keynote for presentations, Numbers for spreadsheets, and Pages for word processing and page formatting) on both the iPhone and iPad.

The biggest challenge in making a killer app for iOS is to design for the iOS *experience.* For example, according to Douglas Adams, the *Encyclopedia Galactica* describes *alcohol* as "a colorless volatile liquid formed by the fermentation of sugars" and also notes "its intoxicating effect on certain carbon-based life forms." On the other hand, *The Hitchhiker's Guide to the Galaxy* not only tells you what *alcohol* is, but it also says "the best drink in existence is the Pan Galactic Gargle Blaster," describes its effect as "like having your brains smashed out by a slice of lemon wrapped round a large gold brick," tells you which planets have bars that offer it and at what prices, and then shows you how to mix one yourself. As Adams points out, "*The Hitchhiker's Guide to the Galaxy* sells rather better than the *Encyclopedia Galactica.*"

Figure 1-1:
The iPad
runs iOS
(left) and
offers a
larger display to show
content
such as a
newspaper
(right).

If the explosion of new iOS apps since its introduction is any indication, you'll want to leverage its fabulous touch-sensitive interface and other features. Because the iPad evolved from the iPhone design, the iPad has design advantages that make netbooks and laptops feel like the dull *Encyclopedia Galactica.* Most iOS apps are designed to take advantage of the iPhone's Multi-Touch display; accelerometer (which detects acceleration, rotation, motion gestures, and tilt); and location services for detecting its physical location — or all three.

However, you can create iOS apps that aren't just a little bit better than their desktop counterparts, but a *lot* better, with an interface that's simpler to use than a Mac or a PC.

Providing an immersive experience

An iPad app can offer a more immersive experience compared with an iPhone app by adding *more content* — full pages from the Internet or in memory, maps you can zoom in to, full-screen videos and slide shows with music, and so on. People can enjoy this content while away from their desks — on living room couches, in coffee shops, on the train, in outer space — and more easily share it with others than they can by using an iPhone or iPod touch. On the other hand, people always have their smartphone with them, so you find many benefits to an iPhone version of your app.

Whenever possible, add a realistic, physical dimension to your application. When I demonstrate the iPad to someone, my favorite game to play is Touch Hockey, because it fully immerses you in an experience that resembles the physical game so well. But it's also a good idea to extend some physical metaphors, like the newspaper or book page, to provide a more immersive experience. *The New York Times,* for example, designed an iPad app that looks like a newspaper and also includes embedded, fully functional videos (not just videos that appear in a separate window). In the iBooks app, you swipe the page to go to the next one, just like a real book, but you can also search the entire text, add bookmarks, and change the font size.

Playing Need for Speed Shift for the iPad from Electronic Arts feels like you're driving the display with your hands as you steer the car using the iPad like a steering wheel. The high-definition screen is just inches from your face — the field of view and the sensation of speed you get are incredible. The full-screen display is also fully touch sensitive — you can tap a car to see inside it, flick a lifelike gear shifter to shift gears, and tap the rearview mirror to look behind you.

Even utility apps can be rethought to be a better experience. On the iPhone, the Contacts app is a streamlined list, but on the iPad, Contacts is an address book with a beautifully tangible look and feel. The more true to life your application looks and behaves, the easier it is for people to understand how it works and enjoy using it. But again, the iPhone Contacts app is always with you, while your poor iPad often gets left home all alone.

The best approach for many apps is to have a portable iPhone version and an immersive iPad version. This book shows you how to develop both versions in a single universal app — built from a single universal Xcode project.

Making content relevant

The iPad's large display may tempt you to consider a design for your app that would look good on a laptop. But you shouldn't forget the first rule of iPhone design: Make its content and functions *relevant to the moment.* The iPad, like the iPhone, adds mobility to the party. This ability to run apps wherever you are and whenever you want makes it possible to have the information you need (as well as the tools you'd like to use) constantly available. But it's not just about the fact that the app you need is ready to run right there on your iPhone or iPad; it's (as importantly) about how the app is designed and implemented. It needs to require as little as possible from the user in terms of effort when it comes to delivering results.

An iOS app can present information relevant to where you are, what time it is, what your next activity might be, and how you're holding the device (in Portrait or Landscape orientation, tilting and shaking it, and so on).

The iOS platform offers a strong foundation for pinpointing the device's current location on a map, controlling views, managing data, playing multimedia content, switching display orientations, and processing gestures. Because the iOS platform can do all that, an app can know your current location, the hotels or campgrounds you're going to stay at, and the planets you're planning to visit. It can even show videos and play the music of the stars all at the same time. While searching maps and brochures, you can know at a glance where you are, how to get to your destination, and what the weather's like so that you know what to wear.

Designing for the larger iPad screen

The important design decision to make, whether you're starting from scratch with a new iPad app or evolving one from an iPhone app, is whether to use the large iPad screen and the new user interface elements to give people access to more information in one place. Although you don't want to pack too much information into one screen, you do want to prevent people from feeling that they must visit many different screens to find what they want.

An iPad app can offer the primary content on the Main view and provide additional information or tools in an auxiliary view (such as a *popover* that appears above the Main view) to give users access to functions without requiring them to leave the context of the Main view.

The large iPad screen also gives you a lot more room for multifinger gestures, including gestures made by more than one person. An iPad app can react to gestures and offer touch controls and pop-up settings that are relevant to what you're actually doing in the app and where you place your fingers. With a display the size of a netbook, you have a lot more screen real estate to allow dragging and two-finger gestures with graphics and images, and depending on what you're doing, a tap or gesture on a particular part of the screen can have a particular function. For example, in the Gameloft version of the first-person shooter called *Nova* (as adapted to the iPad), the display size gives you more flexibility than the iPhone version, with more controls and objects such as mini-maps, and you can slide two fingers across the screen to throw grenades.

With all this in mind, you need to consider at least two things — besides functionality, of course — when it comes to creating a great iPad or iPhone app:

✔ Creating a compelling user experience
✔ Exploiting the platform and ecosystem

I've already talked about the compelling user experience; now it's time to dive into exploiting the platform.

Exploiting the iOS Platform

Okay, enough talk about the iPad's unique experience. Just what exactly is the iOS platform, and what are its features?

Note: The best thing is that the iOS 6 platform runs on both the iPhone and iPad, and uses many of the same views, controls, and code, as you will see in this book.

Exploiting advantages of the system

One of the keys to creating a great app is taking advantage of what the device offers. In the case of a new platform with new possibilities, exploiting advantages is especially important. The combination of hardware and system software opens up design advantages that depart from the typical design approach for desktop and laptop applications. For example:

✔ **Multifinger gestures:** Applications respond to multifinger gestures, not mouse clicks. If you design an app that simply uses a single finger tap as if it were a mouse click, you may be missing an opportunity to design a better user experience.

✔ **Movement and orientation:** The iPhone and iPad have an accelerometer, so you can design apps that detect accelerated movement, as well as change the display for different orientations.

✔ **Split views and unique keyboards:** You can use a Split view on an iPad to display more than one view onscreen at a time. Either device provides a special keyboard unique to the task, such as the numbers-and-formulas keyboard that appears in the Numbers app.

✔ **Internet access:** Users can send and receive e-mail and browse the web; sync contacts, calendars, and notes over the Internet; and download content from Apple stores. With quick and easy access, your app doesn't need to store lots of data — all it really needs to do is jump on the Internet and grab what it needs from there.

✔ **Television or projection system connection:** Users can connect the iPhone or iPad to an HDTV or projection system to show content to larger audiences. With iOS's AirPlay feature and an Apple TV, users don't even need a physical connection.

✔ **Consistent system environment:** The Home button quits your app, and the volume controls take care of audio, just like you'd expect them to. User preference settings can be made available in the Settings application to avoid cluttering your app's user interface. And your native iOS apps can coexist with web services and apps created in HTML5.

✔ **Breathtaking imagery:** Photos and video already look fantastic on this display, but the artwork you create yourself for your app should be set to 24 bits (8 bits each for red, green, and blue), plus an 8-bit alpha channel to specify how a pixel's color should be merged with another pixel when the two are overlaid one on top of the other. In general, the PNG format is recommended for graphics and artwork that are included as part of your iOS app.

In the following sections, you get to dive into some of the major features, grouped into the following major areas:

✔ Accessing the Internet

✔ Tracking location

✔ Tracking motion

✔ Supporting multifinger gestures and touches

✔ Playing content

✔ Accessing the content of Apple's supplied apps (such as Contacts and Photos)

✔ Taking advantage of the display

Accessing the Internet

An iOS device can access websites and servers on the Internet through Wi-Fi or optional 3G or 4G services. This Internet access gives you the capability to create apps that can provide real-time information. An app can tell a user, for example, that the next tour at the Tate Modern in London is at 3 p.m.

This kind of access also allows you, as the developer, to go beyond the limited memory and processing power of the device and access large amounts of data stored on servers, or even offload the processing. You don't need all the information for every city in the world stored on the device, nor do you have to strain the device processor to compute the best way to get someplace on the Tube. You can send the request to a server for all that information, especially information that changes often.

This technique is called *client-server computing* — a well-established software architecture where the client provides a way to make requests to a server on a network that's just waiting for the opportunity to do something. A web browser is an example of a client accessing information from other websites that act as servers.

Knowing the location of the user

You can create an app that can determine the device's current location or even be notified when that location changes, using iOS location services. As people move, it may make sense for your app to tailor itself to where the user is, moment by moment.

Many iPad and iPhone apps use location information to tell you where the nearest coffeehouse is or even where your friends are.

When you know the user's location, you can even put it on a map, along with other places he or she may be interested in. You find out how easy it is to add a map to your app in Chapter 17.

Tracking orientation and motion

All iOS devices contain an *accelerometer with three-dimensional data* — a component that detects changes in movement. The accelerometer measures change along one of the primary axes in three-dimensional space. An app can, for example, know when the user has turned the device from vertical to horizontal orientation, and it can change the orientation from Portrait to Landscape if doing so makes for a better user experience. Newer devices add a gyroscope and — together with the accelerometer — improve the ability of the device to measure in the direction you are moving it in space.

You can also determine other types of motion such as a sudden start or stop in movement (think of a car accident or a fall) or the user shaking the device back and forth. It makes some way-cool features easy to implement — for example, the Etch A Sketch metaphor of shaking the device to undo an operation. You can even control a game by moving the iPhone or iPad like a controller — such as the aforementioned Need for Speed Shift game for the iPad (Electronic Arts), in which you drive the car by using the device like a steering wheel.

Tracking users' fingers on the screen

People use their fingers to select and manipulate objects on the device screen. The moves that do the work, called *gestures,* give the user a heightened sense of control and intimacy with the device. Several standard gestures — tap, double-tap, pinch-close, pinch-open, flick, and drag — are used in the applications supplied with iOS.

You may want to stick with the standard gestures in your app, just because folks are already aware of (and comfortable with) the current pool, but iOS Multi-Touch gesture support lets you go beyond standard gestures when appropriate. Because you can monitor the movement of each finger to detect gestures, you can create your own.

Playing content

Your iOS app can easily play audio and video. You can play sound effects or take advantage of the multichannel audio and mixing capabilities available. You can even create your own music player that has access to all the audio synced to the device from the user's iTunes Library, or from Apple's iCloud service. You can also play back many standard movie file formats, configure the aspect ratio, and specify whether controls are displayed. You can put up pages that look like web pages or book pages if you want, and you can easily mix content for an immersive experience.

Accessing information from Apple's apps

Your app can access the user's information in the Contacts app and display that information in a different way or use it as information in your application. For example, a user could enter the name and address of a hotel, and the application would file it in the user's Contacts database. Then, when the user arrives in New York City, for example, the application can retrieve the address from the Contacts app and display directions. What's more, your app can also present standard interfaces for picking and creating contacts.

What you can do with Contacts, you can do in a similar fashion with the Calendar app. Your app can remind a user when to leave for the airport or create calendar events based on what's happening this week in New York. These events show up in the Calendar app and in other apps that support that framework.

Your app can also access the Photo library in the Photos app, not only to display photos but also to use or even modify them. For example, Apple's Photos app lets you add a photo to a contact, and many applications enable you to edit your photos on the device itself. You can develop your own photo-editing app for the iPhone or iPad using, for example, Apple's Core Image framework.

Copying, cutting, and pasting between apps

iOS (the iPad and iPhone operating system) provides support for Copy, Cut, and Paste operations within and between applications. It also provides a context-sensitive Edit menu that can display the Copy, Cut, Paste, Select, Select All, and Delete system commands. That means that while each iOS application is generally expected to play only in its own sandbox, you actually do have ways to send small amounts of data between applications.

Multitasking, background processing, and notifications

Although iOS doesn't have true multitasking, it has instant-on task switching that reduces application startup and makes it easier to continue right where you left off. For certain kinds of applications, you can also process events in the background. Such applications include the following:

- ✔ **Audio:** Many apps play audio in the background.
- ✔ **Location:** Many apps process *location events* (information the iOS sends to your app about changes in location) in the background.
- ✔ **VoIP:** Many apps provide the ability for the user to make Voice over Internet Protocol calls — turning a standard Internet connection into a way to place phone calls.
- ✔ **Newsstand-Content:** The Newsstand apps download and process content in the background.
- ✔ **External-Accessory:** Some apps work with a hardware accessory that delivers updates.

iOS also offers *push* notifications for receiving alerts from your remote servers even when your app isn't running, and *local* notifications that you can use in your app to alert users of scheduled events and alarms in the background (no servers required). You can use local notifications to get a user's attention; for example, a driver navigation application running in the background can use local notifications to alert the user when it's time to make a turn. Applications can also schedule the delivery of local notifications for a future date and time and have those notifications delivered even if the application isn't running.

Living large on the big screen

The iPad display offers enough space to show a laptop-style application (which is one reason why web pages look so great). You can organize your app with a master list and detailed list of menu choices, or in a layout for Landscape orientation with a source column on the left and a view on the right — similar to the OS X versions of iTunes and iPhoto and exemplified by the Contacts app on the iPad.

Note: Although the iPhone screen is smaller than the iPad screen, don't think of the iPhone screen as being "tiny." The iPhone 5 screen, for example, at 1136 x 640 pixels, displays more pixels (on a smaller physical screen) than the original Macintosh screen (512 x 342 pixels). The first Mac had a 0.18-megapixel monochrome display. The iPhone 5 clocks in at a 0.73-megapixel (four times larger) dazzling full-color display. Progress is a wonderful thing, eh?

If you're familiar with iPhone apps and OS X applications, the iPad is somewhere in between. With the iPad touch-sensitive display, you no longer have to create different screens of menus (as you might for an iPhone app) or deploy drop-down menus and toolbars (as you might for an OS X app) to offer many functions.

For example, to crop and mask out parts of an image in Apple's Keynote app for the iPad (the app that lets you create slide shows), you don't have to select a photo and then hunt for the cropping tool or select a menu item — just double-tap the image, and a mask slider appears. In Apple's Numbers app for the iPad, if you double-tap a numeric formula, the app displays a special numeric-and-function keyboard rather than a full-text keyboard — and the app can recognize what you're doing and finish the function (such as a Sum function) for you.

These are examples of redesigning a known type of application to get rid of (or at least minimize) that modal experience of using a smartphone app — that sinking feeling of having only one path of communication to perform a task or supply a response. iPad applications should allow people to interact with them in nonlinear ways. Modality prevents this freedom by interrupting a user's workflow and forcing the user to choose a particular path.

Lists are a common way to efficiently display large amounts of information in iPhone apps. Lists are very useful in iPad apps, too, but you should take this opportunity to investigate whether you can present the same information in a richer way on the larger display.

Embracing Device Limitations

Along with all those features, however, the iPhone, and even the iPad, have some limitations. The key to successful app development — and to not making yourself too crazy — is to understand those limitations, live and program within them, and even learn to love them. (It can be done. Honest.) These constraints help you understand the kinds of applications that are right for this device.

Often, it's likely that if you *can't* do something (easily, anyway) because of device limitations, maybe you shouldn't.

The iPad evolved from the iPhone and iPod touch, and you need to consider related limitations, as well as a few things left out. So learn to live with and embrace some facts of iPad life:

- **Users have fat fingers.** You may think that the iPad's larger display makes that relatively easy to deal with, but keep in mind that you may want to design a multiuser app for the iPad that takes into account multiple fingers. (Anyone for a nice game of Touch Hockey?)

- **Memory and battery power are limited.** This limitation may or may not be a decisive factor, depending on what kind of app you want to create, but smaller apps generally perform better.

- **You can use only one app at a time.** Although users can switch from one app to another instantly, and apps can continue where a user left off, only one application actually runs at a given time, with some apps capable of running in the background to serve notifications or play music.

The next sections help get you closer to a state of iOS enlightenment.

Designing for fingers

Although the Multi-Touch interface is a feature of the iPad, iPhone, and iPod touch, it brings with it some limitations.

First of all, fingers aren't as precise as a mouse pointer, which makes some operations even more difficult on an iPhone or iPod touch than on an iPad (text selection, for example). Still, due to fat fingers, user-interface elements need to be large enough and spaced far enough apart so that users' fingers can find their way around the interface comfortably. Apple recommends that anything a user has to select or manipulate with a finger be a minimum of 44 x 44 points in size.

Because it's so much easier to make a mistake using fingers, you also need to ensure that you implement a robust — yet unobtrusive — Undo mechanism. You don't want to have your users confirm every action (it makes using the app tedious), but on the other hand, you don't want your app to let anybody mistakenly delete a page without asking, "Are you *sure* this is what you *really* want to do?" Lost work is worse than tedious. Fortunately, the iPad supports the same shake-to-undo feature as the iPhone.

Balancing memory and battery life

As an app designer, you have several balancing acts to keep in mind:

- ✔ **Limited memory:** When compared to the original Macintosh's standards, the computer power and amount of memory on the iPad may seem significant . . . but that is so yesterday. No ifs, ands, or buts; the computer power and amount of memory on the iPhone and iPad are limited. But this is an issue much more with older devices. The newer iPhones and iPads do have fairly large amounts of memory.

- ✔ **Limited battery power:** Access to the Internet can mitigate the device's power and memory limitations by storing data and (sometimes) offloading processing to a server, but those Internet operations eat up the battery faster.

  While it's true that the iOS power-management system conserves power by shutting down any hardware features that aren't currently being used, a developer must manage the trade-off between all those busy features and a shorter battery life. Any app that takes advantage of Internet access, core location, and the accelerometer is going to eat up the batteries.

iOS devices are particularly unforgiving when it comes to memory usage. If you run out of memory, in order to prevent corruption of other apps and memory, the system will simply *shut down your app* (unfortunately not to the tune of "Shut Down" by the Beach Boys).

It just goes to show that not *all* limitations can be exploited as "features."

Why Develop iOS Applications?

Because you can. Because it's fun. And because the time has come (today!). iOS apps are busting out all over, and developers have been very successful. Even high-profile magazines such as *Wired* and *The New Yorker* now offer app versions.

Developing iOS apps can be the most fun you've had in years, with very little investment of time and money (compared with developing for platforms like Windows). Here's why:

- ✔ **iOS apps are usually bite-sized, which means that they're small enough to get your head around.** A single developer — or one with a partner and maybe some graphics support — can do them. You don't need a 20-person project team with endless procedures and processes and meetings to create something valuable.

- ✔ **The applications tend to be crisp and clean, focusing on what the user wants to do at a particular time and/or place.** They're simple but not simplistic. This makes application design (and subsequent implementation) much easier and faster.

- ✔ **The apps use the most innovative platform available for mobile computing.** The iPhone was a game changer in 2007. The iPad is a still a game changer. It's completely changing the Internet as a publishing medium, the software industry with regard to applications, and the mobile device industry with regard to the overall digital media experience.

- ✔ **The free iOS Software Development Kit (SDK) makes development as easy as possible.** This book reveals the SDK in all its splendor and glory in Chapter 2. If you can't stand waiting, you *could* register as an iOS developer, and download the SDK . . . but (fair warning) jumping the gun leads to extra hassle. It's worth getting a handle on the ins and outs of iPad app development beforehand.

iOS has these three other advantages that are important to you as a developer:

- ✔ **You can distribute your app through the App Store.** Apple will list your app in the App Store in the category you specify, and the store takes care of credit-card processing (if you charge for your app), hosting, downloading, notifying users of updates, and all those things that most developers hate doing. Developers name their own prices for their creations or distribute them free; Apple gets 30 percent of the sales price of commercial apps, with the developer getting the rest. However, keep in mind that Apple must approve your app before it appears in the App Store.

- ✔ **Apple has a robust yet inexpensive developer program.** To place your app in the store and manage it, you have to pay $99 per year to join the Individual or Company version of the iOS Developer Program (which includes iPhone and iPad development support). (Apple also offers an Enterprise version for $299 per year to develop proprietary, in-house iOS applications that you can distribute to employees or members of your organization, and a free University version for educational institutions to include iOS development as part of a curriculum.) But that's it. You don't find any of the infamous hidden charges that you often encounter, especially when dealing with credit-card companies. Go to the Apple iOS Developer site (`http://developer.apple.com/programs/ios`) and click the Enroll Now button to get started.

✔ **It's a business and productivity tool.** Both the iPhone and iPad have become acceptable business and individual productivity tools, in part because they have tight security as well as support for Microsoft Exchange and Office, but even more for their designs as handheld mobile computers. Using an iPad with a customer to interact with information is a lot more engaging and cool, and it helps salespeople close the deal faster. Automobile finance companies can begin the credit-application process while customers are standing near a vehicle. Doctors and nurses at hospitals are beginning to use iPads to view X-rays and CT scans and read medical records while standing next to the patient. This happy state of affairs expands the possible audience for your application.

Developing with Apple's Expectations in Mind

Just as the iPhone and iPad can extend the reach of the user, the device possibilities and the development environment can extend your reach as a developer. To make sure that you're reaching in the right direction, it helps to understand Apple's perspective on what iOS apps should be — the company clearly has done some serious thinking about it, far longer than anybody else out there, having taken years to bring iOS devices to market under a veil of secrecy.

So what does Apple think? Spokespeople often talk about three different application styles:

✔ **Productivity applications use and manipulate information.** The RoadTrip sample app that I show in this book is an example, and so are Bento and FileMaker Go (FileMaker), and Apple's iWork apps — Keynote, Pages, and Numbers. Common to all these apps is the use and manipulation of multiple types of information. (I'm not talking about the Productivity category in the App Store — that's a marketing designation.)

✔ **Utility applications perform simple, highly defined tasks.** Google's YouTube app is an example — it deals only with the YouTube videos. The Brushes app for painting (by Steve Sprang) is considered a utility, as it performs a simple, highly defined task. (Again, I'm not talking about the Utilities category in the App Store, although many of those apps are considered utility apps because they perform simple, highly defined tasks.)

✔ **Immersive applications are focused on delivering — and having the user interact with — content in a visually rich environment.** A game is a typical example of an immersive application.

Although these categories help you understand how Apple thinks about iOS apps (at least publicly), don't let them get in the way of your creativity. You've probably heard *ad nauseam* about stepping outside the box. But hold on to your lunch; the iOS "box" isn't even a box yet. So here's a more extreme metaphor: Try diving into the abyss and coming up with something really new.

An Application Ecosystem

The iPad, of course, has an older albeit smaller brother — the iPhone. In one corner, you have a light, small, mobile device that you can take with you — one that almost disappears as it becomes part of a user's daily life. In the other corner, you have a device that shines at presentation and can immerse the user in content — a device you can think of as somewhere in between an iPhone and a Mac.

But often, it's not one or the other. I would, for example, want to use an iPad to research and plan a road trip, but while I'm traveling, I'd like to be able to access all that information on my iPhone, which is a lot easier to take along as I explore. What I don't want is one app for planning and a different app for traveling. Instead I want a seamless integration between the two, and although I may prefer to do one task on one device versus the other, I also want to be able to do either on both. It's a function of user interface design and primary versus secondary functionality based on what the device does best.

What's more, you should keep the laptop and desktop in the picture as well (yes, personal computers do still have a place in this brave new world). Although the PC isn't a subject I cover in this book, don't ignore the laptop or even the desktop. If a user has to engage in a lot of manipulation or data entry, the PC is far better to work with than the iPad.

All these devices combine to serve the user in what I call an *application ecosystem.* The idea of an application ecosystem, which I depict in Figure 1-2, is to distribute functionality to the device that does it best. To do that, it helps to understand what application functionality is best suited for which device.

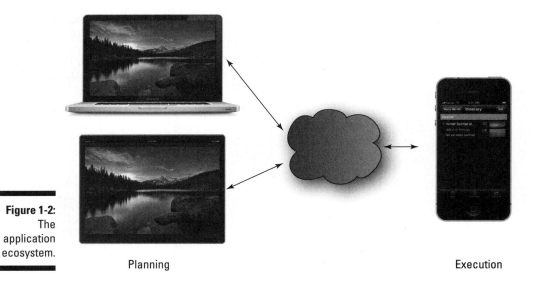

Figure 1-2: The application ecosystem.

Planning   Execution

For example, imagine an application aimed at photographers. The app could show you the best sites to photograph, the best time of day to photograph them, and the best setting to use on your camera. The app could even map the locations to take them from. On an iPad, the user could take advantage of the large display to go through the photographs and decide which ones she wanted to take. She could select those photographs to create a shot list that she could order by time of day and location. Then when she was done, she could access that shot list from her iPhone. She could carry just the iPhone with her, and as she took the photographs, she could update the ones she had taken with the actual settings and time of day, and then be able to access that information from her iPad.

Or imagine a road trip. A user would plan it on his iPad and then access directions, maps, hotel reservations, and places to eat from his iPhone. He could even take notes on his phone about his experience, and add his own photographs from his phone to document his trip. He could then use his iPad to create his own trip album.

The possibilities are endless.

If you want to provide applications for the right device and the right function, and you want seamlessness and consistency across all platforms, does that mean one universal app, or two or three apps with lots of duplicate functionality? Fortunately, you won't need lots of apps — that's where the cloud comes in.

Enter the Cloud

Apple, of course, created a great deal of excitement when it announced iCloud. However, iCloud is more than just an integral part of the built-in applications; it can also be used by developers to implement at least part of the application ecosystem I discuss in the previous section.

iCloud lets you create applications that share data between two devices. For example, you could create a RoadTrip application that allowed the user to plan a trip on an iPad, and then access and even update that data on an iPhone.

But although iCloud does let you share *data* between the same applications running on different devices (which in itself is great), it doesn't allow you to share business logic, nor, at this point, allow you to access that data from a web application, an Android device, or a Windows Mobile device. What's more, it doesn't allow multiple users to access shared data (something you would want in a social networking or calendar application, for example).

At this point, the easiest and best way to implement an application ecosystem is by using web services and an architecture that supports them. These services can be hosted on a third-party cloud-hosting solution, or they can be hosted on enterprise-based servers with an infrastructure bus that can access other services or data (as some of my clients are doing).

Developing an App the Right Way Using the Example App in This Book

Although iCloud, web services, and the application ecosystem are where certain kinds of apps are going, they certainly aren't the place for most developers of iOS applications to start. Also, I don't want to imply that an app necessarily needs to be cloud based. You find lots of opportunities for apps that live only on the device. But if you're thinking about an app that can take advantage of an application ecosystem, I want to pique your curiosity and give you a frame of reference to start thinking in those terms.

So this book is about apps that live on the device, and that's the place to start. And after you've mastered that, you can think about the cloud.

As I mention in the Introduction of this book, the point of this book isn't to find out how to program in Objective-C using the iOS frameworks. Instead, the point is to discover how to build applications, and that's what you'll be doing — finding out the *right way* to develop iOS applications.

The best way I can think of to show you how to build an app is to build one, and I take you through doing that throughout this book. The app you build is called RoadTrip, and it's based on an application I started to develop many years ago, and still think is a good idea. Although the original version that I envisioned had more features, this one isn't too shabby. It allows you to check the weather, see the events happening at your destination, and see the destination, sights, and your current location on a map, as well as display any location by entering the address or the name of a point of interest. You can also choose between destinations.

As simple as it is, RoadTrip shows you how to do many of the tasks that are common to iOS apps. You add animation and sound, display views and navigate through them, and use controls such as buttons, as well as use the Navigation controllers like the kind you find in the Music app and many "industrial strength" applications on the iPhone and the split screen on the iPad that allows you to see two views side by side, or one view with another in a popover window.

As you build the RoadTrip app, you even find out how to display a web page and navigate its links (and return). You also download and display data from the Internet.

In addition, I have you build what's known as a *universal app* — one that can run either on the iPad or iPhone. The advantage of using a universal app is that it becomes the basis of an app that you can extend to take advantage of both iCloud and web services — which I show you how to do in my book *iOS Cloud Development For Dummies.*

Let's get started!

What's Next

You must be raring to go by now and just can't wait to download the Software Development Kit (SDK). That's exactly what many new developers do — and later are sorry that they didn't spend more time up front understanding the iOS user experience, how applications work in the iOS environment, and the guidelines that Apple enforces for apps to be approved for the App Store.

So be patient. *The Hitchhiker's Guide to the Galaxy,* that wonderful fantasy of an iPhone or iPad from 1979, suggests that space is "big, really big . . . you just won't believe how vastly hugely mind-bogglingly big it is" and suggests that you bring a towel. The guide says a towel "is about the most massively useful thing an interstellar hitchhiker can have." (Again with Douglas Adams? But I promise not to get into the meaning of life, the universe, and every-thing, or the ultimate question — for which the answer is [spoiler alert] 42.) This book is your towel for the journey. The following chapters cover all the aspects of development you need to know before you spend time coding. Then, I promise, it's off to the stars.

Chapter 2

Getting to Know the SDK

1'll admit it. In my coding life up until quite recently, I never really considered Xcode to be a true partner in the development process. Using it was like having to include your little brother when you went out to play with your friends because your parents made you.

With Xcode 4, that has changed. Xcode, if you finesse it a bit, can make your development much easier with fewer errors. In this chapter, I take you on a guided tour of the features you'll find in Xcode — giving you the view from 30,000 feet. If you have never used Xcode before, some of its features may not make all that much sense — but not to worry, I'll be going through it all in detail as you use it. The point of this chapter is to provide a frame of reference as you move forward, and a complete reference for you to look back on.

Developing Using the SDK

The iOS Software Development Kit (SDK) provides support for developing iOS applications and includes the complete set of Xcode tools, compilers, and frameworks for creating applications for iOS and Mac OS X. These tools include the Xcode IDE (its integrated development environment) and the Instruments performance analysis tool, among many others.

Xcode 4.5 (the latest version) is now an application you simply download from the Mac App store. (You will need OS X 10.7.3 or better.) You should also become a registered developer. To do that, first go to http://developer.apple.com/devcenter/ios, look for (and then click) the link to become a registered developer, fill out some registration information, and then start reaping the benefits of being a registered developer, starting with access to tons of documentation sample code and a lot of other useful information). *Note:* If you want to actually run your application on your iPhone or iPad and submit it to the App Store, you need to join the official iOS Developer Program, which you can do right after you become a registered developer.

Apple links do change from time to time, so if a link I provide in this book doesn't work, you can always start at http://developer.apple.com and navigate to the iOS Dev Center from there.

Xcode 4 is the latest iteration of Apple's IDE, a complete toolset for building Mac OS X and iOS applications. With Xcode 4, you can develop applications that run on any iPhone, iPad, or iPod touch running iOS. You can also test your applications using the included iOS Simulator, which supports iOS 5 and iOS 6.

The Xcode IDE includes a powerful Source editor, a sophisticated graphical user interface editor, and many other features, including source code repository management. Moreover, as you code, Xcode can identify mistakes in both syntax and logic, and even suggest fixes.

Xcode includes everything you need to create your app — which is both the good news and the bad news. The good news is that it has everything you need. The bad news is that because it has everything you need, it can be pretty complex. But again, not to worry: I guide you through everything involved in creating an app, step by step.

To start with, I give you an overview of Xcode and how you'll use it to develop your app. As you move from step to step, I provide more detail on how to use Xcode to specifically do what you need to do in any given step.

Using Xcode to Develop an App

To develop an iPhone, iPod touch, or iPad app, you have to work within the context of an *Xcode project*. Although I don't explain any particular development methodologies in this book, I can tell you that Xcode supports the following activities that are parts of developing your application:

- ✔ Creating an Xcode project
- ✔ Developing the application (designing the user interface using a storyboard, coding, and running and debugging the code)
- ✔ Tuning application performance
- ✔ Distributing the application

The following sections tell you more about each of these tasks.

Creating an Xcode project

To develop an iOS application, you start by creating an Xcode project. A project contains all the elements needed to create an application, including the source files, a graphical representation of the user interface, and build settings needed to build your application. You work on your project in the *Workspace window,* which allows you to create all of these elements as well as build, run, debug, and submit your application to the App Store.

Developing the application

You have a lot to do to develop an application. You need to design the user experience and then implement what you came up with as a user interface. You need to write code to implement the features of the app. You also need to test and debug the app.

Designing the user interface using a storyboard

Xcode's Interface Builder is the editor you use to assemble your application's user interface with the help of preconfigured objects found in the Library. The objects include windows, controls (such as switches, text fields, and buttons), and the views you'll use, such as Image, Web, and Table views. The Interface Builder editor allows you to add objects, configure their properties, and create connections not only between user interface objects, but also between user interface objects and your code.

When you use a storyboard (which you do in this book), most of if not all your screens end up being displayed in the storyboard, and Interface Builder saves your storyboard in a storyboard file (with the .storyboard extension). When you don't use a storyboard, each screen is saved separately as a nib file (with the .xib extension). Either way, these files contain all the information iOS needs to reconstitute the user interface objects in your application at runtime.

Interface Builder saves you time and effort when it comes to creating your application's user interface. You don't have to code each object (thereby saving you a lot of work), and what's more, because Interface Builder is a visual editor, you get to see what your application's user interface will look like at runtime.

Coding

To code, you use the Source Code editor, which supports features such as code completion, syntax-aware indentation, and source code folding (to hide "code blocks" temporarily). You can get context-based help to assist you, and if you need information about a particular symbol, you can either get a summary of a symbol's documentation directly in the editor, or you can opt for more extensive documentation in the Organizer (more on the Organizer later).

Xcode's Live Issues and Fix-it features work together to point out mistakes as you enter your code and offer to fix those mistakes for you.

Running and debugging

When you run your application to debug or test it, you can run it in the iOS Simulator on your Mac and then on an iOS-based device (if you're in the developer program). Using the simulator, you can make sure your application behaves the way you want. You can also get debugging information — as you run — in the Debug area. By running your app on a device connected to your Mac (still using the debugger, if you like), you can observe the actual user experience and see how the app will perform.

Tuning application performance

The Instruments application enables you to analyze the performance of your application as it runs in the simulator or on a device. The Instruments application gathers data from your running application and presents that data in a graphical timeline.

Among other measurements, you can gather data about your application's memory usage, disk activity, network activity, and graphics performance. This data enables you to analyze your application's performance and identify performance and resource usage problems.

In-depth coverage of Instruments is beyond the scope of this book.

Distributing the application

Xcode provides various kinds of application distribution, including:

- Ad Hoc Distribution for testing on up to 100 iOS devices.
- The App Store for distributing to hundreds of millions of iOS device users. You can give your apps away for free or let Apple sell them for you.
- Custom B2B Apps for distributing business-to-business apps directly to your business customers who have a Volume Purchase Program account.

You create an archive of your application that contains debugging information, making it easier to track down bugs reported by testers (and users) of your application. When your application is ready to go, you submit it to the App Store. (Before you submit your app to the store, you can even run some of the same software-validation procedures on your applications that Apple does passing these tests makes your application's approval process as fast as possible).

The Workspace Window

Command central for Xcode is the Workspace window, where you'll do all the things you need to do to develop your app.

In this section, I present only an overview — more or less the map of what's in the Workspace window and what each bar and button is and does. I came up with this as a way to provide a quick reference to the Workspace window so you can see all its elements, including the various bars and buttons and what they do.

Figure 2-1 shows a "map" of the window. (If you like, bookmark this page so you can refer to this figure at any time when reading the book.) At first glance, it may seem overwhelming, but take a deep breath and don't worry: I explain each part. As I take you through using Xcode to develop your app, I go into more detail as needed. So for now, take a quick read through the upcoming sections just to familiarize yourself with the lay of the land and then return to Figure 2-1 as needed for quick reference.

Figure 2-1:
The Xcode Workspace window.

Although I have added shadings to the Workspace window components in this chapter for easy reference, figures in the remainder of the book show the components as they appear on your screen.

The Workspace window consists of

✔ Workspace areas

✔ The toolbar

✔ An optional tab bar

The following sections describe each of these elements — the heart of Xcode.

Workspace areas

The Workspace is divided into four *areas,* as follows:

✔ Editor area (always shown)

✔ Navigator area

✔ Utility area

✔ Debug area

You can configure the Workspace area in a number of ways. Right off the bat, you can choose to hide and/or show various areas in various combinations. (Note that the Editor area is always present.). The Debug and Utility areas are already configured with panes, but in the Debug area, you can select the pane configuration.

Editor area (always present)

The Editor *area* is always present. If you want, you can show or hide various "editors" contained within the Editor area; you do so using the Editor selector, the group of buttons in the toolbar you can see in Figure 2-2.

Figure 2-2:
The Editor
selector.

The term *editor* here is really a misnomer, even though that's the term used in the documentation. The "editors" you can select in the Editor area are really editor area *configurations,* within which you use the *content* editors available to you. (See the "Editor area content editors" section, later in this chapter, for more on this distinction.)

The editors (configurations) you have available are as follows:

 ✔ **Standard editor:** The button for this Editor area configuration is on the left side of the Editor selector. The Standard editor displays a single pane for editing and is always shown.

 ✔ **Assistant editor:** Select this Editor area (configuration) using the center button. This adds an additional pane to the Editor area, with a content editor in each. The additional Assistant pane has some navigation features that I explain in Chapters 7 and 9. You can further split this pane into two panes.

 ✔ **Version editor:** Open this editor using the right button on the Editor selector. This enables you to compare two different versions of files you have saved in repositories. (Repositories and the Version editor are beyond the scope of this book.)

I later explain the tasks you can perform within these areas.

Additional areas to view as needed

You use the View selector (see Figure 2-3) to toggle between showing and hiding any of the optional areas. By *optional,* I mean that you can open and close these areas as needed. These areas are as follows:

Figure 2-3:
The View
selector.

 ✔ **Navigator area** (left button): No further configuration is possible (you don't divide this area into other views).

 ✔ **Debug area** (center button): Displays various panes depending on what you need to see (the Console pane, which displays debugging information or program output for example, or the Variables pane which displays your program's variables and their values); you change panes using the Debug area Scope bar, shown in Figure 2-4.

Figure 2-4:
The Debug
area Scope
bar.

The Debug area Scope bar toggles from one to another of the following:

- *Variables pane only* (left button)
- *Both Variables and Console panes* (center button)
- *Console pane only* (right button)

 ✔ **Utility area** (right button): Is further configured with two panes (either can be expanded to hide the other):

- *Inspector pane*
- *Library pane*

I explain what you see in each of those panes when I explain the Utility area section, later in the chapter.

 When you hover your mouse pointer over a toolbar button, a tooltip describes its function.

Displaying an area's content

Each area displays certain content, and each area has its own way of displaying its content:

- ✔ **The Navigator area** has navigators.
- ✔ **The Editor area** has content editors.
- ✔ **The Utility area** has
  - *Quick Help* or *Inspectors* in the Inspector/Quick Help pane.
  - *Libraries* in the Library pane.
- ✔ **The Debug area** has
  - *Debugger variables* in the Variables pane.
  - *Debugger output* in the Console pane.

The following sections tell you about these areas in more detail.

Navigator area navigators

The Navigator area contains a host of navigators that organize the tasks and components you use within your Xcode project. You use a Navigator selector bar to select the navigator you need. Figure 2-5 shows the various navigators you can choose from, and the following bullet list explains what each navigator does:

Figure 2-5:
The
Navigator
selector.

 ✓ **Project navigator:** Here's where you manage all the files in your project. You can add files, delete files, and even organize your files by placing them into groups. Selecting a file in the Project navigator launches the appropriate editor in the Editor area.

 ✓ **Symbol navigator:** Lets you zero in on a particular *symbol* — an element such as a variable, method, or function name — in your project. Selecting a symbol highlights it in the editor.

 ✓ **Search navigator:** Finds any string within your projects and frameworks.

 ✓ **Issue navigator:** Displays issues such as diagnostics, warnings, and errors that arise when you're coding and building your project.

 ✓ **Debug navigator:** Displays the *call stack* — information about what method has called what method — during program execution.

 ✓ **Breakpoint navigator:** Manages and edits the *breakpoints* — markers you add to your code that stop program execution at a certain point in your program — in your project or Workspace.

 ✓ **Log navigator:** Examines the logs that Xcode generates when you run and debug your application.

Editor area content editors

The Editor area has a number of editors you use to edit specific content. Content editors are context based, meaning that the selection you make in a Navigator or Editor *jump bar* — the toolbar that appears at the top of each Editor area pane and is used to navigate through the files and symbols in your project — determines the Content editor. The following bullet list names each Content editor and outlines the tasks associated with each one (note that not all tasks are applicable to iOS application development):

✓ **Source editor:** Write and edit your source code; set, enable, or disable breakpoints; and control program execution.

✓ **Project editor:** View and edit settings such as build options, target architectures, and code signing.

✓ **Interface Builder:** Graphically create and edit user interface files in storyboards (and XIB files if you are not using a storyboard).

✓ **Property list editor:** View and edit various types of small, highly structured property lists (plists). (You'll use one for some of your program's data.)

- ✔ **Rich text editor:** View and edit rich text (.rtf) files, much as you would with Text Edit.

- ✔ **Core Data model editor:** Implement or modify a Core Data model. (iOS's persistent object store is beyond the scope of this book).

- ✔ **Mapping model editor:** Graphically create and edit a mapping between an old Core Data store and a new one.

- ✔ **Script editor:** Create and edit AppleScript script files.

- ✔ **Scripting dictionary editor:** Create and edit the scripting definition (.sdef) file — used by AppleScript — for your application.

- ✔ **Viewer:** Display files for which there is no editor (some audio, video, and graphics files, for example) using the same Quick Look facility used by the Finder.

Utility area

The Utility area has two panes: the Inspector pane and the Library pane. You can expand either pane to hide the other.

When working within the Inspector pane, you click a button in the Inspector selector (shown in Figure 2-6) to select a particular inspector. (Note that a previous navigator selection or Content editor selection may determine which inspectors are available.) Your choices are as follows:

Figure 2-6:
The
Inspector
selector.

- ✔ **File inspector:** For viewing (and managing) file metadata, such as a file-name, type, and path.

- ✔ **Quick Help (second button):** For viewing (applicable) details about what has been selected in an editor, such as an abstract or concise description, where and how it is declared, and selection-based information such as an element's scope, the parameters it takes, its platform and architecture availability, references, sample code, and so on. The following selections are supported:

  - *Symbols,* in the Source editor

  - *Interface objects,* in Interface Builder

  - *Build settings,* in the Project editor

Additional inspectors are available in some editors; for example, Interface Builder offers the following:

- ✔ **Identity inspector:** For viewing (and managing) object metadata such as an object's class, runtime attributes, label, and so forth.

- ✔ **Attributes inspector:** For configuring the attributes specific to the selected interface object. For example, some text field attributes include text alignment and color, border type, and editability.

- ✔ **Size inspector:** For specifying characteristics such as the initial size and position of an interface object, its minimum and maximum sizes, and various autosizing rules for the object.

- ✔ **Connections inspector:** View the outlets and actions for an interface object, make new connections, and delete existing connections. (Connections "connect" your program code to user interface objects you create in Interface Builder.)

When working within the Library pane, you click a button in the Library selector bar (shown in Figure 2-7) to select a library of resources you can use in your project. The following libraries are available:

Figure 2-7:
The Library selector.

- ✔ **File templates:** These templates are for the common types of files listed as choices in the New File menu. To add a file of that type to your project, drag it from the library to the Project navigator.

- ✔ **Code snippets:** These are short pieces of source code for use in your application. To use one, drag it directly into your source code file.

- ✔ **Objects:** This library contains the kinds of interface objects you'd use to make up your user interface. To add one to a view, drag it directly into your storyboard or nib file in the Interface Builder editor.

- ✔ **Media files:** This library contains a whole slew of graphics, icons, and sound files. To use one, drag it directly to your storyboard or nib file in the Interface Builder editor.

Debug area

The Debug area is where you'd try to track down the bugs in your code and squash them. A selection in the Debug area Scope bar (refer to Figure 2-4) determines the information the debugger displays:

> ✔ **Variables Pane Only:** Left button
>
> ✔ **Both Variables and Console Panes:** Center button
>
> ✔ **Console Pane Only:** Right button

The pop-up menu in the Variables Pane Scope bar lets you display in the following ways:

> ✔ **Auto:** Display recently accessed variables.
>
> ✔ **Local:** Display local variables.
>
> ✔ **All:** Display all variables and registers.

All Output ▲▼ The pop-up menu in the Console Pane Scope bar lets you display

> ✔ **All Output:** Target and debugger output
>
> ✔ **Debugger Output:** Debugger output only
>
> ✔ **Target Output:** Target output only

You also find other controls and filters for what is displayed; explore them on your own.

Xcode has extensive contextual help articles that you can view by Control-clicking in the Workspace window in the context you need help on.

The toolbar and Tab bar

The *toolbar* (see Figure 2-8) includes Workspace-level tools for managing and running *schemes* (instructions on how to build your application), viewing the progress of (executing) tasks, and configuring the Workspace window. That's a lot of tools, so to keep things straight, it's best to think of the toolbar as actually having three parts: A Flow control part, an Activity Viewer part, and a Workspace Configuration part.

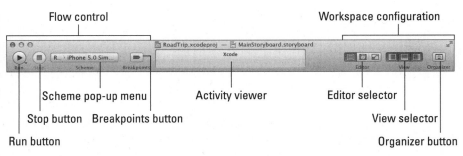

Figure 2-8: The toolbar with the Tab bar.

Flow controls are for defining, choosing, running, and stopping projects. A *scheme* defines characteristics such as build targets, build configurations, and the executable environment for the product to be built in.

The Flow controls are as follows:

- ✔ **Run button:** Clicking the Run button builds and runs the targets. (A *target,* in this context, is the product you want to build as well as the instructions for building that product from a set of files in a project or Workspace for the currently selected scheme). Pressing and holding the mouse button opens a menu (which is also available in the Product menu) that allows you to run, test, profile, or analyze your application.

- ✔ **Stop button:** Terminates your executing application in either the Simulator or the device.

- ✔ **Scheme menu:** Lets you select the scheme and build destination to use.

- ✔ **Breakpoints button:** Activates or deactivates all breakpoints.

The Activity Viewer part of the toolbar shows the progress of tasks currently executing. This viewer displays status messages, build progress, and other information about your project. Click the Issues icon in the Activity viewer to open the Issue navigator (explained earlier in this chapter, in the "Navigator area navigators" section).

You use the final part of the toolbar — the Workspace Configuration part — to configure the Xcode Workspace window to suit your needs. You can use these controls to select an editor type, show or hide optional view areas, and open the Organizer window. (See the "Displaying an area's content" section, earlier in the chapter, for more on your choices here.)

The Tab bar is great for keeping track of where you've been and what you might want to go back to. Note, however, that showing the Tab bar is optional. If you decide that the Tab bar is something you just can't do without, choose View➪Show Tab Bar from Xcode's main menu. You can reorder tabs, close them individually, or drag them out of the bar to create a new window.

If you lose the toolbar (or Tab bar), you can always add it back to any window by selecting View➪Show Toolbar (or View➪Show Tab Bar). The View menu also allows you to configure the Workspace window.

The Organizer window

The Organizer window (see Figure 2-9) enables you to do the supplemental tasks associated with development, such as accessing documentation and managing devices, archives, and project-related metadata.

Organizers

Figure 2-9:
The
Organizer
window.

To display the Organizer window, click the Organizer button on the Workspace window toolbar (refer to Figure 2-8) or choose Window➪Organizer from Xcode's main menu. The Organizer window includes five individual organizers, which enable you to do the following:

- **Devices organizer:** Provision a device, manage your developer profile, install iOS on the device, and manage your application and data on a device.

- **Repositories organizer:** Create, view, and manage Git and Subversion repositories for your Workspace. These are where your various project versions are managed.

- **Projects organizer:** Lets you locate your projects without having to remember where they are in the file system) and offers *snapshots* — a Save feature that enables you to save different versions of your projects).

- **Archives organizer:** Submit your application to the App Store or testers and manage your product archives.

- **Documentation organizer:** Access documentation and sample code from within Xcode.

Each of these organizers includes task-oriented contextual help that you get by Control-clicking an organizer's content pane.

Chapter 3

The Nuts and Bolts of an Xcode Project

*A*s I explain in Chapter 2, to use Xcode to create an app, you need to create an Xcode project. An Xcode project includes all the files, resources, and information required to build your application. It's your partner in creating your application, and the sooner you make friends with it, the easier your life will become.

In this chapter, I show you how to create an Xcode project and then build and run your app in the Simulator.

Creating Your Project

Because developing an iPhone and/or an iPad app requires you to work in an Xcode project, it's time to create one. The app you'll be building is called RoadTrip (and will also be the name of the project). The app, as I mention in the introduction to this book, is like a travel guide on your iOS device. Here's how you get your RoadTrip project off the ground:

1. **Launch Xcode.**

   With Xcode 4.5, Xcode is now an application in the Mac App Store, which, right from the start, makes your life simpler. (You used to have to download a .dmg, or *D*isk I*mage* file, and then run an installer). Simply go the Mac App Store, search for Xcode 4, click the FREE button, and then click the INSTALL APP button that the Free button transmogrifies into, and you are done. After the download you'll find the Xcode in your Applications folder. Double-click to launch it.

   Here are a couple of hints to make Xcode handier and more efficient right from the start:

   - *Create a shortcut.* Control-click the Xcode icon that appears in the Dock and then choose Options⇨Keep in Dock. You'll be using Xcode a lot, so it wouldn't hurt to be able to launch it from the Dock.

   - *Nix the Welcome to Xcode screen if you'd like.* When you first launch Xcode, you see the Welcome to Xcode screen with several links. (After you use Xcode to create projects, your Welcome screen lists all your most recent projects in the right column.) If you don't want to be bothered with the Welcome screen in the future, deselect the Show This Window When Xcode Launches check box.

     You can also just click Cancel to close the Welcome screen.

     If you ever want to see the Welcome screen again, you can access it through the Window menu or by pressing Shift+⌘+1.

2. **Click the Create a New Xcode Project link on the left side of the Welcome screen, or choose File⇨New⇨New Project to create a new project.**

   Alternatively, you can just press Shift+⌘+N.

   No matter how you decide to start a new project, you're greeted by the Choose a Template for Your New Project sheet (a "sheet" is also known as a "document-modal dialog"). Its purpose in life is pretty clear: It's there to let you choose a new template for your new project. Note that the leftmost pane has two sections: one for iOS and the other for OS X (Apple's latest name for the Macintosh operating system).

3. **In the upper-left corner of the Choose a Template dialog, select Application under the iOS heading (if it isn't already selected).**

   After clicking Application, the main pane of the Choose a Template sheet refreshes, revealing several choices. (See Figure 3-1.) Each choice is actually a template that, when chosen, generates code to get you started.

Figure 3-1:
Choose a
template
first.

4. **Select Master-Detail Application from the template choices displayed (as I have in Figure 3-1) and then click Next.**

   After you click Next, the Choose Options for Your New Project sheet appears.

   This Master-Detail Application template provides a starting point for the appropriately named Master-Detail application. What you get is a skeleton app with a Split view. (I explain all about split views in the "The iPad's Split views" section, later in this chapter.) A Split view is what you see in the Mail application. In Landscape orientation on the left is a *Master view,* and on the right is a *Detail view.* In Portrait orientation you see the Detail view with a button that enables you to display the Master view in a popover.

   Note that when you select a template, a brief description of the template is displayed underneath the main pane. (Again, refer to Figure 3-1 to see a description of the Master-Detail Application template.) In fact, go ahead and click some of the other template choices just to see how they're described as well. Just be sure to click the Master-Detail Application template again when you're done, and then click Next, to follow along with developing the RoadTrip app.

These template names do change from time to time, so don't be surprised if yours are a little different from the ones I refer to in this book. For the most part, the kinds of application they build tend to stay the same.

5. **In the Choose Options for Your New Project sheet (see Figure 3-2), enter a name for your new project in the Product Name field, and add a company name (or your name) in the Company Identifier field.**

I named this project RoadTrip. (You should do the same if you're following along with developing RoadTrip.)

Class prefix is something that will get prepended to the classes the template will generate, so enter **RT** (for RoadTrip) in the Class Prefix field.

If you don't enter a prefix here, the template will create generically named classes that seem to have no connection to your project.

6. **Select Universal from the Devices Family pop-up menu (if it isn't already selected).**

Doing so creates a skeleton app that will be configured to run on the iPad, iPhone, or iPod touch.

By choosing Universal, you're creating an app that can run on iPhone (and iPod touch) and iPad.

Figure 3-2:
Choose
project
options.

While any iPhone application will run on the iPad, it doesn't work the other way around unless you create a Universal application.

I have you select Universal because, with the introduction of storyboards in iOS 5 and Xcode 4.2, creating a universal application has become much easier.

Other options to select or deselect in this sheet are the following:

- *Use Storyboard:* Whatever you do, be sure to select this check box. The Use Storyboard option enables you to create the entire user interface flow graphically.

- *Use Core Data:* Deselect this check box. In some of the templates, you can also choose to generate the code necessary to use Core Data. The Core Data framework supports object persistence and is beyond the scope of this book. You can find quite a bit of sample code in the iOS Dev Center that does a good job of illustrating how to use it.

- *Use Automatic Reference Counting:* Select this check box. As I explain in Chapter 6, this option makes memory management much easier.

- *Include Unit Tests:* Deselect this check box. Although unit testing is a valuable feature, covering it is beyond the scope of this book. *Unit tests* are part of a style of programming that involves writing test cases before writing the code to be tested. You can set requirements in concrete before writing any code. I don't use unit testing for RoadTrip because it would make the process of explaining Xcode more complicated. The feature is worth examining on your own, however.

7. **Click Next and choose a location to save the project (the Desktop or any folder works just fine), deselect the Source Control: Create Local Git Repository for This Project check box, and then click Create.**

Git is a software control management (SCM) system that keeps track of changes in the code and saves multiple versions of each file on your hard drive. Git can be used as a local repository — thus the Create Local Git Repository for This Project option — or you can install a Git server on a remote machine to share files among team members. Git is beyond the scope of this book — but if you want to find out more about it, check out the Xcode 4 User Guide (choose Help➪Xcode User Guide).

After you click Create, Xcode creates the project and opens the Workspace window for the project — which should look like what you see in Figure 3-3.

Xcode will remember your choices for your next project.

Figure 3-3:
The Xcode
Workspace
window.

Exploring Your Project

Not to sound like a broken record, but to develop an iOS app, you have to work within the context of an Xcode project, very much like the one shown in Figure 3-3. This is, in effect, Command Central for developing your app; it displays and organizes your projects, source files, and the other resources needed to build your apps.

The project

If the project isn't open, go ahead and open it in Xcode by tracking down the project file — on the Desktop, in a folder, wherever — and double-clicking it. As I explain in Chapter 2, when your project is launched in Xcode, the Navigator area appears on the left side of the Workspace window. When using the Master-Detail Application template — you did select the Master-Detail Application template when you created your project, right? — the following options are selected for you by default:

✔ The Utility and Debug areas are hidden.

✔ The Navigator area is shown, with the Project navigator selected by default in the Navigator selector.

✔ The project (RoadTrip, in this case) is selected in the Project navigator.

And as a result, the Project editor displays the RoadTrip project information in the Standard editor.

Long story short, when you launch your RoadTrip project in Xcode, what you see in the editor is the Project editor displaying the RoadTrip project.

When I refer to (or ask you to select) the *RoadTrip project in the Project Navigator,* I am referring to the RoadTrip project that you see selected in Figure 3-3.

The Project editor

Having your RoadTrip project selected in the Navigator area's Project navigator (refer to Figure 3-3) sets a couple of balls rolling. In the first column of the Project editor, under the Project heading, you see the project itself. (It turns out that a workspace can actually have more than one project, but you won't be doing that in this book.) A bit below the Project heading, you see the Targets heading. (Yes, there's room for more than one target here as well.) Any project you create defines the default build settings for all the targets in that particular project. (Note that each target can also specify its own build settings, which could potentially override the project build settings.)

A *target* is really just the *app* (the product you are building) and includes the information that Xcode requires to build the product from a set of files in a project or workspace — stuff like the build settings and build phases which you can see and edit in the Xcode project editor. A target inherits the build settings for the project, but you can override one or more of them by specifying different settings at the target level. There is one active target at a time, with the Xcode scheme (iPad Simulator for example) specifying the target.

The Project editor shows tabs across the top; clicking these tabs opens panes that enable you to examine and change project settings. Most of the default settings will work for your needs, but as you develop the example project in Chapter 8, you'll be changing a setting in the Compile Sources section in the Build Phases tab. (Won't that be exciting!) The tabs are as follows:

✔ **Summary:** Each setting in the Summary tab is actually found in one of the other tabs. When you edit a setting, Xcode updates the data in the appropriate tab automatically (which is where the data really resides), meaning you probably won't have to go into the other tabs.

The iOS Application Target and iPhone/iPad Deployment Info sections of the Summary tab display settings based on the choices you made when you first created the RoadTrip project. (Notice that one of the settings is Deployment Target. While you must compile your project using the current SDK, you can target it to run on earlier iOS versions. I cover that in more detail in a document on my website — Running Sideways and Backwards (which also explains the business about universal applications).

There's a section on the Summary tab for adding an app icon — you'll be doing that for the RoadTrip app in the "Adding Application Icons" section, later in this chapter — as well as a section for adding a launch image for your app. (The *launch image* is what is displayed while your app is launching — kind of like provisional eye candy that hangs around until the app is ready to use.)

The Summary tab is also your go-to place for adding a new framework to your app — I cover adding a new framework in Chapter 9 — as well as for setting Entitlements. (Entitlements confer specific capabilities or security permissions to your app, and are beyond the scope of this book.)

✔ **Info:** If you listened to my advice and actually created the RoadTrip project earlier in this chapter and were then to open the disclosure triangle next to the Supporting Files folder in the Project navigator, you'd see a file called `RoadTrip-Info.plist`. The Info tab contains more or less the same information as that file. An *information property list file* contains essential configuration information for a *bundled executable* (the executable code and the accompanying resources, such as the storyboard, nibs, images, sounds, and so on). The system uses these keys and values to obtain information about your application and how it's configured. As a result, all bundled executables (plug-ins, frameworks, and applications) are expected to have an information property list file.

✔ **Build Settings:** Most developers can get by with the default build settings, but if you have special requirements — ones that require anything from tweaking a setting or two to creating an entirely new build configuration — you'll take care of them in this tab.

✔ **Build Phases:** This tab has a number of sections that control how Xcode builds your products. For example, Xcode detects when one of your products is dependent on another and automatically builds those products in the correct order. However, if you need to tweak the order in which Xcode builds your products, you can use the Build Phases tab to create explicit target dependencies.

✔ **Build Rules:** Xcode processes your source files according to file type using a set of built-in rules. For example, property list (`plist`) files are copied into the product using the CopyPlistFile script located in the Xcode directory. Because the built-in rules are fine for almost all circumstances, you won't need to mess with this particular tab for a long time — and if you're lucky, never.

The Project navigator

After your project is created, the Xcode workspace displays the Project navigator. I introduce the Project navigator in Chapter 2, but give you a full tour here.

Xcode has a lot of context-based help. Whenever you're curious about what something does, try Control-clicking in an area, and you'll likely find a menu with a Help selection. In Figure 3-4, for example, I Control-clicked in the Project navigator to bring up a shortcut menu from which I can choose the Project Navigator Help menu.

The Navigator area is an optional area on the left side of the Workspace window where you can load different navigators — including the Project navigator — with the help of the Navigator selector. To hide or show the Navigator area, click the left View selector button in the workspace toolbar, shown in Figure 3-5.

The Navigator area includes the Navigator selector bar, the Content area, and the Filter bar. It can also include other features specific to the selected navigator.

Figure 3-4: Project navigator help.

Click to view the Navigator area.

Figure 3-5:
The View
selector
in the
workspace
toolbar.

 The Project navigator enables you to do things like add, delete, group, and otherwise manage files in your project or choose a file to view or edit in the Editor area. (Depending on which file you choose, you'll see the appropriate editor, as I explain in Chapter 2.) In Figure 3-6, for example, you can see that I've decided to open all the disclosure triangles so that the Project navigator displays all the files in the project.

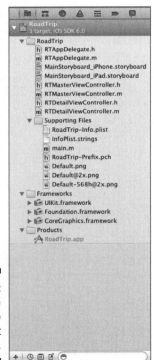

Figure 3-6:
The
RoadTrip
Project
navigator.

The *Filter bar* lets you restrict the content that's displayed — such as recently edited files, unsaved files, or filenames.

Making your way down the folder structure shown in the Project navigator (refer to Figure 3-6), the first folder listed is labeled RoadTrip. This folder contains all the source elements for the project, including source code, resource files, graphics, and a number of other pieces that will remain unmentioned for now (but I get to those in due course). Although each template organizes these source elements in different ways, the Master-Detail Application template organizes the interface header and implementation code files (along with the Storyboard file(s) and a Supporting Files folder) inside the RoadTrip folder. (For good measure, the RoadTrip folder also includes a Frameworks folder and a Products folder.)

Here's the kind of stuff that gets tossed into folders for projects like the RoadTrip project:

- ✔ **AppDelegate files:** The `RTAppDelegate.h` and `RTAppDelegate.m` files contain the code for app-specific behavior that customizes the behavior of a framework object (so that you don't have to subclass it — as I describe in Chapter 6). A behavior-rich framework object (used as is) delegates the task of implementing one of its responsibilities to an application delegate for a very specific behavior. The *delegation* pattern of adding behaviors to objects is described in more detail in Chapter 6.

- ✔ **Storyboard:** The storyboard files live in your project as the `MainStoryboard.storyboard_iPad` file and the `MainStoryboard.storyboard_iPhone` file (for a universal app), or just as a lone `MainStoryboard.storyboard_whatever` file (for a device-specific app). With a storyboard, you can create and implement an overall view of the flow of your application and the user interface elements. I go into great detail on storyboards in Chapter 4. Soon you'll like the `.storyboard` files as much as I do.

- ✔ **View controllers:** The `RTMasterViewController.h` and `RTMasterViewController.m` files contain the code to control the initial view of the RoadTrip (based on the Master-Detail Application template). You'll do a lot more with view controllers in later chapters.

- ✔ **Supporting Files:** In this folder, you typically find the precompiled headers (header files that are compiled to reduce your application compilation time) of the frameworks you'll be using — such as `RoadTrip_Prefix.pch` — as well as the property list (`RoadTrip-Info.plist`) and `main.m`, your application's main function. You may even find images and other media files, and some data files. The `InfoPlist.strings` file is used for localization (translating the text in your app to the user's language preference).

✔ **Frameworks:** This folder holds the code libraries that act a lot like prefab building blocks for your app. (I talk about frameworks in Chapter 4.) By choosing the Master-Detail Application template, you let Xcode know that it should add the UIKit, Foundation, and CoreGraphics frameworks to your project, because it expects that you'll need them in this kind of application.

You'll be adding more frameworks yourself in addition to these three in developing RoadTrip. You find out how to add more frameworks in Chapter 8.

✔ **Products:** The Products folder is a bit different from the others. In it, you'll find the final RoadTrip.app file — not the source code of the app, but rather the *built* version of the app, which means that it has been translated from the source code into the object code for the iPad's processor to execute. At the moment, this file is listed in red because the file can't be found.

When a filename appears in red, this means that Xcode can't find the underlying physical file. And because you've never compiled the RoadTrip app, it makes sense that the RoadTrip.app file (the app itself) is missing.

You may notice that some items in the Project navigator look like folders, but you'll soon discover that they often don't act like folders. If you just happen to open the RoadTrip folder on your Mac — outside of the Xcode context — you won't see all the "folders" that appear in the Xcode window. That's because those folders are simply groupings that help organize and find what you're looking for.

Setting Your Xcode Preferences

Xcode gives you options galore. I'm guessing that you won't change any of them until you have a bit more programming experience under your belt, but a few options are actually worth thinking about now — so in this section, I show you how to set some of the preferences you might be interested in.

Follow these steps to set some of the preferences you'll find useful:

1. **With Xcode open, choose Xcode⇨Preferences from the main menu.**

2. **Click the Behaviors tab at the top of the Preferences window to show the Behaviors pane.**

   The Xcode Preferences window refreshes to show the Behaviors pane.

   The left side of the pane shows the Events pane (the check marks indicate events for which settings are set), while the right side shows the possible actions for an event.

3. **Select (Running) Generates output in the left column and then choose the Show, Hide, or If No Output Hide option from the Debug area pop-up menu to the left of the debugger in the right pane.**

   This step controls what appears while you run your app. By default, you'll find that the check box for showing the debugger in the Debug area is selected. (See Chapter 8 for more about debugging.)

4. **Select other options from the left column (perhaps (Build) Starts, (Build) Generates new issues, (Build) Succeeds, and (Build) Fails)) and experiment with the options available.**

   You can link an event with playing a sound (something I like to do) or have an event trigger the Xcode icon bouncing up and down in the Dock. You can change many options in the Behaviors pane — too many to cover in this chapter! But take a look through them and experiment — they can make your life much easier.

   Figure 3-7 shows the behaviors I have chosen if the run pauses. (By *pause,* I mean the run hits, say, a breakpoint; I cover breakpoints in Chapter 8.) I like to have a sound inform me in case I'm busy daydreaming (submarine seems like the appropriate sound to play here).

   Figure 3-8 shows the behaviors I have chosen if a build fails. I like to use a sound for this occurrence as well. I also want to have the Issue navigator display. (See Chapter 8 for more about the value and use of the Issue navigator.) I also want it to navigate to the first new issue.

5. **Click the Downloads tab at the top of the Preferences window and then select Documentation in the segmented control.**

6. **Select the Check for and Install Updates Automatically check box, and then click the Check and Install Now button.**

   This step ensures that the documentation remains up-to-date and allows you to load and access other documentation.

7. **(Optional) Click the Fonts & Colors tab at the top of the Preferences window and use the options to change your workspace theme.**

   When I get bored, I sometimes change the theme to Midnight to get a black background.

8. **(Optional) Click the Text Editing tab at the top of the Preferences window and set your text editing preferences.**

   I set the Indent width to 2 in the Indentation settings to get as much code on a line as possible.

9. **Click the red Close button in the top-left corner of the window to close the Xcode Preferences window.**

Figure 3-7:
Setting
behaviors.

Figure 3-8:
Choosing
a behavior
for when a
build fails.

Building and Running Your Application

As I mention in Chapter 2, the Xcode toolbar (see Figure 3-9) is where you do things like run your application. I spell out the process a bit more here.

Figure 3-9: The Xcode toolbar.

The Flow controls are for defining, choosing, running, and stopping projects. They consist of the following:

- ✓ **Run button:** Clicking the Run button builds and runs the *targets* — a target is a product to build and the instructions for building the product from a set of files in a project or workspace for the currently selected scheme. Pressing and holding the mouse button opens a menu — also available in the Product menu — that allows you to run, test, profile, or analyze your application.

  Holding various modifier keys while clicking the Run button allows you to select these other run options:

  Control key: Run without building.

  Shift key: Build without running.

  Option key: Edit the scheme and run.

- ✓ **Stop button:** Terminates your (executing) application in the Simulator or the device.

- ✓ **Scheme menu:** A *scheme* defines characteristics such as build targets, build configurations, and the executable environment for the product to be built. The *scheme menu* lets you select which scheme and which build destination you want to use. (I describe schemes in greater detail in the next section of this chapter.)

- ✓ **Breakpoints button:** Activates or deactivates all breakpoints. The Breakpoints button turns breakpoints on and off. (A *breakpoint* tells Xcode to stop execution at a point in the code — I explain breakpoints more fully in Chapter 8.)

The *Activity viewer* shows the progress of tasks currently executing by displaying status messages, build progress, and other information about your project. For example, when you're building your project, Xcode updates the Activity viewer to show where you are in the process — and whether or not the process completed successfully. If an Issues icon appears in the Activity viewer, click it to open the Issues navigator and look there for messages about your project. (None exist yet in Figure 3-9, so you won't see an Issues icon there.)

The *Workspace configuration* includes the Editor and View controls (which I explain in Chapter 2) as well as the Organizer window button.

Building an app

Building an app in Xcode means compiling all the source code files in the project. It's really exciting (well, I exaggerate a bit) to see what you get when you build and run a project that you created from a template. Building and running an app is relatively simple; just follow these steps:

1. **In the Flow Controls section of the toolbar, choose a scheme from the Scheme pop-up menu.**

   A *scheme* tells Xcode the purpose of the built product. The schemes in the Scheme pop-up menu specify which targets (actual products) to build, what build configuration to use when building them, which debugger to use when testing them, and which executable to launch when running them on the device or Simulator.

   Xcode automatically creates several schemes with configurations for you, and you can create more schemes and edit any of the schemes.

   To work with the example app I came up with for this book (the RoadTrip app), you just want to make sure that the scheme is set either to the Simulator or the device and that the proper SDK has been selected. Remember that when you download an SDK, you actually download multiple SDKs — a Simulator SDK and a device SDK for each of the current iOS releases. You should use the Simulator SDK for iOS 6.0 (as of this writing) for apps that you want to submit to the App Store — until a newer version of iOS is released.

   In a document on my website, I show you how to switch to the device SDK and transfer your app to a real-world iOS device. But before you do that, you need to be a card-carrying member of the iOS Developer Program. (Only members can run an app on a device, even on your very own iPhone or iPad.) Go to http://developer.apple.com/ios to learn about enrolling in the program if you haven't done so already.

REMEMBER

2. **Choose Product⇨Run from the main menu to build and run the application.**

   You can also click the Run button in the top-left corner of the Work-space window. The Activity viewer (shown previously in Figure 3-9) tells you all about the build progress, flags any build errors (such as compiler errors) or warnings, and (oh, yeah) tells you whether the build was successful.

Figure 3-10 shows you what you'll see in the Simulator (in the Portrait mode), and then you tap the Master button. I know it's not much to look at, but it's a start — and it *is* a functioning iPad app.

Figure 3-10: Not much of an app, but it *is* yours.

If you rotate the Simulator by choosing Hardware⇨Rotate Left, in the Simulator menu you see a nice Split view (as shown in Figure 3-11). (I talk more about the mechanics behind this — the use of a split view controller — in the next section, and in even more detail in Chapter 13.)

The iPad's Split views

While it's true that on the iPhone you often see only one view at a time, on the iPad you get to see two views, courtesy of the Master-Detail Application template (and something called a split view controller, which I explain in detail in Chapter 13).

If you take another look at Figure 3-11, you can see what I'm talking about. The view on the left displays what is called the master view. While technically it could be any type of view you'd like, in the case of the Master-Detail Application template, you get something called a table view, which displays a list of what is referred to as cells, entries, or rows. On the left side of Figure 3-12, I tapped the + button and you see a timestamp (in Coordinated Universal Time [UTC], the primary time standard and the successor to Greenwich Mean Time [GMT]) in the first cell in the master view. When I tap that cell, as I have on the right side of Figure 3-12, the same timestamp is displayed in the detail view and the cell is highlighted in the master view.

Figure 3-11:
Your app in landscape mode.

Figure 3-12:
Splits aren't
just for
bananas.

All the detail view does right now is display "Detail view content goes here." Well, that's not all it does. When you rotate the iPad into portrait mode, it's also responsible for both displaying a nice Master button as well as for displaying the master view in the popover that you see when you tap the nice Master button. (Refer to Figure 3-10.)

In landscape view, the master view on the left side also includes a toolbar with Edit and + "bar button items" that allow the user to modify content in this particular example program.

Again, it probably doesn't seem like much, but (as you'll see when I explain the RoadTrip app in Chapter 4) this is pretty much all the "infrastructure" you'll need to put together a really cool app.

The Log navigator

If you want to look at how the build works, now is as good a time as any to explain how the Log navigator works.

 Xcode generates a series of logs during the build process, which meticulously record the actions performed. You can view these logs by selecting the Log navigator, either by using the Navigator selector or by choosing View⇨ Navigators⇨Show Log Navigator from Xcode's main menu. In Figure 3-13, you can see a log of all my recent builds.

Debug session

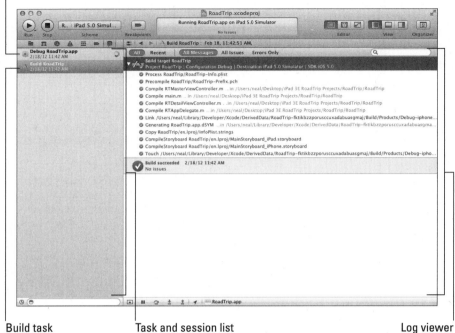

Figure 3-13:
Build
results.

Build task   Task and session list   Log viewer

The Log navigator lists these two types of actions:

✔ **Tasks:** The Task log lists all the operations Xcode performed to carry
out the task, such as building operations, archiving operations, and
source control operations.

✔ **Sessions:** A Session log is the transcript of the events that occurred
during a session (a period during which an activity is performed).
Running or debugging an application, for example, generates a session
log that would include all debugger output.

The Log navigator contains the Task and Session list. When you select an
item in this list, the corresponding log appears in the Log viewer. You can
filter this list with the Filter bar.

It turns out you won't need to use the Log navigator for the example app in
this book, simply because I have you examine all debug activity in the Debug
area instead and any task-related issues in the Issue navigator.

The ultimate success (or failure) of your build is also displayed in the
Activity viewer.

Running in the Simulator

When you run your app, Xcode installs it on the Simulator (or on a real device if you specified a device as the active SDK) and launches it. Using the Hardware menu and your keyboard and mouse, the Simulator mimics most of what a user can do on a real device, albeit with some limitations that I point out shortly.

At first, the iPad Simulator looks like any iPad model would — kind of like what you can see back in Figure 3-11. If you were to click the Home button at the bottom center of the Simulator window once, you'd quit your app. The app would then appear on the Home screen with a standard blank icon. Click the blank icon once to launch the app again.

Interacting with your simulated hardware

Any simulator worth its salt has to be able to duplicate the actions you'd expect from a real device. The Xcode Simulator — no surprise here — can mimic a wide range of activities, all accessed from the Simulator Hardware menu. The Hardware menu items allow you to control various simulator behaviors, including:

- **Choose a device.** Switch the simulated device to an iPad, any model iPhone, or the Retina display found on iPhone 4, iPhone 4S, and fourth-generation iPod touch models.

- **Choose a version.** Switch to a different version of iOS.

- **Rotate left.** Choosing Hardware⇨Rotate Left rotates the Simulator to the left. If the Simulator is in Portrait view, it changes to Landscape view; if the Simulator is already in Landscape view, it changes to Portrait view.

- **Rotate right.** Choosing Hardware⇨Rotate Right rotates the Simulator to the right. Again, if the Simulator is in Portrait view, it changes to Landscape view; if the Simulator is already in Landscape view, it changes to Portrait view.

- **Use a shake gesture.** Choosing Hardware⇨Shake Gesture simulates shaking the device.

- **Go to the Home screen.** Choosing Hardware⇨Home does the expected — you go to the Home screen.

- **Lock the Simulator (device).** Choosing Hardware⇨Lock locks the Simulator, which then displays the Lock screen.

- **Send the running app low-memory warnings.** Choosing Hardware⇨Simulate Memory Warning fakes out your app by sending it a (fake) low-memory warning.

- ✔ **Simulate the hardware keyboard.** Choose Hardware⇨Simulate Hardware Keyboard to check out how your app functions when the device is connected to an optional physical keyboard dock or paired with a Bluetooth keyboard.

- ✔ **Choose an external display.** To bring up another window that acts like an external display attached to the device, choose Hardware⇨TV Out and then choose 640 x 480, 1024 x 768, 1280 x 720 (720p), or 1920 x 1080 (1080p) for the window's display resolution. Choose Hardware⇨TV Out⇨Disabled to close the external display window.

Making gestures

On the real device, a gesture is something you do with your fingers to make something happen in the device — a tap, a drag, a swipe, and so on. Table 3-1 shows you how to simulate gestures using your mouse and keyboard.

Table 3-1	Gestures in the Simulator
Gesture	*iPad Action*
Tap	Click the mouse.
Touch and hold	Hold down the mouse button.
Double tap	Double-click the mouse button.
Two-finger tap	1. Move the mouse pointer over the place where you want to start.
	2. Hold down the Option key, which makes two circles appear that stand in for your fingers.
	3. Click the mouse button.
Swipe	1. Click where you want to start and hold down the mouse button.
	2. Move the mouse slowly in the direction of the swipe and then release the mouse button.
Flick	1. Click where you want to start and hold the mouse button down.
	2. Move the mouse quickly in the direction of the flick and then release the mouse button.
Drag	1. Click where you want to start and hold down the mouse button.
	2. Move the mouse slowly in the drag direction.

Gesture	iPad Action
Pinch	1. Move the mouse pointer over the place where you want to start.
	2. Hold down the Option key, which makes two circles appear that stand in for your fingers.
	3. Hold down the mouse button and move the circles in (to pinch) or out (to unpinch).

Uninstalling apps and resetting your device

You uninstall applications on the Simulator the same way you do on the iPad, except you use your mouse instead of your finger. Follow these steps:

1. **On the Home screen, place the pointer over the icon of the app you want to uninstall and hold down the mouse button until all the app icons start to wiggle.**

2. **Click the app icon's Remove button — the little *x* that appears in the upper-left corner of the icon — to make the app disappear.**

3. **Click the Home button — the one with a little square in it, centered below the screen — to stop the other app icons from wiggling and finish the uninstall.**

On a separate note, you can always reposition an app's icon on the Home screen by clicking and dragging it around with the mouse.

You can remove an application from the background the same way you'd do on the iPad, except that you use your mouse instead of your finger. Follow these steps:

1. **Double-click the Home button to display the applications running in the background.**

2. **Place the pointer over the icon of the application you want to remove, and hold down the mouse button until the icon starts to wiggle.**

3. **Click the icon's Remove button — the red circle with the *x* — that appears in the upper-left corner of the application's icon.**

4. **Click the Home button to stop the icons from wiggling and then click once again to return to the Home screen.**

To reset the Simulator to the original factory settings — which also removes all the apps you've installed — choose iOS Simulator⇨Reset Content and Settings, and then click Reset in the warning dialog that appears.

Living with the Simulator's limitations

Keep in mind that, despite the Simulator's many virtues, running apps in the Simulator is still not the same thing as running them on the iPad. Here's why:

- **Different frameworks:** The Simulator uses Mac OS X versions of the low-level system frameworks, instead of the actual frameworks that run on the device. That means that occasionally some code may run fine in the Simulator but not on actual iOS devices. Although the Simulator is useful for testing functionality, there's no substitute for debugging the app on the device itself if you want to find out how it will really run.

- **Different hardware and memory:** The Simulator uses the Mac hardware and memory. To accurately determine how your app will perform on an honest-to-goodness iOS device, you have to run it on a real iOS devices.

- **Different installation procedure:** Xcode installs *your* app in the Simulator automatically when you build the app using the iOS SDK. It's a different kettle of fish to install your app on the device for testing. And, by the way, you don't have a way to get Xcode to install apps from the App Store in the Simulator.

- **Lack of GPS:** You can't fake the Simulator into thinking that it's lying on the beach at Waikiki.

    You can, however, choose to simulate a location in the Debug area. I tell you more about simulating a location in Chapter 15.

- **Two-finger limit:** You can simulate a maximum of two fingers. If your application's user interface can respond to touch events involving more than two fingers, you need to test that on an actual device. (The motion of two fingers in itself is a tad limited in the Simulator — you can't do two-figure swipes or drags.)

- **Accelerometer differences:** You can access your computer's accelerometer (if it has one) through the UIKit framework. Its reading, however, will differ from the accelerometer readings on an actual iPad (for some technical reasons that I don't have the space to go into).

- **Differences in rendering:** OpenGL ES (Open Graphics Library for Embedded Systems, in other words) is one of the many 3D graphics libraries that works with the iOS SDK. It turns out that the renderers it uses on devices are slightly different from the ones it uses in the iPad Simulator. As a result, a scene on the Simulator and the same scene on a device may not be identical at the pixel level.

- **Telephony:** You can't make a phone call on the iPhone simulator.

Adding the Image and Sound Resources and an Application Icon

If you select the Home button — either on the Simulator or the iPad itself — you can't help but notice that the icon assigned to your fledgling app is rather undistinguished looking, to say the least.

Even though your app doesn't do anything yet, you can have a nice, shiny app icon by following these steps:

1. **Download the iOS 6 RoadTrip Resources folder from my website at** www.nealgoldstein.com/support/downloads.

   Store the folder somewhere handy where you'll be sure to find it again.

   This folder includes not only the application icon but also a number of other resource files (images and sound) you'll be using in your application.

   You'll start by adding the resources you'll need.

2. **Control-click RoadTrip project in the Project Navigator, choose Add Files to "RoadTrip" from the contextual menu, use the dialog that appears to navigate to the RoadTrip Resources folder you downloaded, and then select the RoadTrip Resources folder. Or choose File⇨Add Files to RoadTrip, as shown in Figure 3-14.**

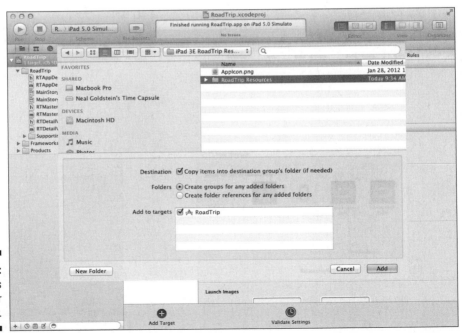

Figure 3-14: Adding files to your project.

Xcode asks you (via a check box in the aforementioned dialog) whether you want to make a copy of the file. If you don't select the check box, Xcode creates a pointer (alias) to the file. The advantage of using an alias is that if you modify the file later, Xcode will use that modified version. The disadvantage is that Xcode won't be able to find the file if you move it.

3. **Select the Copy Items into Destination Group's Folder (If Needed) check box, make sure the check box in front of Road Trip in the Add to Targets section is selected, and then click Add to copy the files.**

   This adds the resource files you need. Now you can turn your attention to getting the application icon to show up on the Home screen.

You can also drag files into the Project navigator.

Standard and Retina display images

Starting with iOS 4, you can include two separate files for each image resource. (You'll just be using a single file in this book, however.) One file provides a standard-resolution version of a given image, and the second provides a high-resolution version of the same image (for the *Retina display*). The naming conventions for each pair of image files are as follows:

- ✔ **Standard:** <ImageName><device_modifier>.<filename_extension>
- ✔ **High resolution:** <ImageName>@2x<device_modifier>.<filename_extension>

The <ImageName> and <filename_extension> portions of each name specify the usual name and extension for the file. The <device_modifier> portion is optional and contains either the string ~ipad or ~iphone. You include one of these modifiers when you want to specify different versions of an image for the iPhone and iPad. The inclusion of the @2x modifier for the high-resolution image lets the system know that the image is the high-resolution variant of the standard image.

When creating high-resolution versions of your images, place the new versions in the same location in your application bundle as the original images.

If you click one of the resources, you see it displayed in the Editor area. Because Xcode doesn't have a graphics editor, as I explain in Chapter 2, Xcode uses the same quick-look functionality as used by the Finder.

Adding the application icons

Ideally, you should provide four different-sized applications icons, with descriptive filenames (you can actually use any filenames you like) such as

- ✔ `Icon57.png`: 57x57 pixels in PNG format for normal iPhone
- ✔ `Icon114.png`: 114x114 pixels in PNG format for Retina iPhone
- ✔ `Icon72.png`: 72x72 pixels in PNG format for normal iPad
- ✔ `Icon144.png`: 144x144 pixels in PNG format for Retina iPad

I created icons matching those measurements in a graphics program, and you can find them in the RoadTrip Resources folder (the one you downloaded in Step 1 in the previous section). To add those icons and have them used as your application icons, do the following:

1. **Select the Project navigator by clicking the first icon in the Navigator selector bar — the one that looks like a folder.**

   The Project navigator displays the RoadTrip project container and the files and resources in your project.

2. **Select the RoadTrip project container — the first item in the Project navigator.**

   The Project editor launches.

3. **Control-click the first selection box in the App Icons subsection of the iPhone Deployment info section (be sure to click outside the No Image Specified image but within the selection box), and choose Select File.**

4. **Using the dialog that appears, navigate back to the RoadTrip Resources folder you downloaded, select** `Icon57.png` **for the normal iPhone icon, and click Choose.**

   The Prerendered check box you see back in Figure 3-9 allows you to specify that you don't want the shine and glossy effect applied to your icon. I chose to select the box, although it's your choice on whether you like the look.

5. **Repeat the process using** `Icon144.png` **for the Retina iPhone,** `Icon72.png` **for the iPad, and** `Icon144.png` **for the Retina iPad.**

6. **If you'd like, drag all the app icons into the Resources group (I will) to get them out of the way.**

App icons are very important if you want to sell apps in the App Store. People are unlikely to buy an app with an ugly icon — no one believes that "beauty is only skin deep." It is generally good practice to pay a professional artist to create a family of app icons, unless you are a professional artist along with being a rock-star programmer.

Run your project with its new icon

To run your project with its new icon, select Run for the iPhone on the Xcode toolbar. Then click the Home button, and you should see your application icon. Then repeat for the iPad version. (Check out Figure 3-15 to see how the icons look on both platforms.)

It is generally a good idea to make your iPad icons look a bit different than your iPhone icons, which is why I added *HD* to the iPad icons. This helps the user know that he is running the iPad version when on the iPad.

Figure 3-15:
The app icon in all its glory.

Part II
Building RoadTrip

The 5th Wave   By Rich Tennant

"I build bookshelves and Bernice buys an iPad."

In this part . . .

Killer iOS apps start with the user experience. This goes beyond a pretty interface and includes how people use your app to accomplish want they want.

Of course, the boys and girls at Apple really understand that and have included the Interface Builder editor — which is much more than your run-of-the-mill program for building graphical user interfaces — in Xcode to enable you to build a real interface. In this part, you also discover the storyboard, which is the icing on the Interface Builder cake. The storyboard lets you lay out the entire application flow and saves you a lot of coding, to boot.

In this part, you find out how to use Xcode to lay out the Test Drive screen of your application. That's where you can test drive a '59 pink Cadillac Eldorado Biarritz convertible by having it drive up and down the screen. You see how to develop a storyboard for the iPad and another storyboard for the iPhone — both in a single universal app.

You add background images and controls that can be a new user's first experience with your application.

Of course, you need code to make your application do something beyond just sitting there and looking nice. The iOS frameworks provide what you need to actually make your code do something useful.

Therefore, in this part, you take a brief tour of the RoadTrip app, the one you'll be building in this book. You see not only what the app will do, but also how it uses the frameworks and SDK to do it.

Chapter 4

Storyboards and the User Experience

*A*s I mention in the Introduction, my goal for this book is for you to understand the *right way* to develop applications for the iPhone and iPad. Because you'll be using the knowledge I impart to you to develop my RoadTrip application, now is probably a good time to explain the application — what it actually does, how it is organized, and what the program architecture looks like.

One thing that makes iOS software development so appealing is the richness of the tools and frameworks provided in the iOS Software Development Kit (SDK). In this regard, the frameworks are especially important. Each one is a distinct body of code that actually implements your application's generic functionality — in other words, frameworks give the application its basic way of working. This is especially true of one framework in particular: the `UIKit` framework, which is the heart of the user interface.

In this chapter, you get an overview of the iPad's user interface architecture, meaning you'll find out what the various pieces are, what each does, and how they interact with each other. The idea here is for this chapter to lay the groundwork for developing the RoadTrip app's user interface, while succeeding chapters take you to the next level(s).

I also go through what classes and frameworks are available in the SDK — well, at least the main ones you'll need to know about in order to build the RoadTrip app as well as a number of other classes and frameworks any self-respecting app developer would need to know in order for her to build her own apps. For added measure, I also talk about something Apple calls *design patterns,* or programming paradigms that the frameworks are based on.

But the place I want to start is a feature that was new to Xcode 4.2 — the storyboard — which allows you to lay out the user interface and the *application flow* (the relationships between various screens) in a "white board" sort of way.

Introducing the Storyboard

I really like Xcode's Storyboard feature. When I saw a storyboard for the first time, it was like a dream come true. (Well, okay, not quite.) To me, the Storyboard feature represented exactly what I needed — not only for building my own apps but also for teaching other people how to build their own apps.

I mention back in Chapter 1 that using a storyboard is analogous to sketching the user interface and app flow on a white board, and then having that sketch turn into something your app can use. That means working with a storyboard can save you lots of time and effort by reducing the code you have to write. Moreover, it can really help when it comes to fully understanding the app flow. If you haven't developed before, you'll find that using a storyboard makes it easier to get a more complex app up and running.

The idea behind a storyboard is that you'd use it to lay out the entire flow of your application. Figure 4-1 shows you what the iPad storyboard for a finished application would look like. You'll find that, when you lay out an app in a storyboard, you can actually run your program before you even add any content, so you can get a sense of how the user experience will unfold.

To get to the storyboard so you can actually edit it, you use the Project navigator and select the storyboard file you're interested in. Doing so brings up the Interface Builder editor. You'll use the Utility area as well to add user interface elements, use the inspectors to set attributes, and so on.

Telling your story

As you develop your application, you use Interface Builder to graphically add user interface elements to each one of your *views* in the storyboard. (I tell you more about views in the "Working with Windows and Views" section, later in this chapter; for now just think of views as containers for displaying what you see on the iPad screen.) In this context, user interface elements include things like controls, images, and placeholders for content you'll display. After you've added the elements you need, all you have to do is fill in code where it's needed. If you've used Xcode to program in the past, you'll find that you have to write a lot less *plumbing code* — code that is specifically designed to do things like launch view controllers — and, in some cases, no plumbing code at all.

Figure 4-1:
The completed RoadTrip storyboard.

Typically, I lay out the entire flow of my application early on in the development process, but for the example app developed for this book, I decided not to do that because I wanted to first show you all the basics of developing an app with Xcode. That means you'll see some of the storyboard stuff now but will have to wait until Chapter 14 to storyboard the rest of the RoadTrip app. I promise, though, that when you do an app of your own, you'll be ready to start with the storyboard and design your application flow the way it should be done — in one fell swoop.

Ready for a storyboard tour? To follow along with me, go back to Xcode and select the `MainStoryboard_iPad.storyboard` file for your sample project in the Project navigator. This is the iPad storyboard, one of the storyboards that Xcode created for you when you used the Master-Detail Application template, selected the Universal Device Family, and selected the Use Storyboard check box. (See Chapter 3 for more on the specifics of the Master-Detail Application template.) The name *Main* in the `MainStoryboard_iPad.storyboard` file implies that, of course, there can be *other* storyboards. (In this case, you'll notice there are two `MainStoryboards` — one for the iPad and one for the iPhone.)

Selecting the `MainStoryboard_iPad.storyboard` file in the Project navigator opens that file in the Interface Builder editor, as shown in Figure 4-2. While all this may look a bit daunting at first, I promise you that by the time you're finished with this book, it will seem like old hat. (For a detailed explanation of what's going on in Figure 4-2, see Chapter 13.)

In the olden days (pre-storyboards, and thus pre-iOS 5 and pre-Xcode 4.2), you used *nib* files to define your user interface one view controller at a time. The term *nib* (with its corresponding file extension .xib) is an acronym for NeXT Interface Builder, a bit of software originally developed at NeXT Computer, whose OPENSTEP operating system was used as the basis for creating Mac OS X. A nib file is a special type of resource file that you use to store the iOS user interface you create with the Interface Builder editor. Storyboards are actually just a series of connected nib files.

View controllers manage what you see on the iPad or iPhone screen. For more on view controllers, check out the section "View Controllers — the Main Storyboard Players," later in this chapter.

Working with object graphs

Continuing with the storyboard tour, note that as you create your storyboard, you create an *object graph* that is then archived when you save the file. When you load the file, the object graph is unarchived.

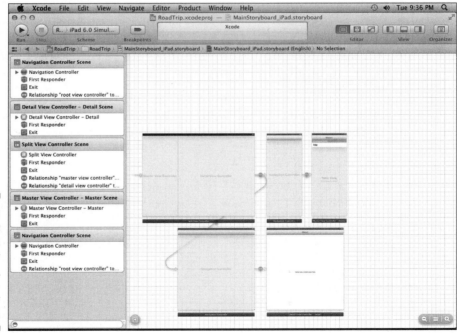

Figure 4-2:
RoadTrip
Main
Story
board_
iPad.
story
board.

So, what's an *object graph?* Here's the short answer: Object-oriented programs are made up of complex webs of interrelated objects. They are linked to one another in a variety of ways. One object can contain another object, for example, or it can own it, or it can reference it. All the items that you see in your storyboard (and some items that you don't see) are all objects and are part of that web of objects. The Interface Builder editor allows you to create this network graphically and then, at runtime, it makes the connections for you.

A storyboard file can capture your entire user interface in one place and lets you define both the individual view controllers and the transitions between those view controllers. As a result, storyboards capture the flow of your overall user interface in addition to the content you present.

If you are creating new applications, the Xcode templates have an option for you to use storyboards. For other applications, you can add storyboards, but you won't need to do that in this book.

In the application you build in this book, you use just one storyboard file to store all the view controllers and views for each device. Behind the curtain, however, Interface Builder takes the contents of this one storyboard file and divides it into discrete pieces that can be loaded individually for better performance.

That's the 100-yard-dash tour of the storyboard and its purpose. For you to truly get a feel for the essence of the storyboard, however, you need to see how the storyboard replicates the way an iOS application is structured — in other words, you need an in-depth look at the iOS application architecture. The best way to do that is within the context of a real application. So, before I get into even more detail about working in the storyboard, I want to give you a sense of the basic functions and purpose of the application developed throughout this book — the app I've affectionately named RoadTrip.

Defining What You Want an Application to Do: The RoadTrip Application

Necessity is the mother of invention, and the RoadTrip project was inspired by a necessity of a sort. My evil twin, Skippy, was about to leave on a 7,000-mile road trip around the United States in the family's pink 1959 Cadillac Eldorado Biarritz convertible. (Driving a car that gets only 8 miles per gallon is merely one of the reasons we call him evil.)

I walked in one day and found him on his living room floor, with maps and tour books spread out every which way. "Okay, brother," he said, "since you're so smart, can't you figure out a way so that when I'm traveling, I don't have to spread out these maps and paper all over my car? Can't I just keep all the stuff I need on my iPad?"

Being the good brother that I am, I started to give the idea some thought.

To make RoadTrip a useful application, I had to move from Skippy's problem — all those maps and tour books all over his car — to the app's solution, which is to present information that's relevant to one of the following questions:

✔ Where are you?

✔ Where do you plan to be?

✔ What do want to do, or where do you want to go when you get there?

By concentrating on what is truly relevant, you reduce the app to the amount of information you need to deal with at any one time.

Guided by the app's purpose — as well as by what the iPad or iPhone does best — I developed a clearer picture of what Skippy would want the app to do. That clearer picture comes into focus in Figure 4-3, where — there on the left side — you can see the application functionality in what Xcode calls the Master view. The pane on the right — displaying the appropriately named Detail view — gives my evil twin brother the chance to watch his car go back and forth onscreen (with sound effects no less — he is easily amused). (For more on Master and Detail views, check out Chapter 13.)

Figure 4-3:
A real-live example of the Master view/Detail view combination.

The iPad's split-view interface allows the user to sometimes see a Master view and a Detail view at the same time. The iPhone's smaller screen requires that you design your user interface to only show one or the other at a given time. We'll use the iPad storyboard file as the example in this chapter, but the storyboard for the iPhone is basically similar – it just differs in some of the details. You'll see how to manage both iPad and iPhone user interfaces in later chapters.

This division into Master view and Detail view is an elegant way of allowing the user to pick a task from the navigation tree on the left and see the content associated with that task on the right. The tasks I came up with for my RoadTrip app are as follows:

- ✔ **Get real-time weather access.** Snow in New York in August? Not likely, but these days you never can tell. You can see real-time weather access at work in Figure 4-4.

- ✔ **Find out what's going on wherever you are.** Figure 4-5 shows an event that Skippy might be interested in.

- ✔ **Bring up a map based on the destination.** The map shows Skippy's destination and points of interest, and even allows him to zero in on his current location. (See Figure 4-6.)

Figure 4-4:
The weather in New York on the iPad screen.

Figure 4-5:
RoadTrip
describes
some things
for you to do
while in a
city.

Figure 4-6:
Finding your
way with
pinpoint
accuracy.

> ✔ **Find some place on a map.** If Skippy has an address that he wants to find on the map, he should be able to do that *and* get its GPS coordinates as well. (I threw that last bit in because Skippy is a map freak). Figure 4-7 gives an example of finding a point of interest on a map.

There are of course a lot of other features you'd want to add to this app to make it worth the $.99 you'll be charging, and I talk about some of those in Chapter 21, as well as how this app fits into an Application Ecosystem of the kind I explain in Chapter 1.

Given the user interface described in this section, the big questions are a) how do you create an application from your knowledge of the problem, and b) how do you want the app to help solve it?

The answers to those questions can be found in the application architecture.

In the Apple Human Interface Guidelines, Apple suggests the current selection in the Master view (left pane) should be indicated. While this is critical for something like Mail, where you would like to know which e-mail in the list of e-mails is currently shown in the Detail view (right pane), I (and other people who have reviewed this design) don't think it is necessary in all cases. It is your choice, and in Chapter 13 I'll give you the option of having the current Master View selection remain highlighted.

Figure 4-7:
Where is Radio City Music Hall anyway?

Creating the Application Architecture

At a basic level, the RoadTrip application is made up of the following:

✔ **Models:** Model objects encapsulate the "application" logic and content (data) of the application.

✔ **Views:** Data content is useless if your user never sees it. *Views* are the windows to your content — the pathway to the user experience — and it's up to you to decide what information to display and how to display it. Part of the decision will involve what *kind* of view best serves your content. (Xcode offers you a number of different ways to display both information and navigation choices.)

✔ **View controllers:** View controllers manage the user experience. They connect the views that present the user experience with the models that provide the necessary content. View controllers also manage the way the user navigates the application.

The MVC (Model-View-Controller) model is pretty much the basis for all iPad application development projects. I explain MVC in more detail in the "The Model-View-Controller (MVC) design pattern" section, later in this chapter. The trick here is to come up with just the right views, view controllers, and model objects to get your project off the ground.

What You Add Where

The following table summarizes the chapters in which you will add new Objective-C classes and new view controller scenes to your project. The Chapter 3 classes and storyboard scenes are built with Apple's Master-Detail template, but the rest are up to you as you work through this book.

Chapter	Create Objective-C Class	Add Storyboard Scene
3	RTAppDelegate	Master View controller
	RTMasterViewController	Detail View controller
	RTDetailViewController	
5		Test Drive controller
9	TestDriveController	
11	Trip	
	Destination	

Chapter	Create Objective-C Class	Add Storyboard Scene
14		Weather controller
		Map controller
		Find controller
		Destination Controller
15	WeatherController	
16	EventsController	
	EventPageController	
	Events	
19	FindController	
20	DestinationController	

But before you decide what you need to build your application, you'll need to understand what's available. *Frameworks* supply the classes you have to work with in your application — classes like UIView, UIViewController, UIControl, and a whole lot more.

Using Frameworks

A *framework* offers common code that provides generic functionality. The SDK provides a set of frameworks for incorporating technologies, services, and features into your apps. For example, the UIKit framework gives you event-handling support, drawing support, windows, views, and controls that you can use in your app.

A framework is designed to easily integrate the code that runs, say, an app or game or that delivers the information your user wants. A framework is similar to a software library, but with an added twist: It also implements a program's *flow of control* (in contrast to a software library, whose components are arranged by the programmer into a flow of control). So, when working within a framework, the programmer doesn't have to decide the order in which things should happen — such as which messages are sent to which objects and in what order when an application launches, or when a user touches a button on the screen. Instead, the order of those events, or flow of control, is a part of the framework.

When you use a framework, you provide your app with a ready-made set of basic functions; essentially you've told it "Here's how to act," and it's in a position to take the ball and run with it. With the framework in place, all you need to do is add the specific functionality that you want in the app — the content as well as the controls and views that enable the user to access and use that content.

The frameworks and iOS provide pretty complex functionality, such as

- ✔ Launching the app and displaying a window on the screen
- ✔ Displaying controls on the screen and responding to a user action — changing a toggle switch, for example, or scrolling a view, such as the list of your contacts
- ✔ Accessing sites on the Internet, not just through a browser but also from within your own program
- ✔ Managing user preferences
- ✔ Playing sounds and movies

Some developers talk in terms of "using a framework" — but in reality, your code doesn't use the framework so much as the framework uses your code. Your code provides the functions that the framework accesses; the framework needs your code to become an app that does something other than start up, display a blank window, and then end. This perspective makes figuring out how to work with a framework much easier.

If this seems too good to be true, well, okay, it is — all that complexity (and convenience) comes at a cost. It can be really difficult to get your head around the whole thing and know exactly where (and how) to add your app's functionality to the functionality that the framework supplies. That's where design patterns, which I discuss next, come in. Understanding the design patterns behind the frameworks gives you a way of thinking about a framework — especially UIKit because it's based on the MVC design pattern — that doesn't make your head explode.

Using Design Patterns

When it comes to iOS app development, the UIKit framework does a lot of the heavy lifting for you. That's all well and good, but working with that framework is a little more complicated than just letting it do its work. The framework is designed around certain programming paradigms, also known as *design patterns*. The design pattern is a model that your own code must be consistent with.

To understand how to take best advantage of the power of frameworks — or (better put), figuring out how the framework objects want to best use your code — you need to understand design patterns. If you don't understand them or if you try to work around them because you're sure that you have a "better" way of doing things, your job will actually end up being much more difficult. (Developing software can be hard enough, so making your job more difficult is definitely something you want to avoid.) Getting a handle on the basic design patterns that the framework uses (and expects) will help you develop an app that makes the best use of the framework. This means doing the least amount of work in the shortest amount of time.

The design patterns can help you to understand not only how to structure your code but also how the framework itself is structured. They describe relationships and interactions between classes or objects, as well as how responsibilities should be distributed among classes so that the iPad does what you want it to do. In programming terms, a design pattern is a commonly used template that gives you a consistent way to get a particular task done.

The iOS design patterns

To develop an iOS app, you need to be comfortable with the following basic design patterns:

- Model-View-Controller (MVC)
- Delegation
- Block Objects
- Target-Action
- Managed Memory Model

Of these, the Model-View-Controller design pattern is the key to understanding how an iPad or iPhone app works and is the focus of the following section. I explain the remainder of the patterns as they're put to use in this book.

Another basic design pattern exists as well: Threads and Concurrency. This pattern enables you to execute tasks concurrently (including the use of Grand Central Dispatch, that aiding-and-abetting feature introduced in OS X Snow Leopard for taking full advantage of all that processing power available, even on the smaller iPad and much smaller iPhone). The Threads and Concurrency design pattern — as well as Grand Central Dispatch — is way beyond the scope of this book.

The Model-View-Controller (MVC) design pattern

The iOS frameworks are *object oriented*. An easy way to understand what that really means is to think about a team working in an office. The work that needs to get done is divided up and assigned to individual team members (in this case, objects). Each team member has a job and works with other team members to get things done. What's more, a good team member doesn't care how other members do their work, just that they do it according to the agreed upon division of labor. Likewise, an object in object-oriented programming takes care of its own business and doesn't care what the object in the virtual cubicle next door is doing, as long as it will do what it's supposed to do when asked to do it.

Object-oriented programming was originally developed to make code more maintainable, reusable, extensible, and understandable by encapsulating all the functionality behind well-defined interfaces. The actual details of how something works (as well as its data) are hidden, which makes modifying and extending an application much easier.

Great — so far — but a pesky question still plagues programmers:

Exactly how do you decide on the objects and what each one does?

Sometimes the answer to that question is pretty easy — just use the real world as a model. (Eureka!) In the RoadTrip app, for example, some of the classes of model objects are `Trip`, `Events`, `Destination`, and so on. But when it comes to a generic program structure, how *do* you decide what the objects should be? That may not be so obvious.

The MVC pattern is a well-established way to group application functions into objects. Variations of it have been around at least since the early days of Smalltalk, one of the very first object-oriented languages. The MVC is a high-level pattern — it addresses the architecture of an application and classifies objects according to the general roles they play in an application, rather than drilling down into specifics.

The MVC pattern creates, in effect, a miniature universe for the application, populated with three distinct kinds of objects. It also specifies roles and responsibilities for all three types of objects and specifies the way they're supposed to interact with each other. To make things more concrete (that is, to keep your head from exploding), imagine a big, beautiful, 60-inch, flat-screen TV. Here's the gist:

✔ **Model objects:** These objects together comprise the content "engine" of your app. They contain the app's data and logic — making your app more than just a pretty face. In the RoadTrip application, for example, the model maintains a list of events and sights, as well as the name and location of the destination and a background image to use.

   You can think of the *model* (which may be one object or several that interact) as a particular television program, one that, quite frankly, doesn't give a hoot about what TV set it's shown on.

   In fact, the model shouldn't give a hoot. Even though it owns its data, it should have no connection to the user interface and should be blissfully ignorant about what's done with its data.

✔ **View objects:** These objects display things on the screen and respond to user actions. Pretty much anything you can see is a kind of view object —

the window and all the controls, for example. Your views know how to display information they receive from the model object and how to get any input from the user the model may need. But the view itself should know nothing about the model. It may handle a request to display some events, but it doesn't bother itself with what that request means.

You can think of the *view* as a television screen that doesn't care about what program it's showing or what channel you just selected.

The UIKit framework provides many different kinds of views, as you find out in the next section.

If the view knows nothing about the model, and the model knows nothing about the view, how do you get data and other notifications to pass from one to the other? To get that conversation started (Model: "I've just updated my data." View: "Hey, give me something to display," for example), you need the third element in the MVC triumvirate, the controller.

✔ **Controller objects:** These objects connect the application's view objects to its model objects. They supply the view objects with what they need to display (getting it from the model) and also provide the model with user input from the view.

You can think of the *controller* as the circuitry that pulls the show off of the cable and then sends it to the screen or requests a particular pay-per-view show.

The basic application architecture looks like Figure 4-8.

Figure 4-8: The Model-View-Controller.

When you think about your application in terms of model, view, and controller objects, the UIKit framework starts to make sense. Understanding the framework this way also begins to lift the fog hanging over where to make at least part of your application-specific behavior go. Before you delve into that topic, however, you need to know a little more about the classes that the UIKit provides, because these are the guys you will task with implementing the MVC design pattern — window classes, view classes, and view controller classes.

Throughout this book, I'll be talking about both classes and objects, and now is as good a time as any to remind you of the difference between the two.

In Objective-C, classes include instance variables, properties, and methods (that can access the instance variables of a class). Classes are about files in your project that contain code. Classes are *types* in your program.

Objects, on the other hand, exist at runtime and are *instances* of a class. You can think of a class as a blueprint to build an object of that type.

Working with Windows and Views

iPad apps have a single window, so you won't find additional document windows for displaying content. When your application is running — even though other apps may be hibernating or running in the background — your app's interface takes over the entire screen.

Looking out the window

The single window that you see displayed on the iPad or iPhone is an instance of the UIWindow class. This window is created at launch time, either programmatically by you or automatically by UIKit when you use a storyboard. In general, after you create the Window object (that is, if you create it instead of having it done for you), you never really have to think about it again.

A user can't directly close or manipulate an iOS window. It's your app that programmatically manages the window.

Although your application never creates more than one window at a time, iOS can support additional windows on top of your window. The system status bar is one example. You can also display alerts on top of your window by using the supplied Alert views.

Admiring the view

In an iOS app world, view objects are responsible for the view functionality in the Model-View-Controller architecture. A *view* is a rectangular area on the screen (on top of a window).

In the UIKit framework, windows are really a special kind of view, but for the purpose of this discussion, I'm referring to views that sit on top of the window.

What views do

Views are the main way for your app to interact with a user. This interaction happens in two ways:

- ✔ **Views display content.** This happens, for example, by making drawing and animation happen onscreen. In essence, the view object displays the data from the model object.

- ✔ **Views handle touch events.** Views respond when the user touches a button, for example. Handling touch events is part of a responder chain (which I explain in Chapter 6).

The view hierarchy

Views and subviews create a view hierarchy. You have two ways of looking at it (no pun intended this time): visually (how the user perceives it) and programmatically (how you create it). You must be clear about the differences or you'll find yourself in a state of confusion that resembles the subway at rush hour.

Looking at it visually, the window is at the base of this hierarchy with a *Content view* on top of it (a transparent view that fills the window's Content rectangle). The Content view displays information as well as allowing the user to interact with the application, using (preferably standard) user-interface items such as text fields, buttons, toolbars, and tables.

In your program, that relationship is different. The Content view is added to the window view as a *subview.* But the Content view can also have its own subviews, and so on. Possible relationships include:

- ✔ Views added to the Content view become *subviews* of it.

- ✔ Views added to the Content view become the *superviews* of any views added to them.

- ✔ A view can have one (and only one) superview and zero or more subviews.

It seems counterintuitive, but a subview is displayed *on top of* its parent view (that is, on top of its superview). Think about this relationship as containment: A superview *contains* its subviews. Figure 4-9 shows an example of a view hierarchy.

Controls — such as buttons, text fields, and so on — are actually view subclasses that become subviews. So are any other display areas that you may specify. The view must manage its subviews, as well as resize itself with respect to its superviews. Fortunately, much of what the view must do is already coded for you. The UIKit framework supplies the code that defines view behavior.

The visual hierarchy   ...   translates to a structural one.

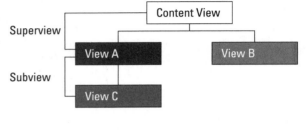

The view hierarchy also plays a key role in both drawing and event handling. I explain event handling in Chapter 6.

You create or modify a view hierarchy whenever you add a view to another view, either programmatically or with the help of the Interface Builder. The UIKit framework automatically handles the relationships associated with the view hierarchy.

Developers typically gloss over this visual-versus-programmatic-view-hierarchy stuff when starting out — and without understanding these concepts, it's really difficult to get a handle on what's going on.

The kinds of views you use

The UIView class defines the basic properties of a view, and you may be able to use it "as is" — as you'll do in the Test Drive screen of the RoadTrip app — by simply adding an image view and some controls.

In the Detail view shown back in Figure 4-3, the user can take a test drive by tapping the Test Drive button. (Later in the book, in Chapter 10, I show you how to animate the car so that it leisurely drives to the other side of the screen, turns around, drives back, and then turns around one more time so that it's back to where it started on the screen.)

The UIKit framework also provides you with a number of other views that are subclassed from UIView. These views implement the kinds of things that you as a developer need to do in the user interface.

It's important to think about the view objects that are part of the UIKit framework. When you use an object such as a UISlider or UIButton, your slider or button behaves just like a slider or button in any other iOS app. This enables the consistency in appearance and behavior across apps that users expect. (For more about why this kind of consistency is one of the characteristics of a great app, see Chapter 1.)

Container views

Container views are a technical (Apple) term for content views that do more than just lie there on the screen and display your controls and other content. The UIScrollView class, for example, adds scrolling without you having to do any work. Most of the time, Container views just do their thing in the background (as part of other views you use — Table views, for example), and I don't explain any more about them in this book because you won't need to use or manage them explicitly.

UITableView inherits this scrolling capability from UIScrollView and adds the ability to display lists and respond to the selections of an item in that list. Think of the Contacts application on your iPad (and a host of others, come to think of it). UITableView is one of the primary navigation views on the iPad.

Table views are used a lot in iPad applications to do these two things:

- ✓ **Display hierarchal data:** For an example, think of the Music application, which gives you a list of albums and, if you select one, a list of songs.

- ✓ **Act as a table of contents:** Now, think of the Settings application, which gives you a list of applications that you can set preferences for. When you select one of those applications from the list, it takes you to a view that lists what preferences you're able to set as well as a way to set them.

In the RoadTrip app, the *List* views — such as the ones in the Master view shown earlier in Figure 4-3 — are Table views. The List view shown in the figure acts as an introduction to the application; it provides the user with a way to decide where he or she wants to go, for example, by selecting Destination in the Table view.

Another Container view, the UIToolbar class, contains button-like controls, which you find everywhere on the iPad. In the Mail app, for example, you tap an icon on the bottom toolbar to respond to an e-mail. In RoadTrip, you find such controls at the top of the Map view (refer to Figure 4-6) to allow you to decide on how you want the map to be displayed.

Controls

Controls are the fingertip-friendly graphics that are used extensively in a typical application's user interface. Controls are actually subclasses of the UIControl superclass, a subclass of the UIView class. They include touchable items such as buttons, sliders, and switches, as well as text fields in which you enter data. You use them in your views, including, as you just saw, in a toolbar.

Controls make heavy use of the Target-Action design pattern, which is used when you touch the Test Drive button as shown in Figure 4-10.

I explain the Target-Action pattern in detail in Chapter 9.

Display views

Think of *Display views* as controls that look good but don't really do anything except, well, look good. These include the following: `UIImageView` (check out the background to the Master view shown earlier in Figure 4-3 for an example); `UILabel` (for adding labels to buttons and other controls); `UIProgressView`; and `UIActivityIndicatorView`. I like to add an activity indicator to those views where I download data so folks have something to watch while waiting.

Text and Web views

Text and *Web views* provide a way to display formatted text in your application. The `UITextView` class supports the display and editing of multiple lines of text in a scrollable area. The `UIWebView` class provides a way to display HTML content. These views can be used as the Main view, or as a sub-view of a another view. (You encounter `UIWebView` in the RoadTrip app as Weather views.) `UIWebView` is also the primary way to include graphics and formatted text in Text Display views.

Figure 4-10:
A button is the tip of the Target-Action design pattern.

The views that display content — such as the Detail views shown previously in Figures 4-4 and 4-5 — are *Web* views, for some very good, practical reasons, which I'll now list:

✔ **Some views must be updated regularly.** *Web views,* in that context, are the perfect solution; they make it easy to access data from a central repository on the Internet. (Client/server is alive and well!)

✔ **Web views can easily display formatted data that's locally stored.** Real-time access isn't always necessary — sometimes it's perfectly fine to store some data on the iPad or iPhone. Web views have no problem with locally stored data, which is very handy.

✔ **Web views can access websites!** Don't overlook the obvious: Web views open the door to websites, which means you have the whole Internet at your beck and call. If users want more detailed weather information, for example, they can get to the ten-day forecast by simply touching a link.

Alert views and Action sheets

Alert views and *Action sheets* present a message to the user, along with buttons that allow the user to respond to the message. Alert views and Action sheets are similar in function but look and behave differently from one another. For example, the UIAlertView class displays a blue alert box that pops up on the screen, and the UIActionSheet class displays a box that slides in from the bottom of the screen.

I have you add an Alert view to the RoadTrip app in Chapter 9 to inform the user when the Internet isn't available. Figure 4-11 shows what the user would see if no Internet connection is available.

Navigation views

Tab bars and Navigation bars work in conjunction with view controllers to provide tools for navigating in your app. (For more on navigation bars, see Chapter 5.) Normally, you don't need to create a UITabBar or UINavigationBar directly — it's easier to let Interface Builder do the job for you or configure these views through a Tab bar or Navigation controller, respectively.

The window

You'll remember this one: The *window* provides the surface for drawing content and is the root container for all other views.

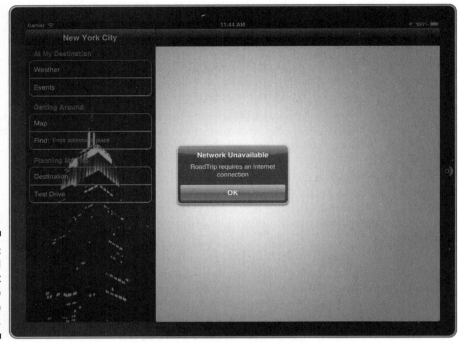

Figure 4-11:
Users need
the Internet
alert, so
be sure to
include it.

View Controllers — the Main Storyboard Players

Early in this chapter, I provide an overview of the *storyboard* — the white board, so to speak, on which you lay out the flow of the elements, or *design pattern,* of your application. In this book, the example application developed throughout — RoadTrip — uses the Model-View-Controller (MVC) design pattern, and in this particular design pattern, it's the *view controllers* that implement the pattern's controller component. These controller objects contain the code that connects the app's view objects to its model objects. Whenever the view needs to display something, the view controller goes out and gets what the view needs from the model. Similarly, view controllers respond to controls in your Content view and may do things like tell the model to update its data (when the user adds or changes text in a text field, for example), compute something (the current value of, say, your U.S. dollars in British pounds), or change the view being displayed (like when the user presses the Detail Disclosure button on the iPod application to find out more about a song).

View controllers, as you can see in Figure 4-12, are the objects that control what is displayed and that respond to user actions. They are the heart and soul of the storyboard.

Figure 4-12:
It's all about
the view
controller.

As I explain in more detail in Chapter 9, a view controller is often the (target) object that responds to the onscreen controls. The Target-Action mechanism is what enables the view controller to be aware of any changes in the view, which can then be transmitted to the model.

Imagine that an iPad user launches the RoadTrip app. On the left side (or in a popover), he or she sees a Table view and on the right side a Detail view (the Weather for example). (Refer to Figure 4-4.) The user may tap an entry (cell) in the Table view to display events. The Events controller is then launched and sends a message to the appropriate method in the model to get the events. The model object returns a list of URLs, and so on. The controller then delivers that information to the view, which promptly displays the information to the user.

If your imaginary user now launches the RoadTrip app on the iPhone (or iPad Touch), the user will see a full-screen table view. The screen will shift to a detail view when the user taps a cell in the table. The same information is available in the iPhone version as in the iPad version, but the user interface has to be slightly different.

You will be pleased to know that you can build one set of Objective-C classes that works with both the iPhone and iPad storyboard files, so you only need one set of code to build your Universal app.

The sequence of events is as follows:

1. A message is sent to that view's view controller to handle the request.
2. The view controller's method interacts with the `Trip` model object.
3. The model object processes the request from the user for the current events.
4. The model object sends the data back to the view controller.
5. The view controller sends the data to the view to display the information.

View controllers have other vital iPad responsibilities as well, such as the following:

- **Managing a set of views:** This includes creating the views as well as flushing them from memory during low-memory situations.

- **Responding to a change in the device's orientation:** If, say, the user causes the iPad to switch from landscape to portrait orientation, the view controller responds by adjusting its views to match the new orientation.

- **Creating a Modal (not model) view:** A Modal view is a child window that displays a dialog that requires the user to do something (tap the Yes or Cancel button, for example) before returning to the application.

  You use a Modal view to ensure that the user has paid attention to the implications of an action (for example, "Are you *sure* you want to delete all your contacts?").

- **Display a popover:** A popover is a transient view that is shown when people tap a control or an onscreen area. Popovers are used in a variety of ways, including displaying the Master view when a Split View app (like RoadTrip) is in Portrait orientation, or displaying additional information about a selection.

- **Respond to user input and navigation:** While the view processes a touch using the Target-Action pattern, it is almost always the view that is the target of the action — responding to the touch appropriately (like having a '59 Cadillac Eldorado Biarritz convertible drive right up the center of the screen — sound effects included).

View controllers are also typically the objects that serve as delegates and data sources for Table views (more about those in Chapter 19) as well as for other kinds of framework views.

In addition to the base `UIViewController` class, `UIKit` includes the following:

- ✔ subclasses such as `UITabBarController` (to manage the Tab bar)
- ✔ `UITableViewController` (which you use to manage Table views)
- ✔ `UINavigationController` (which implements navigation back and forth between view controllers)
- ✔ `UIPageViewController` (to allow users to navigate between view controllers using the specified transition)
- ✔ `UIImagePickerController` (to access the camera and Photo library on the iPad)
- ✔ `UISplitViewController` (which you'll be using on the iPad — only — to display the side-by-side views you see in Figure 4-3, for example).

What About the Model?

As this chapter shows (and as you'll continue to discover), much of the functionality you need in an application is already in the frameworks.

But when it comes to the *model objects* — the things you build to actually hold the data and carry out the logic for your app — you're on your own for the most part. In the RoadTrip app, for example, you're going to need to create a `Trip` object that owns the data and logic and uses other objects to perform some of the actions it needs.

I talk about the model and model classes in more detail in Chapter 11. That's where you'll also find much more on implementing model objects.

You may find classes in the framework that help you get the nuts and bolts of the model working. But the actual content and specific functionality are up to you.

To implement the structure that enables me to include several destinations in the RoadTrip app, I need to have the data. I use *property lists* (XML files, in other words) to take care of that because they're well suited for the job, and (more importantly) support for them is built in to the iPad frameworks. (For more on property lists, see Chapter 11.)

iOS now includes a `UIDocument` class for managing the data associated with a user's documents. If you're implementing a document-based application, you can use this class to reduce the amount of work you must do to manage your document data. If you're implementing an application that supports iCloud storage, the use of document objects makes the job of storing files in iCloud much easier. I don't cover the `UIDocument` class in this book.

Using naming conventions

When creating your own classes, methods, and variables, it's a good idea to follow a couple of standard naming conventions:

✔ **Class names** (such as `View`) should start with a capital letter.

✔ The names of **methods** (such as `view DidLoad`) should start with a lowercase letter and additional words within the name should start with an uppercase letter (`viewDidLoad`).

✔ The names of **instance variables** (such as `frame`) should start with a lowercase letter.

When you follow these conventions, you can tell from the name what something actually is. A few more such conventions are good to know, and I explain them as they arise in the course of the book.

It's Not That Neat

It would be nice (not to mention amazing) if everything fit neatly into model, view, or controller, but it doesn't work that way.

You really need to know about one other kind of class. The `UIApplication` class handles routing of incoming user events, dispatches action messages from controls, and deals with numerous other basic plumbing functions that aren't the responsibilities of a model, view, or controller. It typically works with an *application delegate,* a piece of code that allows you to customize how your application responds to events such as application launch, low-memory warnings, and application termination. The app delegate (as it's often referred to) is also the place where you'll create your model. I explain the mysteries of the `UIApplication` class as well as the role of the application delegate in Chapter 6.

Taking a Look at Other Frameworks

So far, almost all the things that I've talked about can be found in the `UIKit` framework, whose sole purpose in life is to provide a developer with all the classes an application needs in order to construct and manage its user interface. The `UIKit` framework does a majority of the heavy lifting for you, but developers don't live by the `UIKit` framework alone; quite a few other frameworks get put into play as well. The next few sections give you a rundown of some of the other frameworks you may encounter.

The Foundation framework

The Foundation framework is similar to the UIKit framework in that it defines general-purpose classes. The difference is that whereas UIKit limits itself to classes that implement the user interface, the Foundation framework stakes a claim on all the other stuff — the non–user-interface stuff — you need in your app. In practical terms, this means that the Foundation framework defines basic object behavior, memory management, notifications, internationalization, and localization.

The Foundation framework also provides *object wrappers* or *equivalents* (for numeric values, strings, and collections) and *utility classes* (for accessing underlying system entities and services, such as ports, threads, and file systems as well as networking, and date and time management).

The CoreGraphics framework

The CoreGraphics framework contains the interfaces for the Quartz 2D drawing API and is the same advanced, vector-based drawing engine that's used in Mac OS X. It provides support for path-based drawing, anti-aliased rendering, gradients, images, colors, coordinate-space transformations, and PDF document creation, display, and parsing. Although the API is C based, it uses object-based abstractions to make things easier for you. While it is the basis for many things you see on the screen, you won't be using it directly in this book.

Even more frameworks

Besides the UIKit, Foundation, and CoreGraphics frameworks, you use a handful of others in this book's example application, as well as (I'm sure) in your own applications down the road. They are as follows:

- ✔ MapKit: Lets you embed a fully functional map interface into your application. The map support provided by this framework includes many of the features normally found in the Maps application.

- ✔ AVFoundation: Provides an Objective-C interface for managing and playing audio-visual media in your iOS application.

- ✔ AudioToolbox: Contains the APIs that provide application-level services — for playing sounds, for example.

- ✔ MediaPlayer: Provides basic functionality for playing movie, music, audio podcast, and audiobook files, as well as access to the iPod Library.

✔ SystemConfiguration: Contains interfaces for determining the network configuration of a device.

✔ CoreLocation: Provides location data to support functionality such as social networking. It also includes classes to do both forward and reverse geocoding (which I explain in Chapter 18).

You can find many, many more frameworks for your apps in iOS Technology Overview Appendix B: iOS Frameworks, which you can find in the iOS Developer Library, at http://developer.apple.com/library/ios/navigation/index.html; then enter iOS Technology Overview. Be advised that if you want to be able to do something, there's probably a framework to support it.

Understanding the MVC in the Project

As one might expect, when you create an Xcode project, any and all classes added to the project by the template correspond to the Model-View-Controller design pattern. No surprises there.

If you look carefully, you can actually see how the features of the MVC model end up getting translated into a real, live project. Start by checking out the Project navigator, where you see RTMasterViewController .h and .m files, RTDetailViewController .h and .m files, and RTAppDelegate .h and .m files. (Remember that, because everything in the iPad version is built using a split view, you're going to see two controllers — one for the Master view and one for the Detail view. I explain that in detail in Chapter 13.)

The interface (.h file) contains the class declaration and the methods and properties associated with the class. But although the interface file has traditionally also included the instance variables, you're actually going to include all instance variables in the implementation file instead, so you can keep them away from prying eyes. (You can find more on hiding the instance variables in Chapter 6.)

The implementation (.m file) contains the actual code for the methods of the class and — as just mentioned — also includes your instance variables.

The RTMasterViewController and RTDetailViewController correspond to the controllers I explain in the "View Controllers — the Main Storyboard Players" section, earlier in this chapter. But where are the classes that correspond to the views?

To find out, select the `MainStoryboard_iPad` file in the Project navigator and you see two view controllers in the Document Outline. Each view controller in a storyboard file manages a single scene. Select the disclosure triangle to expand the Master View controller and you see its view, shown in Figure 4-13.

When you click the view controller in the Document Outline, you see a (blue) line around the window to represent the view controller.

If you can't see the Document Outline, you can use the Hide/Show Document Outline control, shown in Figure 4-14. You can also zoom in and out of a storyboard by double-clicking in the Interface Builder editor or using the zoom control shown in Figure 4-14.

Now click the view in the Document Outline, and you'll see a display of the view itself — waiting for you to add all sorts of interesting images and controls (which you do in the next chapter). You can see that in Figure 4-14.

You see, of course, that the window changes — the view has been highlighted on the Canvas — but I explain more about that when I have you actually add the user interface elements in Interface Builder.

So now that you have controllers and views, what about models? (The design pattern is called Model-View-Controller, after all.) Well, the models aren't there . . . at least not yet. For that other shoe to drop, you'll have to go to Chapter 11, where I explain in great detail all about model classes and how to add them.

You can also see some of the other parts of the application infrastructure I mention earlier in the *Project navigator.* The `RTAppDelegate` `.h` and `.m` files in the Project navigation area correspond to the app delegate.

You'll see one other element in the Document Outline — the first responder: This object is the first entry in an app's dynamically constructed responder chain (a term I explain along with more about the application infrastructure at runtime in Chapter 6) and is the object designated to be the first handler of events other than touch events, such as motion events and a few other events you won't be working with in this book.

But because the responder chain of an application can't be determined at design time, the first responder proxy acts as a stand-in target for any action messages that need to be directed at the application's responder chain.

Although you might use the first responder mechanism quite a bit in your apps, you don't have to do anything to manage it. It's automatically set and maintained by the `UIKit` framework.

Figure 4-13:
The view
controller
highlighted
on the
Canvas.

Figure 4-14:
The view
in the
storyboard.

Chapter 5

Creating the RoadTrip User Interface

In This Chapter

▶ Seeing how storyboards work

▶ Working in the Utility area

▶ Understanding and adding navigation controllers

▶ Using Interface Builder to add objects to your storyboard

*I*f you've read the preceding chapters, you have the foundation for understanding the tools you need to build an app, with particular focus on the example app developed in this book. Now you're ready to find out how to add a user interface to your app via the storyboard.

In this chapter, I show you how to add items to the `TestDrive Controller`'s view using both Interface Builder and the user interface objects available to you in the Library pane in the Utility area. You first add these items to your iPad storyboard and then add similar items to your iPhone storyboard.

Creating Your User Interface in the iPad Storyboard

In the Project navigator, select the `MainStoryboard_iPad.storyboard` file and you'll see several view controllers in the Document Outline (Split View Controller, Master View Controller, and Detail View Controller). Each view controller in a storyboard file manages a single *scene* (a scene, in this sense, is really just a view controller). On the iPad, courtesy of the Split View controller (which I explain in more detail in Chapter 13) or a popover controller, you can have multiple scenes on a screen. (On the iPhone, alas, generally you can see only one scene on a screen at a time). In the Document Outline, select the disclosure triangle next to the Master View Controller in the Master View Controller – Master Scene to expand the view controller and you'll see its view.

If you can't see the Document Outline, you can use the Hide/Show Document Outline control shown in the lower-middle of Figure 5-1. You can also zoom in and out of a storyboard by double-clicking in the storyboard's Canvas, or by using the zoom control shown in the lower-right in Figure 5-1. The = sign returns the storyboard to full size, which is the only way views are editable.

To add user interface elements, select the view you want to work with under the view controller heading listed in the Document Outline.

It's about the view controller

Selecting a storyboard file in the Project navigator launches Interface Builder, which is the editor you use to edit the storyboard files for your application. Most applications need only one storyboard file, but because you're creating a *universal* app, you'll have two storyboards, one for the iPad user interface (`MainStoryboard_iPad.storyboard`) and one for the iPhone user interface (`MainStoryboard_iPhone.storyboard`). Each storyboard file you create has its own *initial view controller,* which serves as the entry point into the storyboard. For example, in your application's main storyboard file, the initial view controller would be the first view controller presented by your application.

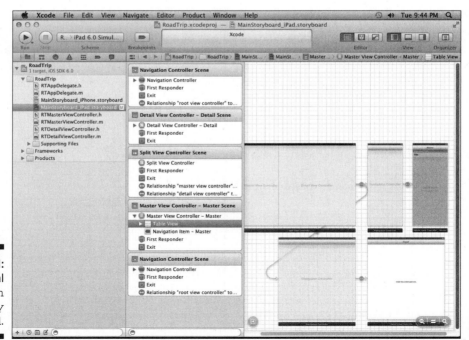

Figure 5-1:
The initial
Main
Story
board.

The view controller is the big kahuna here, and each view controller in a story-board file, as I said, manages a single scene. For iPhone applications, a scene manages one screen's worth of content, but for iPad applications, the content from multiple scenes can be onscreen simultaneously. To add new scenes to your storyboard file, all you have to do is drag a view controller from the Library to the storyboard canvas. You can then add controls and other views (such as Image, Web, or even Table views) to the view controller's view.

Besides the ability to lay out your application as a whole, storyboards also reduce the amount of code you have to write. Say you want to create a transition from one view controller to another; all you would need to do is Control-click a button or Table View cell in one view controller and drag it to the other. Dragging between view controllers creates a *segue,* which appears in Interface Builder as a configurable object. Segues support all the same types of transitions available in UIKit, such as navigation and modal transitions. A segue also enables you to define custom transitions.

I explain more about segues and view controller transitions in Chapter 14, when you add more scenes and segues to the RoadTrip app.

Using Interface Builder to add the user elements

Xcode's Interface Builder enables you to create a storyboard by letting you lay out your user interface graphically in each view controller. You use Interface Builder to design your app's user interface and then save what you've done as a resource file, which is included in your app and loaded into your app at runtime. This resource file is then used to automatically create the window and your app's view controllers, as well as all your views and controls.

If you don't want to use Interface Builder, you can also create your objects programmatically — creating views and view controllers and even things like buttons and labels using your very own application code. I show you an example of creating a button programmatically in Chapter 15.

So how do you actually get those cute little controls into the view that lives in the view controller scene? For that, you use another area of the workspace — the Utility area.

As I explain in Chapter 2, you use the View selector on the toolbar to display or hide the Utility area. The Utility area is an optional area on the right side of the Workspace window. To hide or show the Utility area, click the Utility button on the View selector on the right on the Workspace toolbar. (In Figure 5-2, I'm using the View selector to open the Utility area.)

Figure 5-2:
The View
selector.

When you hover your mouse pointer over a toolbar button, a tooltip describes its function.

Figure 5-3 shows the Utility area in all its glory. I have resized the Library window and also selected the Icon view in the Library pane's View selector (the right segmented control selection at the top right of the Library pane). Personally, I find that easier to work with.

Figure 5-3:
The Utility
area.

Inspector selector bar

Inspector pane

Library selector bar

View selector

Filter bar

Category menu

As you can see, this area includes two panes, the top one for Quick Help and other inspectors (the Attributes inspector is selected here), and the bottom one for libraries of resources.

Working within the Utility Area

The Utility area consists of the Inspector and Library panes and their corresponding Inspector and Library selector bars. The idea is to use the Inspector pane to view and access Quick Help and other inspectors, and to scour the Library pane for ready-made resources you want to use in your project. You'll be using both the Inspector and Library panes in this chapter.

Inspector and Quick Help pane

You use the Inspector selector (shown in Figure 5-4) to toggle on the particular inspector you want to use. (Xcode makes the decision-making process a bit easier by having your choice of Navigator or Content editor predetermine which inspectors in fact show up in the Inspector selector.)

Figure 5-4:
The
Inspector
selector.

Utility area inspectors perform a variety of tasks. Following is a list of important inspectors and what you use them for:

✔ **File inspector (first button):** Lets you view and manage file metadata such as its name, type, and path.

✔ **Quick Help (second button):** Lets you view (applicable) details about what has been selected in an editor. Details include an abstract or concise description, where and how the selected element is declared, its scope, the parameters it takes, its platform and architecture availability, references, sample code, and so on. Different editors support different elements for selection, as follows:

   • *Symbols,* available for selection in the Source editor

   • *Interface objects,* available for selection in Interface Builder

   • *Build settings,* available for selection in the Project editor

Additional inspectors are available in some editors; for example, Interface Builder offers the following:

 ✓ **Identity inspector:** Lets you view and manage object metadata such as its class, runtime attributes, label, and so forth.

 ✓ **Attributes inspector:** Lets you configure the attributes specific to the selected interface object. For example, some text field attributes include text alignment and color, border type, and editability.

✓ **Size inspector:** Lets you specify characteristics such as the initial size and position, minimum and maximum sizes, and autosizing rules for an interface object.

✓ **Connections inspector:** Lets you view the outlets and actions for an interface object, make new connections, and delete existing connections. The Connections inspector is where you'll find things like outlets and targets that I explain in Chapter 9.

Library pane

A selection in the Library selector in the Library pane does the obvious: It selects a particular library of resources that you can then use in your project. Figure 5-5 shows the choices offered by the Library selector; the following list gives the details:

Figure 5-5:
The Library
selector.

 ✓ **File templates:** Click here to find templates for the common types of files you create using the New File menu. To add a file of that type to your project, simply drag it from the File Templates library to the Project navigator.

✓ **Code snippets:** Need just a smidgeon of code? Click here to find short pieces of source code you can then use in your application. Just drag the bit you found directly into your source code file.

 ✓ **Objects:** This library consists of interface objects you can use as part of your user interface. To add one to a particular view, drag it directly into your storyboard or nib file in Interface Builder.

 ✓ **Media files:** Here's where you'll find graphics, icons, and sound files. To use one, drag it directly to your storyboard or nib file in Interface Builder.

You can filter out what gets displayed in a selected library by entering your Search text into the text field in the Filter bar at the bottom of the Library pane.

Understanding iPad Navigation

Although the iPhone and iPad are very similar, one area in which they often differ is in how a user can navigate through an application.

For example, in iPhone apps that use a master-detail architecture, a Back button is prominently displayed as the user moves from a detail view to back to the Master view. (Figure 5-6 shows what I mean.) An iPad app that uses Split view functionality for the master-detail architecture will not need that Back button. But there are many other user interface designs on the iPad where a Back button is often used.

Apple has built this ability into the iOS architecture and has made it an integral part of the view controller architecture, as personified in the Navigation controller. (Okay, I know it isn't a "person," but you get the idea.)

Figure 5-6:
An iPhone
application
sequence.

A Navigation controller is a Container view controller that enables the user to navigate back and forth between view controllers. A Navigation controller is an instance of the `UINavigationController` class, which is a class you use "as is" and don't subclass. The methods of this class provide support for managing a stack-based collection of custom view controllers. This stack represents the path taken by the user through the application, with the bottom of the stack reflecting the starting point and the top of the stack reflecting the user's current position in the application.

Apple's `UIKit` framework (part of the Cocoa Touch frameworks) generally uses class names that begin with *UI*, such as `UIView`, `UIViewController`, `UIImageView`, `UIButton`, and many more. To avoid confusion, you should not use the UI prefix for your own class names. Apple also has special prefixes for many other frameworks. For example, the Core Image framework includes classes such as `CIColor`, `CIContext`, `CIFaceFeature`, and so on. These naming conventions provide hints so that when you come across an Apple class named `CIImage`, you can expect to find it in the Core Image framework.

Some developers adopt their own special prefixes for all their custom classes, including simple schemes such as using the RT prefix, so that class names could be `RTMasterViewController` (which is used in the RoadTrip sample), `RTMapController`, `RTWeatherController`, and so on. It's not necessary to use a unique prefix for every custom class name, but you should avoid using Apple's class names for your own classes.

A *stack* is a commonly used data structure that works on the principle of "last in, first out." Imagine an ideal boarding scenario for an airplane: Passengers would start being seated in the last seat in the last row, and they'd board the plane in back-to-front order until they got to the first seat in the first row, which would contain the seat for the last person to board. When the plane reached its destination, everyone would deplane (is that really a word?) in the reverse order. That last person on — the person in row one, seat one — would be the first person off.

A computer stack works on the same concept. Adding an object is called a *push* — in this case, when you tap the Travel button, for example, the view controller for that view is pushed onto the stack. Removing an object is called a *pop* — touching the Back button pops the view controller for the view being displayed. When you pop an object off the stack, it's always the last one you pushed onto it. The controller that was there before the push is still there and now becomes the active one.

Although the Navigation controller's primary job is to act as a manager of other view controllers, it also manages a few views. Specifically, it manages a *Navigation bar* that displays information about the user's current location in the data hierarchy, a Back button for navigating to previous screens, and any custom controls the current view controller needs.

Take another look at Figure 5-6 and notice that, when the user taps Events in the iPhone version of RoadTrip, the Navigation controller (courtesy of the storyboard) pushes the next view controller onto the stack. The new view controller's view slides into place and the Navigation bar items are updated appropriately. When the user taps the Back button on the Navigation bar, the current view controller pops off the stack, that view slides off the screen, and the user finds himself back in the previous view.

The Navigation controller maintains the stack of view controllers, one for each of the views displayed. The very first view controller that the Navigation controller pushes onto its stack when a Navigation controller is created is called the *Root view controller*. It remains active until the user selects the next view to look at.

Navigation bars enable a user to navigate the hierarchy. Here's what you need to know in order to make that work:

- ✔ The view beneath the Navigation bar presents the current level of the application.

- ✔ A Navigation bar includes a title for the current view.

- ✔ If the current view is lower in the hierarchy than the top level, a Back button appears on the left side of the bar; the user can tap it to return to the previous level. (Back in Figure 5-6, these buttons are named Road Trip and New York City and are shaped like a left-pointing arrow; the text in the Back button tells the user what the previous level was.)

- ✔ A Navigation bar may also have an Edit button on the right side — used to enter Editing mode for the current view — or even custom buttons.

On the iPad, the Master-Detail Application template has not one, but *two* Navigation controllers already included in the storyboard — one for the Master View controller and the other for the Detail View controller, as you can see in Figure 5-7.

The only "problem" right now is that each Navigation controller has only one view controller to manage, which means you won't be able to select anything and see a new view, with its accompanying Back button.

In this chapter, you get to fix that for the Detail View controller, at least.

As you can see in Figure 5-8, when you tap the first cell in the Master View controller (you'll add the Test Drive label shortly), a new view controller slides its view into place. If you select the Back button, you slide back to the previous Detail view.

Figure 5-7:
The
Navigation
controllers
are already
in.

Figure 5-8:
Navigating
in RoadTrip
on the iPad.

You have other (even slicker) iPad navigation options at your disposal, and I get to them in Chapter 13, where you get a chance to change from navigation that uses the Navigation controller to something a bit more appropriate for the RoadTrip application. For now, though, you'll go with the Navigation controller approach, just to get you off and running.

So, on your mark, get set, and go. Time to add a new view controller.

Adding a New View Controller

Your first step in adding a new view controller is to select the iPad storyboard file in the Project navigator. With the storyboard displayed, you then make sure that the Utility area is visible by clicking its icon in the Xcode toolbar's View selector. With that done, you can now hide the Project navigator by clicking *its* icon in the Xcode toolbar's View selector. (See Figure 5-9; remember, the button is a toggle, as I explain in Chapter 2.) Doing so gives you a little more real estate onscreen. (If you are blessed with a large monitor, though, you can keep the Project navigator open.)

Figure 5-9:
Hiding the
Navigator
area.

Because I have limited space on a book page, I'm hiding the Navigator area, as you can see in Figure 5-10. (When I work on my large-screen monitor, I usually keep the Navigator area shown.)

Figure: 5-10:
Drag in a
view
controller.

As the last step in getting your canvas ready, click the Attributes inspector button in the Inspector selector in the Utility area.

To add the `Test Drive controller` (which manages the view that will allow you to have RoadTrip's little car drive up the screen, turn around, and then go back to its original position, all with sound effects), you need to do the following:

1. **Select Objects in the Utility area's Library pane, and then drag a new view controller from the pane into your storyboard.**

   If you are using Icon view (like I do), the View Controller object is the first icon in the first row. (Selecting it will display a window describing what it is.)

   While you can add controls and other views to views only when the storyboard elements are full size, you can add view controllers (and, as you'll soon see, segues) at any zoom level.

   A new scene is created, as shown in Figure 5-10.

2. **Select the Table view in the Master View Controller – Master Scene (as I have in Figure 5-11) and then select the Attributes inspector.**

   If you look at the Canvas, you see a Table view with Prototype Cells, and a cell with the text of Title.

   You'll notice that, in the Table View section of the Attributes inspector, the Dynamic Prototypes option is selected.

   Right now, if you select a cell, nothing happens. That's because with Dynamic Prototype cells, you have to implement a method in your view controller to do something when a cell is selected (as you will in Chapter 20, where you create cells based on the information for each destination in the `Destinations` plist).

   For now, all I want to do is to be able to launch a Test Drive controller when the first cell is selected (and I really don't care about the time stamp). To do that in the most expeditious way possible, I'll have you use the Attributes inspector to change the Master view from Dynamic Prototypes to Static Cells.

   Static cells were a new feature in iOS 5.0 — and are used when you know in advance what needs to be displayed in a cell. Instead of having to implement a method in your view controller to return the cell with the text you want, you can format the cells in the storyboard. But more importantly, you can create a segue from a static cell that will launch the Test Drive Controller for you when the cell is tapped.

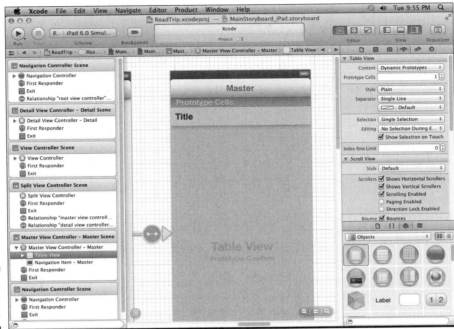

Figure 5-11:
The Table
view.

That's all I am going to say about static cells for now — I really want to get on with explaining how to create the user interface in the storyboard using Interface Builder, but I promise I'll return to static cells in detail in Chapter 12, because they are a feature that you'll probably be using often.

3. **In the Attributes inspector, select Static Cells from the Content drop-down menu, as I have in Figure 5-12.**

   You'll notice a change in the Table view. The heading Prototype Cells will disappear and you'll see three cells each with the text Title.

4. **In the Outline view, expand the disclosure triangle next to the table view and you'll see a Table View section.**

   Expand the Table View section and you'll see three Table View cells. Expand the first Table View cell and you'll find a label. Select the label, and in the Attributes inspector Title field, enter **Test Drive** as I have in Figure 5-13.

Figure 5-12:
Make them
static cells.

Figure 5-13:
Your Test
Drive cell.

5. **Select the first Table View cell (the cell, not the Test Drive label) in the Document Outline, and Control-drag from the cell in the Master View controller to the view controller you just added, as shown in Figure 5-14. Then release the mouse button.**

   Control-clicking from a button or Table View cell and dragging to the view controller you want displayed creates a selection segue or an accessory action. When you release the mouse button, you'll see the Storyboard Segues contextual menu, which pops up onscreen. You'll learn more about segues in this section and in Chapter 14. We won't be using an accessory action, but it's a another way to trigger a segue — from an accessory button in a table view.

6. **Select Push from the Selection Segue pop-up menu, as shown in Figure 5-15.**

   A *segue* performs the visual transition between two view controllers and supports push (navigation), modal, and custom transitions.

   A *push* segue changes the scene — and the user sees the new view controller's view (with its Back button) slide into place when the user taps a button; the Navigation bar items are updated appropriately. (See the "Understanding iPad Navigation" section, earlier in this chapter, for more on adding a Navigation controller.)

Figure 5-14: Drag from the Test Drive cell to the Table view controller.

In contrast to a push segue, a *modal* segue presents the view controller modally, with the transition style you specify, and requires the user to do something (tap Save or Cancel, for example) to get back to the previous view controller. As for custom transitions, segues support the standard visual transition styles such as Cover Vertical, Flip Horizontal, Cross Dissolve, and Partial Curl.

Segue objects are used to prepare for the transition from one view controller to another, which means segue objects contain information about the view controllers involved in a transition. When a segue is triggered — but before the visual transition occurs — the storyboard runtime calls the current view controller's prepareForSegue:sender: method so that it can pass any needed data to the view controller that's about to be displayed.

You'll notice that selecting Push from the Storyboard Segue's pop-up menu causes the Navigation bar to appear but also shrinks the view. I explain that in Chapter 13.

7. **Select the Push segue in the Master View Controller scene. After making sure that *Push* appears on the Style menu in the Attributes inspector, enter** TestDrive **in the inspector's Identifier field, as I have in Figure 5-16; then press return (or enter).**

Figure 5-15: Creating a push segue.

You won't always use the identifier, but it's good practice to name it so that you can identify the segue.

The field in the storyboard isn't updated until you press return, or sometimes until you click in another field *in that inspector.*

8. **Choose Detail Split from the Attributes inspector's Destination drop-down menu, as I have in Figure 5-16.**

   The size of the view in the Test Drive controller changes.

9. **Finally, select the two unused Table View cells in the Document Outline and delete them by pressing Delete. (You won't be using them.)**

   The default destination was set to Current, which meant that it was set to the Master view, because that's where you were dragging from. With that default, the view controller had been resized for the Master view, which is 320 points wide in the standard Split view controller. But you want the destination to be in the Detail view; choosing Detail Split in this step takes care of that for you.

   If you look closely at Figure 5-16, you can see that the view has now been sized down and that a Navigation bar has been added to the top of the view. If you expand the view controller in the View Controller Scene in the Document Outline, you can see that a Navigation bar added there as one would expect.

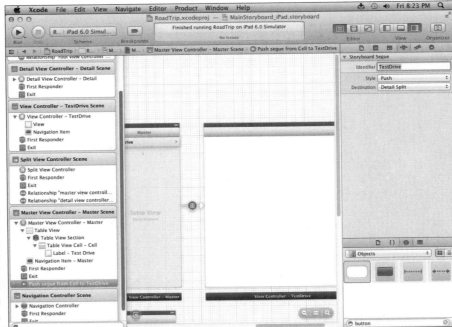

Figure 5-16: Make the destination a Detail view and add an identifier.

You'll also notice that a Disclosure Indicator (the *chevron* — a right-arrowhead-like shape on the right side of the Test Drive cell) has also been added. For now we'll leave it there, but in Chapter 13, I explain how to remove or change it if you'd like.

When you select the Detail cell and create the Push segue with the Detail view as the destination, the new Test Drive controller becomes *embedded* in the Detail view's Navigation controller. This Navigation controller manages the view controller stack for everything in the Detail view of the Split view controller.

Danger Will Robinson

If you were to build and run RoadTrip for iPad at this point, the app would crash because Apple's Master-Detail template has added code for dynamic table cells that can't be used for our static table cell. You will soon delete that unwanted code, so the app will work properly by the end of this chapter.

Once the unwanted code is deleted, there are two ways to test the app for iPad.

First, you could choose Landscape orientation, and select Test Drive, which would allow a new view controller's view to slide into place, Back button and all. If you then selected the Back button, the old Detail view would slide back into place.

However, in Portrait orientation, if you selected the Master button and then selected Detail, you'd see the new controller with a Back button as well. The Master button, however, will only appear again after you have selected Back and returned to the Detail View controller (the Root View controller). You'll find out how to fix that annoying bit of business in Chapter 13.

Before you go any further, take a look at the View Controller – Test Drive in the Attributes inspector, which I have selected in the Inspector selector bar in the Utility area in Figure 5-17. As you can see, the controller has properties that you can set using Interface Builder (including a title and identifier which I explain next).

The Attributes inspector is the place where you'll set properties of the view controllers, controls, and other view objects you add to the view.

Figure 5-17:
Adding a
title and
identifier.

Adding an identifier to the view controller

If you take another look at Figure 5-17, you can see that I've set Interface Builder's zoom to full size, clicked on the view controller I just created, selected the Attributes inspector in the Inspector selector bar, and then entered **TestDrive** in the Title field in the View Controller section. I then selected the Identity Inspector tab, and set the Storyboard ID to **TestDriveID.** The Title string is used in the Outline view, while the Storyboard ID string is used from code in the app.

I did all that for one simple reason: If you want to do *anything* special with a view controller in a storyboard, you need to be able to find it, and the easiest way to keep tabs on a view controller is by giving it a name using the identifier. While you may not need an identifier for every view controller, it's a good idea to get in the habit of adding it just in case you do. As for the name you enter in the Title field, it enables you to distinguish which view controller is which in the storyboard. You'll notice that in the Document Outline, the selected view controller is now named View Controller – TestDrive and the scene now is named View Controller – TestDrive Scene.

Whatever you type in a field isn't really added until you press Return or click in another field.

Adding the User Interface Objects

At this point, I could continue building out my storyboard by adding more elements such as views and segues, just like I did in the previous section. But by now I'm itching to really *do* something, which would require me getting some actual objects into the storyboard. When an itch comes, I scratch, so get ready to start editing and adding some objects.

To edit an object in the TestDrive view in the storyboard, select `MainStoryboard_iPad.storyboard` in the Project editor to open Interface Builder. Expand the View Controller – TestDrive in the View Controller – TestDrive Scene in the Document Outline. Select the View, and then select the Attributes inspector in the Inspector selector.

The Attributes inspector enables you to set various object properties. For example, to change the color of the view's background, you'd choose the background color from the Background pop-up menu.

If you select Default from the pop-up menu or just click in the current color displayed in the Background field, you see the Colors palette (shown on the right side in Figure 5-18).

Figure 5-18:
Pick a color,
any color.

The toolbar at the top of the Colors palette gives you a number of options for selecting a color. These are the standard options available for choosing a color on the Mac, and I'll leave you to explore them on your own.

Changing the background color for a view is kind of neat, but the real fun comes from your ability to add your own view object as a background image. That's what you're going to do next. (Feel the excitement!)

View Layout

Before you start to add another view — which will be a subview of the view that's already there — it's necessary to talk about view layout options. View layout is particularly important on mobile devices because the pesky user might rotate her device. So why is that an issue? Let's take the specific case of the original iPad. When held in Portrait orientation, the screen is 768 pixels wide by 1024 pixels tall. But when rotated to Landscape position, the screen becomes 1024 pixels wide, but only 768 pixels tall.

If your app handles rotation properly, then components such as buttons, text fields, images, and so on usually need to move and resize. In other words, you need a layout strategy, so that subviews are moved and resized correctly when their containing superview is resized.

Here are three strategies for view layout:

- ✔ **Hard-coded layout.** Here, you set the location, width, and height of each view yourself, and change those properties when the device is rotated. This is a really bad idea for most apps. It's difficult, error-prone, and inflexible.

- ✔ **Use iOS Autosizing.** Autosizing has existed since early versions of the iOS SDK and provides a mechanism for automatically moving and resizing a view in response to changes in its superview's position or size. You can set the default Autosizing behavior for your views from the Size pane of the inspector. The Size inspector contains an Autosizing section with springs and struts, which is described later in the chapter. The great advantage to using Autosizing is that it works on older devices running iOS 4.3, iOS 5, and iOS 6, so it is the technique I use in this book for the RoadTrip sample. Apps released before iOS 6 generally used Autosizing.

- ✔ **Use iOS 6 Auto Layout.** You use the Auto Layout system to define layout constraints for user interface elements. Constraints represent relationships between user interface elements. Auto layout improves upon Autosizing's "springs and struts" model in some ways, but is only available in iOS 6. I did not use Auto Layout in the Road Trip sample because of this limitation, but I do show you how to use Auto Layout at the end of this chapter.

Turn off Auto Layout

For now, follow these steps to turn off Auto Layout and use Autosizing:

✔ Turn off Auto Layout by selecting the iPad storyboard file in the project Navigator.

✔ Show the File inspector pane in the Utilities view.

✔ Uncheck the Use Auto Layout checkbox.

✔ Repeat these steps for the iPhone storyboard file.

Back to Adding User Interface Objects

Any view object you end up using has *properties* such as color (sometimes), a background image, or the ability to interact with the user — respond to touches, in other words. You generally set these properties using either the Attributes inspector in Interface Builder or programmatically.

To see those properties, you need to zoom to full size or select it in the Document Outline (which zooms it to full size). Full size is the only time view objects are editable.

To add a background image, follow these steps:

1. **Scroll down in the Library window and drag an Image view (the one selected in the Library in Figure 5-19) from the Library onto the view.**

   An Image view is a view that's used to display an image. (See Chapter 4 for more on views.)

   If you click an object in the Library, up pops a dialog telling you what it is. The dialog even tells you what class it is, as you can see in Figure 5-19. Click Done to dismiss it.

   What you just did is add an Image view as a *subview* of the RoadTrip controller's view, the one created for you by the template.

   Except for the view controllers up top and a few gesture recognizers scattered around the middle of the gallery, most of the "objects" you see in the Library are derived from the View class.

   You can add horizontal and vertical guides to help you line things up by choosing Editor⇨Add Horizontal Guide or Editor⇨Add Vertical Guide, respectively.

Figure 5-19:
Adding an
Image view.

2. **Select the Image view you just added, either in the Document Outline or on the Canvas.**

   Doing so changes what you see in the Attributes inspector. It now displays the attributes for the Image view.

3. **Using the Attributes inspector's Image drop-down menu, scroll down to select SeeTheUSA_iPad, as shown in Figure 5-20.**

   Doing so adds the image you want to use to the Image view, as shown in Figure 5-21. (You added this image in Chapter 3 — it was in the RoadTrip Resources file you downloaded and added to your RoadTrip project.)

   The preferred format for the image is `.png`. Although most common image formats display correctly, Xcode automatically optimizes `.png` images at build time to make them the fastest and most efficient image type for use in iPad applications.

4. **Drag in another Image view and place it at the bottom-center of the Image view you just added, as shown in Figure 5-22.**

Figure 5-20:
Selecting a
background
image.

Figure 5-21:
The image
selected
and in
place.

5. **Return to the Attributes inspector's Image drop-down menu, but this time select CarImage.png.**

   The image you selected is added to the Image view.

6. **Select the Image view you just added and choose Editor➪Size to Fit Content from the main menu.**

   The Image view is resized so that it better fits the enclosed content. (See Figure 5-23.) If you look closely, you'll recognize the vintage pink 1959 Cadillac Eldorado Biarritz convertible my evil twin Skippy plans to drive cross country to New York; the thought of driving it, much less parking it in New York, staggers the imagination.

7. **With the car Image view still selected, choose Editor➪Add Horizontal Guide and Editor➪Add Vertical Guide.**

   I'll take any help I can get when it comes to positioning objects, and these guides can help me keep track of a particular location on the larger scene.

Figure 5-23:
The family car — Skippy's pride and joy.

In Chapter 10, I show you how to animate Skippy's Eldorado Biarritz so it leisurely drives to the top of the screen, turns around, drives back, and then turns around one more time so that it's back where it started.

Autosizing

Because you're sure to decide — as all good app developers have decided and will continue to decide in perpetuity — that the RoadTrip app needs to function well in both Portrait and Landscape orientations, you'll need to make sure that, when you rotate the view, the car (subview) remains positioned at the bottom of the screen.

Luckily for you, most of that work gets done for you in `UIViewController` — the class from which we've derived `TestDriveController`. (The technical term for this bit of work is *autosizing*.) The only thing you have to do is tell the view controller exactly how you want it to move things around when the view changes orientation. You can make such wishes known in the storyboard using the Size inspector.

Figure 5-24 shows what happens when you select the Image view you want to work with and then select the Size inspector. Based on the way the CarImage view is currently configured, it's set to maintain its distance from the top and left of the SeeTheUSA view. How do I know that? Because that's what the Autosizing pane tells me.

Take another look at Figure 5-24. The Autosizing pane in the Size inspector has in its outer square a set of four indicators called *struts* — a line with two perpendicular lines at each end. These struts surround an inner square that contains two indicators referred to as *springs* (a line with an arrow head at each end). These struts and springs are set and unset with a click; when they're enabled, they're solid and bright red, and when disabled, dim and dashed.

You decide which struts to enable. If you do select one, that indicates to the Autosizing mechanism that you want to maintain a fixed distance on that particular side between the edge of this view (the CarImage view) and the edge of the enclosing superview (SeeTheUSA). In Figure 5-24, it's set up so that the CarImage will maintain a fixed distance to the top and left of the SeeTheUSA Image view (its superview).

Figure 5-24:
The current resizer setting.

The springs work similar to the struts, but are designed to indicate to the Autosizing mechanism how to resize the view when it rotates. (You won't need to use springs here, but you will use them in Chapter 16, which is why I'm giving you the heads-up now.)

With the Autosizing settings the way they're set up in Figure 5-24, if you built and compiled the app, started it up in Landscape orientation, and then rotated the view, you'd get what you see in Figure 5-25 — a car image no longer correctly lined up at the starting gate, as it were.

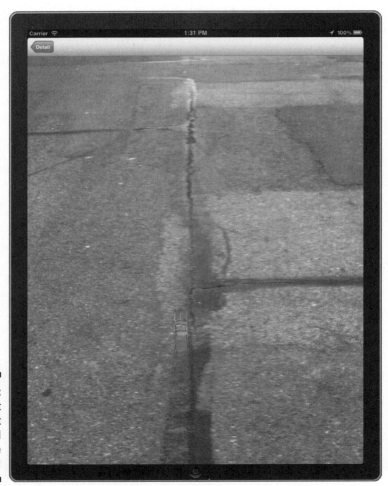

Figure 5-25:
But I want to start at the start and be in the middle!

For some technical reasons, when you have the Test Drive view displayed, you won't be able to rotate the Simulator to Portrait orientation when upside down and have the Test Drive view rotate. In addition, when you have the Test Drive view displayed, you won't be able to rotate the Simulator back to Portrait orientation and have the Master view and the Test Drive view rotate — you'll have to select the Detail button and return to the Detail view to have the views rotate correctly.

If you want to have the car maintain the same distance from the bottom and stay nicely centered in the view no matter which orientation you choose, you need to toggle off the top and left struts in the Autosizing pane to disable them, as shown in Figure 5-26.

Now, when you build and run your app and then rotate the view from landscape to portrait, you'll see the car maintain the position you want. (See Figure 5-27.)

Figure 5-26:
Maintaining
the distance
from the
bottom.

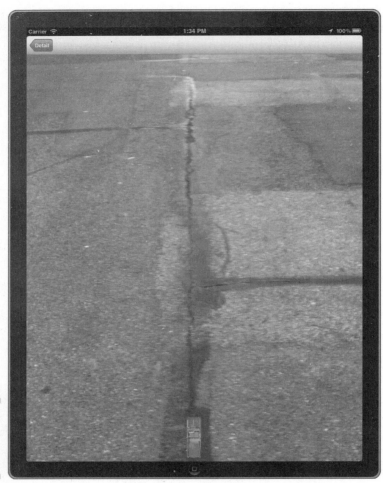

Figure 5-27:
Starting
at the
beginning.

Adding the Test Drive button

I say the more objects, the merrier. I want to add a nice Test Drive button which, when clicked, will send our 1959 Cadillac Eldorado Biarritz convertible on its merry way. Here's how it's done:

1. **Select the Round Rect button in the Library and drag it onto the view.**

2. **Click the Attributes Inspector button on the Inspector selector bar.**

   The button attributes you're going to set using the Attributes inspector are all Objective-C properties. Note that you can also set these properties programmatically; I show you how to do that in Chapter 8.

As you can see in Figure 5-28, the Type pop-up menu in the Attributes inspector is set to Rounded Rect — no surprise there. The button is shown in its default State configuration — in this case, unselected and unhighlighted. If you were to click the State Config pop-up menu and choose another configuration, such as Highlighted or Selected, you'd be able to change the font, text color, shadow, background, and other attributes in the Attributes inspector for the selected state.

This particular Rounded Rect button, being distinctly generic, is remarkably unexciting. To liven things up just a tad, I'm going to have you replace the Rounded Rect button with an image I created. (You'll find that image in the RoadTrip Resources folder that you should have downloaded and added to your project in Chapter 3.)

3. **In the Attributes inspector, choose Custom from the Type pop-up menu, as shown in Figure 5-29.**

Admittedly, you could just add an image to the Rounded Rect button, but doing so would simply place the image within the generic button, which strikes me as small beer. In this case, I say go for broke and replace the generic button altogether.

Figure 5-28:
Adding a button.

TIP

Choosing Custom from the menu causes the image of the button to disappear from the view. Just keep it selected so you can still manipulate the button itself. (It still is selectable, if you can find it.) If you happen to lose track of your (now invisible) button, just select the Button entry under the View subheading in the Document Outline and you'll see the button's resize handles.

4. Choose Button.png from the Background drop-down menu, as shown in Figure 5-30.

So why are you using the Background drop-down menu rather than the Image drop-down menu to place an image as your button? When you choose an image from the Background drop-down menu, you're simply doing that — setting the image for the button. You'll still add the title and so on using the Attributes inspector. If you were to choose from the Image drop-down menu, you would have included the title as part of the image and you wouldn't have been able to add it in the Inspector.

5. Using the button's resize handles, resize the button to 96 points by 37 points.

REMEMBER

You can also select the Size inspector, as I have in Figure 5-31, and enter the width and height in the fields provided.

You'll have to recenter the button after you resize it in the Size inspector.

Figure 5-29:
Creating a custom button.

Figure 5-30:
Choose
a custom
image for
the button.

Figure 5-31:
Using
the Size
inspector.

6. **Give this button a title (buttons don't have text; they have titles) by going back to the Attributes inspector, entering** Test Drive **in the Title field, and pressing Return.**

   You could double-click the button and enter the Title there and press Return as well. In my experience, though, doing so may cause the button to resize itself.

You could select a different Background image and title for each button state by cycling through the State Config choices and repeating Steps 2 through 5. I'll leave that for you to explore on your own.

Whenever you enter text, be sure to press Return. Anything you enter won't change the current setting unless you press Return or click in another field.

Massaging the Template Code

If you have been playing around with the code generated for you by the Master-Detail Application template, you've probably discovered that not only can you select the + (plus sign) button to create a timestamp displayed both in the Master and Detail views, but you can also select the Edit button and delete the timestamp entry in the Master (and consequently) Detail views.

All this functionality is built into the template courtesy of the `UITableViewController`. I explain how Table views work in Chapter 20, but because you are using a segue and static cells in the Master view, you won't need that functionality in the Master view. But not only don't you need it, it also actually interferes with the functioning of the segue, which you'll also understand when I explain Table view (and its `UITableViewDelegate` and `UITableViewDataSource` protocols) in detail in Chapter 20.

To deal with this issue, I want you to delete the code in Listing 5-1. Here we're talking about the code in `RTMasterViewController` starting with the `#pragma mark - Table View` statement and up to — but not including — the `@end` statement. This is the code that implements the Table View functionality, and also another method, `prepareForSegue`, that lets you pass data to the view controller you are transitioning to — unused here, but explained in detail in Chapter 13.

Listing 5-1:   Delete This Code from RTMasterViewController.m

```
#pragma mark - Table View

- (NSInteger)numberOfSectionsInTableView:(UITableView *)
        tableView
{
  return 1;
}

- (NSInteger)tableView:(UITableView *)tableView numberOf
        RowsInSection:(NSInteger)section
{
  return _objects.count;
}

- (UITableViewCell *)tableView:(UITableView *)tableView
        cellForRowAtIndexPath:(NSIndexPath *)indexPath
{
    UITableViewCell *cell = [tableView dequeueReusableCell
        WithIdentifier:@"Cell"];

  NSDate *object = [_objects objectAtIndex:indexPath.row];
  cell.textLabel.text = [object description];
    return cell;
}

- (BOOL)tableView:(UITableView *)tableView canEditRowAt
        IndexPath:(NSIndexPath *)indexPath
{
    // Return NO if you do not want the specified item to
        be editable.
    return YES;
}

- (void)tableView:(UITableView *)tableView commitEditing
        Style:(UITableViewCellEditingStyle)editingStyle
        forRowAtIndexPath:(NSIndexPath *)indexPath
{
    if (editingStyle == UITableViewCellEditingStyleDelete)
        {
        [_objects removeObjectAtIndex:indexPath.row];
        [tableView deleteRowsAtIndexPaths:[NSArray
        arrayWithObject:indexPath] withRowAnimation:UI
        TableViewRowAnimationFade];
    } else if (editingStyle ==
        UITableViewCellEditingStyleInsert) {
        // Create a new instance of the appropriate class,
        insert it into the array, and add a new row to
        the table view.
    }
```

(continued)

Listing 5-1 *(continued)*

```
}

/*
// Override to support rearranging the table view.
- (void)tableView:(UITableView *)tableView
         moveRowAtIndexPath:(NSIndexPath *)fromIndexPath
         toIndexPath:(NSIndexPath *)toIndexPath
{
}
*/

/*
// Override to support conditional rearranging of the
         table view.
- (BOOL)tableView:(UITableView *)tableView canMoveRowAt
         IndexPath:(NSIndexPath *)indexPath
{
    // Return NO if you do not want the item to be
         re-orderable.
    return YES;
}
*/

- (void)tableView:(UITableView *)tableView didSelectRowAt
         IndexPath:(NSIndexPath *)indexPath
{
    if ([[UIDevice currentDevice] userInterfaceIdiom] ==
         UIUserInterfaceIdiomPad) {
        NSDate *object = [_objects
            objectAtIndex:indexPath.row];
        self.detailViewController.detailItem = object;
    }
}

- (void)prepareForSegue:(UIStoryboardSegue *)segue
         sender:(id)sender
{
    if ([[segue identifier]
            isEqualToString:@"showDetail"]) {
        NSIndexPath *indexPath = [self.tableView
            indexPathForSelectedRow];
        NSDate *object = [_objects
            objectAtIndex:indexPath.row];
        [[segue destinationViewController]
            setDetailItem:object];
    }
}
```

You'll also need to delete some code in the viewDidLoad method. This code
adds the edit and + (plus) buttons to the Navigation bar. Delete the code in
Listing 5-2 that I've commented out in bold, underline, and italic in view
DidLoad in RTMasterViewController.m.

Listing 5-2:   Delete the Code in viewDidLoad

```
- (void)viewDidLoad
{
  [super viewDidLoad];
// Do any additional setup after loading the view,
          typically from a nib.
//self.navigationItem.leftBarButtonItem =
                              self.editButtonItem;
//UIBarButtonItem *addButton = [[UIBarButtonItem alloc]
    initWithBarButtonSystemItem:UIBarButtonSystemItemAdd
        target:self action:@selector(insertNewObject:)];
//self.navigationItem.rightBarButtonItem = addButton;
//self.detailViewController = (RTDetailViewController *)
    [[self.splitViewController.viewControllers lastObject]
                          topViewController];
}
```

Finally, in Listing 5-3, delete the insertNewObject: method in RTMasterViewController.m (the action method specified in the + button created in viewDidLoad, which was the selector used).

Listing 5-3:   Delete insertNewObject:

```
- (void)insertNewObject:(id)sender
{
    if (!_objects) {
        _objects = [[NSMutableArray alloc] init];
    }
    [_objects insertObject:[NSDate date] atIndex:0];
    NSIndexPath *indexPath =
            [NSIndexPath indexPathForRow:0 inSection:0];
    [self.tableView insertRowsAtIndexPaths:
        [NSArray arrayWithObject:indexPath]
      withRowAnimation:UITableViewRowAnimationAutomatic];
}
```

Autosizing the Button

Just as with the car image, you'll have to specify how you want the button to act when the view rotates.

If you were to select the button and call up the Size inspector right now, you'd see that the button, like the car image before it, is set to keep a fixed left and top margin. (Refer back to Figure 5-31.)

To have the button reposition itself so it stays in the center of the view no matter which orientation is displayed, deselect the top and right struts, as shown in Figure 5-32.

If you compile and run now, and in Landscape orientation, select Test Drive in the Master view, you'll end up with what you see Figure 5-33.

Figure 5-32:
Keep it centered.

Figure 5-33:
Select the Test Drive cell.

Choose Hardware⇨Rotate Left (or whatever direction moves it to Portrait orientation, right side up) in the Simulator menu and you'll see Figure 5-34, where the button maintains its position at the center of the view.

If you select the Detail button, it will take you back to the originating Detail View controller, which you will then be able to rotate back to Landscape orientation.

After you've added an object to your storyboard, you can check the results of your efforts at any time to see how things look. To do so, click Run on the Xcode toolbar and make sure you have the iPad Simulator scheme selected.

Occasionally you might make a change to your app (usually having to do with a resource) and then, when you run your app, nothing seems to have changed. When you click Run, Xcode does only what it needs to do to the parts of your app that have changed, and if it gets "confused" (yes, there are bugs in Xcode), your change won't be linked into the app. If you think that has happened, choose Product⇨Clean, and Xcode will recompile all the pieces of your app.

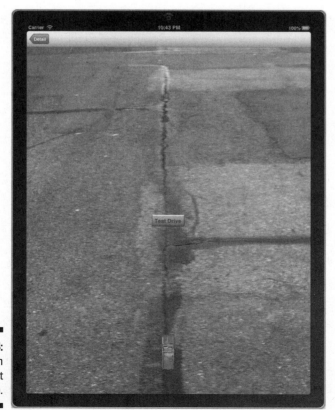

Figure 5-34:
The view in Portrait orientation.

Creating the iPhone User Interface

All the code that you write in Chapters 1 through 5 for the iPad will work fine for the iPhone. That will also be true for later chapters in this book.

All you need to do is add the following items to your iPhone storyboard file, in a very similar manner to what you just did for the iPad storyboard:

- Drag a `UIViewController` into the iPhone storyboard. Change its class name to `TestDriveController` and its Storyboard ID to TestDrive.

- Add a `UIImageView`, using the `SeeTheUSA_iPhone.png` image.

- Add a `UIImageView`, using the `CarImage.png` image.

- Add a Test Drive button.

- Select the Master View Controller scene in the iPhone storyboard.

- Select the Table view in the Master View Controller.

- Use the Attributes inspector to change the Master view from Dynamic Prototypes to Static Cells.

- Select the Label in the first Table View cell, and change its text to Test Drive.

- Control-drag from the Table View cell to the `TestDriveController`; choose a Push segue from the pop-up menu.

- Select the unused Table View cells from the Table view and delete them.

Now the iPhone app should work in a similar manner to the iPad app.

A Quick Auto Layout Example.

Follow these steps to try iOS6 Auto Layout:

1. **Create a new project from Xcode's File menu.**

2. **Choose an iOS** `Single View Application` **template.**

3. **Make the following changes:**

    a. **In the Product Name text field, enter** AutoLayout.

    b. **In the Devices pop-up menu, enter** iPhone.

    c. **Check the Use Storyboards checkbox.**

    d. **Check the Use Automatic Reference Counting checkbox.**

    e. **Make sure the Include Unit Tests checkbox is unchecked.**

4. **Save the project.**

5. **Select the Storyboard file in the Project Navigator.**

6. **Choose a** `Round Rect Button` **in the Object library.**

7. **Drag a button into the View Controller in the Storyboard.**

8. **Open the view controller outline in the Storyboard, and select the button you just dropped into the scene.**

9. **With Button selected, click the icon for adding a constraint, as shown in Figure 5-35.**

10. **Choose** `Horizontal Center in Container` **from the pop-up menu, as shown in Figure 5-36.**

11. **Click the same icon you chose in Step 9, and choose** `Vertical Center in Container` **from the pop-up menu.**

   Now the button has two constraints, so it will always be centered in its enclosing view both horizontally and vertically. Figure 5-37 shows the resulting View Controller Scene with both constraints on the button.

Figure 5-35:
Preparing to
add a
constraint.

Click here to add a constraint.

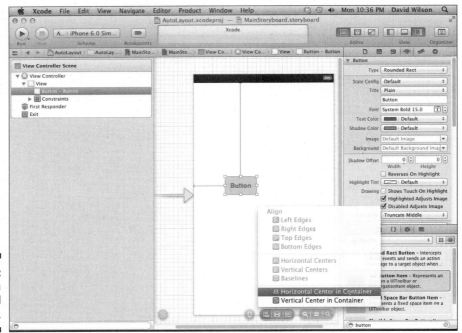

Figure 5-36:
Adding a
Horizontal
constraint.

Figure 5-37:
The button
with two
constraints.

12. **Add a label near the top, and add a constraint to center it horizontally, with the result shown in Figure 5-38.**

The resulting rotation behavior is shown in Figure 5-39.

Figure 5-38:
A label and
a button
with their
constraints.

Figure 5-39:
Auto Layout
in action

Final thoughts

As you can see, Auto Layout can also be easy to use. Just remember that it only works on iOS 6 or later, so you can't use it for apps intended for older devices, or ones that have not been updated to iOS 6.

Later chapters in this book will stick with trusty Autosizing, rather than using new-fangled Auto Layout.

Chapter 6

The Runtime, Managing Memory, and Using Properties

In This Chapter

▶ Understanding the application life cycle

▶ Handling interruptions

▶ Using Automatic Reference Counting to manage memory

▶ Understanding the five rules of memory management

▶ Customizing framework behaviors

▶ Taking advantage of the power of declared properties

*P*revious chapters provide you with at least a basic understanding of how to graphically build your user interface. Now it's time to add some code to have your application actually do something. But before you do that, I want to explain three things about writing iPad apps.

First, a lot of what you'll be doing is customizing and extending the behavior of framework classes. You customize and extend the behavior of these classes through *subclassing, delegation,* and using a powerful Objective-C feature called *declared properties.*

Second, on the iPhone or iPad, like any other device, you create objects to do your bidding — which means that you allocate memory, which happens to be a scarce resource on the iPad. Running out of memory is the main cause of applications crashing (not to mention being rejected from the App Store), so you need to understand *memory management.*

And finally, to know what message to send to what objects at what time, as well as what messages will be sent to your app at runtime, you need to understand the *application life cycle.*

Dealing with these three aspects of writing iOS apps is your pass to the Successful iOS Programmers' Secret Society, and in this chapter, you start your initiation. And because you'll find all this stuff easier to understand if you understand the overall context, I begin with the application life cycle.

This chapter is like the Classic Comics version of several hundred pages of Apple documentation, reference manuals, and how-to guides. Although a lot is left unsaid (though less than you might suspect), what's in this chapter is enough to get you started and also keep you going as you develop your own iPad apps. It provides a frame of reference on which you can hang the concepts I throw around with abandon in upcoming chapters — as well as the groundwork for a deep enough understanding of the application life cycle to give you a handle on the detailed documentation.

So relax. Get yourself a cup of coffee (or something stronger if you want) and be prepared to be entertained.

Stepping through the App Life Cycle

Although simple for the eventual user, the birth, life, and death of an application is a pretty complex process. In this section, I explain what happens throughout the time that the user launches the app from the Home screen, uses the app, and then stops using the app, either because she is done or decides to respond to an interruption such as an SMS message.

The life of an iOS app begins when a user launches it by tapping its icon on the Home screen. The system launches your app by calling its `main` function — which Xcode kindly lets you peek at if you go to the Project navigator, open the disclosure triangle next to the Supporting Files group, and select `main.m`.

The details of the implementation shown here may change, but the overall architecture will stay the same from one iOS version to another.

```
#import <UIKit/UIKit.h>
#import "RTAppDelegate.h"

int main(int argc, char *argv[])
{
  @autoreleasepool {
      return UIApplicationMain(argc, argv, nil, NSStringFr
          omClass([RTAppDelegate class]));
  }
}
```

The `main` function is where a program starts execution. This function is responsible for the high-level organization of the program's functionality and typically has access to the arguments given to the program when it gets executed.

The `main` function does only these two things:

1. Sets up an autorelease pool:

```
@autoreleasepool {
```

   This is a piece of memory-management plumbing that you don't need to use in this book (other than here), or perhaps ever, but feel free to investigate on your own if you are interested.

2. Calls the `UIApplicationMain` function to create the application object and delegate and set up the event loop:

```
return UIApplicationMain(argc, argv, nil,
            NSStringFromClass([RTAppDelegate class]));
```

   This is your entrance into the entire application startup process and its underlying architecture.

UIApplicationMain

The `UIApplicationMain` function creates the *application object* (a singleton — the only — `UIApplication` object) and the *application delegate* (a class created for you by the Xcode template). It also sets up the *main event loop*, including the application's *run loop* (which is responsible for polling input sources) and begins processing events.

In the following section, I explain the role of each of these elements in the application life cycle.

UIApplication provides application-wide control

The `UIApplication` object provides the application-wide control and coordination for an iOS application. It's responsible for handling the initial routing of incoming user events (touches, for example) as well as for dispatching action messages from control objects (such as buttons) to the appropriate target objects. The application object sends messages to its application delegate to allow you to respond in an application-unique way to occurrences such as application launch, low-memory warnings, and state transitions such as moving into background and back into foreground.

Delegation is a mechanism used to avoid subclassing complex UIKit objects, such as the UIApplication object. Instead of subclassing and overriding methods in a framework or other object, you go ahead and use that object unmodified and opt for putting your custom code inside a delegate object instead. As interesting events occur, the framework or other object sends messages to your delegate object. You use these methods to execute your custom code and implement the behavior you need. I explain the delegation pattern more in "The Delegation pattern" section, later in this chapter.

The Application Delegate object (the AppDelegate you see in the template) is responsible for handling several critical system messages and must be present in every iOS application. The object can be an instance of any class you like, as long as it adopts the UIApplicationDelegate protocol. In the template, you'll find that it's a subclass of UIResponder, which enables it to respond to and handle events. (UIApplication is also derived from UIResponder.)

The methods of this protocol correspond to behaviors that are needed during the application life cycle and are your way of implementing this custom behavior. Although you aren't required to implement all the methods of the UIApplicationDelegate protocol, you'll often find yourself writing code to handle the following:

✔ Initialization in your application delegate's application:didFinishLaunchingWithOptions: method.

✔ State transitions such as moving in and out of background and foreground. I explain these in more detail in the section "Knowing what to do when the normal processing of your application is interrupted," later in this chapter.

✔ Low-memory warnings, which I cover in the section "Observing Low-Memory Warnings," later in this chapter.

The UIApplication is a singleton object (there is just the one). To get a reference to it, you send the class message. (In Objective-C, you can send messages to classes, which are really objects on their own.) Sending the UIApplication object the delegate message gives you a pointer to the delegate object:

```
RTAppDelegate *appDelegate =
           [[UIApplication sharedApplication] delegate];
```

You'll be doing that a lot, so much so, in fact, that it should become second nature to you.

UIApplicationMain loads the storyboard

If the application's `Info.plist` file specifies a storyboard file (or a main nib file), as RoadTrip's `Info.plist` file does, the `UIApplicationMain` function loads it. The application's `Info.plist` file provides a map to the high-level structure of the application.

To see the `RoadTrip-Info.plist` file, select RoadTrip-Info.plist under the Supporting Files heading in the Project navigator, as shown in Figure 6-1. The file dutifully appears in the Editor area.

A *nib* file is a resource file that contains the specifications for one or more objects and is used to graphically create your user interface using Interface Builder in applications when you've opted not to use a storyboard. (A storyboard consists of a series of linked nib files created for you; for more on storyboards, see Chapters 4 and 5.)

If you're using a storyboard, the initial view controller is instantiated for you. As you can see in the Attributes inspector in Figure 6-2, the Initial View Controller setting is a standard View Controller property and is set for you by Interface Builder. (You usually don't even have to think about it.) In the iPad storyboard file, the initial view controller is a Split view controller that was included by the template. The nib-loader will also instantiate both Navigation controllers as well as their Root view controllers. (I explain Navigation controllers and Root view controllers in Chapter 5.)

Figure 6-1:
The Road Trip-Info. plist file.

Figure 6-2:
The initial
view
controller is
specified for
the iPad
storyboard.

In the iPhone storyboard file, the initial view controller is a Navigation controller that uses a Table View controller as its root view controller.

UIApplication sends the application:didFinishLaunchingWithOptions: message to its delegate

If the method is implemented in the application delegate, the `application`
`:didFinishLaunchingWithOptions:` message is sent to the application
delegate.

Launch time is a particularly important point in an application's life cycle. In
addition to the user launching an application by tapping its icon, an application can be launched to respond to a specific type of event. For example, it
could be launched in response to an incoming push notification, it could be
launched to open a file, or it could be launched to handle some background
event that it had specified it wanted to handle (a location update, for example). In all these cases, an Options dictionary passed to the `application:`
`didFinishLaunchingWithOptions:` method provides information about
the reason for the launch. (An application launched by the system for a specific reason — other than the user tapping its icon — is beyond the scope of
this book.)

The `application:didFinishLaunchingWithOptions:` message is sent
to the delegate when the application has launched and its storyboard has

been loaded. In this step, as you will see, you initialize and set up your application. At the time this message is sent, your application is in the inactive state. At some point after this method returns (completes) — unless your application does some kind of background processing — your application will become active and will receive the `applicationDidBecomeActive:` message when it *enters the foreground* (becomes the application that the user sees on the screen).

The class interface (usually declared in the .h file) lists the messages to which an object of that class can respond. The actual code for implementing a message is called a method and will be found in the associated .m file. When you want to have an object execute a method, you send it a message. In other words, the message is *what* you want done, while the method is how to do it.

Your goal during startup is to present your application's user interface as quickly as possible — and quick initialization equals happy users. Don't load large data structures that your application won't use right away. If your application requires time to load data from the network (or perform other tasks that take noticeable time), get your interface up and running first and then launch the task that takes a longer time on a background thread. Then you can display a progress indicator or other feedback to the user to indicate that your application is loading the necessary data or doing something important.

In the templates that don't use a storyboard, the `application:didFinish LaunchingWithOptions:` method allocates and initializes the window and the Split view controller (as well as its initial view controllers), adds it all to the window, and makes the window visible.

In a storyboard-based application, this is all done by the storyboard for you, and the `application:didFinishLaunchingWithOptions:` method does nothing other than return `YES` (the usual return).

You would return `NO` only if your application was launched because another application opened a URL that's owned by your application and your application can't handle the URL.

You will be adding some code to this method in Chapter 8.

Handling events while your application is executing

Most events sent to an application are encapsulated in an event object — an instance of the `UIEvent` class. In the case of touch-related events, the event object contains one or more touch objects (`UITouch`) representing the fingers that are touching the screen. As the user places fingers on the screen, moves them around, and finally removes them from the screen, the system reports the changes for each finger in the corresponding touch object.

Distributing and handling events is the job of responder objects, which are instances of the `UIResponder` class. The `UIApplication`, `UIViewController`, `UIWindow`, and `UIView` classes (and your own `RTAppDelegate`) all inherit from `UIResponder`. After pulling an event off the event queue, the application dispatches that event to the `UIWindow` object where it occurred. The window object, in turn, forwards the event to its first responder, designated to be the first recipient of events other than touch events. In the case of touch events, the first responder is typically the view object (`UIView`) in which the touch took place. For example, a touch event occurring in a button is delivered to the corresponding button object.

If the first responder is unable to handle an event, it forwards the event to its next responder, which is typically a Parent view or view controller. If that object is unable to handle the event, it forwards it to its next responder, and so on until the event is handled. This series of linked responder objects is known as the *responder chain*. Messages continue traveling up the responder chain — toward higher-level responder objects, such as the window, the application, and the application's delegate — until the event is either handled or discarded.

The responder object that handles an event often sets in motion a series of programmatic actions by the application — such as when you drag an image of a 1959 Cadillac Eldorado Biarritz convertible across the screen as I describe in Chapter 10.

The following list provides the chronology of what actually happens when the user taps something:

1. You have an event — the user taps a button, for example.

   The touch of a finger (or the lifting of a finger from the screen) adds a touch event to the application's event queue, where that event is *encapsulated* in — placed into, in other words — a `UIEvent` object. A `UITouch` object exists for each finger touching the screen, so that you can track individual touches. As the user manipulates the screen with his or her fingers, the system reports the changes for each finger in the corresponding `UITouch` object.

2. The run loop monitor dispatches the event.

   When something occurs that needs to be processed, the event-handling code of the `UIApplication` processes touch events by dispatching them to the appropriate *responder* object — the object that has signed up to take responsibility for doing something when an event happens (when the user touches the screen, for example). As mentioned previously, responder objects can include instances of `UIApplication`, `UIWindow`, and `UIView` (and any of its subclasses), as well as `UIViewController` (and any of *its* subclasses). All these classes inherit from `UIResponder`.

3. A responder object decides how to handle the event.

   For example, a touch event occurring with a button in a view is delivered to the button object. The button object handles the event by sending an action message to another object — in this case, the UIViewController object. This enables you to use standard button objects without having to muck about in their internals — you just tell the button what method you want to have invoked in your target (usually the view controller as I explain in Chapter 9), and you're basically set.

   Processing the message may result in changes to a view, a new view altogether, or some other kind of change in the user interface. When one of these results occurs, the view and graphics infrastructure takes over and processes the required drawing events.

4. Your application then returns to the run loop.

   After an event is handled or discarded, application control passes back to the run loop. The run loop then processes the next event or puts the thread to sleep if it has nothing more to do.

But because your application isn't alone on the device, it can be interrupted by an SMS message, or the user touching the Home button. When your application is interrupted, you'll have to take care of some things before control is switched to another application.

Knowing what to do when the normal processing of your application is interrupted

On an iOS device running iOS 4.2 or newer versions, various events besides termination can interrupt your app to allow the user to respond — for example, calendar alerts or the user pressing the Sleep/Wake button — and your app moves into the *inactive state*. If the user chooses to ignore an interruption, your app moves back into the *active state* and continues running as before. If the user decides to tap the alert to deal with it (or if the interruption was from the user touching the Home button to switch out of your application), your app then moves into its *background state,* where it's suspended but remains in memory.

iOS sends you a number of messages to let you know exactly what's happening as well as to give you the opportunity to take actions such as save user data and *state information,* which means saving at the point where the user was in the application. (If an app needs to continue running, it can request execution time from the system.) Because the app is in the background (running or suspended) and still in memory, relaunching is nearly instantaneous. An app's objects (including its windows and views) remain in memory, so they don't need to be re-created when the app relaunches. If memory becomes constrained, iOS may purge background apps to make more room for the foreground app.

Because these interruptions cause a temporary loss of control by your app, touch events are no longer sent to your app. When developing your app, you need to take this fact into account. For example, if your app is a game, you should pause the game when your game is interrupted. In general, your app should store information about its current state when it moves to the inactive state and be able to restore itself to the current state upon a subsequent relaunch.

In all cases, the sequence of events starts the same way — with the `applicationWillResignActive:` message sent to your application delegate when the application is about to move from active to inactive state. In this method, you should pause ongoing tasks, disable timers, throttle down OpenGL ES frame rates (that is, you should use this method to pause the game), and generally put things on hold.

What happens after this depends on a) the nature of the interruption, and b) how the user responds to the interruption. Your application may be either moved to the background or reactivated. I explain these occurrences next.

Before I do that, however, check out Figure 6-3, which shows the application life cycle and how interruptions are handled.

If the user responds to the interruption (the SMS message for example) or has launched another application, your application is moved to the background.

When the user accepts the notification or interruption, or presses the Home button (or when the system launches another application), your application moves into the background state, where it's suspended. (If an app needs to continue running, it can request execution time from the system.)

The next two bullets explain the messages your application can respond to after it's been moved into the background:

> ✔ **The** `applicationDidEnterBackground:` **message:** When your app first enters the background state, it's sent the `applicationDidEnter` `Background:` message. In this method, you should save any unsaved data or *state* (where the user is in the app — the current view, options selected, and stuff like that) to a temporary cache file or to the preferences database "on disk." (Okay, I know that Apple calls the iOS storage system a *disk* even though it is a solid-state drive, but if Apple calls it that, I probably should too, just so I don't confuse too many people.)
>
> Even though your application enters the background state, you have no guarantee that it will remain there indefinitely. If memory becomes constrained, iOS will purge background apps to make more room for the foreground app. You need to do everything necessary to be able to restore your application in case it's subsequently purged from memory so that the next time the user launches your app, your application can use that information to restore your app to its previous state. You also have to do additional cleanup operations, such as deleting temporary files.

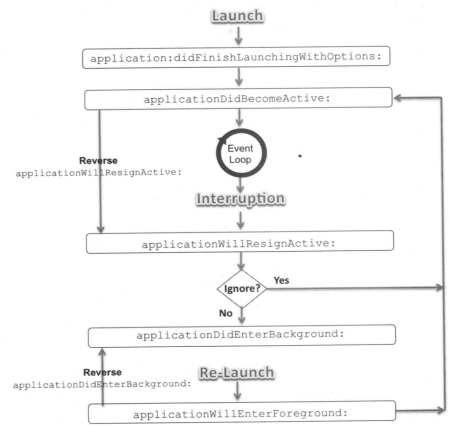

Figure 6-3:
The application life cycle.

If your application is purged when it's in this suspended state, *it receives no notice that it's removed from memory.* You need to save any data beforehand!

When your delegate is sent the `applicationDidEnterBackground:` method, your app has an undocumented amount of time to finish things up. If the method doesn't return before time runs out (or if your app doesn't request more execution time from iOS), your app is terminated and purged from memory.

If your application requests more execution time or it has declared that it does background execution, it's allowed to continue running after the `applicationDidEnterBackground:` method returns. If not, your (now) background application is moved to the *suspended* state shortly after returning from the `applicationDidEnterBackground:` method.

If the application is in the background, it then may be relaunched. This can happen if the user selects the app from the Home screen or the multitasking bar, or it's launched by the system if the app processes events in the background or monitors a significant location change, for example.

✔ **The** `applicationWillEnterForeground:` **message:** When your application is relaunched from the background, it's sent the `application WillEnterForeground:` message. In this method, you need to undo what you did in the `applicationDidEnterBackground:` method (not `applicationWillResignActive`; you undo that next).

If the user ignores the SMS message, or the app is relaunched from the background, your application is reactivated and starts getting touch and other events.

When your application is reactivated, it's sent the `applicationDid BecomeActive:` message.

You can use the `applicationDidBecomeActive:` method to restore the application to the state it was in before the interruption. Here you undo what you did in the `applicationWillResignActive` method, such as restart any tasks that were paused (or not yet started) while the application was inactive. If the application was previously in the background, you might need to refresh the user interface.

While an application is in the suspended state, the system tracks and coalesces (really *nets out*) events that might have an impact on that application when it relaunches. As soon as your application is up and running again, the system delivers those events to it. For most of these events, your application's existing infrastructure should just respond appropriately. For example, if the device orientation changed, your application's view controllers would automatically update the interface orientation in an appropriate way.

Apps are generally moved to the background when interrupted or when the user quits. But if the app was compiled with an earlier version of the SDK, or is running on an earlier version of the operating system that doesn't support multitasking — or if you decide that you don't want your app to run in the background and you set the `UIApplicationExitsOnSuspend` key in its `Info.plist` file — iOS terminates your app.

Even if your application supports multitasking (almost all do at this point), you must still be prepared for your application to be killed without any notification. The user can kill applications explicitly using the multitasking bar. In addition, if memory becomes constrained, the system might remove applications from memory to make more room. If it does remove your *suspended* application, *it doesn't give you any warning, much less notice!* However, if your application is currently running in the background state, the system does call the `applicationWillTerminate:` method of the application delegate.

When your application delegate is sent the `applicationWillTerminate:` message in nonmultitasking applications, or those running in the background, you need to do the same kinds of things you do in `application DidEnterBackground:`, except this time you do them knowing that your application won't be returning from the background.

Your `applicationWillTerminate:` method implementation has a limited (albeit undocumented) amount of time to do what it needs to do and return. Any longer than that and your application is terminated and purged from memory. (The Terminator doesn't kid around.)

An overview of the view controller life cycle

View controllers have a life cycle just as applications do, but I don't need to go into much detail about it here. The important part to know is that certain messages sent as views are displayed and hidden.

The two methods you need to know about in order to work with views are the following:

- ✔ `viewDidLoad`
- ✔ `viewWillAppear:`

The `viewDidLoad` message is sent to your view controller. This message is sent after the view controller has loaded its associated views into memory. This method is used to perform additional view initialization on views loaded from the storyboard or nib file, and the message isn't *necessarily* sent every time the view appears. If, for example, the user makes a selection in the view that causes a new view controller to load and slide its view into place, and the user then taps the Back button, this message isn't sent when the originating view reappears. That's the job of `viewWillAppear:`.

The `viewWillAppear:` message is sent when the view is about to become visible. The first time it's sent is after the `viewDidLoad` message, and then whenever the view reappears, such as when you tap the Back button, for example. You use this method to do the things that are necessary to present the view. For example, if you are displaying the location of the nearest book store that carries *iOS 6 Application Development For Dummies*, update that information in this method.

Numerous other methods are also placed in the view controller for you as stubs. I leave you to explore them on your own.

Of course, aside from all this system stuff that happens, your application will be chugging along doing what the user wants it to do. And in responding to user requests, you'll create objects to do the user's bidding — which means that you allocate memory. And because memory is a scarce resource on the iPad, you need to understand *memory management,* discussed in the next section.

Working within the Managed Memory Model Design Pattern

As powerful as it is, the iPhone — and even the iPad — is limited in resources, and the most critical of these resources is memory. To truly understand how to manage memory correctly in your application, you need to understand how the iOS memory works.

Understanding memory management

Whenever you (or a framework object) create an object using Objective-C, you allocate memory for the object. Although iOS devices and the Mac all use what's known as *virtual memory,* unlike the Mac, virtual memory in iOS is limited to the actual amount of physical memory. So when it begins to run low on memory, the Memory Manager frees memory pages that contain read-only content (such as code); this way, all it has to do is load the "originals" back into memory when they're needed. In contrast to what the Mac does, the iPad doesn't temporarily store "changeable" memory (such as object data) to the disk to free space and then read the data back later when it's needed. This state of affairs limits the amount of available memory.

So as you can see, when one object is done using memory, it's critical that the memory be released for use by other objects.

If memory continues to be limited, the system may also send notifications to the running application, asking it to free additional memory. This is one of the critical events that all applications must respond to, and I explain this process in the section "Observing Low-Memory Warnings," later in this chapter.

In Objective-C, memory is managed in iOS apps by *reference counting* — keeping the system up-to-date on whether an object is currently being used. Read on for all the details.

Using reference counting

In many ways, Objective-C is like the coolest guy in your school who now makes a seven-figure income surfing, bungee jumping, and skateboarding during the summers and then snowboarding around the world in the winter. In other ways, though, Objective-C is like the nerd in your class who grew up to be an accountant and reads the *Financial Times* for fun. Memory management falls into this category. In fact, memory management is simply an exercise in counting. To manage its memory, Objective-C (actually the iOS memory manager) uses a technique known as *reference counting*. Every object has its own reference count, or *retain count*. As long as the retain count is greater than zero, the memory manager assumes that someone cares about that object and leaves it alone. When an object's retain count goes to zero, the memory manager knows that no one needs it anymore and sends the object a `dealloc` message, and after that, its memory is returned to the system to be reused.

That process sounds pretty straightforward, but how does the retain count get incremented and decremented? Until Xcode 4.2 and iOS 5.0, you had to manage the retain count in your application. When an object is created via `alloc` or `new` or through a `copy` or `mutableCopy` message (which creates a copy of an object but has subtleties beyond the scope of this book), the object's retain count is set to 1. When your application uses one of those methods, ownership is transferred to the object that sent the message — that is, the object has been retained and that object that sent the message becomes a nonexclusive *owner* of the object. *Ownership* here means that the object will be there to use until it's explicitly released by sending it a `release` message when it's no longer needed (although if other active owners exist, it wouldn't be deallocated until all of them have released it).

Before Xcode 4.2 and iOS 5.0, if you didn't create an object by one of those methods but you wanted to become an owner, thereby making sure that the object stayed around for you to use until you were done with it, it was up to you to send a `retain` message to increase the retain count, and when you were done, to send a `release` message. This was because the creator of the object (which caused the retain count to be set to 1) may have autoreleased it — sent an object a release message that will cause it to be released later (usually the next tine the run loop is entered). This is useful in situations in which you want to relinquish ownership of an object but avoid the possibility of its being deallocated immediately (such as when you return an object from a method). In either instance, you were maintaining a pointer to the object so that it could be used.

Although this approach was simple in theory, it was a real headache for programmers. The vast majority of system crashes occurred because apps ran out of memory and were shut down by the system. In some of these cases, the application *didn't* respond to the memory warning methods and manage the low-memory warnings I explain in the section "Observing Low-Memory Warnings," later in this chapter.

Most of the time, however, even if the application responded to the low-memory warnings, it was limited to what it could do because the memory was *leaked.* Memory was actually available because some objects were not being used, but those objects' memory had not been released back to the system. In fact, there were no longer pointers to these objects (for a variety of reasons), so they *couldn't* be released and then deallocated and the memory reused.

You have ways to manage memory automatically. One is *garbage collection,* which scans through memory and releases objects that have no pointers to them. Garbage collection for Objective-C is available on the Mac (and for many other languages on other platforms), but garbage collection has a few problems. It can start up and pause your applications at the most inopportune time, and it affects performance and the user experience because you have no control, or any idea, when it will occur.

Having to do all this memory management in your application has changed with the latest version of the Objective-C compiler, which now comes with *automatic reference counting (ARC),* which you can enable whenever you create a project. (For more on options when creating a project, see Chapter 3.) ARC does for you in the compiler what you used to have to do on your own. It handles all those `releases`, `autoreleases`, and `retains` for you. I tell you much more about ARC in the next section.

Automatic Reference Counting (ARC)

Automatic reference counting (ARC) is a compiler-level feature that simplifies the process of managing the lifetimes of Objective-C objects. Instead of you having to remember when to retain or release an object, ARC evaluates the lifetime requirements of your objects and automatically synthesizes the appropriate method calls at compile time. It isn't a new runtime memory model — and it isn't a garbage collector. All the action takes place in the compiler.

ARC takes care of the process of retaining and releasing objects by taking advantage of (and having the compiler enforce) naming conventions. It also relies on new object pointer ownership qualifiers (more on that later).

Lest you worry, ARC is actually much faster (has better performance) than doing memory management on your own.

ARC doesn't automate `malloc()` and `free()` (C functions I won't get into here) and doesn't automate `CoreFoundation` (CF) or `CoreGraphics` (CG). You'll be using some of those kinds of functions, and I talk about them in Chapter 10.

To be able to manage memory for you, ARC imposes some restrictions — primarily enforcing some best practices and disallowing some other practices. You won't have to worry about most of this in an application that was created to use ARC. You may see some things in non-ARC samples, but hopefully my discussion here will help you figure out how to work within the ARC restrictions.

In the following, I explain the rules that you have to follow to use ARC in your application.

- ✔ **Rule 1: Don't call the** `retain`, `release`, **or** `autorelease` **methods.** In addition, you can't implement custom `retain` or `release` methods.

    If you're new to Objective-C programming, this rule won't mean anything to you because it isn't something you'll have been doing in your existing applications. The only reason you'll need to know about this rule is to understand what non-ARC code is doing to manage memory. If you're an old hand, you'll have been using these methods, and you'll be happy to be told *not* to use them.

    You can provide a custom implementation of `dealloc` if you need to manage other resources — but I don't have you do that for the example app developed in this book.

- ✔ **Rule 2: Don't store object pointers in C structures.** Because the compiler must know when references come and go, you can't store object pointers in. For most readers, that won't be a problem because you'll be using objects rather than C structures.

- ✔ **Rule 3: Inform the compiler about ownership when using Core Foundation–style objects.** In iOS applications, you often use the `CoreFoundation` framework. An example is in Chapter 10, when you add sound to your application.

    `CoreFoundation` objects are anything beginning with a `CF` — things like the address book functions, for example. A `CoreFoundation` object would look like this:

    ```
    AudioServicesCreateSystemSoundID(
        (__bridge CFURLRef)burnRubberURL, burnRubberSoundID);
    ```

    ARC doesn't automatically manage the lifetimes of `CoreFoundation` types, and there are `CoreFoundation` memory management rules and functions you can use, such as `CFRetain` and `CFRelease` (or the corresponding type-specific variants).

    In this book, and most of the time, you don't have to worry about memory management because you usually will be casting an Objective-C object to a `CoreFoundation` type object, or vice versa — with the result that you end up with no `CoreFoundation` memory management in your code. You still have to let the compiler know about any memory management implications, though.

Again, in this book, and much of the time elsewhere, you simply tell ARC not to worry by using a __bridge cast. (You'll use a __bridge cast in Chapter 10.)

If you do have CoreFoundation memory management, macros such as CFBridgingRetain or CFBridgingRelease will transfer ownership between ARC and CoreFoundation. (This topic is beyond the scope of this book, however.)

✔ **Rule 4: Use the @autoreleasepool keyword to mark the start of an autorelease block.** This isn't something you'll be concerned about — or will ever do, for that matter. But it's a rule nonetheless.

✔ **Rule 5: Follow the naming conventions.** The compiler knows whether to retain an object based on what gets returned. Sometimes the object being returned by a method is retained, and sometimes it's autoreleased later. If the object is going to be autoreleased, the object needs to be retained. If it's already retained, you don't want the compiler to do anything.

The only way the compiler knows whether an object has been retained when it's returned is through certain naming conventions. Under ARC, these naming conventions are now part of the language, and you must follow them.

The compiler knows that a retained object has been returned when the first word in the first part of the *selector* (the method name) is alloc, new, copy, mutableCopy, or init. These methods transfer ownership — where *transferred ownership* means that the object has been retained for you. An example is the NSString initWithFormat: method.

In addition, you can't give a property a name that begins with new.

✔ **Rule 6: Just follow the rules.** That's it — no retaining releasing or autoreleasing. Just follow the rules and code to your heart's content without worrying about memory management.

Except, of course, in some situations, you'll need to explicitly tell the compiler about what you want to do. In those cases, you'll have to tell the compiler explicitly about an object's lifetime. I explain how to do that in the next section.

Working with variable types according to ARC

Because the reference to an object lives in a variable, object pointers can be qualified using ownership type or lifetime qualifiers. These qualifiers determine when the compiler can deallocate an object to which a pointer points. These qualifiers are as follows:

```
__strong
__weak
__unsafe_unretained
__autoreleasing
```

The following sections describe the function of each of these qualifiers.

- ✔ __strong **variables retain their values.** __strong is the default. You almost never have to specify it, and all stack local variables, including parameters, are __strong. A __strong pointer to an object will cause that object to be retained while it's in scope (or not set to nil). No more *dangling references* (objects that have been deallocated that you expect to be there)!

- ✔ __weak **variables don't retain values.** __weak variables don't cause an object to be retained (that is, you don't use them in the reference count) and are, in fact, set to nil (zeroed) as soon as the referenced object starts deallocating. You need to be concerned with these only to prevent retain cycles, which I explain shortly.

- ✔ __unsafe_unretained **variables don't retain values and aren't zeroed.** Some Apple-provided classes (only on the Mac and some third-party libraries) don't work with zeroing weak references. These have to be cleared in a dealloc method elsewhere.

  Using ARC, __strong, __weak, and __autoreleasing stack variables are now implicitly initialized with nil.

- ✔ __autoreleasing **for indirect pointers.** These variables aren't for general use. They're used for out parameters that pass values back to the calling routine. They're retained and then autoreleased when they're read into, and are beyond the scope of this book.

Understanding the deadly retain cycle

ARC works very well to manage memory except in one circumstance. In this section, I explain how that circumstance can arise, and what you'll need to do to keep it from happening.

When you create an object, the compiler makes sure that ownership is transferred and all is well. The compiler will release that object when it goes out of scope, so if it's an instance variable, it will stay in scope until the object itself is deallocated.

I take you through this process using a little program called RetainCycle that I wrote to illustrate the retain cycle.

I create a new RetainIt object in the viewDidLoad method of my RetainCycleViewController object. It will be released only when the retainIt variable goes out of scope (it's __strong by default). In this case, it will be released and then deallocated (assuming that no other object takes ownership) at the end of viewDidLoad because the retainIt variable will go out of scope:

```
-  (void)viewDidLoad
{
   [super viewDidLoad];
   RetainIt* retainIt = [[RetainIt new]init];
}
```

But when I create the RetainIt object, in the RetainIt class's initialization method, init (see the following), I create a Cycle object and assign it to the cycle instance variable I declared. As you might expect, the Cycle object will be retained until the RetainIt object is deallocated because it's referenced by an instance variable, which stays in scope until the object is deallocated:

```
-  (id)init
{
   self = [super init];
   if (self) {
      self.cycle = [[Cycle new] init];
      cycle.retainIt = self;
   }
   return self;
}
```

I also, however, assign to the Cycle object's retainIt property a reference back to the RetainIt object. The Cycle class looks like this:

```
@interface Cycle : NSObject

@property (strong, nonatomic) RetainIt* retainIt;

@end
```

At the end of the day, it looks like Figure 6-4.

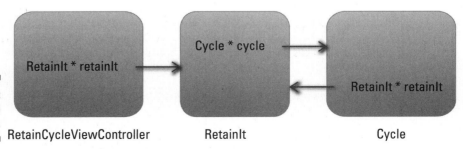

Figure 6-4:
The retain cycle.

RetainCycleViewController   RetainIt   Cycle

This means that the `RetainIt` object won't be deallocated until the `Cycle` object is deallocated, and the `Cycle` object will be deallocated only when the `RetainIt` object is deallocated. Whoops!

Although this example may appear a bit contrived, it actually can occur in real life when you have one object with a back pointer to the object that creates it (either directly or through a chain of other objects, each with a `strong` reference to the next leading back to the first).

The __weak lifetime qualifiers for objects take care of this. Although I haven't explained properties yet, the solution is to make the lifetime qualifier back pointer __weak.

```
@property (weak, nonatomic) RetainIt* retainIt;
```

I explain this more when I explain property attributes later in this chapter.

Observing Low-Memory Warnings

Even if you've done everything correctly, in a large application, you may simply run out of memory. When that situation occurs, the system dispatches a low-memory notification to your application — and it's something you must pay attention to. If you don't, it's a reliable recipe for disaster. (Think of your low-fuel light going on as you approach a sign on the highway that says, "Next services 100 miles.") UIKit provides several ways for you to set up your application so that you receive timely low-memory notifications:

- Override the `viewDidUnload` and `didReceiveMemoryWarning` methods in your custom `UIViewController` subclass.
- Implement the `applicationDidReceiveMemoryWarning:` method of your application delegate.
- Register to receive the `UIApplicationDidReceiveMemoryWarning Notification:` notification.

The viewDidUnload method

When a low-memory condition occurs, one way to free some memory is to remove views that aren't being used. You don't have to worry about that, however, because it's handled in the view controller class from which you derive your view controllers — `UIViewController`.

What you do have to worry about, though, is managing any references to the view or its subviews that you have. This includes managing the outlets you create in Chapter 9.

That's why Interface Builder will so kindly add (in Chapter 9, where you add the `car` and `testDriveButton` outlets) the following code to your project:

```
- (void)viewDidUnload
{
    [self setCar:nil];
    [self setTestDriveButton:nil];
    [super viewDidUnload];
}
```

Here you set the references to the outlets you will create to `nil`, which will tell ARC to generate the code to release these references and which will enable them to be released from memory. You can also use this method to release any objects that you created to support the view but that are no longer needed now that the view is gone, by setting them to `nil` as well. You shouldn't use this method to release user data or any other information that can't be easily re-created.

The didReceiveMemoryWarning method

The `didReceiveMemoryWarning` method is sent to the view controller when the application receives a memory warning. The default implementation of this method checks to see whether the view controller can safely release its view. If the view can be released, this method releases it and sends the `viewDidUnload` message (see the preceding section).

You should override this method to release any additional memory used by your view controller, but be sure to send the `[super didReceiveMemory-Warning]` to allow the view controller to release its view.

The applicationDidReceive MemoryWarning: method

Similar to `viewDidUnload`, your application delegate should set any references to objects it can safely free to `nil`.

The UIApplicationDidReceiveMemory WarningNotification: notification

Low-memory notifications are sent to the Notification Center, where all notifications are centralized. An object that wants to get informed about any notifications registers itself to the Notification Center by telling which notification it wants to be informed about, and a *block* (to be explained in Chapter 10) to be called when the notification is raised. A model object, for example, could then release data structures or objects it owns that it doesn't need immediately and can re-create later by setting references to nil. However, this approach is beyond the scope of this book.

For those of you who are curious, in your model object (which you create in Chapter 11), you could add the following:

```
[[NSNotificationCenter defaultCenter] addObserverForName:
   UIApplicationDidReceiveMemoryWarningNotification
   object:[UIApplication sharedApplication] queue:nil
   usingBlock:^(NSNotification *notif) {
                                                          //
         your code here
}];
```

You can test `applicationDidReceiveMemoryWarning:` and `UIApplicationDidReceiveMemoryWarningNotification:` in the Simulator by choosing Hardware⇨Simulate Memory Warning.

Picking the right memory-management strategy for your application

Each of these strategies gives a different part of your application a chance to free the memory it no longer needs (or doesn't need right now). How you actually get these strategies working for you depends on your application's architecture, so you'll have to explore that on your own.

Not freeing enough memory will result in iOS sending your application the `applicationWillTerminate:` message and shutting the app down. For many apps, though, the best defense is a good offense, which means you need to manage your memory effectively and eliminate any memory leaks in your code by following the ARC rules.

Customizing the Behavior of Framework Classes

Although you'll be creating classes of your own (especially model classes), often you're going to want to customize the behavior of a particular framework class. You have three ways to go about it:

- ✔ Subclassing
- ✔ Delegating
- ✔ Declared properties

In this section, I'll cover the first two, and the third in the following section.

Subclassing

Objective-C, like other object-oriented programming languages, permits you to base a new class definition on a class already defined. The base class is called a *superclass;* the new class is its *subclass.* The subclass is defined only by its extension to its superclass; everything else remains the same. Each new class that you define *inherits* methods and instance variables of its superclass.

Some framework classes are expected to be subclassed. Among them are view controllers, which you'll be subclassing quite a bit. Others aren't expected to be subclassed because you're going to need to customize their behavior; in those situations, you use *delegation* instead.

The Delegation pattern

Delegation is a pattern used extensively in the iOS frameworks, so much so that, if you want to do any serious app development work, you're going to have to get your head around it. In fact, when you *do* understand it, your life will instantly become much easier to manage.

Delegation, as I mention in the previous section, is a way of customizing the behavior of an object without subclassing it. Instead, one object (a framework or any other object) delegates the task of implementing one of its responsibilities to another object. You're using a behavior-rich object supplied by the framework *as is* and putting the code for program-specific behavior in a separate (delegate) object. When a request is made of the framework object, the method of the delegate that implements the program-specific behavior is automatically called.

The iOS frameworks have been designed to (mostly) use delegation rather than subclassing (for technical reasons, which are beyond the scope of this book).

For example, the `UIApplication` object handles most of the actual work needed to run the application. But, as you saw, it sends your application delegate the `application:didFinishLaunchingWithOptions:` message to give you an opportunity to create model objects that are unique to your app.

When a framework object has been designed to use delegates to implement certain behaviors, the behaviors it requires (or gives you the option to implement) are defined in a *protocol.*

Protocols define an interface that the delegate object implements. In iOS, protocols can be formal or informal, although I concentrate solely on the former because formal protocols include support for things like type checking and runtime checking to see whether an object conforms to the protocol.

In a formal protocol, you usually don't have to implement all the methods; many are declared optional, meaning that you have to implement only the ones relevant to your app. Before a formal protocol attempts to send a message to its delegate, the host object determines whether the delegate implements the method (via a `respondsToSelector:` message) to avoid the embarrassment of branching into nowhere if the method isn't implemented.

Delegation and protocols are the preferred way to manage model views (so says Apple, after much trial and error), and you create your own protocol to manage model views in Chapter 19.

Understanding Declared Properties

Although properties and instance variable access and accessors are often mashed together in the minds of programmers, I want to make sure that you understand the unique nature of properties and how they really work.

Whereas *methods* are concerned with sending messages to objects to get things done, *properties* are concerned with the state of the objects. Frameworks and other objects behave based on what they find in their properties (hence you can modify object behavior by changing a property); for example, a button's background image is a property you set (indirectly, in Interface Builder) in Chapter 5.

You also may want to know something about the state of the object, such as its color, or about a window's Root view controller.

In Chapter 12, I discuss creating a model object — `Trip`. Your app's view controllers, which act as a bridge between the views and the model, need to be able to find the `Trip` object to get data and send it updates. All of this is done using properties.

As I discuss when creating an outlet in Chapter 9, a property looks like the following:

```
@property (strong, nonatomic) IBOutlet UIImageView *car;
```

But not all properties are outlets. If you select the `RTAppDelegate.h` file in the Project inspector, you can see that it includes a `window` property:

```
@property (strong, nonatomic) UIWindow *window;
```

And in Chapter 11, you add a `trip` property to `RTAppDelegate`:

```
@property (nonatomic, strong) Trip *trip;
```

As you can see, the order of the attributes (`strong, nonatomic` vs. `non-atomic, strong`, which I explain in the later section "Setting attributes for a declared property") doesn't matter.

What comprises a declared property

A declared property has two parts: its declaration and its implementation.

The declaration uses the `@property` keyword, followed by an optional parenthesized set of attributes, the type information, and the name of the property.

Access to properties is implemented by accessor methods (although within the class that declares the property, the property can be accessed directly, just as instance variables are). You can write your own accessor methods or you can let the compiler do it for you. To have the compiler do it for you, you use the `@synthesize` directive to tell the compiler to create the accessor methods. The code it generates matches the attributes you've specified. (I explain the attributes in the upcoming "Setting attributes for a declared property" section.)

However, starting with Xcode 4.4, the Objective-C compiler automatically calls `@synthesize` for properties with no explicit accessor methods, so you no longer need to add `@synthesize` statements to your `.m` files. Therefore, you will not see any `@synthesize` statements used in this book.

The default names for the getter and setter methods associated with a property are *whateverThePropertyNameIs* for the getter and *setWhateverThePropertyNameIs:* for the setter. In the case of `trip`, the getter method is `trip`, and the setter method is `setTrip:`.

To access the `trip` property in the `appDelegate`, you would use

```
RTAppDelegate* appDelegate =
            [[UIApplication sharedApplication] delegate];
Trip* thisTrip = [appDelegate trip];
```

or to set that property, use

```
RTAppDelegate* appDelegate =
            [[UIApplication sharedApplication] delegate];
[appDelegate setTrip:newTrip];
```

`delegate`, by the way is a `UIApplication` property

As I said, the `UIApplication` is a singleton object (there is just the one). To get a reference to it, you send the `class` message (in Objective-C, you can send messages to classes, which are really objects on their own). Sending the `UIApplication` object the `delegate` message gives you a pointer to the delegate object.

Using dot syntax

Objective-C provides a dot (`.`) operator that offers an alternative to square bracket notation (`[ ]`) to invoke accessor methods. You use dot syntax in the same way you would when accessing a C structure element:

```
Trip* thisTrip = appDelegate.trip;
```

or to set that property, use

```
appDelegate.trip = newTrip;
```

When used with objects, however, dot syntax acts as "syntactic sugar" — it's transformed by the compiler into an accessor message. Dot syntax doesn't directly get or set an instance variable. The code examples using it are the exact equivalent to using the bracket notation.

Many programmers like the dot syntax because it may be more readable; just think of those bracket notation situations where you're accessing a property that is a property of another object (that is a property of another object, and so on). The real advantage of dot syntax, though, is that the compiler will generate an *error* when it detects an attempt to write to a read-only declared property. This is so much better than having to settle for an undeclared method *warning* because you invoked a nonexistent setter method, with the app subsequently failing at runtime.

When you use the compiler to create accessor methods for you, the compiler creates an instance variable of the type you have declared that it will then use to store and retrieve the property value with the name of the property. For example for the following property:

```
@property (weak, nonatomic) IBOutlet UIImageView *car;
```

the statement

```
@synthesize car;
```

generates an instance variable with the name of `car` of type `UIImage`.

However, if you let the compiler automatically generate an `@synthesize` statement for you, it actually uses an instance variable name beginning with an underscore character, so you would get the following code generated:

```
@synthesize car = _car;
```

This allows you to distinguish between the property name (accessed by `self.car`) and the instance variable name (accessed simply as `_car`).

Apple recommends that you use the property reference (`self.car`) in normal methods, but use the `_car` variable in init methods.

Setting attributes for a declared property

I mention earlier in this chapter that you can set certain property attributes when you declare a property. I cover some of those attributes in this section.

Setter semantics/ownership

These properties specify how instance variable storage should be managed (see the earlier section "Working with variable types according to ARC" for more):

✔ `strong` (similar to `retain`, which was used previous to ARC) creates an accessor method that means that the object this property points to will be retained while it is in scope (or whenever it's set to `nil` or some other value).

✔ weak (similar to assign, which was used previous to ARC) creates an accessor that uses simple assignment. This attribute is the default, and you typically use this attribute for scalar types such as NSInteger and CGRect, or (in a reference-counted environment) for objects you don't own — delegates, for example — and to avoid retain cycle problems, as I explain in "Understanding the deadly retain cycle," earlier in this chapter.

✔ copy specifies that a copy of the object should be used for assignment. The previous value is sent a release message.

The copy is made by invoking the copy method. This attribute is valid only for object types, which must implement the NSCopying protocol (and is beyond the scope of this book).

For object properties, you must explicitly specify one of the types listed previously; otherwise, you get a compiler warning. So you need to think about what memory management behavior you want, and type the behavior explicitly.

Writability

The following attributes specify whether a property has an associated set accessor. They are mutually exclusive.

✔ readwrite indicates that the property should be treated as read/write. This attribute is the default. With the @synthesize directive, the getter and setter methods are synthesized; otherwise, both a getter and setter method are required.

✔ readonly indicates that the property is read-only. With the @synthesize directive, only a getter method is synthesized. Otherwise, only a getter method is required. If you attempt to assign a value using the dot syntax, you get a compiler error.

Accessor method names

You'll remember that the default names for the getter and setter methods associated with a property are propertyName and setPropertyName:, respectively. For example, for the property trip, the accessors are trip and setTrip:. You can, however, specify custom names instead. They're both optional and can appear with any other attribute (except for readonly in the case of setter =):

✔ getter = getterName specifies the name of the get accessor for the property. The getter must return a type matching the property's type and take no parameters.

✔ setter = setterName specifies the name of the set accessor for the property. The setter method must take a single parameter of a type matching the property's type and must return void.

Typically, you should specify accessor method names that are key-value coding compliant (which is beyond the scope of this book). A common reason for using the getter decorator is to adhere to the `isPropertyName` convention for Boolean values.

Atomicity

You can use this attribute to specify that accessor methods aren't `atomic`. (No keyword denotes `atomic`.) This has to do with currency and thread issues that are way beyond the scope of this book. If you specify `nonatomic`, a synthesized accessor for an object property simply returns the value directly. Otherwise, a synthesized get accessor for an object property uses a lock and retains and autoreleases the returned value. You use `nonatamic` throughout this book and on the iPad in general.

Writing your own accessors

You don't have to use the accessors generated by the compiler; and, sometimes, it even makes sense to implement them yourself (although such times don't arise in this book). If you implement the accessor methods yourself, you should make sure that your approach matches the attributes you've declared. (For example, if you specify `copy`, you must make sure that you do copy the input value in the setter method.)

For example, if you have a lot of overhead to create an object that might not be used, you can create your own getter accessor that creates the object the first time it's accessed. In addition, writing your own accessor means you don't have to have an instance variable associated with the property. The `UIView frame` property, for example, is actually computed based on the `bounds` and `center` properties.

Accessing instance variables with accessors

If you don't use `self`, you access the instance variable directly. In the following example, the set accessor method for `currentDestinationIndex` isn't invoked:

```
currentDestinationIndex = [[NSUserDefaults
  standardUserDefaults]objectForKey:CurrentDestinationKey];
```

The preceding isn't the same as

```
self.currentDestinationIndex = [[NSUserDefaults
  standardUserDefaults]objectForKey:CurrentDestinationKey];
```

To use an accessor, you must use `self`.

Hiding Instance Variables

When properties were first developed, they were looked at as a way to avoid the tedium of writing accessors for instance variable-based properties.

People used to think about properties as a way to access instance variables. In fact, instance variables shouldn't be equated to properties, and more important, instance variables shouldn't be made public. (Doing so violates the object-oriented principle of encapsulation, but that's a conversation for a different time.) In fact, Apple's new approach is to put instance variable declarations in the implementation file of the class.

Before the new Objective-C compiler that comes with Xcode 4.2 came about, programmers declared instance variables in the header file in the `@interface` class declaration. In the old times, you would've added the following bolded code to the `TestDriveController.h` file:

```
@interface TestDriveController : UIViewController
                    <DestinationControllerDelegate> {

  AVAudioPlayer *backgroundAudioPlayer;
  SystemSoundID burnRubberSoundID;
  BOOL touchInCar;
}
```

This approach made instance variables (`ivars`) visible to everyone and everything and was, as I mentioned, at odds with the principle of encapsulation (even if the variables couldn't be accessed).

Starting with Xcode 4.2, you can now hide instance variables by declaring them in the implementation file in one of two ways. The first is as a *class extension,* which you create by adding a second interface block in the implementation file followed by open and close parentheses:

```
@interface TestDriveController () {

  AVAudioPlayer *backgroundAudioPlayer;
  SystemSoundID burnRubberSoundID;
  BOOL touchInCar;
}
@end
```

The second way is by declaring the instance variable in the `@implementation` block of the class:

```
@implementation TestDriveController

AVAudioPlayer *backgroundAudioPlayer;
SystemSoundID burnRubberSoundID;
BOOL touchInCar;
```

A class extension is a variation of an Objective-C category, which is beyond the scope of this book.

The approach you use is your choice; I prefer the class extension because I think it makes the variables easier to distinguish.

You can also use class extensions to have a publicly declared set of methods and then declare additional methods for use solely by the class:

```
@interface TestDriveController () {

  AVAudioPlayer *backgroundAudioPlayer;
  SystemSoundID burnRubberSoundID;
  BOOL touchInCar;
}
- (void) privateMethod;
@end
```

These methods are not really private, but are not visible in the header file. They are "private APIs."

Chapter 7

Working with the Source Editor

In This Chapter

▶ Using the Standard source editor to add code

▶ Fixing syntax errors as you code

▶ Getting the help you need from the documentation and other forms of help

▶ Searching and finding symbols

*I*f you've been reading through the chapters in order, by now you may be beginning to hate me because I haven't shown you much in the way of coding yet. Isn't developing apps about coding? Well, yes and no.

Think of painting a room in your house. So much time and effort needs to be spent in the prep work because you know that if you prepare correctly, the job will take you less time in the long run by saving you a lot of rework.

That's what the chapters in this book have been doing so far — preparing you to code by showing you the ins and outs of Xcode and the UIKit framework. At this point, all you have left to do is find out about the Xcode source editor and a few other features. After that, you'll be ready to code, and take my word for it, you will.

In this chapter, I tell you how to navigate the files in your project using the Jump bar and the navigators, as well as how to work with the source editor to enter code. And for when you are confused, or simply just curious, I explain how to access the documentation and Xcode's Help system. This chapter finishes the explanation on how to use Xcode, and you'll know what you need to know to make it easy to start coding in the next chapter.

Navigating in the Xcode Source Editors

In previous chapters, I give you quite a bit of information about the Xcode Workspace, albeit primarily focusing on storyboards. I mention the Assistant as well, and in this chapter, I want to extend that knowledge and describe most of the rest of the tasks you need to be able to do in Xcode.

As you've seen, most development work in Xcode is done in the Editor area, the main area that's always visible within the Workspace window. The Editor area can also be further configured, with the Standard editor pane always shown, as well as an optional Assistant pane that shows related content. (If you select an interface [.h] header file, the Assistant pane shows the corresponding implementation [.m] code file, and vice versa; I don't talk about the Version pane, but showing that area is also an option.) I use the term *pane* (Standard editor *pane* and Assistant *pane*) to refer to certain configurations, even though Apple doesn't use that term. I do this to distinguish between the *Editor area* configuration (the Standard editor isn't actually an editor at all, but simply a single pane configuration in the editor area) and the built-in *editors* — an editor operates in an *Editor area*. The main editors are the following:

- ✔ **Source editor:** You use this editor to write and edit your source code, as well as to set and enable (or disable, for that matter) breakpoints as well as to control program execution.

- ✔ **Project editor:** With this editor, you view and edit project and target settings, such as build options, target architectures, and code signing characteristics.

- ✔ **Interface Builder:** Here, you graphically create and edit user interface files in storyboards and .xib files.

The editor you use is determined by what you have selected in the Project navigator. An editor pane appears for that (selected) item in the Editor area.

So far, you've worked primarily in the Interface Builder editor, but when you code, you do the bulk of your work in the source editor in the Standard editor pane, with some forays, as needed, in the Assistant editor pane and an occasional excursion into the Utility area as well.

As described earlier in the book, you use the View selector in the Workspace toolbar to hide or show the Navigator, Debug, and Utility areas. (To review the Xcode workspace landscape, see Chapter 2.) If you like, you can hide the other areas and see just the source editor (and perhaps the Assistant).

Figure 7-1 shows the Project navigator. Because I selected RTMasterViewController.m, you see the *source editor* displaying that file in the Standard editor pane. (If you were to select one of the storyboard files in the Project navigator, you'd see Interface Builder as your editor of choice; that's the editor I highlight in Chapter 5.) In Figure 7-1, I also selected the Assistant in the Editor selector and split the panes using the split controls (the next to the last "+" icon on the right in the Jump bar).

Notice that when I selected the Assistant, the RTMasterViewController.h file opened. That's because the Assistant editor pane automatically (depending how you have set it — see the next section) shows the related content for whatever I select in the Project navigator so that you can edit both easily.

You then see `RTMasterViewController.m` (the implementation code file) in the Standard source editor pane and `RTMasterViewController.h` (the header file) in the Assistant editor pane. Clicking the split controls opens a second pane as well.

The Standard editor pane (the left editor pane, or the top one if you have a horizontal split) is the one that's affected by changing your selection in the Project navigator.

The interface (`.h`) header file defines the class's interface by specifying the following:

✔ **The class declaration (and what it inherits from).**

✔ **Methods.**

✔ **Any *instance* variables (that is, variables defined in a class).** Note that Apple has suggested moving away from declaring instance variables in the interface and moving those declarations to the implementation file to keep them more private, as I explain in Chapter 6.

Assistant editor pane   Jump bars   Split controls

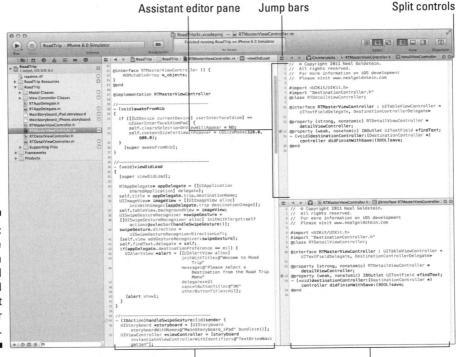

Figure 7-1: The source editor with Standard and Assistant editor panes.

Standard editor pane   Assistant editor pane

The implementation (.m) code file, on the other hand, contains the code for the class, which includes each method definition. It also can contain the instance variable declarations. See Chapter 6 for more on this topic as well.

By default, the Assistant editor pane appears to the right of the source editor pane. To change the orientation of the Assistant editor pane to the source editor pane, choose View➪Assistant Layout and then choose a layout. If the header file doesn't appear for you, navigate to it using the Jump bar, as explained in the next section.

Using the Jump bar

A Jump bar appears at the top of each Editor area pane to provide an alternative way to navigate through the files and symbols in your project. You can use the Jump bar to go directly to items at any level in the Workspace.

A *Jump bar* is an interactive, hierarchical mechanism for browsing items in your workspace. Each editor area includes a Jump bar, as do Interface Builder and the documentation organizer. The configuration and behavior of each Jump bar is customized for the context in which it appears.

The darker Jump bar you see in Figure 7-1 indicates that the Standard editor pane is the active pane.

The Standard editor Jump bar

The Standard editor Jump bar has the *basic configuration,* which includes the following:

- ✔ **Context-related items:** Click the Related Items menu (represented by an icon showing a cluster of tiny rectangles on the far left side) to see additional selections relevant to the current context, such as recently opened files or the interface (.h) header file for an implementation (.m) code file you're editing.

- ✔ **Previous and Next buttons:** These are the left- and right-arrow buttons on the left side of the Jump bar. You use these to step back and forth through your navigation history.

- ✔ **A hierarchical path menu:** This menu shows the same structure that you see in the Project navigator, down to individual files and the symbols inside the files. The path you would see in the source editor in the Standard editor pane is shown in Figure 7-2.

The hierarchical path menu lets you quickly choose a file. For example, in Figure 7-3, I get an overview of all the RoadTrip files when I select the RoadTrip project in the hierarchical path menu.

Selecting the last item in the hierarchical path menu provides a list of all the symbols in that file, as shown in Figure 7-4.

Hierarchical path menu

Figure 7-2:
The hierarchal path menu in the Standard editor pane.

Figure 7-3:
A file hierarchy.

Figure 7-4:
A tour of RT Master View Controller.m.

Another example of a Jump bar with the basic configuration is in the Documentation Organizer. It simply allows you to select documents from installed libraries. Other Jump bars have more components.

The Assistant modes and the Jump bar

When you use the Assistant, you'll find that the Jump bar differs somewhat from the Jump bar of the Standard editor. The Assistant's Jump bar has two modes: Tracking (or Automatic) mode and Manual mode.

- **Tracking mode:** The default behavior for the Assistant is to display the counterpart of the file displayed in the Standard editor pane. That is, if you've opened an implementation file, Assistant displays the corresponding header file, and vice versa. You can choose any of several other possible criteria to be used by the Assistant with the help of the Assistant pop-up menu (the first item in the path shown in the Jump bar above the Assistant editor). As you can see in Figure 7-5, the choices offered depend on the type of file being edited (a source file, for example, as shown, or the storyboard).

- **Manual mode:** You select the file to display in the Assistant pane on your own, rather than have the Assistant choose for you. (As mentioned previously, you can also split the Assistant editor pane to create multiple assistant editors.)

Hold down the Option key when selecting an item in the Project navigator to open the Assistant and display that item in the Assistant editor pane.

If you have any questions about what something does, just position the mouse pointer above the icon; a tooltip appears to explain it.

Figure 7-5: Assistant options in the source editor.

Organizing your code using the #pragma mark statement

While you're here, this is a good time to introduce the #pragma mark statement. If you look in the RTDetailViewController, you can see how this statement can be used to group things in your file; such statements are also displayed in the list of symbols.

You use the # pragma mark statement with a label (such as View life cycle or Animation) to add a category header in the Methods list so that you can identify and keep separate the methods that fit logically in the list.

For example, in the RTDetailViewController template, I added

```
#pragma mark - Managing the detail item
```

The first part of the statement (with a space and a dash) places a horizontal line in the Methods list. The second one places the text "View life cycle" in the Methods list.

This is a useful trick for finding code sections, organizing your code, and adding new code in the proper sections.

Using the Xcode Source Editor

The main tool you use to write code for an iPad application is the Xcode source editor, which appears as the Standard editor pane in the editor area on the right side of the Xcode Workspace window after you select a source code file in the Project navigator. It also appears as the Assistant editor in a second pane if you click the Assistant Editor button — the middle Editor selector button in the top-right corner of the Workspace window.

Apple has gone out of its way to make the source editor as useful as possible by including the following:

- ✔ **Code completion:** Code completion is a feature of the editor that shows symbols — arguments, placeholders, and suggested code — as you type statements. Code completion can be really useful, especially if you're like me and forget exactly what the arguments are for a function. When code completion is active (as it is by default), Xcode uses the text you typed — as well as the context within which you typed it — to provide inline suggestions for completing what it thinks you're *going to* type. You can accept inline suggestions by pressing Tab or Return. You can also see a pop-up list of suggestions by clicking an item in the suggestion list or clicking the up and down arrows to select an item. As you do so, the inline suggestion changes depending on what you selected. Press the Esc key, or Control+spacebar, to cancel a code completion operation. You can turn off code completion, or set options for code completion, by choosing Xcode⇨Preferences and clicking the Text Editing tab.

- ✔ **Automatic indenting, formatting, and closing braces:** As I explain in Chapter 3 in the section on preferences, the source editor indents the text you type according to rules you can set in the Text Editing preferences pane. It also uses fonts and colors for the various syntax elements (variables, constants, comments, and so on) according to the settings in the Fonts & Colors pane of Xcode preferences. As for closing braces, anytime you type an opening brace ({) and then press Return, Xcode automatically adds a closing brace (}) — unless you've deactivated the Automatically Insert Closing "}" option in the Text Editing preferences.

✓ **Code folding in the Focus ribbon:** With code folding, you can collapse code that you're not working on and display only the code that requires your attention. You do this by clicking in the Focus ribbon column (see Figure 7-6) to the left of the code you want to hide (between the gutter, which displays line numbers and breakpoints, and the editor). A disclosure triangle appears, and clicking it hides or shows blocks of code.

✓ **Opening a file in a separate window:** Double-click the file in the Project navigator to open the file in a new window.

Figure 7-6:
The Gutter and Focus ribbon.

Gutter   Focus ribbon

Using Live Issues and Fix-it

The Apple LLVM compiler engine wants to be your best friend, so *Live Issues* continuously evaluates your code in the background and alerts you to coding mistakes. Before this feature came along, you had to build your app first, and trust me, this new way saves lots of time and effort.

But not only is Live Issues happy to point out your mistakes (like someone else I know, but I won't go there), *Fix-it* will also offer (when it can) to fix the problem for you. Clicking the error displays the available Fix-its, such as correcting an assignment to a comparison, repairing a misspelled symbol, or appending a missing semicolon. With a single keyboard shortcut, you can instantly have the error repaired, and you can continue coding. Fix-it marks syntax errors with a red underline or a caret at the position of the error and with a symbol in the gutter.

For example, in Figure 7-7, the semicolon is missing after the [super view-DidLoad] statement. (Notice the error indicator — the red circle with exclamation point — in the Activity viewer, your Go To place for showing status messages, build progress, and errors.) Pressing Return will automatically fix this problem. This is a very useful feature and will cut down your debugging time significantly (especially if you actually use it).

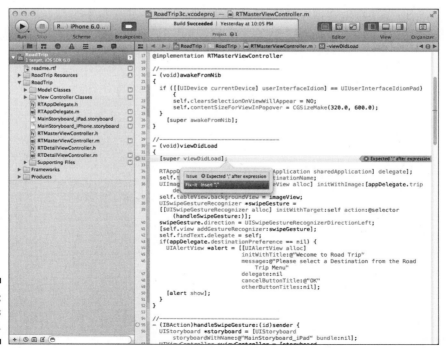

Figure 7-7:
Live Issues
and Fix-it.

Compiler warnings

Although Xcode and the compiler working together are very good at giving you warnings and errors, sometimes they're a little slow on the uptake when you actually get around to fixing the problem. So don't be surprised by random warnings and errors, especially if the compiler for some reason can't find the header file.

If you see a warning or error that you're just sure you've fixed, you can click the Run button. Xcode and the compiler will reset, and the warning will go away. (Unless, of course, it was right all along and you hadn't fixed the problem.)

The Issue navigator

The Issue navigator is one of the navigators provided by Xcode. The error displayed in Figure 7-7, shown previously, also appears in the Issue navigator, as shown in Figure 7-8.

Scope bar   Issue list   Issue stepper

Figure 7-8:
An error message displayed by the Issue navigator.

To get to the Issue navigator, you select it in the Navigator selector bar.

If, in spite of Live Issues and Fix-it (or any other) warnings, you decide to compile the program, the Issue navigator will automatically launch for you.

The Issue navigator displays the error and warning messages generated in a Project or Workspace and is similar to the other navigators you've used so far.

When you select a warning or error in the Issue navigator, an editor displays the item with the issue, and if the error occurs in a source file, the issue message is placed on the line of code with the issue.

Place the pointer over an issue message that ends with an ellipsis (which appears if the pane is too narrow to display the entire message) to get a complete description of the issue.

You can display issues by file or by type using the buttons on the Scope bar (refer to Figure 7-7), filter the issue list with the Filter bar, and even step through issues using the Issue stepper in the Jump bar. Use the Next and Previous buttons in the Jump bar to jump to the previous and next issues.

As you may recall from Chapter 3, I changed Xcode preferences to have the Issue navigator displayed and a sound played when a build fails.

Accessing Documentation

The ability to quickly access documentation is a major feature of Xcode, and one you'll want to use regularly. If you have no idea how to do something, or how something works, you can often find the answer in the documentation.

Being able to figure out what's going on will make your life easier. You saw that Xcode will complete your code for you, which is useful when you can't quite remember the method signature and parameters, but what if you don't even have a clue?

Or like many developers, you may find yourself wanting to dig deeper when it comes to a particular bit of code. That's when you'll really appreciate things like Xcode's Quick Help, the Documentation pane in the Organizer window, header file access, the Help menu, and the Find tools. With these tools, you can quickly access the documentation for a particular class, method, or property.

Getting Xcode help

To see how easy it is to access the documentation, say that you've selected RTMasterViewController.h, as shown in the preceding Figure 7-8. (I've hidden the Assistant to have more room). What if you wanted to find out more about UITableViewController, the super class of RTMasterViewController?

The Quick Help section of the Utility area provides documentation for a single symbol. (To see the Utility area, click the rightmost View selector button in the top-right corner of the Workspace window and select the second button in the Inspector selector bar.) In an editor, click anywhere in the symbol or select the entire symbol, as shown in Figure 7-9.

The Quick Help section of the Utility area shows a description of the symbol and provides links to more information. For example, you can click the UITableViewController Class Reference link near the bottom of the Quick Help section (refer to Figure 7-9) to bring up the class reference definition in the iOS Library Reference in the Documentation pane of the Organizer window, as shown in Figure 7-10. I use class references a lot!

Figure 7-9:
Accessing the Quick Help section of the Utility area.

Figure 7-10:
The class
reference
in the
Organizer
window.

With the Quick Help section open, information is available for three types of elements in your project, depending on your selection in the open editor:

- ✓ **Symbols,** in the source editor
- ✓ **Interface objects,** in Interface Builder
- ✓ **Build settings,** in the Project editor

It may be more convenient to use a Quick Help window if, for example, you prefer to work with the Utility area hidden. To do so, press Option and click one of the following in the open editor:

- ✓ **Symbols,** in the source editor
- ✓ **Build settings,** in the Project editor

As you can see in Figure 7-11, a Quick Help window appears with the pointer indicating the item you selected (in this case, the symbol `UITableViewController`):

If you're like me and want to go directly to the class reference, press Option and double-click the symbol instead.

Figure 7-11:
The Quick
Help
window.

The Organizer window

You can have only one Organizer window (shown in Figure 7-12). You use the organizers in this window to manage all the development resources (projects, the Workspace, repositories, and so forth) on your local system in addition to using documentation, managing devices, and managing archives.

To display the Organizer window, click the Organizer button in the Workspace window's toolbar (you'll see it there on the far right) or choose Window➪Organizer. The window includes five individual organizers, whose tasks I describe in the following list:

✓ **Devices organizer:** Lets you provision a device, manage your developer profile, install iOS on the device, and work with your application and its data. This organizer is present only if the iOS SDK is installed.

✓ **Repositories organizer:** Lets you create, view, and manage Git and Subversion repositories for your Workspace in a single consistent interface.

✓ **Projects organizer:** Lets you find, view, and manage an open project or Workspace, its derived data, and its snapshots.

✓ **Archives organizer:** Lets you view and manage build product archives resulting from your distribution scheme.

✔ **Documentation organizer:** Lets you find documentation and sample code and use them within Xcode. You can search and explore documentation and set bookmarks, and I suggest that you explore these topics further.

Each of these organizers includes task-oriented contextual help articles that you can view by choosing the Organizer and clicking in its content pane while pressing Control.

I explain a bit more about some of the other organizers as you use them in upcoming chapters.

The Help menu

The Help menu's search field (in the Xcode menu bar) also lets you search Xcode Help, the Xcode User Guide, and Documentation and API Reference, all of which open the Documentation pane of the Organizer window. You can also choose Quick Help for *Selected Item,* which displays a Quick Help panel above the selected symbol in the editor.

Figure 7-12:
The
Organizer
window.

Finding and Searching in Your Project

You'll find that, as your classes get bigger, sometimes you'll want to find a symbol or some other text in your project. Xcode provides a number of ways to do that.

Using the Find command to locate an item in a file

Need to track down a single symbol or all occurrences of a symbol in a file or class? You can easily locate what you're looking for by choosing Edit⇨Find⇨Find or pressing ⌘+F, which opens a Find toolbar above the Editor pane to help you search the file in the editor.

For example, as shown in Figure 7-13, I entered **viewDidLoad** in the Find toolbar. Xcode found six instances of `viewDidLoad` in the source editor and highlighted them. (Admittedly, the first highlight is a tad darker.)

You can jump from one instance to the next by pressing ⌘+G. Or you can use the Previous and Next buttons (left and right arrows) on the Find bar.

Figure 7-13: You can use Find to locate something in a file.

Click the Find pop-up menu on Find toolbar and choose Replace to do a file-level replace.

Click the magnifying glass in the Search field in the Find toolbar to display a menu that allows you to show or hide the Find options. For example, you can choose to ignore or match the case of the text in the Search field. Changes you make to this set of options remain persistent for future searches.

Using the Search navigator to search your project or framework

 Whereas the Find command works for locating an item in a file or class, you use the Search navigator (the third button from the left in the Project Navigator toolbar) to find items in your project or even frameworks. You can use Shift+Command+F as a handy keyboard shortcut for the Find command in the Workspace menu item, which also opens the Search navigator pane.

In Figure 7-14, I entered **viewDidLoad** in the Search field. I also clicked the magnifying glass in the Search field to display search options. (Clicking in the Find pop-up menu will also let you choose Replace to perform a global replace).

Figure 7-14: The Search navigator shows a specific use of the search term in the file.

Note how the initial results of my search are displayed in the Search navigator; if I wanted to filter the Results list still further, I could enter text into the field at the bottom of the pane. Any items that don't match the text are removed from the Results list.

To go directly to where the search term appears in a file, click an entry under the file's name in the Search navigator, as shown in Figure 7-14. The file appears in the editor pane on the right, open to the location where the search term appears.

Using the Symbol navigator

 The Symbol navigator allows you to browse through the symbols in your project — just click the Symbol button on the Navigator selector bar. Note that you need to wait until Xcode finishes indexing your project before you can use this feature.

You can display symbols in a hierarchical or flat list using the buttons at the top of the Symbol navigator.

You can specify which symbols are displayed by using the buttons at the bottom of the navigator. Buttons are blue when on and black when off. Use the following buttons in any combination:

✔ **The first button** on the Symbol navigator shows only class symbols and hides global symbol types.

✔ **The middle button** shows only symbols in this project.

✔ **The third button** shows only containers (classes and categories).

You can refine the Results list still more by entering text in the Filter field at the bottom of the navigator.

If you select a symbol to display, its header file definition will be displayed in the source editor. In Figure 7-15, I've hidden everything but the member symbols. In the resulting list, I selected the `RTDetailViewController viewDidLoad` method, and its definition was highlighted in the source editor.

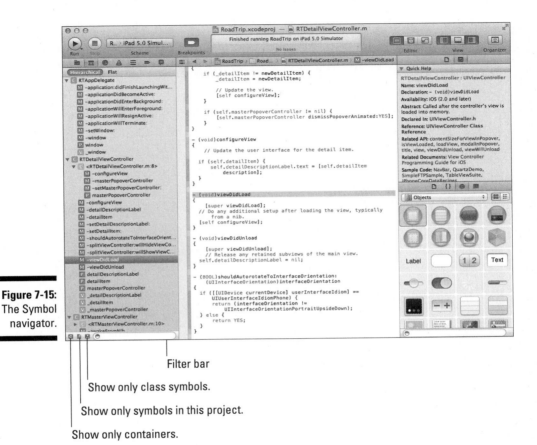

Figure 7-15:
The Symbol
navigator.

Filter bar

Show only class symbols.

Show only symbols in this project.

Show only containers.

You're Finally Ready to Code!

Yes, it's finally time to code, and from here on, it's full-steam ahead.

Part III
Getting Your Feet Wet — Basic Functionality

The 5th Wave   By Rich Tennant

"Hold on, Barbara. I'm pretty sure there's an app for this."

In this part . . .

After you have the foundation in place, you need to make all those controls do something, such as when a user taps a button.

In this part, you start the actual coding process to turn a good idea (an app that you use when you take a road trip) into a real working app.

Because your app will be using the Internet — a lot! — you find out how to determine whether the Internet is available and how to alert the user when it is not.

You also discover how to customize the appearance of the controls provided by the framework to make your application a thing of beauty.

Next, you find out how to connect all those views and controls that you've added in Interface Builder to your code to make them do something — such as have a '59 pink Cadillac Eldorado Biarritz convertible drive up and down the screen.

Finally, you add animation and sound to the opening screen of your app so that when the user taps the Test Drive button, the '59 Cadillac Eldorado convertible takes off with a screech and then drives up and down the screen with a satisfying engine purr.

You also begin to see how to account for the differences between an iPad and an iPhone, and make sure that the app can run flawlessly on whatever device the user has handy.

Chap

It's (Finally) Ti

*Y*es, it's finally time to start coding, although ᵢ
 you going on the RoadTrip app functionality ᵢ
developed in this book). In this chapter, I show you
include to make sure that your app isn't rejected ouₜ

Next, you'll spruce up the Main view by customizing h
and finally, I give you an introduction to your new frieₙ
some of you out there (but not me) may code perfectly,
make some mistakes as they develop an application. For
ger in Xcode starts helping you right from the start — so
stand how to use it as soon as you start coding.

Checking for Network Availability

One of the easiest ways to get your app rejected by Apple is to ᵗ
sure that you have an Internet connection when your app needs ᵢ
fore fail to notify the user that the functionality that requires the ₍
will be unavailable (or even worse, have your app just hang there).

Downloading the Reachability sample

Apple provides a sample application called Reachability that shows hoᵥ
determine whether you have an Internet connection (as well as quite a b
additional network information I won't be going into), and you'll be using
code in the RoadTrip app developed in this book. Here's how to use code
from that valuable sample program:

_____

1. Download the Reachability sample from Apple by clicking **Sample Code** at `http://developer.apple.com/devcenter/ios`.

2. Type Reachability **in the Search field.**

3. **Click the Reachability project in the search results, and in the iOS Developer Library window that appears, click the Download Sample Code button.**

4. **In Safari downloads, double-click the Reachability folder to open it.**

5. **Open the disclosure triangle next to the Classes folder (or open the folder) and drag the** `Reachability.m` **and** `Reachability.h` **files into your project.**

   (I put them in my Supporting Files group just to keep them out of the way.)

6. **Select the check box in front of Road Trip in the Add to Targets section.**

   Be sure to select the Copy Items into Destination Group's Folder option (if it isn't already selected).

In order for you to be able to use this code, you need to add the `SystemConfiguration` framework. To do so, follow these steps:

1. **In the Project navigator, select the project icon (in this case, RoadTrip) at the top of the Project navigator content area to display the Project editor.**

2. **In the Targets section in the Project editor, select RoadTrip.**

3. **On the Summary tab, scroll down to the Linked Frameworks and Libraries section.**

4. **Expand the Linked Frameworks and Libraries section if it isn't already expanded (see Figure 8-1) by clicking the disclosure triangle.**

5. **Click the + (plus sign) button underneath the list of current project frameworks.**

   A list of frameworks appears.

6. **Scroll down and select SystemConfiguration.framework, as shown in Figure 8-2.**

7. **Click the Add button.**

   You'll see the framework added to the Linked Frameworks and Libraries section.

8. **Close the Linked Frameworks and Libraries section.**

Figure 8-1:
Adding a
framework.

Figure 8-2:
Select
`System`
`Config-`
`uration`
`.frame`
`work.`

9. **In the Project navigator (don't do this from the Linked Frameworks and Libraries section!), drag the** `SystemConfiguration.framework` **file (you can see it at the top of the Project Navigator in Figure 8-3) to the Frameworks group, as shown in Figure 8-3.**

You can also add a framework by clicking the Build Phases tab in the Project editor, expanding the Link Binary with Libraries section, and following the same procedure.

When I wrote this chapter, the Reachability sample application hadn't yet been updated to use ARC, which is okay, because it gives me a chance to show you how to use both ARC and non-ARC files in your project.

In order to have both ARC and non-ARC code in a single project, the following steps allow you to remove a file from ARC:

1. **In the Project navigator, select the project icon at the top of the Project navigator area (RoadTrip, in this case) to display the Project editor.**

2. **In the Targets section, select RoadTrip.**

3. **Click the Build Phases tab.**

   You're witnessing here one of the few reasons you would ever have for using any of the other tabs in the Project editor.

4. **Expand the Compile Sources section, as shown in Figure 8-4.**

Figure 8-3:
Drag in the
Project
navigator!

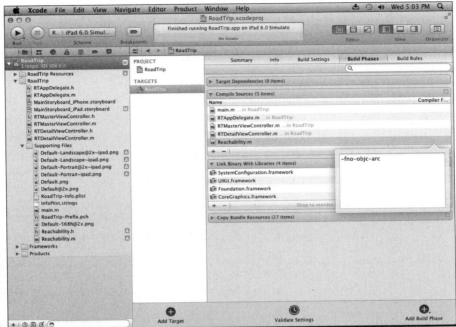

5. **Double-click the** `Reachability.m` **file.**

   A window appears.

6. **In the window's text box, enter** -fno-objc-arc, **as shown in Figure 8-4; then click outside the text box to close it.**

You may also have to choose Product⇔Clean if you tried to compile the project without doing Steps 1–6 because you wanted to see how many errors it would generate.

You have now told the compiler not to use ARC in `Reachability.h` and `.m` and that memory management is done by the Reachability code (which is what it would have been doing all along pre-ARC).

You also need to add the bolded code in Listing 8-1 to `Reachability.h`.

Listing 8-1:   Update the Reachability Interface

```
#import <Foundation/Foundation.h>
#import <SystemConfiguration/SystemConfiguration.h>
#import <netinet/in.h>
```

Adding the code to check for reachability

The place to check for whether you have access to the Internet is right when you start up. The method for doing that is the application delegate protocol method application:didFinishLaunchingWithOptions:.

You also need to include the Reachability.h file to be able to use Reachability, so add the bolded code in Listing 8-2 to the beginning of both the RTAppDelegate.m file and the application:didFinishLaunchingW ithOptions: method.

Listing 8-2:   Updating the RTAppDelegate Implementation and application:didFinishLaunchingWithOptions:

```
#import "RTAppDelegate.h"
#import "Reachability.h"

@implementation RTAppDelegate

@synthesize window = _window;

- (BOOL)application:(UIApplication *)application
        didFinishLaunchingWithOptions:
                                (NSDictionary *)launchOptions
{
  if ([[UIDevice currentDevice] userInterfaceIdiom] ==
                                UIUserInterfaceIdiomPad) {
    UISplitViewController *splitViewController =
        (UISplitViewController *)
                        self.window.rootViewController;
    UINavigationController *navigationController =
        [splitViewController.viewControllers lastObject];
    splitViewController.delegate =
            (id)navigationController.topViewController;
  }
NetworkStatus networkStatus =
  [[Reachability reachabilityForInternetConnection]
                            currentReachabilityStatus];
  if (networkStatus == NotReachable) {
    UIAlertView *alert = [[UIAlertView alloc]
      initWithTitle:@"Network Unavailable"
      message:@"RoadTrip requires an Internet connection"
      delegate:nil
      cancelButtonTitle:@"OK"
      otherButtonTitles:nil];
    [alert show];
  }
  return YES;
}
```

I'll have you ignore the code not in bold for the time being. I explain it in detail in Chapter 13.

In the main bolded section of Listing 8-2, you start by creating a `Reachability` object and then send it the `currentReachabilityStatus` message:

```
NetworkStatus networkStatus =
  [[Reachability reachabilityForInternetConnection]
                            currentReachabilityStatus];
```

`reachabilityForInternetConnection` is an initializer that creates a `Reachability` object that checks for the availability of an Internet connection. As I said, Reachability has a lot of functionality, but all you really care about right now is whether you can reach the Internet.

Next, check to see whether you have network access:

```
if (networkStatus == NotReachable) {
```

If you don't have network access, you post an alert:

```
UIAlertView *alert = [[UIAlertView alloc]
      initWithTitle:@"Network Unavailable"
      message:@"RoadTrip requires an Internet connection"
      delegate:nil
      cancelButtonTitle:@"OK"
      otherButtonTitles:nil];
[alert show];
```

This is the standard way to configure and then show an alert. You have filled in the various (self-explanatory) parameters required by the initialization method. Configured this way, the alert will have a single button.

The `show` message to the `alert` object causes the alert to be displayed in the window, and when the user taps Cancel, the alert is dismissed.

If you had added other buttons to give the user a choice of responses, you would have had to make the object posting the alert (the `RTAppDelegate`, in this case) a `UIAlertViewDelegate`, assigned the delegate parameter to `self`, and added the title of the other buttons using a `nil` terminated list. You would then have needed to implement the `alertView:clickedButtonAtIndex:` method in the delegate.

Explaining how Reachability works is beyond the scope of this book, but by examining the code, you can easily figure out how to get any other network status information you want.

If you run the application now, and either turn off your Internet connection on the computer (if you're running the Simulator) or turn on Airplane mode or turn off your Wi-Fi connection on the iPad, you see the message shown in Figure 8-5.

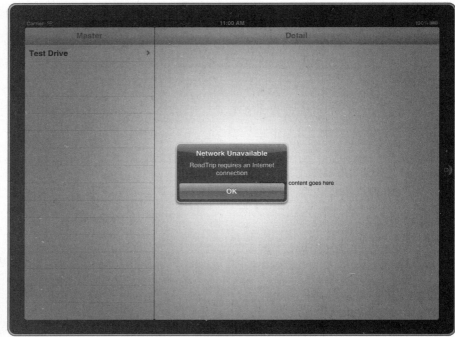

Figure 8-5:
Checking
the network
connection.

You can also temporarily change the

```
if (networkStatus == NotReachable) {
```

to

```
if (networkStatus != NotReachable) {
```

so that the test works in reverse. Just be sure to change it back!

Of course, in a real app, you would want to do something further here, such as give the user options and so on. I'll leave that up to you.

Congratulations! It's time for your first (real) adventure in coding land.

Sprucing Up the Main View

Now that you have some rudimentary code written, it's time to pick up the pace. If you look underneath the alert in Figure 8-5, or if you dismiss the alert, you can see that you are close to the user interface I showed you in Chapter 4, but not quite there. While some of what you'll need to do to get to this user interface could be accomplished in Interface Builder, some can't, and I want to explain how to set the appearance of controls programmatically in your app.

Users appreciate consistency of the user interface on their iPad. If you just use the interface objects "as is," however, your app looks sort of generic.

To allow developers to spice up the look of its apps, Apple provides three basic ways to customize a control's appearance:

- ✔ **By setting properties in Interface Builder:** You use this approach when you create the custom button in Chapter 5, in the section about adding user interface objects.

- ✔ **By setting properties in your program:** These include some of the same properties that you could have set in Interface Builder, and some that can only be set programmatically.

- ✔ **By customizing the appearance of an entire class:** An example is a `UIButton`, which you can customize by using the `UIAppearance` protocol to get the appearance proxy for a class and then customize the appearance of instances of a class by sending appearance modification messages to the class's appearance proxy.

In this section, I show you how to use the last two approaches.

You start by adding the bolded code in Listing 8-3 to the `application:did FinishLaunchingWithOptions:` method and deleting the commented-out code in bold, underline, and italic. In this method, you work on changing the appearance of the Navigation bar and the bar's button items.

Listing 8-3: Updating application:didFinishLaunchingWithOptions:

```
- (BOOL)application:(UIApplication *)application
          didFinishLaunchingWithOptions:
                             (NSDictionary *)launchOptions
{
  UINavigationController *navigationController;
  if ([[UIDevice currentDevice] userInterfaceIdiom] ==
                             UIUserInterfaceIdiomPad) {
    UISplitViewController *splitViewController =
      (UISplitViewController *)
                         self.window.rootViewController;
    //UINavigationController *navigationController =
         [splitViewController.viewControllers lastObject];
    //splitViewController.delegate = (id)
           navigationController.topViewController;
    splitViewController.presentsWithGesture = NO;
    UINavigationController *detailNavigationController =
         [splitViewController.viewControllers lastObject];
```

(continued)

Listing 8-3 *(continued)*

```
  splitViewController.delegate =
      (id)detailNavigationController.topViewController;
  navigationController =
  [splitViewController.viewControllers objectAtIndex:0];
  }
  else {
  navigationController = (UINavigationController *)
                      self.window.rootViewController;
  }
NetworkStatus networkStatus = [[Reachability
        reachabilityForInternetConnection]
        currentReachabilityStatus];
  if (networkStatus == NotReachable) {
    UIAlertView *alert = [[UIAlertView alloc]
      initWithTitle:@"Network Unavailable"
      message:@"RoadTrip requires an Internet connection"
      delegate:nil
      cancelButtonTitle:@"OK"
      otherButtonTitles:nil];
    [alert show];
  }
  [[UIApplication sharedApplication]
    setStatusBarStyle:UIStatusBarStyleBlackOpaque
                                animated:NO];
  navigationController.navigationBar.barStyle =
                                UIBarStyleBlack;
  [navigationController.navigationBar
    setTitleTextAttributes:
      [NSDictionary dictionaryWithObject:
        [UIColor yellowColor]
                        forKey:UITextAttributeTextColor]];
  [[UIButton appearance] setTitleColor:
    [UIColor greenColor] forState:UIControlStateNormal];
  [[UIBarButtonItem appearanceWhenContainedIn:
    [UINavigationBar class], nil]
    setTitleTextAttributes:
      [NSDictionary dictionaryWithObject:
                                [UIColor yellowColor]
    forKey:UITextAttributeTextColor]
    forState:UIControlStateNormal];
  [[UIButton appearanceWhenContainedIn:
    [UIAlertView class], nil] setTitleColor:
    [UIColor whiteColor] forState:UIControlStateNormal];
  [[UIToolbar appearance] setBarStyle:UIBarStyleBlack];

  return YES;
}
```

These changes are for the Navigation bar elements, and other application-wide classes. The fact that they're application wide makes it convenient to set them all up here. In addition, we want to disable the Split View gesture recognizer (which slides the Master View controller in from the left) because we'll be using a popover, as you'll see in Chapter 13.

Taking a closer look at Listing 8-3, you see that you start by taking into account the fact that this is a universal app, and the way you access the Navigation bar on the iPhone is different from the iPad when you use a split view. That may not make much sense now, but it will when I get into the detailed explanation of split views in Chapter 13 — so I'll ask you to just enter the bolded code into the `application:didFinishLaunchingWithOpti ons:` method as described earlier, and wait until Chapter 13 for more details. I normally don't like to defer explanations like this (and I generally don't), but the explanation is rather long and detailed.

```
UINavigationController *navigationController;
  if ([[UIDevice currentDevice] userInterfaceIdiom] ==
                                 UIUserInterfaceIdiomPad) {
    UISplitViewController *splitViewController =
      (UISplitViewController *)
                        self.window.rootViewController;
    UINavigationController *detailNavigationController =
        [splitViewController.viewControllers lastObject];
    splitViewController.delegate =
        (id)detailNavigationController.topViewController;
    navigationController =
    [splitViewController.viewControllers objectAtIndex:0];
  }
```

Starting with the next block of (bolded) code, you begin customizing a control's appearance by setting properties in your program. To start with, you set the status bar at the very top of the window to black:

```
[[UIApplication sharedApplication]
    setStatusBarStyle:UIStatusBarStyleBlackOpaque
                                        animated:NO];
```

You send the `setStatusBarStyle:animated` message to the `UIApplication` object, which "owns" the status bar. As you may recall from Chapter 6, you only have one `UIApplication` object. You get a reference to it by sending the class message `sharedApplication` (also explained in Chapter 6, in the section on `UIApplicationMain`).

In Objective-C, every class is also an object, so you can define methods that are responded to by the class.

`setStausBarStyle:animated` allows you to set the status bar to the default (white), black translucent, and black opaque, either with an animated action or immediately. I chose "black opaque" and "immediately" (`animated:No`) here.

Next, you set some of the properties of the Navigation bar, which means that you'll need a reference to the Navigation bar object. The Navigation bar is a property of the Navigation controller, which means that you'll of course need a reference to the Navigation controller. (I learned all this by going through the Xcode documentation for each of the classes, which I did by pressing Option and clicking the class name in the Source editor. I recommend that you explore those classes as well.)

You set the Navigation bar style to black:

```
navigationController.navigationBar.barStyle =
                                   UIBarStyleBlack;
```

This code sets not only the Navigation bar style but also the bar button elements (such as the Back button) to black.

Now that you have a nice black Navigation bar, set the title text to yellow. Setting the title text requires creating a dictionary to pass the parameters for the title text. Each key in the dictionary corresponds to a different text style attribute. (You can discover such facts by pressing Option while double-clicking the `setTitleTextAttributes` symbol in the Source editor to read the method documentation.) Here's the code that sets the title text to yellow:

```
[navigationController.navigationBar
    setTitleTextAttributes:
      [NSDictionary dictionaryWithObject:
        [UIColor yellowColor]
                    forKey:UITextAttributeTextColor]];
```

Several different title text attributes are available for you to set, including font, text shadow color, and a text shadow offset, each with its own key. In this case, you specify a text color.

The `UITextAttributeTextColor` key specifies a text color and requires a `UIColor` object as its value.

A `UIColor` object represents color and can also represent opacity (alpha value). `yellowColor` (along with a number of similar methods) is a class method that returns a color object whose RGB values are 1.0, 1.0, and 0.0 and whose alpha value is 1.0. You find similar class methods for other colors, such as `redColor`, `clearColor`, and so on, as I discovered by pressing Option while double-clicking `UIColor` and reading the class reference documentation. (You should be getting the picture by now about reading the documentation, so I won't belabor the point.)

If you don't like the boring black background for the Navigation bar that you get when you set the bar style to black, you have the option of adding a background image. `setBackgroundImage:forBarMetrics:`, as you might guess, enables you to set a background image. You have to provide the image using `UIImage` (as you do in Chapter 5 in the section about adding user interface objects):

```
[navigationController.navigationBar setBackgroundImage:
    [UIImage imageNamed:@"NavBarImage.png"]
                      forBarMetrics:UIBarMetricsDefault];
```

You use the `imageNamed:` method to find an image in your program's bundle (which contains the application executable and any resources used by the application, such as the application icon and aforementioned image). The `imageNamed:` method first looks to see whether the image has already been loaded (because you've used it previously) and cached. If not, it loads the image data, caches it, and then returns the resulting object. Of course, you'll have to add that image to the project.

On a device running iOS 4 or later, the behavior is identical if the device's screen has a scale of 1.0. If the screen has a scale of 2.0 (which means you're using the Retina display on either the iPhone or iPad), this method first searches for an image file with the same filename with an `@2x` suffix appended to it. For example, if the file's name is `button`, the method first searches for `button@2x`. If it finds an image with `2x` in the filename, it loads that image and sets the scale property of the returned `UIImage` object to 2.0. Otherwise, it loads the unmodified filename and sets the scale property to 1.0.

`UIBarMetricsDefault` says use this image for both Landscape and Portrait orientation. You can set a different image for Landscape orientation if you'd like.

After you have your background image installed (if you want one), you can customize the appearance of your controls using the following code. Until now, you've been customizing a control's appearance by setting properties in your program. In this next chunk of code, I show you how to customize a control's appearance by customizing the appearance of an entire class:

```
[[UIButton appearance] setTitleColor:
    [UIColor greenColor] forState:UIControlStateNormal];
```

This code takes advantage of a feature in `UIKit` called Custom Appearance for UIKit Controls. It enables you to customize the appearance of many `UIKit` views and controls to give your application a unique look and feel. You can set the tint color, background image, and title position properties (among others) on a number of objects, including toolbars, navigation bars, search bars, buttons, sliders, and some other controls.

You set the default attributes to use for a class by using an *appearance proxy* — an object supplied by UIKit that you can use to modify the default appearance of views and controls in classes that adopt the UIAppearance protocol. (You can see whether a class conforms to the UIAppearance protocol by looking in the class reference for the class.) If you were to look up the UIButton class, you would see, as shown in Figure 8-6, that it does.

Figure 8-6:
The UI
Button
class con-
forms to
the UI
Appear-
ance
protocol.

To modify the default appearance of such a class, you need to first get its appearance proxy object by sending the appearance class message to the class:

```
[UIButton appearance]
```

Next, you send a message to the appearance proxy object to set new default values. For example, you can use a proxy object to change the default title color of the UIButton class to green by using setTitleColor, as follows:

```
[[UIButton appearance] setTitleColor:
      [UIColor greenColor] forState:UIControlStateNormal];
```

This statement modifies the titleColor for all buttons. This approach works well if you want all buttons to have this title color. It also means that *every* button title — including the Back button in the Navigation bar and the OK button in the alert you post when you don't have an Internet connection — will be green. But you can fix that situation if you don't want to include those items.

If you want the text for all Bar Button items (such as the Back button) in the alert to be yellow and not green, or to be set to any other color you want instead of the one you're using for the `appearance` object, you can use the `appearanceWhenContainedIn:` object to set the tint color, background, image, and title position properties (among others) for all Bar Button items that are *subviews* (not subclasses) contained in a Navigation bar to yellow:

```
[[UIBarButtonItem appearanceWhenContainedIn:
    [UINavigationBar class], nil] setTitleTextAttributes:
    [NSDictionary dictionaryWithObject:
                                [UIColor yellowColor]
        forKey:UITextAttributeTextColor]
        forState:UIControlStateNormal];
```

To make the title of the OK button in an alert another color (white, in this example), you can use the `appearanceWhenContainedIn:` object again:

```
[[UIButton appearanceWhenContainedIn:
    [UIAlertView class], nil] setTitleColor:
    [UIColor whiteColor] forState:UIControlStateNormal];
```

This code sets the font color for all Bar Button items that are subviews of the `UIAlertView`.

Finally, you set the appearance of all toolbars to black. (I know you don't have a toolbar yet, but you will have one when Chapter 13 rolls around.)

```
[[UIToolbar appearance] setBarStyle:UIBarStyleBlack];
```

Figure 8-7 shows the before and after results on the iPad of the code you just added. Because this book is in black and white, you'll have to take my word for it that the Navigation bar is black, the Navigation bar title is yellow, the Test Drive button title is green, and the Back button title is yellow.

Figure 8-7:
Before and after control customization on the iPad.

Notice that the Navigation bar for the Detail view has stayed the same; I get around to fixing that in Chapter 13, when I replace the Navigation bar with a toolbar sporting the black tint you specified earlier in Listing 8-3.

Finally, you'll also want to be able to set the title in the Navigation bar for the view. You could have done that in Interface Builder, but I'm showing you how to do it programmatically because you want to be able to set the title of the view based on where the user is going.

To set the RTMasterViewController title, add the bolded code in Listing 8-4 to viewDidLoad in RTMasterViewController.m.

Listing 8-4:   Updating viewDidLoad

```
- (void)viewDidLoad
{
    [super viewDidLoad];
    self.title = @"Road Trip";
}
```

How did I know to put this code here, rather than in some other section of the code? As I explain in Chapter 7, viewDidLoad is the message sent when the view is loaded for the first time, but before it's displayed. If you want a title, you want to see it here, before the view is displayed.

Understanding Autorotation

In Chapter 5, I said I would explain more about view rotation when the orientation changes.

One of the responsibilities of the UIViewController class is to work with the application's window to handle device rotation (also known as *device orientation changes*). Although the UIViewController class itself already includes the functionality to animate the transition from the current orientation to the new one (which you can override if you need to lay out the view again for the new orientation), it must also communicate to the application window whether it in fact wants to support a particular orientation.

In earlier versions of iOS, you had to override certain UIViewController methods to control autorotation, but you can manage this now by simply choosing your desired Supported Interface Orientations in the Target's Summary Deployment Info sections, as shown in Figure 8-8.

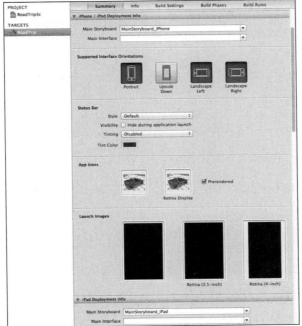

Figure 8-8:
The Target's
Supported
Interface
Orientations.

Writing Bug-Free Code

Although some developers think that writing code is where they spend the vast majority of their time when they're developing an app, debugging is actually right up there as a very close second. (And yes, I know that the title of this section is wishful thinking.)

Because debugging plays such a crucial role in writing workable code, I want to use this section to emphasize two points:

- App developers should strive to write code with as few bugs as possible (duh!).
- App developers need to know how to use the debugger so they can track down the inevitable bugs they do introduce into their code as efficiently as possible.

With the release of Xcode 4, Apple has made it easier to write code with fewer bugs, as well as use the debugger to track down bugs you do have.

Because the best defense is a good offense, I want to start with the tools that Xcode provides that help you to write less buggy code. Xcode has figured out that the best way to make sure your code has as few bugs as possible is by giving you the opportunity to fix the code as you write it. Such opportunities come in the form of Xcode's various compiler warnings. More specifically, by taking advantage of the Live Issues and Fix-it features, which I explain in Chapter 7, you'll catch many of your errors before you even run your program, and fixing them will be easy. (Well, some of them, at least.) Live Issues continuously evaluates your code in the background and alerts you to coding mistakes, and Fix-it will also offer to fix the problem for you. I suggest that unless you are crystal clear about what you're doing, don't run your app without first resolving any outstanding compiler warnings.

Of course, Live Issues and Fix-it are really only good at fixing syntax errors — they're usually not much help in detecting logic errors or coding mistakes that cause runtime errors (such as dividing by zero). For those errors, you need to become facile at using the debugger — or, more precisely, the Debug area and the Debug navigator.

Working in the Debug area and Debug navigator

The Debug area consists of the Debug bar, partnered with the Variables pane and the Console pane, each of which has a Scope bar fitted out with a pop-up menu. You usually use the Debug area in conjunction with the Debug navigator.

You access the Debug area by selecting it in the Xcode toolbar's View selector (as shown in Figure 8-9). You select the Debug navigator by showing the Navigator area and then selecting the Debug navigator in the Navigator selector bar. Truth be told, though, there's nothing much to see in the Debug area or Debug navigator unless your application is actually running. And although the Debug area's Variables and Console panes will retain the results from your last program execution, the Debug navigator shows content only when your application is paused.

If you get a runtime error (or if you click the Pause button or a breakpoint is triggered), the Debug area and the Debug navigator open automatically.

Figure 8-10 show what happens when you hit a breakpoint (which I explain shortly) in your program.

Show the Debug area

Figure 8-9:
Accessing
the Debug
area.

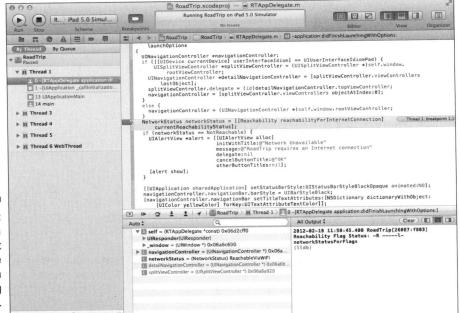

Figure 8-10:
Hitting a
breakpoint
displays the
Debug area
and Debug
navigator.

What you see in the Debug area is controlled by using the Debug area Scope bar, shown in Figure 8-11. You use this bar to toggle between the Variables pane only (left button), both Variables and Console panes (center button), and Console pane only (right button).

Debug area scope bar

Figure 8-11:
Use the
Debug area
Scope bar
to control
what pane
you see in
the Debug
area.

The Variables pane and the Console pane have their very own Scope bars as well. The pop-up menu in the Variables pane Scope bar lets you display

✔ **Auto:** Recently accessed variables

✔ **Local:** Local variables

✔ **All:** All variables and registers

The pop-up menu in the Console pane Scope bar lets you display

✔ **All Output:** Target and debugger output

✔ **Debugger Output:** Debugger output only

✔ **Target Output:** Target output (program logging to the debugger, for example) only

Xcode offers other controls and filters for what gets displayed that I encourage you to explore on your own.

Managing breakpoints

You can use the debugger to pause execution of your program at any time and view the state of the running code.

As mentioned previously, you won't find much to see in the Debug area and Debug navigator unless your program is stopped at a breakpoint or paused (and not much at those points, either). The debugger is more useful to you if you set breakpoints to stop at known points and then view the values of the variables in your source code. Given that fact, it's probably time to show you how to set a breakpoint and explain what a breakpoint is.

A *breakpoint* is an instruction to the debugger to stop execution at a particular program instruction. By setting breakpoints at various methods in your program, you can step through its execution — at the instruction level — to see exactly what it's doing. You can also examine the variables that the program is setting and using. If you're stymied by a logic error, setting breakpoints is a great way to break that logjam.

To set breakpoints, open a file in the Source editor and click in the Gutter — the column between the Navigator area and the Focus ribbon that is adjacent to the Editor area in Figure 7-6 — next to the spot where you want execution to stop. You can toggle the state (on or off) of all the breakpoints in your program at any time by clicking the Breakpoints button in the Xcode toolbar (to the left of the Activity viewer).

To disable an individual breakpoint, click its icon in the gutter. To get rid of a breakpoint completely, simply drag it off to the side. You can also right-click (or Control-click) the breakpoint and choose Remove Breakpoint from the pop-up menu that appears.

In Figure 8-12, I've added a breakpoint to the statement after I check network status. You'll also notice that I've displayed the Breakpoint navigator by selecting the appropriate icon in the Navigator selector bar. The Breakpoint navigator lets you see all breakpoints at once; if you select a given breakpoint in the Breakpoint navigator, it displays in the Source editor (where you can also edit it).

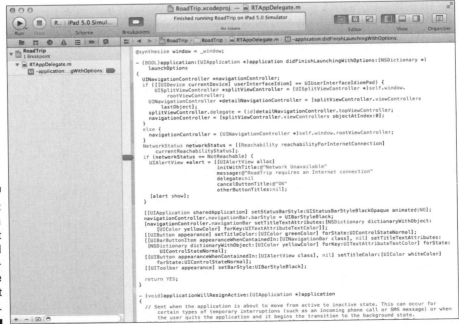

Figure 8-12:
Setting a breakpoint and displaying the Breakpoint navigator.

You can set several options for each breakpoint by Option-clicking the breakpoint and choosing Edit Breakpoint from the shortcut menu that appears, as shown in Figure 8-13.

Doing so opens the Edit Breakpoint window, where you can set the actions and options you want for breakpoints added in the Breakpoint editor. As shown in Figure 8-14, you can set a condition for a breakpoint, ignore it a set number of times before stopping, add an action, and automatically continue after evaluating actions.

In Figure 8-15, I selected the Click to Add an Action check box and then chose to add a sound. I also set a condition that I want the breakpoint to be triggered only if the `networkStatus` isn't equal to `notReachable`. In this case, as you can see in Figure 8-15, I had to specify

```
networkStatus != 0
```

This is because `networkStatus` is not a symbol the debugger has access to, but rather an enumerated type (a set of named values that behave as constants). If you examine the `Reachability.h` file you'll find

```
typedef enum {
        NotReachable = 0,
        ReachableViaWiFi,
        ReachableViaWWAN
} NetworkStatus;
```

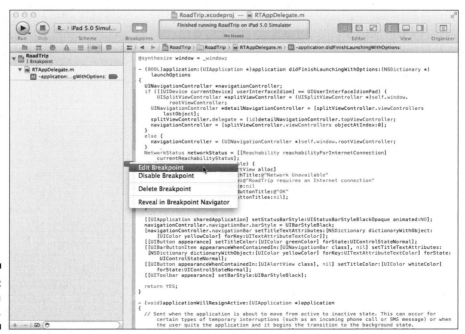

Figure 8-13:
Editing a
breakpoint.

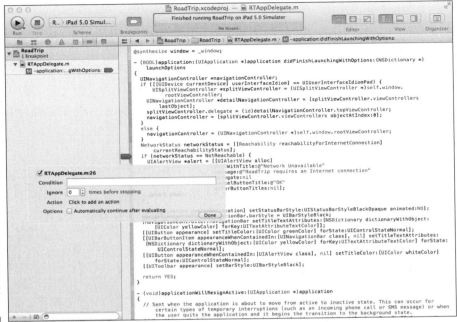

Figure 8-14:
Some
breakpoint
options.

Figure 8-15:
Fine-
tuning the
breakpoint.

The "normal" condition, of course, would be to set the breakpoint to stop when the condition is something you don't expect, like the `networkStatus` *equal to* `NotReachable`. But I want to keep my Mac connected to my network (which connects the Simulator as well), so I set it this way so it would stop at the breakpoint every time (unless of course my network unexpectedly goes down).

Set this breakpoint and run your program in Xcode. As you can see in Figure 8-16, you'll be stopped at the breakpoint.

Figure 8-16:
The compiler stops at the breakpoint I set.

As you can see in the figure, when the breakpoint is reached, the Debug area is displayed and the Debug navigator opened automatically. (As I mention in Chapter 3, you can change that response in the Behaviors tab of Xcode Preferences.) It stopped because the condition I set (`networkStatus != 0`) evaluated `YES`.

What you'll find in the Debug area

As you can see in Figure 8-16, on one side of the Debug area you have the Variables pane (which displays the values of variables), and on the other side, you have the Console pane. That's the configuration I've selected in the Debug area Scope bar (the middle button).

The Variables pane

The Variables pane displays the variables you're interested in. Click the disclosure triangle next to `self` to see the instance variables in the object. You'll see the local variables to a method as well. As mentioned earlier, you can specify which items to display by using the pop-up menu in the top-left corner of the Variables pane:

- ✔ **Auto:** Displays only the variables you're most likely to be interested in, given the current context.
- ✔ **Local:** Displays local variables.
- ✔ **All:** Displays all variables and registers.

You can also use the Search field on the toolbar to filter the items displayed in the Variables pane.

The Console pane

The Console pane displays program output. Again, as mentioned earlier, you can specify the type of output you see in the console by using the pop-up menu in the top-left corner of the Console pane:

- ✔ **All Output:** Displays target and debugger output.
- ✔ **Debugger Output:** Displays debugger output only.
- ✔ **Target Output:** Displays target output only.

When you are stopped at the breakpoint you set earlier, what you see is a lot of boilerplate and then this:

```
2012-02-19 12:02:12.486 RoadTrip[26123:f803] Reachability
          Flag Status: -R -----1- networkStatusForFlags
(lldb)
```

Not much of interest here, but in Chapter 11, you'll find out how to *print* (really *display*) the contents of a variable to the Console pane — and in Chapter 15, you'll have the opportunity to examine some runtime error messages.

The (rather boring) stuff you see here is the result of an `NSLog` statement in `Reachability`:

```
2012-02-19 12:02:12.486 RoadTrip[26123:f803] Reachability
          Flag Status: -R -----1- networkStatusForFlags
```

`NSLog` allows you to display information in the Console pane during execution. For example, if you wanted to know how many points of interest your app had to display (the number of elements in the `poiData` array — you find out about `poiData` in Chapter 17), instead of using a breakpoint and displaying a variable, you could add the following `NSLog` statement:

```
NSLog(@"Number of points of interest %i",
                                  [poiData count]);
```

which would display

```
2012-02-19 12:06:52.688 RoadTrip[26145:f803]
                         Number of points of interest 1
```

in the Console pane.

NSLog is pretty useful and uses the same formatting as NSString's string-WithFormat and other formatting methods.

What you'll find in the Debug navigator

Selecting an item in the Debug navigator causes information about the item to be displayed in the Source editor. For example, selecting a method displays the source code for that function in the Source editor.

Each application within iOS is made up of one or more *threads,* each of which represents a single path of execution through the application's code. Every application starts with a single thread, which runs the application's main function. The main thread encompasses the application's main run loop, and it's where the NSApplication object receives events. Applications can add (spawn) additional threads, each of which executes the code of a specific method.

Threads per se are way beyond the scope of this book, but that's okay: Here you'll be concerned with only the main thread.

Every time you send a message (or make a function call), the debugger stores information about it in a *stack frame* and then it stores all such frames in the *call stack.* When you're thrown into the debugger because of an error (or if you pause the application by clicking the Pause button on the toolbar), Xcode displays the thread list, and within each thread the call stack for that thread, putting the most recent call at the top. The call stack shows a trace of the objects and methods that got you to where you are now.

You can do a lot more as far as threads are concerned, but again, that's outside of the scope of this book. (If you don't know whether to be disappointed or relieved, hold that thought.)

Although the trace isn't really all that useful in this particular context, it can be *very* useful in a more complex application — it can help you to understand the path that you took to get where you are. Seeing how one object sent a message to another object — which sent a message to a third object — can be really helpful, especially if you didn't expect the program flow to work that way.

Getting a look at the call stack can also be useful if you're trying to understand how the framework does its job, and in what order messages are sent. As you'll soon see, you can stop the execution of your program at a breakpoint and trace the messages sent up to that point.

Displaying variables in the Source editor

In the Debugger window, you can move your pointer over an object or variable in the Source editor to show its contents and move your pointer over disclosure triangles to see even more information.

In Figure 8-17, for example, I moved the pointer over networkStatus to see its value (information about the current status of the Internet connection).

TIP

When you move your pointer over a variable, its contents are revealed — and if more disclosure triangles appear, you can move your pointer over them to see even more information (which I explain in more detail in Chapter 11).

You see the value of the variable in the Variables pane as well.

In the next section, I show you how to step through your program after it's stopped at a breakpoint.

Figure 8-17: Showing the network-Status.

Tiptoeing through your program

When you build and run the program with breakpoints, the Debug bar appears in the Workspace window as the program runs in the Simulator. The program stops executing at the first breakpoint (if you have set a condition, it stops executing if that condition is met).

To control the execution, you use the Debug bar (located at the top of the Debug area that you see in Figure 8-18). The Debug bar includes buttons to

- ✔ **Open or close the Debug area.** As mentioned previously, you can hide the Debug area if you don't need it for what you're doing right now.

- ✔ **Pause or resume execution of your code.** Click this button to stop your program from executing or continue execution after it stopped when it entered the debugger.

- ✔ **Step over.** Click this button to make the *process counter (PC),* which is identified by the green arrow in the gutter, move to the next line of code to be executed. If that line of code sends a message, it will send the message (and run the method) — but then, from your perspective, it just moves to the next line of code.

- ✔ **Step in.** Click this button to move the process counter to the next line of code to be executed. If the line of code sends a message to a method in your source code, the debugger will step to the method and then return to the next line of code after the line that sends the message.

- ✔ **Step out.** Click this button to step out of the current function or method. The Source editor then displays either the method that sent the message or the function's caller.

- ✔ **Simulate location.** You can have the debugger simulate the location of the iPad for you. I explain this in Chapter 17.

Because I set a condition that I want the breakpoint to be triggered only if the networkStatus isn't equal to NotReachable, when I build and run RoadTrip in Figure 8-18, you can see that the program has stopped executing at the breakpoint. The networkStatus is reachableViaWiFi as you can (barely) see in Figure 8-18 in the Variables pane. If I then want to watch what happens as RoadTrip executes step-by-step, I would select Step In, and the screen shown in Figure 8-19 appears.

Figure 8-18:
The Debug
area and
Debug bar.

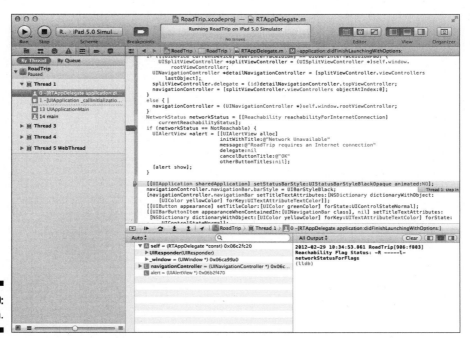

Figure 8-19:
Step in.

You can see that the instruction

```
if (networkStatus == NotReachable) {
```

caused the debugger to move to the line following the code block that would have been executed if the `if` statement evaluated to `YES` and the debugger has paused at the blank line.

That's because the `if` statement evaluated to `NO` — the `networkStatus` was `reachableViaWiFi)` — and the code block was skipped:

```
if (networkStatus == NotReachable) {
  UIAlertView *alert = [[UIAlertView alloc]
      initWithTitle:@"Network Unavailable"
      message:@"RoadTrip requires an Internet connection"
      delegate:nil
      cancelButtonTitle:@"OK"
      otherButtonTitles:nil];
  [alert show];
}
```

Of course you knew that, having displayed the value of the `networkStatus` as reachable in Figure 8-17.

This concludes your introduction to the debugger and Debug navigator. I do want to show you a couple more things, but I need to have you add more code to have them make sense. In Chapter 11, I show you how to print (display) the contents of a variable in the Console pane, and then in Chapter 15, I show you a couple of my favorite runtime errors.

Chapter 9

Adding Outlets and Actions to Your RoadTrip Code

As I explain in Chapter 3, one of the things that the RoadTrip app will be able to do is send the image of a car to the top of the screen, have it turn around, have it move back down the screen, and then have it turn around again so it's back where it started, all from a simple tap of the Test Drive button. Fun times.

For all that to happen, you're going to need to add some logic to your code. You do that in a custom view controller, which gets detailed coverage in this very chapter — especially the bits about adding custom view controllers and connecting them to the view controllers you create in your storyboard. But that's only one part of the story. For all the pieces to fit, you'll need to be able to access the elements stipulated in your storyboard — elements like the car image — and then connect those elements to the code in your custom view controller.

The way you add the logic to connect the view to the model via the view controller in this chapter is going to be the model for how you deal with the rest of the view controllers in the storyboard. Keep in mind that, although you can add all the view controllers you'll ever need to the storyboard graphically, you still need to add some code on your own if you ever want the controller to actually *do* anything, such as get data from the model and send it to the view.

Using Custom View Controllers

The view controller provided by the storyboard is a `UIViewController` (or `UITableViewController`, which is a type of view controller) and is blissfully unaware of what you want to display in a view, or how to respond to view actions (such as the user tapping the Test Drive button). In this section, you create a custom controller that *does* know about its view. (In Chapter 10, you get to add the logic you need to the custom view controller to make the car move and make noise.)

Adding the custom view controller

You start the process of adding a custom view controller to your project by adding the custom view controller class, as follows:

1. **To create a new group to keep your view controller classes in, select the RoadTrip group in the Project navigator and either right-click and choose New Group from the menu that appears or choose File⇨New⇨New Group from the main menu.**

   Note that you need to select the RoadTrip *group,* right there under RoadTrip Resources, and not the RoadTrip *project,* which is at the top of the Project navigator.

   To change a file's group, select the file and drag it to the group you want it to occupy. The same goes for groups as well (after all, they can go into other groups).

2. **(The) New Group should be selected so you can name your new group** View Controller Classes **by typing it.**

   If it is not already selected, or you want to change the name, select the name and name it (this is the same way you would name a folder on the Mac).

3. **In the Project navigator, select the (newly created) View Controller Classes group and either right-click and then choose New File from the menu that appears or choose File⇨New⇨New File from the main menu (or press ⌘+N) to bring up the New File dialog.**

4. **In the left column of the dialog, select Cocoa Touch under the iOS heading, select Objective-C class template in the top-right pane, and then click Next.**

5. **In the Class field, enter** TestDriveController, **choose UIViewController from the Subclass Of drop-down menu, make sure that the Target for iPad option is selected and that the With XIB for User Interface option is deselected, and then click Next.**

Because this is a name unique to my application, as opposed to the genetic `AppDelegate` or `DetailViewController` names the template generates, I am not going to add the RT prefix here. But feel free to continue that naming scheme if you'd like.

Some people also would tell you to call this file `TestDrive`*`View Controller`*, but that seems like overkill to me; personally the shorter the name you can have without losing any information, the better.

6. **In the Save sheet that appears, select a location, and then click Create.**

If you examine the (generated) code added in `TestDriveController`, you'll notice two methods.

The first one I'll draw your attention to is `viewDidLoad` — you'll be adding code to it to do any view controller or view initialization after the view controller and its view have been loaded from the storyboard:

```
- (void)viewDidLoad
{
    [super viewDidLoad];
// Do any additional setup after loading the view,
        typically from a nib.
}
```

Setting up the TestDriveController in the MainStoryboard for iPad

Now that you have a custom view controller (it doesn't do anything yet, but it will), you need to let the storyboard know that you want to load your custom view controller rather than a `UIViewController`.

In the Project navigator, select the `MainStoryboard_iPad` file, and in the Document Outline, select View Controller – TestDrive in the View Controller – TestDrive Scene. (I had you enter **TestDrive** in the Title field way back when, and now you're actually using it.)

Using the Inspector selector bar, open the Identity inspector in the Utility area and then choose `TestDriveController` (replacing `UIViewController`) from the Class drop-down menu in the Custom Class section, as I have in Figure 9-1. This means that when the Detail cell in the Master Controller is tapped, your custom controller — the `TestDriveController` — will be instantiated and initialized, meaning it will now receive events from the user and connect the view to the `Trip` model you'll create in Chapter 11.

Figure 9-1:
Connecting the view controller object in the iPad story-board to the `Test Drive Controller` class.

When you write your own code, it's pretty obvious how a program works: You create an object, initialize it, and then send it messages. When you work with storyboards, however, how your program works may not be so obvious. How do you go from the objects you added to your user interface in Interface Builder to code that enables you to access these objects? How do you get an Image view to change its image or receive a message that the user has tapped a button, for example?

The objects in your user interface must communicate with each other and with your source code if your program is to allow the user to interact with it. In order to access a user interface object and specify which messages are sent and received, you use Interface Builder to create connections. There are two basic types of connections you can create:

- ✔ **Outlet connections,** which connect your code to Interface Builder objects that enable you to get and set *properties* (change the image in an Image view, for example)

- ✔ **Action connections,** which specify the message to be sent to your code when the control is *interacted with* (the user taps a button, for example)

In this chapter, I explain how to create both outlets and actions in your code.

Understanding Outlets

An *outlet* is a way to connect your code to an object you added to a view in your storyboard that you've decided will become part of your user interface at runtime. The connections between your code and its outlets are automatically reestablished every time the object referenced by the outlet is loaded.

The object containing an outlet is usually a custom controller object such as the view controller generated for you by the template. In the class declaration of that custom controller, you declare an outlet as a property with the type qualifier of IBOutlet.

Listing 9-1 shows you what the TestDriveController class extension (in the .m file) will look like after you're done mucking about with it at the end of this chapter.

Listing 9-1:   Outlets (and Actions) Declared

```
@interface TestDriveController () {
  AVAudioPlayer *backgroundAudioPlayer;
  SystemSoundID burnRubberSoundID;
  BOOL touchInCar;

}
@property (weak, nonatomic) IBOutlet UIImageView *car;
@property (weak, nonatomic)
                         IBOutlet UIButton *testDriveButton;
- (IBAction)testDrive:(id)sender;
@end
```

An outlet is a property that points to another object, enabling an object in an application to communicate with another object at runtime. Using an outlet, you have a reference to an object defined in the storyboard (or a nib file) that is then loaded from that storyboard file at runtime. You can make outlet connections between any objects that you add to your storyboard in Interface Builder.

For example, in Figure 9-2, you use an outlet to get the text the user typed in the Find text field.

Figure 9-2:
Using an outlet to get the text entered by the user.

```
@interface FindController : MapController
@property (weak, nonatomic) IBOutlet MKMapView*mapView;
@property (strong, nonatomic) NSString*findLocation;
- (IBAction)mapType:(id)sender;

@end
```

But before you go setting up outlets for anything and everything, make sure that you really need one. You don't have to use outlets to be able to access all Interface Builder objects. Instead, as you saw in Chapter 8, you can access the Navigation bar to change its background indirectly through other connections established by the nib loader.

Adding Outlets

To recap from the previous section, outlets are the way your code can *access* — either by sending messages or setting properties — the Interface Builder objects in your storyboard. In previous versions of Xcode, you had to declare an outlet in the header file of a class and make a connection between the outlet and another object using Interface Builder. Now, however, you can do all this graphically in Interface Builder, and the required code is generated for you. Read on to find out more about how this works.

Opening the Assistant editor

To create an outlet, you need to connect the interface object in Interface Builder with your code. Although you have a couple of ways to make this connection, the easiest and most clear-cut way is to use the Assistant editor to automatically display the code file that's most relevant to the interface element you're working with. To make the Assistant editor automatically display a likely code file, follow these steps:

1. **Select the MainStoryboard_iPad.storyboard file in the Project navigator.**

2. **Close the Utility area if it's open (and you need the space) by deselecting it in the View selector in the Xcode toolbar.**

3. **In Interface Builder, select the View Controller – TestDrive in the View Controller – TestDrive Scene (see, it is handy to actually label things) in the Document Outline; then click the Assistant Editor button in the Editor selector on the toolbar (see Figure 9-3).**

   The Assistant editor pane opens and displays the header file for that particular view controller, as shown in Figure 9-4.

The Assistant editor has two modes: tracking (or automatic) mode and manual mode. In automatic mode, the Assistant selects the file or files that best meet the selected criterion and opens those files in the Assistant pane of the Source editor. In manual mode, you select the file to display using the Assistant pane Jump bar.

Figure 9-3:
Select the
Assistant
editor.

If the Assistant editor doesn't automatically display the header file you want, use the Assistant editor pane's Jump bar to track down the file you need. On that bar, you select the source file by first choosing Manual from the Assistant pop-up menu to put the editor in manual mode and then drilling down through your folder hierarchy to make your selection. (When you're done, you can choose Automatic from the same pop-up menu to get back to automatic mode.)

Figure 9-4:
The view
controller
in the story-
board and
the Test
Drive
Con-
troller
.h file
in the
Assistant
editor.

A *Jump bar* (a handy thing to know about) appears at the top of each Editor area pane and gives you a way to navigate through the files and symbols in your project. The configuration and behavior of each Jump bar is customized for the context in which it appears. In addition to a hierarchical path that enables you to navigate to a file or symbol in your project, the basic configuration of a Jump bar includes the following:

✔ The **Related Items menu** (accessed by clicking the icon shown in the left margin) grants you access to additional selections relevant to the current context, such as recently opened files or the interface (.h) header file for an implementation (.m) code file you're editing.

✔ **Previous and Next buttons** enable you to step back and forth through your navigation history.

I explain the Jump bar in detail when discussing the Standard editor in Chapter 7.

Creating the outlet

After you have the TestDriveController interface displayed (as I do in Figure 9-4), either by having the Assistant editor display it automatically or by navigating to it using the Jump bar, the actual creating-an-outlet business using the Interface Builder editor is very straightforward and pretty easy. You do it by Control-dragging from the element you're interested in to the TestDriveController interface, as detailed in the following steps:

1. **Control-click and drag from the element in the view (the car image, in this example) to the** TestDriveController.h **file between the** @interface **and** @end **statements, as shown in Figure 9-5.**

2. **In the dialog that appears, name this outlet** car **(see Figure 9-6) and then click the Connect button.**

   The outlet is added as a property. (I explain properties in Chapter 6.)

   Figure 9-7 shows your new outlet in all its glory.

A connection between an object and its outlets is actually stored in a nib file. (Come to think of it, a storyboard is really just a series of nib files.) When the nib file is loaded, each connection is reconstituted and reestablished, thus enabling you to send messages to the object. IBOutlet is the keyword that tags an instance-variable declaration so that the Interface Builder application knows that a particular instance variable is an outlet — and can then enable the connection to it.

Figure 9-5:
Control-drag
from an
object to
create an
outlet.

Figure 9-6:
Name the
outlet *car*.

Freedom of outlet reference choice

You actually have a choice — you can add the outlet reference to the public class interface declared in the .h file (as you did earlier in this chapter), or you can add the outlet reference to the private class interface declared in the .m file. An outlet declared in the .h file will be a public property that can be used by methods in other classes in your app. An outlet declared in your .m file can only be used by methods defined in that .m file. A general programming guideline is to keep things private unless they need to be public, so you might keep your outlet references in the .m file. On the other hand, Xcode's Assistant editor will usually open the .h file, so you might just use that public reference — as we generally do in this book.

When you create an outlet in the way I just explained, Xcode also adds some code to the corresponding .m file to support the new outlet. Select `TestDriveController.m` in the Project navigator or just press Control+⌘+up arrow when `TestDriveController.h` is displayed to get the file's *counterpart* — the counterpart to the Interface (.h) file is the Implementation (.m) file, and vice versa.

Figure 9-7:
The outlet you just created.

Figure 9-8 shows the code in the .m file. What might surprise you is that no code has been added to that file. In the old days, you needed to have an @synthesize method in the .m file for each property, but that is no longer necessary.

3. **Go back to the Interface file and create an outlet for the Test Drive button (name it** testDriveButton**).**

    Drag the button to the TestDriveController interface in the same way as you do the car image (between the @interface and @end statements).

The only reason you need to create an outlet for a button (normally you'll attach an action to the button, which you'll do in the later section "Working with the Target-Action Design Pattern") is to change a Button property. You'll be using this outlet in Chapter 10 to make the button blink on and off.

Figure 9-8: The generated code.

The Connections inspector

While clicking and dragging is the easy way to go, you should know that you can make the same outlet connections using the Connections inspector in the Utility area, with a bit more work. But the real value of the Connections inspector is that it shows you what the outlets (and received actions — covered next — and the segues actually are). To use the Connections inspector, follow these steps:

1. **Select Standard editor on the View selector in the toolbar.**

   The Assistant editor closes.

2. **Show the Utility area by selecting it in the View selector.**

3. **Select the Connections inspector by clicking its icon in the Inspector selector bar. (The icon is shown here in the left margin.)**

4. **In the Document Outline, select the View Controller in the Test Drive Controller – Test Drive Scene.**

In Figure 9-9, you can see that in the Outlets section of the Connections inspector, the view controller contains both `car` and `testDriveButton` outlets (as should yours, if you followed along and created them). You'll also see in the Referencing Storyboard Segues section a Push from Table View Cell – Cell.

Figure 9-9:
The Connections inspector and window.

You can also Control-click the view controller in the Document Outline to get a similar picture in the Connections window.

Besides showing the outlets, if you need to change what an existing outlet points to, the Connections inspector or window is the way to go. Just drag from the circle at the end of the connection in the Outlets section in the Connections inspector or Connections window to the Interface Builder object you want that outlet to point to.

If you wanted to create an outlet without all this dragging, you would simply enter the code that Interface Builder created for you in the view controller's @Interface (the property — don't forget the IBOutlet):

```
@property (weak, nonatomic) IBOutlet UIImageView *car;
```

The new outlet will show up in the Connections inspector and window, and then all you need to do is drag from the circle at the end of the connection in the Outlets section to the Interface Builder object you want that outlet to point to.

When you add outlets, you have some memory management considerations, not to mention the entire subject of properties, both of which I explain in Chapter 6. But in this chapter, I'm keeping the focus on what you need to know about interacting with Interface Builder objects in a storyboard. That interaction also includes working with a design pattern called Target-Action, which I explain next.

Working with the Target-Action Design Pattern

The other requirement of a user interface that I mention at the beginning of this chapter is being able to deal with situations where you want to connect a button to your code so that when a user taps the button, something happens. This requirement involves using the *Target-Action pattern,* which is one of the key design patterns in iOS programming.

You use the Target-Action pattern to let your app know that it should do something when prompted. A user might tap a button or enter some text, for example, and the app must respond in some way. The control — a button, say — sends a message (the Action message) that you specify to the target (the receiving object, which is usually a view controller object) that you have selected to handle that particular action.

Using the Target-Action pattern: It's about controls

When a user acts on the control by, say, tapping a button, the iPhone or iPad generates an event. The event triggering a particular action message can be anything, just as the object sending the message can be any object. For example, a gesture-recognizer object might send an action message to another object when it recognizes its gesture. However, the Target-Action pattern is usually found with controls such as buttons and sliders.

The event as such probably doesn't tell you much, but Target-Action provides a way to send an application-specific instruction to the appropriate object.

If you wanted to develop an app that could start a car from an iOS device (not a bad idea for those who live in a place like Hibbing, Minnesota in winter), you could display two buttons, Start and Heater. You could use Interface Builder to specify that when the user taps Start, the target is the CarController object and the method to invoke is ignition. Figure 9-10 shows the Target-Action mechanism in action.

The Target-Action mechanism enables you to create a control object and tell it not only which object you want handling the event but also the message to send. For example, if the user taps a Ring Bell button onscreen, you want to send a Ring Bell message to the view controller. But if the Wave Flag button on the same screen is touched, you want to be able to send the Wave Flag message to the same view controller. If you couldn't specify the message, all buttons would have to send the same message. It would then make the coding more difficult and more complex because you would have to identify which button sent the message and what to do in response. It would also make changing the user interface more work and more prone to errors.

Figure 9-10:
The Target-Action mechanism.

You set a control's action and target using Interface Builder. You get to specify what method — in which object — should respond to a control without having to write any code.

You can also change the target and action dynamically by sending the control or its cell `setTarget:` and `setAction:` messages.

Action methods have a certain *signature* (format, in other words):

```
- (IBAction)testDrive:(id)sender;
```

The type qualifier `IBAction`, which is used in place of the `void` return type, flags the declared method as an action so that Interface Builder is aware of it. (This is similar to the `IBOutlet` tag, used in the "Creating the outlet" section, earlier in this chapter.) And just as with outlets, you can actually make the connections in the Interface Builder editor, and Xcode will generate the necessary code for you.

The `sender` parameter is the control object sending the action message. When responding to an action message, you may query the sender to get more information about the context of the event triggering the action message.

You can set the action and target of a control object programmatically or in Interface Builder. Setting these properties effectively connects the control and its target via the action. If you connect a control and its target in Interface Builder, the connection is archived in a nib file. When an application later loads the nib file, the connection is restored.

`IBAction` is like `IBOutlet` — it does nothing in the code but rather is a tag used by Interface Builder.

Adding an action

After you have the `TestDriveController` interface displayed, either by having the Assistant editor display it automatically or by navigating to it using the Jump bar, the actual business of creating an outlet is pretty straightforward. From within the Interface Builder editor, just Control-drag from the element you're interested in (the Test Drive button, in this case) to the `TestDriveController` interface, as detailed in the following steps:

1. **In the Project navigator, select the** `MainStoryboard_iPad.storyboard` **file.**

2. **Close the Utility area by deselecting it in the View selector.**

   You don't need it to create the action.

3. **Open the Assistant editor by clicking its button in the Editor selector in the toolbar.**

   You should see the `TestDriveController.h` interface file displayed in the Assistant editor. If it doesn't appear, navigate to it using the steps in the earlier section "Creating the outlet."

4. **Control-click and drag from the Test Drive button in the view (the car image, in this example) to the `TestDriveController.h` file, right between the `@interface` and `@end` statements.**

5. **In the dialog that appears, choose Action from the Connection drop-down menu, as shown in Figure 9-11.**

6. **In the same dialog, leave Touch Up Inside as the selection in the Event drop-down menu.**

   To create an Action for a control, you need to specify what event triggers the action. In the case of a button, a Touch Up Inside event is the usual choice because Touch Up Inside is the event that's generated when the very last place the user touched *before* lifting his or her finger is still inside the button. (This allows a user to change his or her mind about touching the button by moving his or her finger off the button before lifting it.)

Figure 9-11:
Select Action as the connection type.

7. **Still in the same dialog, name this action** *testDrive* **by entering** test-Drive **in the Name field; then click Connect.**

   As shown in Figure 9-12, a new action method

   ```
   - (IBAction)testDrive:(id)sender;
   ```

   gets added to your code.

Just as it did when you added an outlet, Xcode also adds code for you in the .m file to support whatever it is that you're doing. (In this case, the added code supports the action.) To see what has been added, select the TestDriveController.m file in the Project navigator or press Control+⌘+up arrow in the file to get the .h file's .m counterpart. Figure 9-13 shows the new code that gets added — in this case, a by-now familiar action method - (IBAction)testDrive:(id)sender as a *stub* (the method definition with no code). It's up to you to code what should be done when this message is received, and you'll find out how to make that decision in Chapter 10.

Figure 9-12:
A new action message.

Figure 9-13:
The test
Drive
method
stub.

You can always double-check the status of your Target-Action connections with the help of the Connections inspector, mentioned earlier in this chapter as part of my coverage of outlets. With the Utility area displayed, click the Connections inspector icon in the Inspector selector bar to open the Connections inspector or right-click the view controller in the Document Outline to get a similar picture in the Connections window. In the Received Actions section, you'll see the new action. As I explain earlier, you can change the Interface Builder object you are receiving the action from by dragging from the circle to the new Interface Builder object. You can also add an action by entering the code the Interface Builder would have added for you (the method declaration and definition) in view controller's @interface

```
- (IBAction)testDrive:(id)sender;
```

and @implementation

```
- (IBAction)testDrive:(id)sender {
}
```

and then dragging from the circle in the Received Actions section in the Connections inspector or window to the control and choose an Event type from the contextual menu that appears when you release the mouse button.

I'm sure you've noticed that RoadTrip has a bunch of other buttons that also need connecting. It turns out, though, that you won't be using the Target-Action pattern to connect them. You'll be using a storyboard feature called *segues* to do that for you. I explain using segues in Chapter 14.

How Outlets and Actions Work

At the start of this chapter, I explain that you need to be able to connect the objects you added to your user interface in Interface Builder to code that enables you to access these objects (such as to an Image view to change its image) or receive a message that the user has tapped a button.

In the chapter, I show you how to create outlets and actions to do that, but I haven't really explained how all that is connected at runtime.

As I explain in Chapter 4, storyboards are a collection of (resource) nib files that you use to store the user interface of your application.

A nib file is an Interface Builder document. When you use Interface Builder in Chapter 4 to create your user interface, you create an *object graph* that is saved (archived) as part of the resource file. When you load the file, the object graph is then used to re-create the relationships between the objects in the file, and your program objects as well.

As I explain in Chapter 6, every storyboard file has an initial view controller. At runtime, it's loaded along with its view and all the other Interface Builder objects you added in Chapter 5 — and you get an exact replica of the objects that were in your Interface Builder document. The nib-loading code instantiates the objects, configures them, and reestablishes any inter-object connections *including the outlets and actions* that you created in Interface Builder. Not bad for a bunch of 0s and 1s, right?

Update the iPhone storyboard file

As in previous chapters, the code you added in this chapter works for both the iPhone and iPad. But, as in previous chapters, you now should add objects to the iPhone storyboard file to keep it on an equal footing with its iPad sibling. You don't want the iPhone storyboard to think that you love it less than the iPad.

You created the Test Drive scene way back in Chapter 5. Now make sure that the `TestDriveController` in the iPhone storyboard file has the connections shown in Figure 9-14, which are very similar to the iPad storyboard connections shown earlier in Figure 9-9.

Figure 9-14:
Test
Drive
Con-
troller
connec-
tions in
the iPhone
storyboard
file.

Chapter 10

Adding Animation and Sound to Your App

Although it may take some time before you go on your road trip, as well as complete the building of the app I'm showing you in this book, the least I can do is show you how to take a test drive in your '59 pink Cadillac Eldorado Biarritz convertible.

In this chapter, you find out how to make the car move up the screen, turn around, and move back to its original position — with the appropriate sound effects.

I also show you how to drag the car on the screen to position the ride from wherever you'd like. And to add just a little more pizzazz, I show you how to make the Test Drive button blink.

This chapter provides you with a very good base for understanding animation, sound, and how to manage touches on the screen.

Understanding iOS Animation

Fortunately, most of what you need to do as far as iOS animation is concerned is already built into the framework. Some view properties can be animated (the center point, for example), which means that you just need to tell the view where to start and where to end, and a few other optional parameters, and you're done. The view itself (in the UIView base class) has the functionality to animate the move. To give you some context in which to understand how animation on the iPhone and iPad works, however, I need to explain what goes on under the hood when a framework takes care of the animation chores for you. More specifically, I need to delve a bit deeper into views, their properties, and the coordinate systems on the iPad.

View geometry and coordinate systems

The default coordinate system in UIKit places its origin in the top-left corner and has axes that extend down and to the right from the origin point. Coordinate values are represented using floating-point numbers, and you don't have to worry about the screen resolution; the frameworks take care of that automatically. Figure 10-1 shows this coordinate system relative to the iPad screen. In addition to the screen coordinate system, views define their own local coordinate systems that allow you to specify coordinates relative to the view instead of relative to the screen.

(0,0)

Status Bar height = 20 points

Frame height = 768 points

Figure 10-1:
The coordinate system on an iPad screen (with a split view).

Frame width = 320 points   Frame width = 704 points

Because every view and window defines its own local coordinate system, whenever you're drawing or dealing with coordinates, you'll need to pay attention to which coordinate system you're using. I know that sounds ominous, but it's really not that big a deal after you get into the rhythm of working with the coordinate systems.

Points versus pixels

Okay, so where does the high-resolution display come in?

In iOS, all coordinate values and distances are specified using floating-point values in units referred to as *points*. The measurable size of a point varies from device to device and is largely irrelevant. The main thing to understand about points is that they provide a fixed frame of reference for drawing.

For example, the screen dimensions (width x height) for the iPhone 4s is 480 x 320 *points* and for the iPad are 1024 x 768 *points*.

So although an iPhone 4s with Retina display has a 960-by-640-*pixel* resolution (a pixel density of 326 pixels per inch [ppi]) and a non-Retina display has a 480-by-320-*pixel* resolution (163 ppi), as long as you design your interface to fit the screen sizes *in points,* your views will display correctly on the corresponding type of device. The same principles apply with non-Retina and Retina display on the iPad.

The takeaway here is, "Don't worry about the resolution; concentrate on points and you'll be fine."

A view's size and position

A view object's location in a coordinate system is determined using either its `frame` or its `center` property:

- ✔ The `frame` property contains the frame rectangle, which specifies the size and location of the view in *its super view's coordinate system.* (If you're still hazy about the whole super view/sub view thing, check out Chapter 4.)
- ✔ The `center` property contains the known center point of the view *in its super view's coordinate system.*

In your wanderings, you may someday encounter the `bounds` property. It's tied up with the bounds rectangle, which specifies the size of the view (and its content origin) in the *view's own local coordinate system.* I mention it here for completeness, but you won't be using it in this book.

Figure 10-1 shows the `frame` of the iPad's Main view (not the Image view I have you add in Chapter 5) with an origin of `x = 0` and `y = 20`. Its size is shown as `width = 320` and `height = 460`. The reason that its origin is at `y = 20` is that its frame is in its window coordinates (its super view), and it has to share the window with the status bar which is, as you might deduce, 20 pixels high.

Working with data structures

In addition to knowing what goes where, you'll need to understand how data structures impact how you work with views.

The frame is a CGRect — a struct (a C language type that aggregates conceptually related variables into a single type) with an origin and a size that are comprised of CGPoints. CG here stands for Core Graphics, one of the frameworks included by the Xcode when you selected the Single-View Application template. (See Chapter 4 to remind yourself about frameworks.) The following code shows the CGRect struct:

```
struct CGRect {
  CGPoint origin;
  CGSize size;
};
```

An origin is a CGPoint with an x and y value, and a CGSize is a CGPoint with a width and height value. The following code shows the CGPoint struct:

```
struct CGPoint {
  CGFloat x;
  CGFloat y;
};

struct CGSize {
  CGFloat width;
  CGFloat height;
};
```

Similarly, the center property is a CGPoint. And that's all you need to know about the data structures you'll be using.

Animating a View

Whenever you assign a new value to certain view properties (such as the frame and center properties, as explained in the previous section), the view is immediately redrawn and the change is immediately visible on the screen.

In addition, changes to several view properties (such as those just mentioned) can be animated. This means that changing the property creates an animation that conveys the change to the user over a short period of time — and it's all handled for you by the UIView class. What's more, it takes only one method call to specify the animations to be performed and the options for the animation.

You can animate the following properties of the UIView class (the first three are explained previously):

✔ frame: This property contains the frame rectangle, which specifies the size and location of the view in *its super view's coordinate system.*

✔ bounds: This property contains the bounds rectangle, which specifies the size of the view (and its content origin) in the *view's own local coordinate system.*

✔ center: This property contains the known center point of the view *in its super view's coordinate system.*

✔ transform: I get to this one a bit later in the chapter.

✔ alpha: This property controls the degree of transparency. If you animate it, you can get views to fade in and fade out.

✔ backgroundColor: This property allows you to transition from one color to another.

✔ contentStretch: This property controls how a view's content is stretched to fill its bounds when the view is resized and is often used to animate the resizing of buttons and controls.

Finally, More Code

In this section, you add the code to animate your '59 pink Cadillac Eldorado Biarritz convertible and have it travel up the screen, turn around, travel back down the screen, and then turn around again so that it's back to its original position.

Implementing the testDrive Method

In Chapter 9, you learned how to create an action for the Test Drive button using Interface Builder, which generated a method stub for you. Now it's time to fill that stub with code.

Add the bolded code in Listing 10-1 to the testDrive: method in TestDriveController.m. I'm also having you add the stubs for code you'll be adding later so that you can run your program before you're completely finished with the back and forth of the animation.

Listing 10-1: Updating testDrive: to Move the Car Up the Screen

```
- (IBAction)testDrive:(id)sender {

  CGPoint center = CGPointMake(self.car.center.x,
      self.view.frame.origin.y + self.car.frame.size.
          height/2);
  [UIView animateWithDuration:3 animations:^ {
      self.car.center = center;
    }
    completion:^(BOOL finished){
      [self rotate];
    }];
}

- (void)rotate {
}

- (void)returnCar {
}

- (void)continueRotation {
}
```

Now, run your program and click or touch the Test Drive button. You'll see your car move up the screen. You're on your way!

Looking more closely at Listing 10-1, you see that you start by creating the coordinate (`CGPoint`) of where you would like the car to end up.

A car is just another view. The following code shows how to move the car on-screen by simply moving the center of the view that holds the image of the car.

```
CGPoint center = CGPointMake(self.car.center.x,
    self.view.frame.origin.y + self.car.frame.size.
        height/2);
```

You use the `center` and `frame` properties primarily for manipulating the view. If you're changing only the position of the view (and not its size), the `center` property is the preferred way to do so.

`CGPointMake` is a function that creates a point for you when you specify the `y` and `x` coordinates as parameters. (You'll be setting the car's new `center` point.)

You can leave the `x` coordinate as is. Doing so makes the car drive right up the center of the screen.

```
self.car.center.x
```

Here's the y coordinate:

```
self.view.frame.origin.y + self.car.frame.size.height/2)
```

`self.view.frame.origin.y` is the top of the view, but if you have the center there, half the car is off the screen. To keep it all on the screen, you add back half the car's height by including `car.frame.size.height/2`.

Notice I'm *adding* to the y coordinate because y increases as you move down the screen from the origin.

So, how do you get the sucker to actually move? Listing 10-1 uses the following code:

```
[UIView animateWithDuration:3 animations:^ {
    self.car.center = center;
    }
    completion:^(BOOL finished){
      [self rotate];
    }];
```

`animateWithDuration:animations:completion:` is a `UIView` class method that allows you to set an animation duration and specify what you want animated as well as a completion handler that's called when the animation is complete.

First you specify that you want the animation to take three seconds:

```
animateWithDuration:3
```

and then you pass in an animation *block* with what you want animated:

```
animations:^ {
  self.car.center = center;
}
```

This sets the new center you just computed, taking three seconds to move it from start to finish.

If the preceding syntax seems mysterious (what's the ^ doing there and what's up with the code as part of the message), don't worry: I explain blocks in the next section.

So while that's all there is to get the car to move across the screen, you're not done. You want it to rotate and then drive back across the screen and then rotate again. That's where the completion handler comes in.

Although you can use a completion handler to simply let you know that an animation is finished, you can also use a completion handler to link multiple animations. (In fact, it's the primary way to take care of that task.)

The completion handler that you specify

```
completion:^(BOOL finished){
  [self rotate];
}
```

causes the `rotate` message to be sent when the animation is complete. You do the actual rotation in the `rotate` method.

Of course, right now, the `rotate` method does nothing. I have you add it so that the app will compile and run. I have you add `returnCar` and `continueRotation` to eliminate the Incomplete Implementation `TestDriveController.m` compiler warning.

`animateWithDuration:animations:completion:` is only one of a number of block-based methods that offer different levels of configuration for the animation block. Other methods include

```
animateWithDuration:animations:
```

and

```
animateWithDuration:delay:options:animations:completion
```

`animateWithDuration:animations:` has no completion block, as you can see.

Both `animateWithDuration:animations:completion:` and `animateWithDuration:animations:` run only once, using an *ease-in, ease-out animation curve* — the default for most animations, it begins slowly, accelerates through the middle of the animation, and then slows again before completing. If you want to change the default animation parameters, you must use the `animateWithDuration:delay:options:animations:completion:` method, which lets you customize the following:

- The delay to use before starting the animation
- The type of timing curve to use during the animation
- The number of times the animation should repeat
- Whether the animation should reverse itself automatically when it reaches the end

✔ Whether touch events are delivered to views while the animations are in progress

✔ Whether the animation should interrupt any in-progress animations or wait until those are complete before starting

As you probably noticed (and I even admitted to), one of the things I tiptoed around was an explanation of the animation syntax:

```
[UIView animateWithDuration:3 animations:^ {
  self.car.center = center;
}
```

Animations use *blocks,* which is a primary design pattern in iOS and is becoming increasingly more important. So before I get to the `rotate` completion handler, I want to explain blocks.

Understanding Block Objects

Objective-C blocks are like traditional C functions in that blocks are small, self-contained units of code. They can be passed in as arguments of methods and functions and then used when they're needed to do some work. (Like many programming topics, understanding block objects is easier when you use them, as you do in the previous section.)

With iOS 4 and newer versions, a number of methods and functions of the system frameworks are starting to take blocks as parameters, including the following:

✔ Completion handlers

✔ Notification handlers

✔ Error handlers

✔ Enumeration

✔ View animation and transitions

✔ Sorting

In the code listings in this chapter, you get to use a block-based method to animate the car, but block objects also have a number of other uses, especially in Grand Central Dispatch and the `NSOperationQueue` class, the two recommended technologies for concurrent processing. But because concurrent processing is beyond the scope of this book (*way* beyond the scope, in fact), I leave you to explore that use on your own.

One of the values of using blocks is that you can access local variables (as well as instance variables), which you can't do in a function or a callback. You also don't have to pass data around — a block can modify variables to pass data back. In addition, if you need to change something, there's no API to change, with its concomitant ripple effect.

In the animation explained in the previous section, you passed a block as the argument to a method. You created the block *inline* (it's there in the message you are sending to the UIView to do the animation) because there wasn't that much code, and that's often the way it's done. But sometimes it's easier to follow what's happening by declaring a block variable and passing that as the argument to the method. The declaration syntax, however, is similar to the standard syntax for function pointers, except that you use a caret (^) instead of an asterisk pointer (*).

If you look at animateWithDuration:animations:completion: in the UIView class reference, you'll see

```
+ (void)animateWithDuration:(NSTimeInterval)duration
     animations:(void (^)(void))animations
     completion:(void (^)(BOOL finished))completion;
```

I know this looks a bit advanced for a *For Dummies* book, but I cover it here because Apple is now treating blocks as a primary design pattern, up there with inheritance and delegation — so don't be surprised to find blocks being used more and more.

Nevertheless, because it's a tad advanced, I'll go through the code slowly, and by the end — I promise — you'll be comfortable with blocks, despite the really weird syntax.

To start, this is the syntax that defines animations as a block that has no parameters and no return value:

```
void (^)(void))animations
```

completion is defined as a block that has no return value and takes a single Boolean argument parameter:

```
(void (^)(BOOL finished))completion
```

When you create a block inline, you just use the caret (^) operator to indicate the beginning of a block and then follow with the code enclosed within the normal braces. That's what was going on back in Listing 10-1, with

```
animations:^ {
  self.car.center = center;
}
```

and

```
completion:^(BOOL finished){
  [self rotate];
}
```

Although in this example you use blocks inline, you could also declare them like any other local variable, as you can see in Listing 10-2.

Listing 10-2: Using Declared Blocks

```
- (IBAction)testDrive:(id)sender {

  CGPoint center = CGPointMake(car.center.x,
    self.view.frame.origin.y + car.frame.size.height/2);

  void (^animation)()= ^() {

    self.car.center = center;
  };

  void (^completion)(BOOL) = ^(BOOL finished){
    [self rotate];
  };

    [UIView animateWithDuration:3 animations:animation
                              completion:completion];
}
```

When you declare a block, you use the caret (^) operator to indicate the beginning of a block with the code enclosed within the normal braces, and a semicolon to indicate the end of a block expression.

The declaration in Listing 10-2 is pretty much the same as you see in the following `animateWithDuration:animations:completion:` method declaration, except that the identifiers have been moved around a little. I have bolded both to make that a little easier to see:

```
+ (void)animateWithDuration:(NSTimeInterval)duration
      animations:(void (^)(void))animations
      completion:(void (^)(BOOL finished))completion;
```

Here, you're declaring two block variables by using the ^ operator: one with the name of `animations` that has no return value, and one with the name of `completion` that has no return value and takes BOOL as its single argument:

```
void (^animation)()
void (^completion)(BOOL)
```

This is like any other variable declaration (`int i = 1`, for example), in which you follow the equal sign with its definition.

You use the ^ operator again to indicate the beginning of the *block literal* — the definition assigned to the block variable. The block literal includes argument names (finished) as well as the body (code) of the block and is terminated with a semicolon:

```
void (^animation)() = ^() {
  self.car.center = center;
};

void (^completion)(BOOL) = ^(BOOL finished){
    [self rotate];
};
```

Although the code you add in Listing 10-2 creates the blocks inline, you should actually replace the testDrive method you added with the code in Listing 10-2 because that's the way I have you use blocks for the rest of this book. Inline blocks work fine for small blocks; for large blocks, however, I find that declaring the block makes the code easier to follow.

You'll be using blocks a few more times in this book, so at some point (despite the weird syntax), you'll become comfortable with them. (Frankly it took me a while to get used to them myself.) After you do get the hang of them, though, you'll find all sorts of opportunities to use them to simplify your code, as you discover in Chapter 19.

Rotating the Object

In this section, I show you how to rotate a view (in this case, turn the car around). To do so, you update the rotate code stub you started out with back in Listing 10-2 with the bolded code in Listing 10-3.

Listing 10-3:   Updating rotate

```
- (void)rotate {

  CGAffineTransform transform =
        CGAffineTransformMakeRotation(M_PI);

  void (^animation)() =  ^() {
    self.car.transform = transform;
  };

  void (^completion)(BOOL) = ^(BOOL finished){
    [self returnCar];
  };

  [UIView animateWithDuration:3 animations:animation
        completion:completion];
}
```

This method uses the block declarations I explain in the previous section.

The `CGAffineTransform` data structure represents a matrix used for *affine transformations* — a blueprint for how points in one coordinate system map to points in another coordinate system. Although `CGAffineTransform` has a number of uses (such as scaling and translating a coordinate system), the only one covered here is the rotation method you use in Listing 10-3:

```
CGAffineTransformMakeRotation(M_PI)
```

To rotate a view, you specify the angle (in radians) to rotate the coordinate system axes. Whereas degrees are numbers between 0 and 360, radians, though similar, range from 0 to 2Π. So when you create a rotation that turns an object around one half-circle, that rotation in radians is pi. (`M_PI` is a system constant that represents pi.)

Just to make your life interesting, you should note that in iOS, positive is counterclockwise, but on Mac OS X, positive is clockwise.

The end result of Listing 10-3 is that the car will rotate 180 degrees in three seconds, and when it's done, you send the `returnCar` message in the completion handler.

To return the car to its original position, add the bolded code in Listing 10-4 to the `returnCar` method stub in `TestDriveController.m`.

Listing 10-4:   Updating returnCar

```
- (void)returnCar {

  CGPoint center = CGPointMake(car.center.x, self.view.
          frame.origin.y + self.view.frame.size.height -
          7
          - self.car.frame.size.height/2);


  void (^animation)() =  ^() {
    self.car.center = center;
  };

  void (^completion)(BOOL) = ^(BOOL finished){
    [self continueRotation];
  };

  [UIView animateWithDuration:3 animations:animation
                                completion:completion];

}
```

This approach is pretty much the same as that of the `testDrive` method except that the new `center` is back where the car started. You put the `center` back by computing the bottom of the view

```
self.view.frame.size.height - 7
    - self.car.frame.size.height/2);
```

and then subtracting 7 — because the car isn't quite at the bottom of the view — and then subtracting half the car's height.

But you're not done yet. You need to rotate the car back to its original position (unless you want to drive in reverse from California to New York). Add the bolded code in Listing 10-5 to the `continueRotation` method stub in `TestDriveController.m`.

Listing 10-5:   Updating continueRotation

```
- (void)continueRotation {

  CGAffineTransform transform =
                      CGAffineTransformMakeRotation(0);

  void (^animation)() = ^() {
    self.car.transform = transform;
  };

  [UIView animateWithDuration:3 animations:animation
                                    completion:NULL];
}
```

You need to understand that the transform (in this case, a view rotation) is still there; that is, you created a transform to rotate the car 180 degrees. If you want to get the car back to the original position, you need to return the transform to 0.

You could extend this action by having the car drive around the perimeter of the screen — but I'll leave that up to you.

Working with Audio

Cars make noise, and a '59 Cadillac certainly doesn't disappoint in that respect. So in this section, I show you how to add some sound to the RoadTrip app so that everyone can hear your car coming down the road.

More specifically, I discuss using two different ways iOS has for implementing audio. One is an instance of the `AVAudioPlayer` class — called, appropriately enough, an *audio player* — which provides playback of audio data from a file or memory. You use this class unless you're playing audio captured from a network stream or in need of very low I/O latency (lag time). The AVAudioPlayer class offers quite a lot of functionality, including playing sounds of any duration, looping sounds, playing multiple sounds simultaneously, and having one sound per audio player with precise synchronization among all the players in use. It also controls relative playback level, stereo positioning, and playback rate for each sound you're playing.

The AVAudioPlayer class lets you play sound in any audio format available in iOS. You implement a delegate to handle interruptions (such as an incoming SMS message) and to update the user interface when a sound has finished playing. The delegate methods to use are described in the AVAudioPlayerDelegate Protocol Reference (which you can access in the Organizer window as I explain in Chapter 7).

The second way to play sound is by using System Sound Services, which provides a way to play short sounds and make the device vibrate. You can use System Sound Services to play short (30 seconds or shorter) sounds. The interface doesn't provide level, positioning, looping, or timing control and doesn't support simultaneous playback: You can play only one sound at a time. You can use System Sound Services to provide audible alerts; on some iOS devices, alerts can even include vibration.

To add sound to your app, you start by adding the frameworks. If you need a refresher on how to do that in more detail than I give here, see the section in Chapter 8 about network availability. Or, just follow these steps:

1. **In the Project navigator, select the project icon at the top of the Project Navigator area (RoadTrip) to display the Project editor.**

2. **In the Targets section, select RoadTrip.**

3. **On the Summary tab, scroll down to the Linked Frameworks and Libraries section.**

4. **Expand the Linked Frameworks and Libraries section — if it isn't already expanded — by clicking the disclosure triangle.**

5. **Click the + (plus sign) button underneath the list of current Project frameworks.**

   A list of frameworks appears.

6. **Scroll down and select both AVFoundation.framework and AudioToolbox.framework from the displayed list of frameworks.**

7. **Click the Add button.**

   You'll see the frameworks added to the Linked Frameworks and Libraries section.

8. **Close the Linked Frameworks and Libraries section.**

9. **In the Project navigator, drag the** AVFoundation.framework **and** AudioToolbox.framework **files to the Frameworks group.**

   Be sure to do your dragging in the Project navigator, not from the Linked Frameworks and Libraries section!

The sound files you need for RoadTrip (the aptly named `BurnRubber.aif` and `CarRunning.aif`) are already in the Resources folder that you added to your project. (See Chapter 3 if you haven't already done this.)

You can use Audacity, a free, open source software for recording and editing sounds, to create your own sound files. It's available for Mac OS X, Microsoft Windows, GNU/Linux, and other operating systems.

With the added frameworks in place, you now need to import the necessary audio player and system sound services headers and then add the instance variables you'll be using. To accomplish all this, add the bolded code in Listing 10-6 to `TestDriveController.m`.

Listing 10-6:   Updating the TestDriveController Private Interface

```
#import "TestDriveController.h"
#import <AVFoundation/AVFoundation.h>
#import <AudioToolbox/AudioToolbox.h>

@interface TestDriveController () {
   AVAudioPlayer *backgroundAudioPlayer;
   SystemSoundID burnRubberSoundID;
}
@end

@implementation TestDriveController
```

As you can see, I'm having you take advantage of being able to put instance variables in the implementation file to keep them hidden (as I explain in Chapter 6). In fact, the file template already had added

```
@interface TestDriveController ()

@end
```

for you.

Next, you need to set up the audio player and system sound services. Uncomment out `viewDidLoad` and add the bolded code in Listing 10-7 to `viewDidLoad` in `TestDriveController.m`.

Listing 10-7:   Updating viewDidLoad

```
- (void)viewDidLoad
{
  [super viewDidLoad];

  NSURL* backgroundURL = [NSURL fileURLWithPath:
    [[NSBundle mainBundle]pathForResource:
                    @"CarRunning" ofType:@"aif"]];
  backgroundAudioPlayer = [[AVAudioPlayer alloc] initWith
          ContentsOfURL:backgroundURL error:nil];
  backgroundAudioPlayer.numberOfLoops = -1;
  [backgroundAudioPlayer prepareToPlay];

  NSURL* burnRubberURL = [NSURL fileURLWithPath:
    [[NSBundle mainBundle] pathForResource:
                    @"BurnRubber" ofType:@"aif"]];
  AudioServicesCreateSystemSoundID(
    (__bridge CFURLRef)burnRubberURL, &burnRubberSoundID);
}
```

In Listing 10-7, the first thing you do is load the sound file from the resources in your bundle:

```
NSURL* backgroundURL = [NSURL fileURLWithPath:
  [[NSBundle mainBundle]pathForResource:
                  @"CarRunning" ofType:@"aif"]];
```

"What bundle?" you say? Well, when you build your iOS application, Xcode packages it as a bundle — one containing the following:

- ✔ The application's executable code

- ✔ Any resources that the app has to use (for instance, the application icon, other images, and localized content — in this case, the plist, .html files, and .png files)

- ✔ The RoadTrip-Info.plist file, also known as the _information property list,_ which defines key values for the application, such as bundle ID, version number, and display name

Pretty easy, huh?

Coming back to Listing 10-7, fileURLWithPath is an NSURL class method that initializes and returns an NSURL object as a file URL with a specified path. The NSURL class includes the utilities necessary for downloading files or other resources from web and FTP servers and from the file system.

The sound file you'll be using is a resource, and pathForResource: is an NSBundle method that creates the path needed by the fileURLWithPath: method to construct the NSURL. Just give pathForResource: the name and the file type, and it returns the path that gets packed in to the NSURL and loaded.

Be sure that you provide the correct file type; otherwise, this technique won't work.

Next, you create an instance of the audio player

```
backgroundAudioPlayer = [[AVAudioPlayer alloc] initWithC
        ontentsOfURL:backgroundURL error:nil];
```

and initialize it with the audio file location (NSURL). You'll ignore any errors.

Set the number of loops to -1 (which will cause the audio file to continue to play until you stop it) and tell the player to get ready to play:

```
backgroundAudioPlayer.numberOfLoops = -1;
[backgroundAudioPlayer prepareToPlay];
```

prepareToPlay prepares the audio player for playback by preloading its buffers; it also acquires the audio hardware needed for playback. This preloading minimizes the lag between calling the play method and the start of sound output. Without this preloading, although the player would still play when you send the play message (later) in viewDidLoad, you'll likely notice a lag as it sets up its buffers.

Similarly, you set up the NSURL for the BurnRubber sound:

```
NSURL* burnRubberURL = [NSURL fileURLWithPath:
  [[NSBundle mainBundle] pathForResource:
                    @"BurnRubber" ofType:@"aif"]];
```

You then call a core foundation method to create a system sound object that you later use to play the sound:

```
AudioServicesCreateSystemSoundID((__bridge
        CFURLRef)burnRubberURL, &burnRubberSoundID);
```

CFURLRef (as I explain in Chapter 6 in the section about automatic reference counting [ARC]) is a CoreFoundation object, and ARC doesn't automatically manage the lifetimes of CoreFoundation types. And although you can use certain CoreFoundation memory management rules and functions, you don't need to do that here. That's because all you're doing is casting an Objective-C object to a CoreFoundation type object, and you won't need to use any CoreFoundation memory management in your code. You have to let the compiler know about any memory management implications, however, so you need to use the __bridge cast.

In testDrive, you'll play both the BurnRubber and CarRunning sounds. To do so, add the bolded code in Listing 10-8 to testDrive: in TestDriveController.m.

Listing 10-8:   Updating testDrive

```
- (IBAction)testDrive:(id)sender {


  AudioServicesPlaySystemSound(burnRubberSoundID);
  [self performSelector:@selector(playCarSound)
                            withObject:self afterDelay:.2];

  CGPoint center = CGPointMake(self.car.center.x,
                              self.view.frame.origin.y +
          self.car.frame.size.height/2 );

  void (^animation)() = ^() {

    self.car.center = center;
  };

  void (^completion)(BOOL) = ^(BOOL finished){
    [self rotate];
  };

  [UIView animateWithDuration:3 animations:animation
          completion:completion];
}
```

You also need to add the code in Listing 10-9 to play the CarRunning sound.

Listing 10-9:   Adding playCarSound

```
- (void)playCarSound {

  [backgroundAudioPlayer play];
}
```

I'm having you play the BurnRubber sound first, followed by the CarRunning sound. If you don't wait until the BurnRubber sound is complete before you play the CarRunning sound, the BurnRubber sound is drowned out by the CarRunning sound.

To play the BurnRubber sound, you use a function call to System Sound Services:

```
AudioServicesPlaySystemSound(burnRubberSoundID);
```

After this sound is done, you start the CarRunning sound by using a very useful method that will enable you to send the message to start the audio player after a delay. That method is performSelector:withObject:afterDelay:, and it looks like this:

```
[self performSelector:@selector(playCarSound)
                        withObject:self afterDelay:.2];
```

`performSelector:withObject:afterDelay:` sends a message that you specify to an object after a delay. The method you want invoked should have no return value, and should have zero or one argument.

In Listing 10-9, this method meets these rules:

```
- (void)playCarSound {

  [backgroundAudioPlayer play];
}
```

`@selector(playCarSound)` is a compiler directive that returns a selector for a method name. A *selector* is the name used to select a method to execute for an object; it becomes a unique identifier when the source code is compiled.

Selectors really don't do anything. What makes the selector method name different from a plain string is that the compiler makes sure that selectors are unique. Selectors are useful because at runtime they act like a dynamic function pointer that, for a given name, automatically points to the implementation of a method appropriate for whichever class they're used with.

`withObject:` is the argument to pass to the method when it's invoked. In this case, you're passing `nil` because the method doesn't take an argument.

`afterDelay:` is the minimum time before which the message is sent. Specifying a delay of 0 doesn't necessarily cause the selector to be performed immediately. When you send the `performSelector:withObject:` message, you specify 0.2 seconds because that's the duration of the `BurnRubber` sound.

Sometimes you may need to cancel a selector. `cancelPerformSelectors WithTarget:` cancels all outstanding selectors scheduled to be performed with a given target.

Several other variations exist on the `performSelector:withObject: afterDelay:` method. Those variations are part of the `NSObject` class, which is the root class of most Objective-C class hierarchies. It provides the basic interface to the runtime system as well as the capability to behave as Objective-C objects.

Finally, to play the sound in the `playCarSound` method, you send the audio player the `play` message:

```
[backgroundAudioPlayer play];
```

The `play` message plays a sound asynchronously. If you haven't already sent the `prepareToPlay` message, `play` will send that for you as well (although you should expect a lag before the sound is played).

Next, you need to stop playing the sound in the `continueRotation` animation's completion block (or it gets really annoying). To stop playing the sound, add the bolded code in Listing 10-10 to `continueRotation` in `TestDriveController.m`. (`completion` replaces the previous value that was `NULL`.)

Listing 10-10:   Updating continueRotation to Stop the Sound

```
- (void)continueRotation {

  CGAffineTransform transform =
                    CGAffineTransformMakeRotation(-0);

  void (^animation)() = ^() {
    self.car.transform = transform;
  };

  void (^completion)(BOOL) = ^(BOOL finished){
    [backgroundAudioPlayer stop];
    [backgroundAudioPlayer prepareToPlay];
  };

  [UIView animateWithDuration:3 animations:animation
                    completion:completion];
}
```

In the code in Listing 10-10, you also set up the audio player to play again.

And there you have it. Run your project and you'll notice some very realistic sound effects when you touch the Test Drive button.

Tracking Touches

While Skippy (the inspiration for the RoadTrip app) was pretending to drive across country, he said that it would be nice to be able to drag the car and place it anywhere on the screen. And because his wish is my command, in this section, I explain how to code for dragging an object, as well as how touches work on the iPad.

The touch of a finger (or lifting it from the screen) adds a touch event to the application's event queue, where it's *encapsulated* (contained) in a `UIEvent` object. A `UITouch` object exists for each finger touching the screen, which enables you to track individual touches.

The `touchesBegan:withEvent:` message is sent when one or more fingers touch down in a view. This message is a method of the `TestDriveController`'s superclass, `UIResponder`, from which the view controller is derived. (I explain this in Chapter 6, in the section about `UIApplicationMain`.)

As the user manipulates the screen with his or her fingers, the system reports the changes for each finger in the corresponding `UITouch` object, thereby sending the `touchesMoved:withEvent:` message. The `touchesEnded:withEvent:` message is sent when one or more fingers lift from the associated view. The `touchesCancelled:withEvent:` message, on the other hand, is sent when a system event (such as a low-memory warning) cancels a touch event.

In this app, you need be concerned only with the first two methods just described.

To begin the process of responding to a touch event, add a new instance variable (bolded in Listing 10-11) to the `TestDriveController.m` implementation file.

Listing 10-11: Updating the TestDriveController Implementation

```
@interface TestDriveController () {

  AVAudioPlayer *backgroundAudioPlayer;
  SystemSoundID burnRubberSoundID;
  BOOL touchInCar;
}
@end
```

Next, add the `touchesBegan:` method in Listing 10-12 to `TestDrive Controller.m` to start tracking touches. (You're actually overriding this method because you have inherited it from the `UIResponder` base class.)

Listing 10-12: Overriding touchesBegan:

```
- (void)touchesBegan:(NSSet *)touches withEvent:
                                    (UIEvent *)event
{
  UITouch *touch = [touches anyObject];
  if (CGRectContainsPoint(self.car.frame,
                    [touch locationInView:self.view]))
    touchInCar = YES;
  else  {
    touchInCar = NO;
    [super touchesBegan:touches withEvent:event];
  }
}
```

As mentioned previously, the `touchesBegan:withEvent:` message is sent when one or more fingers touch down in a view. The touches themselves are passed to the method in an `NSSet` object — an unordered collection of distinct elements.

To access an object in `NSSet`, use the `anyObject` method — it returns one of the objects in the set. For our purposes here, you're assuming just one object — but you might want to explore this issue further on your own so that you can understand how to handle additional possibilities.

The following code shows how to set up the `anyObject` method:

```
UITouch *touch = [touches anyObject];
```

Next, have the code determine whether the user's touch event is in the Car (`UIImage`) view:

```
if (CGRectContainsPoint(self.car.frame,
                        [touch locationInView:self.view]))
```

`CGRectContainsPoint` is a function that returns `YES` when a rectangle (view coordinates) contains a point. You specify the car's `frame` as the rectangle:

```
self.car.frame
```

and you specify the point by sending the `locationInView:` message to the touch:

```
locationInView:self.view
```

`locationInView:` returns the current location of the receiver in the coordinate system of the given view. In this case, you're using the Main view, but you might want to change the view if you're trying to determine the location within another view, for example. Maybe the user is touching an itty-bitty gas pedal. (Just to be clear, in our RoadTrip app, the car does *not* have an itty-bitty gas pedal.)

If it's determined that the touch is in the car, you assign `YES` to the `touchInCar` instance variable; if it's not, you assign `NO` and forward the message up the responder chain. You use `touchInCar` later to determine whether the user is dragging the car around or just running his or finger over the screen.

The default implementation of `touchesBegan:` does nothing. However, subclasses derived directly from `UIResponder`, particularly `UIView`, forward the message up the responder chain. To forward the message to the next responder, send the message to `super` (the superclass implementation).

If you override `touchesBegan:withEvent:` without calling `super` (a common use pattern), you must also override the other methods for handling touch events, if only as stub (empty) implementations.

Multiple touches are disabled by default. To allow your app to receive multiple touch events, you must set the `multipleTouchEnabled` property of the corresponding view instance to `YES`.

As users merrily move the car around the screen (perhaps saying *zoom zoom* to themselves), your app is constantly being sent the `touchesMoved:` message. Add the code in Listing 10-13 to `TestDriveController.m` to override that method, which will enable you to move the car to where the user's finger is.

Listing 10-13:   Overriding touchesMoved:withEvent:

```
- (void)touchesMoved:(NSSet *)touches withEvent:
                                    (UIEvent *)event {

  if (touchInCar) {
    UITouch* touch = [touches anyObject];
    self.car.center = [touch locationInView:self.view];
  }
  else
    [super touchesMoved:touches withEvent:event];
}
```

If the first touch was in the `Car` view (`touchInCar` is `YES`), you assign car's `center` property to the touch coordinate. As I explain in the "Animating a View" section, earlier in this chapter, when you assign a new value to the `center` property, the view's location is immediately changed. Otherwise, you ignore the touch and forward the message up the responder chain.

It's interesting to observe that when you position the car next to a button, it will travel under that button when you touch the Test Drive button. This feature illustrates the subview structure that I explain in Chapter 4 in the section about the view hierarchy. Because I had you add the buttons *last* (they're subviews of the Main view), they're displayed *on top* of the subviews (`car`) that you added earlier.

Animating a Series of Images "In Place"

Although I explain animation using the `UIView` methods earlier in this chapter, this section shows you a way to animate a series of images "in place" — you are not moving the image around as you did earlier with the car; instead you are changing the image where it is to make it appear as if it were animated.

To make the Test Drive button blink, for example, add the bolded code in Listing 10-14 to `TestDriveController.m`. As you can see in the listing, only a single line of code is needed to animate the button.

Listing 10-14:   Creating a Blinking Button

```
- (void)viewDidLoad
{
  [super viewDidLoad];

  NSURL* backgroundURL = [NSURL fileURLWithPath:[[NSBundle
          mainBundle]pathForResource:@"CarRunning"
          ofType:@"aif"]];
  backgroundAudioPlayer = [[AVAudioPlayer alloc] initWithC
          ontentsOfURL:backgroundURL error:nil];
  backgroundAudioPlayer.numberOfLoops = -1;
  [backgroundAudioPlayer prepareToPlay];

  NSURL* burnRubberURL = [NSURL fileURLWithPath:[[NSBundle
          mainBundle] pathForResource:@"BurnRubber"
          ofType:@"aif"]];
  AudioServicesCreateSystemSoundID((__bridge CFURLRef)
          burnRubberURL, &burnRubberSoundID);
  [self.testDriveButton setBackgroundImage:[UIImage
          animatedImageNamed:@"Button" duration:1.0 ]
          forState:UIControlStateNormal];
}
```

In Chapter 5, I show you how to add a custom button with a Button background image. You could have also programmatically added the background image by sending the button the `setBackgroundImage:forState:` message. (Chapter 5 explains the control state as well.) Normally, you might think of making the background image a single image. However, `animatedImageNamed:duration:` and some similar methods use instead a series of files, each displayed for a duration you specify. This type of method enables you to animate (this time, in place) not only a button but also any image by simply supplying a series of images:

```
[testDriveButton setBackgroundImage:
   [UIImage animatedImageNamed:@"Button" duration:1.0]
                         forState:UIControlStateNormal];
```

In the `animatedImageNamed:` method, you supply a *base* name of an image to animate. The method appends a 0 to the base name and loads that image (in this case, Button0). After the time that you specify in `duration` has elapsed, the `animatedImageNamed:` method appends the next number (in this case, 1) to the base image name and attempts to load it and the remainder of images (up to 1,024 images) until it runs out of images, and then it starts over.

In the Project navigator, open the disclosure triangle for the RoadTrip Resources group that you created in Chapter 3. If you look in the RoadTrip Resources group, you see two images, Button0 and Button1 — with Button being the base name you specified. This is an "in place" animation, so all images included in the animated image should share the same size and scale.

If you select each image in the Project navigator, you can see that they're slightly different colors, and each will display for 1.0 second (duration:1.0). This makes the button blink and certainly adds some life to the Main view.

iPhone versus iPad

The iOS 6 animation and sound libraries and frameworks are the same for the iPhone and iPad, so the code shown in this chapter works properly on both the iPhone and iPad apps. Very nice.

Part IV
The Model and Application Structure

The 5th Wave   By Rich Tennant

©RICHTENNANT

Accessories

iPadPad

"It's a docking system for the iPad that comes with 3 bedrooms, 2 baths, and a car port."

In this part . . .

Now you begin to get down to the real work. You find out about Split View controllers and popovers (when building the iPad version of the storyboard file) and also add navigation to the application. You also add the application model, which provides both the data and the logic you need to create an application that delivers real value to the user. Finally, you finish the iPad and iPhone storyboard files so that you can see your basic application flow.

Chapter 11

The Trip Model

*I*t's time to add some content to RoadTrip. As I explain in Chapter 4, the owner of RoadTrip's data is the model, so I start this chapter with a look at the data you'll need and how the model will manage it. Then I show you how to add a `Trip` class that will serve as the interface to the model. Finally, you see how to add the `Destination` class — which is one of the objects that will be used by the model but is hidden behind the `Trip` interface.

What's in the Model

In the Model-View-Controller (MVC) design pattern that is the basis for all iPad and iPhone apps, the model owns the application content logic and data. Therefore, to design your model, the best place to start is with the application design I present in Chapter 4 and consider what will be displayed in the views.

In this first version of RoadTrip, the model needs to provide, for each destination, the following:

✔ The destination name

✔ A background image for the destination

✔ The destination latitude and longitude, along with a title and subtitle to be displayed in the annotation on a map

✔ Events that the user might be interested in

✔ The latitude and longitude, along with a title and subtitle of sights or places of interest to be displayed in the annotation on a map

✔ Weather information

I've made the point (several times) that the model is about the data, so where does the data come from? The easy answer is . . . any place you'd like. Given the iOS model, however, you can take several approaches:

✔ **Option 1:** Download the data from a web service (or FTP site) and have the model control it in a file or have Core Data (an iOS object persistence mechanism outside the scope of this book) manage it.

✔ **Option 2:** Have a web service manage your data and get what you need as you need it.

✔ **Option 3:** Include the data as an application resource.

✔ **Option 4:** Access the data on the web as an HTML page.

Although I really like Option 2 (and explain that in *iOS Cloud Development For Dummies,* it is beyond the scope of this book, so the `Trip` model uses both Options 3 and 4.

Although the preceding answers most of the model's "Show me the data" responsibility, yet another question still has to be answered: How does the model know where the data is? The answer to that question lies in a very useful structure that's used extensively by not only iOS but also applications: property lists (more commonly known as *plists*). The RoadTrip plist that you are about to create will have both data used by the `Trip` model object (Option 3) as well as the URLs for the data you download as HTML pages (Option 4).

Adding the Model Data

For situations in which you need to store relatively small amounts of persistent data — say, less than a few hundred kilobytes — a property list offers a uniform and convenient means of organizing, storing, and accessing the data.

Using property lists

A property list (or *plist*) is perfect for storing small amounts of data that consist primarily of strings and numbers. What adds to its appeal is the capability to easily read it into your program, use the data, and (although you won't be doing it in the RoadTrip application) modify the data and then write the property list back out again (see the "Using plists to store data" sidebar, later in this chapter). That's because iOS provides a small set of objects that have that behavior built right in.

Applications and other system software in OS X and iOS use property lists extensively. For example, the Mac OS X Finder stores file and directory attributes in a property list, and iOS uses them for user defaults. You also get a Property List editor with Xcode, which makes property list files easy to create and maintain in your own programs.

Figure 11-1 shows a property list that I show you how to build — one that contains the data necessary for the RoadTrip app.

Figure 11-1: The RoadTrip plist.

After you figure out how to work with property lists, it's actually easy, but like most things, getting there is half the fun.

Property lists hold serializable objects. A *serializable object* can convert itself into a stream of bits so that it can be stored in a file; it can then reconstitute itself into the object it once was when it's read back in. (Yes, the phenomenon of "Beam me up, Scotty" does exist, at least on your computer.)

These objects, called *property list objects,* that you have to work with are as follows, and you find two types (which I explain in an upcoming paragraph):

Primitives:

- ✔ NSData and NSMutableData
- ✔ NSDate
- ✔ NSNumber
- ✔ NSString and NSMutableString

Containers:

- ✔ NSArray and NSMutableArray
- ✔ NSDictionary and NSMutableDictionary

As previously shown in Figure 11-1, the RoadTrip plist is actually an NSDictionary. It has one entry — DestinationData, which is an array of dictionaries — and the data for each one of the destinations is held in a dictionary in that array (Item 0 and Item 1). If you are a little hazy on arrays and dictionaries, check out *Objective-C For Dummies* (written by Neal and published by Wiley), or the Apple documentation.

Now for that explanation of two kinds of property list objects, as follows:

- ✔ **Primitives:** The term *primitives* isn't a reflection on how civilized these property list objects are; rather, it describes the simplest kind of object. They are what they are.
- ✔ **Containers:** *Containers* can hold primitives as well as other containers.

One important feature of property list object containers (such as NSArray and NSDictionary), besides their ability to hold other objects, is that they both have a writeToFile: method that writes the property list to a file, and a corresponding initWithContentsOfFile:, which initializes the object with the contents of a file. So if I create an array or dictionary and fill it chock-full of objects of the property list type, all I have to do to save that array or dictionary to a file is tell it to go save itself — or create an array or dictionary and then tell it to initialize itself from a file.

Primitives NSString and NSData and their mutable counterparts also can write and read themselves to and from a file.

NSData and NSMutableData are wrappers (a *wrapper* is an object whose basic purpose is to turn something into an object) in which you can dump any kind of data and then have that data act as an object.

The containers can contain other containers as well as the primitive types. Thus, you might have an array of dictionaries, and each dictionary might contain other arrays and dictionaries as well as the primitive types.

Adding a property list to your project

Given the versatility of property lists, you're sure to turn to them time and time again. Follow these steps to incorporate a plist into your Xcode project:

1. **In the Project navigator, select the RoadTrip Resources group, right-click the selection, and then choose New File from the menu that appears to get the New File dialog.**

   Or select the RoadTrip Resources group and choose File⇨New⇨New File from the main menu (or press ⌘+N).

2. **In the left column of the New File dialog, select Resource under the iOS heading, select the Property List template in the top-right pane, and then click Next.**

   A Save sheet will appear.

3. **Enter** Destinations **in the Save As field.**

4. **Click Create (and make sure that the Target field has the RoadTrip text box selected).**

5. **In the newly created Property List, right-click in the editor (the blank page) to show the context-sensitive menu; then choose Add Row, as shown in Figure 11-2.**

   You can also choose Editor⇨Add Item to add a row.

   A new row appears, as shown in Figure 11-3.

6. **Enter** DestinationData **in the Key field, replacing New Item (which should be highlighted).**

7. **Click in the up and down arrows in the Type field and then choose Array from the pop-up menu that appears, as shown in Figure 11-4.**

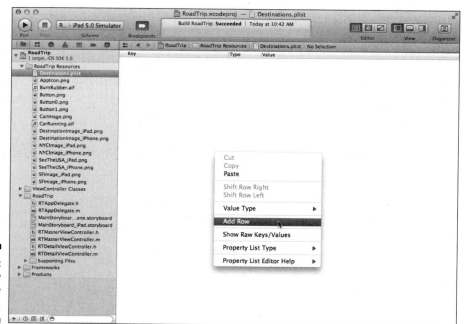

Figure 11-2:
Add a row
to the new
plist file.

Figure 11-3:
A new row.

Change type to Array

Change Key to DestinationData

Figure 11-4:
Change the
New Item to
Array.

8. **Click the disclosure triangle in front of the** DestinationData **key so it is pointing down and click the + (plus) button, as shown in Figure 11-5. A new entry appears.**

   DestinationData is an array of dictionaries that will hold all your destination-specific information, with Item 0 being the first one.

   In Figure 11-5, I've added the row, and you can see the + (plus) button in the new row.

Disclosure triangle open   + button

Figure 11-5:
Add an
entry.

9. **Make Item 0 a dictionary by selecting Dictionary in the Type pop-up menu (in the same way you select Array in Step 7).**

   Your new entry is made into a dictionary, as shown in Figure 11-6.

Figure 11-6:
A dictionary
entry.

10. **Click the disclosure triangle in front of the Item 0 key so that it points down, and click the + (plus) button as you did in Step 7 to add a new entry to the dictionary.**

    You see a new entry under the dictionary like the one in Figure 11-7.

    These disclosure triangles work the same way as those in the Finder and the Xcode editor. The Property List editor interprets what you want to add based on the triangle. So if the items are revealed (that is, the triangle is pointing down), the editor assumes that you want to add a sub item or *child.* If the sub items are not revealed (that is, the triangle is pointing sideways), the editor assumes that you want to add an item at that level *(sibling).* In this case, with the arrow pointing down, you add a new entry — a sub item — to the dictionary. If the triangle were pointing sideways, you would be entering a new entry under the root.

    Only arrays and dictionaries have children.

New item

Figure 11-7:
A new entry
in the
dictionary.

11. **In the Key field of your (newest) entry, enter** DestinationName, **leave the Type as String, and then double-click (or tab to) the Value field and enter** New York City, **as shown in Figure 11-8.**

Change key to DestinationName   Change value to New York City

Figure 11-8:
A dictionary
entry.

12. **Click the + button in the row you just entered, and you get a new entry (a sibling of the previous row). In the Key field, enter** DestinationImage, **leave the Type as String, and then double-click (or tab to) the Value field and enter** NYCImage.

13. **Click the + button in the row you just entered, and you get a new entry (a sibling of the previous row). In the Key field, enter** DestinationLocation **and select Dictionary in the Type pop-up menu.**

14. **Click the disclosure triangle in front of the** DestinationLocation **key so it's facing down, and click the + button.**

    You see a new entry under the dictionary, as you can see in Figure 11-9.

Figure 11-9:
A new dictionary with another entry.

15. **In the Key field, enter** Title, **and enter** New York City **in the Value field.**

16. **Add these three keys with their corresponding type and value:**

Key	*Type*	*Value*
Subtitle	String	A great city
Latitude	Number	40.712756
Longitude	Number	-74.006047

    When you're done, your plist should look like Figure 11-10.

Figure 11-10:
The Destination Location entries.

17. **Click the disclosure triangle to hide the** DestinationLocation **dictionary entries, and add a new array named** *Events* **as a sibling of the** DestinationLocation, **as shown in Figure 11-11.**

Figure 11-11:
The Events
dictionary
entry is an
array.

As explained previously, when the disclosure triangle is closed, you add a sibling entry.

18. Continue filling out the plist to make it match Figure 11-12 and Table 11-1.

Figure 11-12:
The New
York City
destination
entry.

Table 11-1   New York City plist Keys and Values

Key	Type	Value
DestinationName	String	New York City
DestinationImage	String	NYCImage
DestinationLocation	Dictionary	
Title	String	New York City
Subtitle	String	A great city
Latitude	Number	40.712756
Longitude	Number	-74.006047
Events	Array	
Item 0	String	`http://nealgoldstein.com/NYC01.html`

Key	Type	Value
Item 1	String	`http://nealgoldstein.com/NYC02.html`
POIs	Array	
Item 0	String	
Title	String	The Statue of Liberty
Subtitle	String	Pro-democracy and anti-monarchy symbol of freedom
Latitude	Number	40.689244
Longitude	Number	-74.044514
Weather	String	`http://forecast.weather.gov/MapClick.php?zoneid=NYZ072`

After you finish entering these items, close Item 0 under `DestinationData` and go through Steps 8 through 18 again to add the San Francisco entry using the keys and values in Table 11-2. If you want to save some typing, you can copy and paste Item 0 and then expand the new Item 1 and simply replace the values. (That's what I did.)

Table 11-2   San Francisco plist Keys and Values

Key	Type	Value
DestinationName	String	San Francisco
DestinationImage	String	SFImage
DestinationLocation	Dictionary	
Title	String	San Francisco
Subtitle	String	A great city
Latitude	Number	37.7793
Longitude	Number	-122.4192
Events	Array	
Item 0	String	`http://nealgoldstein.com/SF01.html`
Item 1	String	`http://nealgoldstein.com/SF02.html`
POIs	Array	
Item 0	Dictionary	

(continued)

Table 11-2 *(continued)*

Key	Type	Value
Title	String	Golden Gate Bridge
Subtitle	String	An internationally recognized symbol of San Francisco
Latitude	Number	37.819722
Longitude	Number	-122.478611
Weather	String	`http://forecast.weather.gov/MapClick.php?site=mtr&textField1=37.76&textField2=-122.43&smap=1`

Make sure that you spell the entries *exactly as specified* or else you won't be able to access them using the examples in this book. Be especially careful of trailing spaces.

When you're done, refer to Figure 11-1 to see how your plist should look.

You may wonder why you're using this specific data (title and subtitle, for example). You'll understand that when you explore maps in Chapter 17.

Now that you have the information needed by the model to locate the data it's responsible for, it's time to start adding some model classes, which I cover in the following section.

Using plists to store data

Although you won't do it here, you can also modify a plist to store data. The only restriction of note is that you can't modify a plist you've created in your bundle. You need to save it in the file system instead. For example:

```
NSArray *paths = NSSearchPathForDirectoriesInDomains
                    (NSDocumentDirectory, NSUserDomainMask,
    YES);
NSString *documentsDirectory = [paths objectAtIndex:0];
NSString *filePath = [documentsDirectory
                        stringByAppendingPathComponent:
    state];
[updatedDestinations writeToFile:filePath atomically:YES];
```

Adding the First Two Model Classes

The first model class I have you add is the `Trip` class. This will become the only model object visible to the view controllers. Although the `Trip` object will use other objects to carry out its responsibilities, hiding them behind the `Trip` object results in the loose coupling I explain in the next section and in "The importance of loose coupling" sidebar, later in this chapter.

Here is how to create your first two model classes:

1. **Create a new group to keep your model classes in by going to the Project navigator, selecting the RoadTrip group (*not* the RoadTrip project, which is at the top), and right-clicking and choosing New Group from the menu that appears.**

   Or you can select the RoadTrip group and choose File⇨New⇨New Group from the main menu.

   You'll see a new group. (It looks like a folder.)

2. **Name your new group *Model Classes*.**

    To change a file's group, select the file and drag it to the group you want it to occupy. The same goes for groups as well. (After all, they can go into other groups.)

3. **In the Project navigator, select the Model Classes group, right-click the selection, and then choose New File from the menu that appears to open the New File dialog.**

   Or you can select the Model Classes group and choose File⇨New⇨New File from the main menu (or press ⌘+N).

   You'll see a dialog that enables you to select a file type.

4. **In the left column of the dialog, select Cocoa Touch under the iOS heading. Next, select the Objective-C class template in the top-right pane; then click Next.**

5. **In the Class field, enter Trip. In the Subclass Of drop-down menu, select NSObject. Click Next.**

   A Save sheet will appear.

6. **In the Save sheet, click Create.**

7. **Repeat Steps 2–6 to create the `Destination` class.**

You'll also be using the `MapKit` and `CoreLocation` frameworks, so add them as well:

1. **In the Project navigator, select the RoadTrip Project at the top of the Project navigator area to display the Project editor.**

2. **In the Targets section, select RoadTrip.**

3. **On the Summary tab, scroll down to the Linked Frameworks and Libraries section.**

4. **Expand the Linked Frameworks and Libraries section, if it isn't already expanded, by clicking the disclosure triangle.**

5. **Click the + button underneath the list of current project frameworks.**

   A list of frameworks appears.

6. **Scroll down and select both MapKit.framework and CoreLocation.framework from the list of frameworks.**

7. **Click the + button.**

   You'll see the framework added to the Linked Frameworks and Libraries section.

8. **Close the Linked Frameworks and Libraries section.**

9. **In the Project navigator (don't do this from the Linked Frameworks and Libraries section!), drag the** `MapKit.framework` **and** `CoreLocation.framework` **files to the Frameworks group.**

If you make a mistake and want to delete a file, right-click and choose Delete from the menu that appears or select the file and press Delete. Whichever method you choose, you'll see the dialog in Figure 11-13.

Figure 11-13:
What would
you like
to do?

Do you want to permanently delete the file "Trip.h" from disk, or only remove the reference to it?
This operation cannot be undone. Unsaved changes will be lost.

Cancel   Remove Reference Only   Delete

Remove Reference Only removes the file from the Project navigator but leaves it in your project folder on the disk. You can't copy a new file with that name to that project until you delete that file from your project on the disk as well.

When you use the template to create a class, it adds the methods it thinks you may need. As a result, there will be some methods you won't need and that appear to sit around doing nothing. You can delete them or just leave them in case you do need them. This is especially true of initialization methods because initialization in this app will be (mostly) taken care of by the storyboard.

Understanding the Trip Interface

Following is what the `Trip` interface will eventually become:

```objc
#import <Foundation/Foundation.h>
#import <MapKit/MapKit.h>
@class Annotation;

@interface Trip : NSObject

- (UIImage *) destinationImage;
- (NSString *) destinationName;
- (CLLocationCoordinate2D) destinationCoordinate;

- (id)initWithDestinationIndex:(int)destinationIndex;
- (NSString *)weather;
- (int)numberOfEvents;
- (NSString *)getEvent:(int)index;
- (NSArray *)createAnnotations;
- (NSString *)mapTitle;
- (void)addLocation:(NSString *)findLocation
    completionHandler:(void (^)(Annotation *annotation,
                                NSError* error)) completion;
@end
```

As you can see, this code contains a lot of stuff, and I explain it as you add functionality to the `Trip` class along the way.

Earlier in the chapter, I mention that `Trip` is the model interface, and I say this because in many cases more than one class will be involved in delivering the necessary functionality of the model. For example, in this chapter you just added a `Destination` class that will be responsible for the information about your destination. An `Events` class that you will add in Chapter 16 will be responsible for managing the list of things going on at your destination, and an `Annotation` class (coming in Chapter 17) will provide the information you need to plot annotations (places to see) on a map. Hiding additional model objects behind the `Trip` object is known as *loose coupling* and is an important object-oriented design principle (see the nearby "The Importance of loose coupling" sidebar).

You might be tempted to have the view controllers create the model classes they'll use (for example, a `WeatherController` would create the `Weather` object, and so on). The problem with that approach is that it makes the coupling between controller objects and the model much tighter.

One advantage of the Model-View-Controller (MVC) design pattern that I explain in Chapter 4 is that it allows you to assign (most) classes into one of three groups in your application and work on them individually. If each group has a well-defined interface, it encapsulates many of the kinds of changes that are often made so that they don't affect the other groups. This little fact is especially true of the model and view controller relationship.

If the view controllers have minimal knowledge about the model, you can change the model objects with minor impact on the view controllers. So although the `Trip` class will provide this functionality to the various view controllers, as I said, it won't be doing all the work on its own. What makes this possible is a well-defined interface, which I showed you at the start of this section. You create an interface between the model and the controllers by using a technique called *composition,* which is a useful way to create interfaces.

I'm a big fan of composition because it's another way to hide what's really going on behind the curtain. It keeps the objects that use the composite object (in this case, `Trip` is the composite object) ignorant of the objects that the composite object uses and actually makes the components ignorant of each other, allowing you to switch components in and out at will.

So you'll have `Trip` create the model objects, encapsulating the knowledge of what objects make up the model from the object that uses it. `Trip` hides all implementation knowledge from a view controller; it will know only about the `Trip` object. Again, this setup makes everything *loosely coupled* and makes your app more extensible and easier to change.

The importance of loose coupling

While millions of words have been spoken about how to design object-oriented applications, one of the most important is loose coupling. A loosely coupled system is one in which each of its components has little or no knowledge (or makes no use of the knowledge it may have) of other components. The term *loose coupling* refers to the degree of direct knowledge that one class has of another. This isn't about encapsulation or one class's knowledge of another class's attributes or implementation, but rather knowledge of that other class *itself.*

Applying loose coupling means presenting a minimum interface to other objects. The client deals with the fewest number of objects as possible. So although you may want to break down a function into smaller pieces (for example, by using composition), you never want the client to know that. Clients are happy dealing with one object, even if that object then turns around and redistributes that work to other objects.

Implementing the Trip Class

In this chapter, I show you how to implement the `Trip` model functionality that will enable you to choose between multiple destinations (although you won't be doing the choosing until Chapter 20). You also implement the `Trip` functionality that will be needed by the Master View controller (you add that in Chapter 12) — the name of the destination and its background image.

Start by adding the bolded code in Listing 11-1 to `Trip.h`.

Listing 11-1:   Updating the Trip Interface

```
#import <Foundation/Foundation.h>
#import <MapKit/MapKit.h>

@interface Trip : NSObject

- (id)initWithDestinationIndex:(int)destinationIndex;
- (UIImage *) destinationImage;
- (NSString *) destinationName;
- (CLLocationCoordinate2D) destinationCoordinate;
@end
```

As you can see, the code in Listing 11-1 contains an initialization method. This method will enable the `Trip` object to set itself up for the selected destination. (Allow me to explain initialization and a few other things).

Initialization is the logical place to start, but first you need to add some instance variables and import the `Destination` header file if you're going to use it (which you are, in the `Trip` implementation). Add the bolded code in Listing 11-2 to `Trip.m`.

Listing 11-2:   Updating the Trip Implementation

```
#import "Trip.h"
#import "Destination.h"

@interface Trip () {
  NSDictionary *destinationData;
  Destination* destination;
}
@end

@implementation Trip
```

Now you can add the `initWithDestinationIndex:` method in Listing 11-3 to `Trip.m`.

Listing 11-3:   Adding initWithDestinationIndex:

```
- (id)initWithDestinationIndex:(int)destinationIndex {

  if ((self = [super init])) {

    NSString *filePath = [[NSBundle mainBundle]
        pathForResource:@"Destinations" ofType:@"plist"];
    NSDictionary *destinations =
      [NSDictionary dictionaryWithContentsOfFile:filePath];
    NSArray *destinationsArray =
        destinations[@"DestinationData"];
    destinationData =
        destinationsArray[destinationIndex];
  destination = [[Destination alloc]
            initWithDestinationIndex:destinationIndex];
  }
  return self;
}
```

Before I explain the logic in these listings, I want to explain initialization in general. (And yes, you'll see compiler warnings, and you'll be fixing them as you go along.)

Initializing objects

Initialization is the procedure that sets the instance variables of an object (including pointers to other objects) to a known initial state. Essentially, you need to initialize an object in order to assign initial values to these variables. Initialization isn't required in every class in every app; if you can live with all the instance variables initialized to 0 and `nil`, you need do nothing. `Trip`, however, will need to create the objects it will be using, and you'll do that during initialization.

An initialization method doesn't have to include an argument for every instance variable, because some will become relevant only during the course of your object's existence. You must make sure, however, that all the instance variables your object uses, including other objects that it needs to do its work, are in a state that enables your object to respond to the messages it receives.

You may think that the main job in initialization is to, well, initialize the variables in your objects (hence the name), but more is involved when you have a superclass and a subclass chain.

To see what I mean, start by looking at the initializer I use for the `Trip` class in Listing 11-3 (shown previously). By convention, initialization methods begin with the abbreviation `init`. (This is true, however, only for *instance* — as opposed to *class* — methods.) If the method takes no arguments, the method name is just `init`. If it takes arguments, labels for the arguments follow the `init` prefix. As you can see, the initializer in Listing 11-3 has a return type of `id`. You discover the reason for that in the next section.

Initialization involves these three steps:

1. Invoke the superclass `init` method.

2. Initialize instance variables.

3. Return `self`.

The following sections explain each step.

Invoking the superclass's init method

Here is the type of statement you use to get the `init` method up and running:

```
self = [super init];
if (self) {
```

`[super init]` does nothing more than invoke the superclass `init` method. By convention, all initializers are required to assign `self`. `self` is the "hidden" variable accessible to methods in an object that points its instance variables to whatever object you get back from the superclass initializer, which explains `self = [super init]`.

The `if` statement can be a little confusing to people. You may not get an object returned from the super class `init` method. If that's the case, you don't want to do any further initialization.

Although the scenario just described is possible, it isn't common and won't happen in this book (and in general). You might find it in classes that need certain resources to initialize themselves, and if they aren't present, the object can't be created.

There's actually a lot to initialization that I don't cover in this book, but you can find out more in Neal's book *Objective-C For Dummies,* as well as in Apple's Objective-C documentation.

Initializing instance variables

Initializing instance variables, including creating the objects you need, is what you probably thought initialization is about. Notice that you're initializing your instance variable after your superclass's initialization, which you can see in Listing 11-3 (shown previously). Waiting until *after* your superclass does its initialization gives you the opportunity to actually change something your superclass may have done during its initialization, but more importantly, it allows you to perform initialization knowing that what you have inherited is initialized and ready to be used.

In your `initWithDestinationIndex:` method, you start by finding the plist that holds the `Trip` data or location of the data you need:

```
NSString *filePath = [[NSBundle mainBundle]
    pathForResource:@"Destinations" ofType:@"plist"];
```

Next, you create a dictionary to hold the data. You use the method `init WithContentsOfFile:`, which does all the heavy lifting for you. It reads in the `Destinations` plist file and creates a dictionary for you. The plist, as I said previously, is really a dictionary with a single entry with the key `DestinationData`. The `dictionaryWithContentsOfFile:` method creates a dictionary from the plist (and objects and keys for all of its entries) with dictionary keys that are the keys you specified in the plist.

This method also allocates and initializes all the elements in the dictionary (including other dictionaries), so when it's done, you're ready to roll:

```
NSDictionary *destinations =
    [NSDictionary dictionaryWithContentsOfFile:filePath];
```

`NSDictionary`, `NSMutableDictionary`, `NSArray`, and `NSMutableArray` all have the methods `initWithContentsOfFile:` and `writeToFile::` that read themselves in from a file and write themselves out to a file, respectively. This is one of the capabilities that makes property list objects so useful.

Property list containers — and *only* property list containers (and `NSString` and `NSData`) — can read themselves in from and write themselves out to a file. The other property list objects can only store themselves, without any effort on your part, as part of a file.

Your next step in initializing instance variables is to use the `destination Index` to get the right element in the array of dictionaries in the `Destination Data` entry based on the destination chosen by the user. (You'll specify that in the `RTAppDelegate` in Listing 11-11, later in this chapter, where you'll allocate the `Trip` object.)

```
NSArray *destinationsArray =
        destinations[@"DestinationData"];
destinationData =
      destinationsArray[destinationIndex];
```

Finally, you allocate and initialize the `Destination` object:

```
destination = [[Destination alloc]
            initWithDestinationIndex:destinationIndex];
```

Returning self

Earlier in this chapter, I explain that the `self` = statement ensures that `self` is set to whatever object you get back from the superclass initializer. No matter what you get back from invoking the superclass initializer in the initialization method, you need to set `self` to that value and then return it to the invoking method — the method that wants to instantiate the object or a subclass that invoked the superclass's `init` method.

After the code block that initializes the variables, you insert the following:

```
return self;
```

The reason the `return` type is an `id` is that sometimes what you ask for isn't what you get. But don't worry; that becomes transparent to you if you follow the rules for initialization I just explained.

The reason that you may get back a different class than what you asked for is that under certain circumstances when you allocate a framework object, what you may get back may be a class optimized for your use based on the context.

So where do the braces go?

If you look in the code provided by the template, sometimes you see a method implementation that looks like this:

```
- (void)viewDidLoad
{
```

and sometimes you'll see one that looks like this:

```
- (IBAction)testDrive(id)
sender {
```

I personally prefer the latter — with the bracket on the same line as the method — and will use it in the methods I have you add.

Quite frankly, it doesn't matter to the compiler, but it can raise itself to a religious issue among programmers. Do what you'd like.

Initializing the Destination Class

Now it's time to turn to the `Destination` class and its initialization. Add the bolded code in Listing 11-4 to `Destination.h` to update its interface to add the header files, the properties you'll be using, and the method declarations.

Listing 11-4:   Updating the Destination Interface

```
#import <Foundation/Foundation.h>
#import <MapKit/MapKit.h>

@interface Destination : NSObject

@property (nonatomic, readwrite)
                      CLLocationCoordinate2D coordinate;
@property (nonatomic, readwrite, copy) NSString *title;
@property (nonatomic, readwrite, copy) NSString *subtitle;
@property (nonatomic, strong) NSString *destinationName;
@property (nonatomic, strong) UIImage *destinationImage;

- (id)initWithDestinationIndex:
                           (NSUInteger)destinationIndex;
@end
```

As you saw in Chapter 4, you'll be displaying the destination on a map with an *annotation* (that pop-up window that displays information about the location when you touch the pin on the map). Doing that requires a `coordinate` property of type `CLLocationCoordinate2d` (that's why you need to include the `MapKit` and `CoreLocation` frameworks) and optional `title` and `subtitle` properties. Although you won't be doing anything with this part of `Destination` until Chapter 17, I have you initialize `Destination` with what is described in the plist but defer the explanation until Chapter 17.

When you're done, you can add the `initWithDestinationIndex:` method in Listing 11-5 to `Destination.m`.

Listing 11-5:   Add initWithDestinationIndex:

```
- (id)initWithDestinationIndex:
                           (NSUInteger)destinationIndex {

  self = [super init];
  if (self) {

    NSString *filePath = [[NSBundle mainBundle]
```

```
                    pathForResource:@"Destinations" ofType:@"plist"];
    NSDictionary *destinations = [NSDictionary
                    dictionaryWithContentsOfFile:filePath];
    NSArray *destinationsArray =
            destinations[@"DestinationData"];
    NSDictionary *data =
        destinationsArray[destinationIndex];

    NSString *imageName;
    if ([[UIDevice currentDevice] userInterfaceIdiom] ==
                                    UIUserInterfaceIdiomPad)
        imageName =
          [NSString stringWithFormat:@"%@_iPad.png",
                data[@"DestinationImage"]];
    else
        imageName =
          [NSString stringWithFormat:@"%@_iPhone.png",
                data[@"DestinationImage"]];
    self.destinationImage =
                        [UIImage imageNamed:imageName];

    self.destinationName =
                    data[@"DestinationName"];
    NSDictionary* destinationLocation =
            data[@"DestinationLocation"];
    CLLocationCoordinate2D destinationCoordinate;
    destinationCoordinate.latitude =
        [destinationLocation[@"Latitude"] doubleValue];
    destinationCoordinate.longitude =
        [destinationLocation
                    [@"Longitude"] doubleValue];
    self.coordinate = destinationCoordinate;
    self.title =
            destinationLocation[@"Title"];
    self.subtitle =
          destinationLocation[@"Subtitle"];
  }
  return self;
}
```

Destination initializes itself more or less the same way that Trip did. It starts by loading its data:

```
NSString *filePath = [[NSBundle mainBundle]
        pathForResource:@"Destinations" ofType:@"plist"];
NSDictionary *destinations =
    [NSDictionary dictionaryWithContentsOfFile: filePath];
NSArray *destinationsArray =
        destinations[@"DestinationData"];
NSDictionary *data =
      destinationsArray[destinationIndex];
```

Then it uses the dictionary data to initialize its properties:

```
NSString *imageName;
if ([[UIDevice currentDevice] userInterfaceIdiom] ==
                               UIUserInterfaceIdiomPad)
  imageName = [NSString stringWithFormat:@"%@_iPad.png",
               data[@"DestinationImage"]];
else
  imageName = [NSString stringWithFormat:@"%@_iPhone.png",
               data[@"DestinationImage"]];
    self.destinationImage =
                           [UIImage imageNamed:imageName];
```

Because the view sizes are different on the iPhone and iPad, you need different images for the destination. To actually determine the image name, you have to take the name specified in the plist and add an iPad or iPhone suffix.

```
self.destinationName =
                  data[@"DestinationName"];
NSDictionary* destinationLocation =
              data[@"DestinationLocation"];
CLLocationCoordinate2D destinationCoordinate;
destinationCoordinate.latitude =
  [destinationLocation[@"Latitude"] doubleValue];
destinationCoordinate.longitude =
  [destinationLocation
                  [@"Longitude"] doubleValue];
self.coordinate = destinationCoordinate;
self.title = destinationLocation[@"Title"];
self.subtitle =
          destinationLocation[@"Subtitle"];
```

The initialization of the properties is simply done by using the keys you specified when you created the plist, which turn into dictionary keys when you load the dictionary (and its dictionaries) from the plist file.

Now you can add the `Trip` methods `destinationImage`, `destination Name`, and `destinationCoordinate`, which use the `Destination` object. Add the methods in Listing 11-6 to `Trip.m`.

Listing 11-6: Adding destinationImage, destinationName, and destinationCoordinate

```
- (UIImage *) destinationImage {

  return  destination.destinationImage;
}

- (NSString *) destinationName {

  return  destination.destinationName;
```

```
}

- (CLLocationCoordinate2D) destinationCoordinate {

    return destination.coordinate;
}
```

These `Trip` methods will be used by the Master View controller to request the data it needs for its view.

Interestingly, in this case, all `Trip` does is turn around and send the request to the `Destination` object. This is, of course, an example of loose coupling, which I explain earlier.

In this case, there isn't that much for `Destination` to do, so you could've simply had `Trip` manage the data. But in a more robust app (like one worth 99 cents), it would likely have more to do. In fact, you could start by having `Trip` manage all the data and add a `Destination` object when you felt you needed to. And when you did add the `Destination` object, doing so would have no impact on the objects needing that data — ah, loose coupling in action.

Creating the Trip Object

Finally, you have to create the `Trip` object. You need to make it accessible to the view controllers that need to use it, so you'll make it an `RTAppDelegate` property. As you saw earlier, in Chapter 6, any object in your app can find the `RTAppDelegate`, and from it get a pointer to the `Trip` object.

Add the bolded code in Listing 11-7 to `RTAppDelegate.h`.

Listing 11-7: Updating the RTAppDelegate Interface

```
#import <UIKit/UIKit.h>
@class Trip;

@interface RTAppDelegate : UIResponder
            <UIApplicationDelegate>

@property (strong, nonatomic) UIWindow *window;
@property (nonatomic, strong) Trip *trip;

- (void) createDestinationModel:(int)destinationIndex;

@end
```

`createDestinationModel:` is the method that actually creates the `Trip` object.

`@class` is a compiler directive to let the compiler know that `Trip` is a class (or type). You need to import the header to actually use it in your code, however, and you'll do that by adding the bolded code in Listing 11-8 to `RTAppDelegate.m`.

Listing 11-8: Updating the RTAppDelegate Implementation

```
#import "RTAppDelegate.h"
#import "Reachability.h"
#import "Trip.h"

@implementation RTAppDelegate
```

You also declare a method that will actually create the `Trip` object. Add the bolded code in Listing 11-9 to `application:didFinishLaunchingWithOp tions:` in `RTAppDelegate.m` to use that method.

Listing 11-9: Updating application:didFinishLaunchingWithOptions:

```
- (BOOL)application:(UIApplication *)application
        didFinishLaunchingWithOptions:
                          (NSDictionary *)launchOptions
{
  UINavigationController *navigationController;
  if ([[UIDevice currentDevice] userInterfaceIdiom] ==
                          UIUserInterfaceIdiomPad) {
    UISplitViewController *splitViewController =
      (UISplitViewController *)
                          self.window.rootViewController;
    splitViewController.presentsWithGesture = NO;
    UINavigationController *detailNavigationController
        [splitViewController.viewControllers lastObject];
    splitViewController.delegate =
        (id)detailNavigationController.topViewController;
    navigationController =
    [splitViewController.viewControllers objectAtIndex:0];
  }
  else {
    navigationController = (UINavigationController *)
                          self.window.rootViewController;
  }
  NetworkStatus networkStatus = [[Reachability
        reachabilityForInternetConnection]
        currentReachabilityStatus];
  if (networkStatus == NotReachable) {
    UIAlertView *alert = [[UIAlertView alloc]
      initWithTitle:@"Network Unavailable"
```

```
      message:@"RoadTrip requires an Internet connection"
      delegate:nil
      cancelButtonTitle:@"OK"
      otherButtonTitles:nil];
  [alert show];
}
[[UIApplication sharedApplication]
    setStatusBarStyle:UIStatusBarStyleBlackOpaque
                                      animated:NO];
navigationController.navigationBar.barStyle =
                                UIBarStyleBlack;
[navigationController.navigationBar
  setTitleTextAttributes:
      [NSDictionary dictionaryWithObject:
        [UIColor yellowColor]
[[UIButton appearance] setTitleColor:
    [UIColor greenColor] forState:UIControlStateNormal];
[[UIBarButtonItem appearanceWhenContainedIn:
  [UINavigationBar class], nil]
  setTitleTextAttributes:
    [NSDictionary dictionaryWithObject:
                              [UIColor yellowColor]
    forKey:UITextAttributeTextColor]
    forState:UIControlStateNormal];
[[UIToolbar appearance] setBarStyle:UIBarStyleBlack];
[[UIButton appearanceWhenContainedIn:
  [UIAlertView class], nil] setTitleColor:
    [UIColor whiteColor] forState:UIControlStateNormal];
[self createDestinationModel:0];
return YES;
}
```

As you can see, you use the createDestinationModel: method to actually create the model. I have this as a separate method because you'll need to be able to send the RTAppDelegate a message to create a new Trip when the user chooses a new destination in Chapter 20.

Also notice that, for now, you'll be defaulting to the first destination in the plist. You'll fix that in Chapter 20 as well.

Add the createDestinationModel: method in Listing 11-10 to RTAppDelegate.m.

Listing 11-10: Adding createDestinationModel:

```
- (void) createDestinationModel:(int)destinationIndex {

  self.trip = [[Trip alloc] initWithDestinationIndex:desti
        nationIndex];

}
```

All you do is allocate and initialize the `Trip` object and assign it to the `trip` property.

More Debugger Stuff

In this section, I give you something more interesting to look at in the Debugger than you've had up to now for this book's example app. As it stands, you can compile RoadTrip with no errors and it runs, albeit the same way that it did before. So you have no idea if all that code you added really works. Does it really find the `Destinations.plist` file and create all the dictionaries with their entries correctly?

One way to find out is to put a breakpoint in your code and see what's there; so go ahead and set a breakpoint in `Trip.m` on the following line (in the `initWithDestinationIndex:` method) by clicking in the gutter next to (in front of) the line:

```
destination = [[Destination alloc]
            initWithDestinationIndex:destinationIndex];
```

Then set another breakpoint in `Destination.m` (in its `initWith DestinationIndex:` method) on the following line:

```
self.subtitle =
            destinationLocation[@"Subtitle"];
```

Run your application.

If your program execution stops at a breakpoint, you can move your pointer over an object or variable in the Source editor to see its contents. In Figure 11-14, I've done that with `destinationData` (and so should you).

`destinationData` is a pointer to the dictionary that contains the data for the first entry in the Destination plist's `DestinationData` array. You'll have six key/value pairs, as you should have, and if you look in the Variables pane in the Debugger, you'll see two objects in the `destinationsArray`, which is also as it should be.

If you move your pointer into the `destinationData` variable display in the Source editor and Control-click in the up and down arrow, as I have in Figure 11-15, you see a drop-down menu with a Print Description selection.

Figure 11-14:
Display the contents of a variable in the Source editor.

Figure 11-15:
You can print the contents of a variable.

If you select Print Description, you'll see the values in the destination Data dictionary *printed* (displayed) in the Console pane (see Figure 11-16).

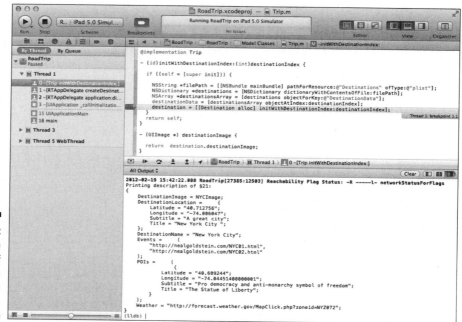

Figure 11-16:
Printing the contents of a variable to the Console pane.

You could also have done the same thing by Control-clicking in the Variables pane. One thing you'll notice is that no instance variables are displayed (at least in this release of Xcode) because you have them in a class extension rather than in the interface. Oh, well, you can't have everything.

If you select Continue Program Execution in the Debug bar, you can print out variables to be sure that the Destination method initWithDestination Index: works as expected.

On a side note, when I was writing this, I found that my code didn't work. I had inadvertently placed a trailing space in the DestinationLocation key, which I found out by printing the contents of the destinationData dictionary. My discovery of that error was what prompted the trailing space warning in the "Adding a property list to your project" section, earlier in this chapter.

Chapter 12

Implementing the Master View Controller

In This Chapter

▶ Working with custom view controllers

▶ Using the Trip model to get data for a view

*W*ith the model in place, you can now return to the Master View controller and transform its view into the user interface you fell in love with way back in Chapter 4. In this chapter, you'll connect the Master View controller for the iPad to the Trip model to create the interface and also to be able to (eventually) respond to user requests. You'll then repeat the process for the iPhone version.

The strategy you adopt in this chapter to add the logic to connect the view to the model via the view controller is the same strategy you'll use for the rest of the view controllers in the storyboard. As always, although you can add the view controllers you'll need to the storyboard graphically, you'll still need to add some code to have the controller actually do anything, such as get data from the model and send it to the view.

Setting Up a Custom View Controller for the iPad

While `RTMasterViewController` already actually does something, I want to develop it for use in RoadTrip by customizing its appearance and having it display (through its entries or cells) a table of contents showing the application functionality. Here's how you'd start things off:

1. **In the Project navigator, select MainStoryboard_iPad.**

2. **In the Document outline, select Master View Controller – Master in the Master View Controller – Master scene, open the disclosure triangle next to the Master View controller in the scene, and select the Table view.**

3. **Using the Inspector selector bar, open the Attributes inspector in the Utility area.**

   You'll notice that, in the Table View section of the Attributes inspector, the Static Cells option is selected in the Content drop-down menu, as shown in Figure 12-1. You changed this Table view to Static cells in Chapter 5.

   As I explain in Chapter 5, static cells were a new feature in iOS 5.0 — used when you know in advance what needs to be displayed in a cell. Instead of having to implement a method in your view controller and return the cell with the text you want (as you will in Chapter 20 where you create cells based on the information for each destination in the `Destinations` plist), you can format the cells in the storyboard.

4. **In the Document outline, open the disclosure triangle next to the Table view, select Table View Section, and delete it.**

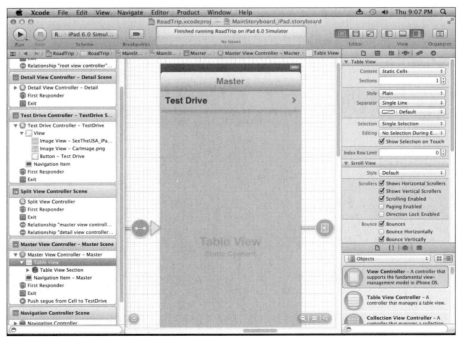

Figure 12-1:
You start with static cells.

You could've left that cell and added cells to that section and more sections, but I want to show you what it's like to start from a clean slate.

Notice that the segue to the Test Drive controller has been deleted as well. That means you can no longer select Test Drive and have the view slide into place. But you'll fix that in Chapter 13.

You are now ready to add the text you want displayed to the cells, but before you do, I want to give you some background on how Table views work.

As I explain in Chapter 20, Table views usually require both a *data source* as well as a *delegate*. The data source supplies the content for the Table view and provides the content for each cell (or row). The delegate manages the appearance and behavior of the Table view and determines what to do when the user selects a cell (or row) — it could, for example, push a view controller onto the stack.

If you're using the Table view only as a type of "table of contents" for your application, selecting Static Cells lets you create the cell content in Interface Builder (as I show you how to do next) and use storyboard segues to specify what happens when a user selects a cell — much easier and a lot less work than coding it yourself! I explain more about this in Chapter 20.

The following steps show you how to customize your Table view:

1. **Select Table View in the Document Outline in the Master View Controller – Master Scene.**

2. **Using the Inspector selector, open the Attributes inspector in the Utility area, select Grouped from the inspector's Style drop-down menu, and then enter 3 in the Sections field.**

   You see three sections with three rows each, as shown in Figure 12-2.

   Note that Table views come in two basic styles:

   - *Plain:* The default style is called *plain* and looks really unadorned — plain vanilla. It's a list: just one darn thing after another. You can index it, though, just as the Table view in the Contacts application is indexed, so it can be a pretty powerful tool.

     A plain view can also have section titles (as I describe shortly) and footers.

   - *Grouped:* The other style is the *grouped* Table view; unsurprisingly, it allows you to lump entries together into various categories.

     Grouped tables can't have an index.

     When you configure a grouped Table view, you can also have header, footer, and section titles. I show you how to do section titles shortly.

Figure 12-2:
Static cells
and three
sections.

The details of what you've just done may change as the storyboard defaults are changed, but you get the picture.

3. **Open the disclosure triangle next to Table View in the Document outline, check out the Table View sections under it, and select the first section.**

   The Attributes inspector refreshes to show the attributes of the first Table View section.

4. **Change the Rows field in the Attributes inspector to 2 (or delete one of the cells) and enter** At My Destination **in the Header field.**

5. **Select the second section and, after the Attributes inspector refreshes, change the Rows field in the Attributes inspector to 2, and enter** Getting Around **in the Header field.**

6. **Select the third section and, after the Attributes inspector refreshes, change the Rows field in the Attributes inspector to 2, and enter** Planning My Trip **in the Header field. (See Figure 12-3.)**

7. **Select the first Table View Cell in the first Table View Section in the Document Outline in the Master View Controller – Master Scene and, after the Attributes inspector refreshes, scroll down (if needed) to the View section and select Clear Color from the section's Background drop-down menu, as shown in Figure 12-4.**

Figure 12-3:
Setting the number of rows and sections with headers that you want.

Figure 12-4:
Make the Table View cell background clear.

8. **Still in the Attributes inspector, choose Basic from the Style menu.**

   The Style menu provides a number of options for how the cell is formatted. Each one formats the text in the cell a little differently in the label(s) it adds to the cell to display the text. (Or you can leave it as Custom, drag in a label(s), and format the label any way you want.)

   When you select Basic, a disclosure triangle gets added next to first Table View Cell in the Document Outline in the Master View Controller – Master Scene. If you open it, you see that a single label has been added for you, as shown in Figure 12-5.

9. **Select the Label in the Document outline.**

   The Attributes inspector displays the Label properties — including the text, which you can change to your heart's content. (Selecting the Text icon in the Font field allows you to change the font as well.)

   In Figure 12-6 on the left, I've entered **Weather** in the Text field (remember to press Return) and on the right, I've changed the Font from System Bold to just plain System by selecting the Font icon (the little T inside the Font field) and choosing System in the pop-up Font menu.

10. **For the Label, select Clear Color from the View section's Background drop-down menu, as shown in Figure 12-7.**

Figure 12-5:
A basic cell with the supplied label.

Figure 12-6:
The formatted cell of a table.

Figure 12-7:
Make the Label Background clear.

11. **Finally, and this is the pièce de résistance, select White Color from the Label section's Text Color drop-down menu.**

    Yes, it is in fact the case that you won't be able to see the text very well, as demonstrated by Figure 12-8.

12. **Repeat Steps 7–11 to format the next two cells, this time entering** Events and Map, **respectively, in the Text field in the Attributes inspector.**

    You have to treat the Find cell a little differently. Rather than just adding a title to the Table View Cell, you're going to add a label and input text field *inside* the table view cell. This is only one example of how you can put almost any view inside a Table View Cell.

    Start by leaving the cell type as Custom in the Style menu. (Because you'll have the user enter the place he or she wants to find in the cell, you'll have to format it on your own.) Continue with the steps that follow.

13. **Drag a label from the Library pane onto the cell.**

14. **With the label selected, go to the Attributes inspector and enter** Find: **in the Text field, change the font to System (if it's not already set to System), make the Label and Table View Cell backgrounds Clear Color, and set the text to White Color (if it's not already set that way), as you did in Steps 7, 10, and 11.**

    If you select the label it should look like Figure 12-9.

15. **Drag a Text Field from the Library pane onto the cell and position it as shown in Figure 12-10.**

16. **At the top of the Text Field section of the Attributes inspector, enter** Enter address or place **in the Placeholder field to help the user understand what this text field is for.**

17. **In the Attributes inspector, select the first Border Style (No Border) in the Text Field section.**

    The text field will seem to disappear, but you can always select it again in the Document outline.

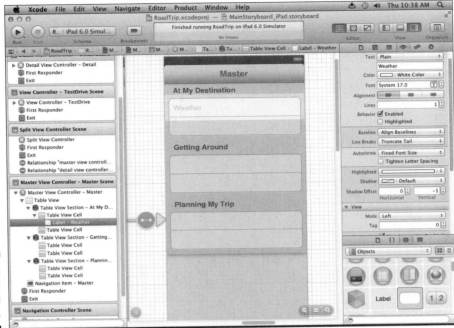

Figure 12-8:
The first cell
and label
are done.

Figure 12-9:
Add a label.

Figure 12-10:
Add a text
field.

18. **Using the appropriate drop-down menus, set the background to Clear Color and the text to White Color.**

    You can see the results in Figure 12-11.

    Text fields enable the user to enter small amounts of text, which is exactly what you need here.

19. **Repeat Steps 7–11 to format the next two cells, this time entering** Destination **and** Test Drive, **respectively, in the Text field in the Attributes inspector.**

20. **Your Master View controller should look more or less like mine does in Figure 12-12.**

If you were to remove the code breakpoint that you set in Chapter 11, and then click the Run button for the iPad version, you would see the screen shown in Figure 12-13. Clicking or tapping in a cell doesn't get you anything yet, but it soon will.

Of course, this user interface isn't particularly exciting; in fact, it's rather pedestrian. Let's fix that. Doing that requires doing some coding in the Master View controller.

Figure 12-11:
The Find cell complete.

Figure 12-12:
The finished Content controller.

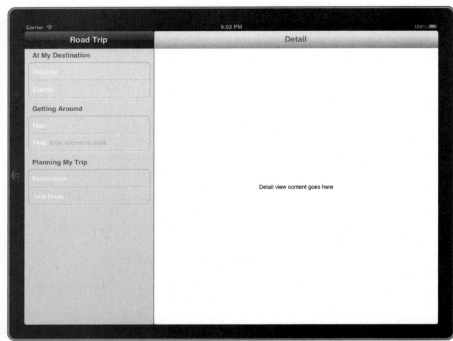

Figure 12-13:
The latest
additions
to the
RoadTrip
app for iPad.

Adding a Background Image and Title

The type of Table view highlighted in this chapter has static cells that you set up in Interface Builder, as I mention in the previous section. However, in this view, everything isn't static — including two things based on the destination. Those two things are the background image and the title. You have to set those programmatically.

Start by hiding the Utility area and then show the Project navigator (if you have hidden it) by making the appropriate selections in the toolbar. Then select `RTMasterViewController.m` in the Project navigator.

You may recall from Chapter 6 that the View Controller method you'd use to customize a view at launch time is `viewDidLoad`, which is the method I'll have you use here as well.

First, import the headers you need by adding the bolded code in Listing 12-1 to `RTMasterViewController.m`.

Listing 12-1: Updating the RTMasterViewController Implementation

```
#import "RTMasterViewController.h"
#import "RTDetailViewController.h"
#import "RTAppDelegate.h"
#import "Trip.h"
```

Now add the bolded code in Listing 12-2 to the viewDidLoad method in RTMasterViewController.m and delete the commented out code in bold, underline, and italic.

Listing 12-2: Updating viewDidLoad

```
- (void)viewDidLoad
{
    [super viewDidLoad];
//self.title = @"Road Trip";
  RTAppDelegate* appDelegate = [[UIApplication
                                sharedApplication] delegate];
    self.title = appDelegate.trip.destinationName;
    UIImageView* imageView = [[UIImageView alloc]
        initWithImage:[appDelegate.trip destinationImage]];
    self.tableView.backgroundView = imageView;
}
```

You want to add two features to the RTMasterViewController's view. The first makes the title in the Navigation bar the name of the destination, and the second adds a background image to the view. This data is owned by the Trip model, so you're finally getting to use the model.

To get the information the Master View controller needs from the (Trip) model, it needs to send a message to the Trip object. You may recall that in Chapter 11, when you created and initialized the Trip object in RTAppDelegate, you assigned its pointer to the trip property to make it accessible to the view controllers.

You find RTAppDelegate just like you previously did: by sending the class message sharedApplication to the UIApplication class and then sending the delegate message to the UIApplication object.

You use the following two methods to place your background image and display the destination name:

✔ destinationImage is a Trip method that returns a UIImage pointer.

✔ destinationName is a Trip method that returns an NSString pointer that contains the destination name. (You added this method in Chapter 11 when you began working with the Trip class.)

Run the application now and select Travel. Be prepared to be impressed with your work, as evidenced by what you see in Figure 12-14.

As I mention in the preceding section, because you deleted the Test Drive cell, the segue was deleted as well. That means you can no longer select Test Drive and have the view slide into place. But you'll fix that in the next chapter.

Figure 12-14:
The Master View controller user interface for iPad.

Updating the iPhone Storyboard File

You can reuse the iPad code you just developed for the iPhone version, but you will have to update the iPhone storyboard file with the same kind of changes you just did for the iPad storyboard. Remember, both the iPhone and iPad versions are your children, and you don't want to hurt the iPhone app's feelings by neglecting it.

The simplest way to update the iPhone storyboard is to review all the directions in this chapter that described how to update the iPad storyboard, and repeat those steps for the iPhone storyboard. But you do not need to repeat the code changes — the ones made in this chapter work fine for both iPad and iPhone.

The iPhone Master View controller interface should now look like Figure 12-15.

Figure 12-15:
The Master View controller interface for the iPhone.

Chapter 13

Working with Split View Controllers and the Master View

This chapter is primarily about the iPad user interface, because Split View controllers aren't supported on the smaller iPhone. In Chapter 5, I explain a bit about iPad navigation using the example of a Navigation controller within a Split View controller. But the iPad has some even slicker ways to navigate, which I get to in this chapter. You'll be happy to know that you're going to be replacing the Navigation controller style of navigation with something more appropriate to the RoadTrip application.

The Problem with Using a Navigation Controller in Detail View

As I explain in Chapter 5, the Master-Detail Application template you're using sets up the iPad's Split View controller in such a way that, when a cell in the Master view is tapped (Test Drive for example), the Navigation controller pushes the next view controller onto the stack. The new view controller's view slides into place, and the Navigation bar items are updated appropriately. The result, as you can see on the right side of Figure 13-1, is a Back button in the Detail view that enables you to return to the previous Detail view. (I'm using the pre–Chapter 12 version of RoadTrip, because it is easier to show you the flow in Figure 13-1.)

Figure 13-1:
On the iPad,
it's back and
forth using a
Navigation
controller
and
Navigation
bar.

But as I explain in Chapter 1, while the user experiences on the iPhone and iPad have similarities, in some ways, the experiences are quite different. And one major and very obvious difference is the screen size — a difference which can have a major impact on the ways you can navigate and display information.

On the iPhone, you go from one view to another using the navigator approach you see in Figure 13-2.

Figure 13-2:
Navigating
with a
Navigation
controller on
the iPhone.

The only difference is that, with the increased real estate on the iPad, you can show both the Table view that you use for navigation as well as the associated content you want to display at the same time, as you see in Figure 13-3.

But while you can take advantage of the larger display using the Navigation controller approach, a problem is lurking in the background that I want to call your attention to.

In the current (unimproved) version of RoadTrip, when you tap the Test Drive cell (before Chapter 12), the Test Drive controller is pushed onto the stack (as I explain in Chapter 5), and the view slides into place. A Back button (labeled Detail) is displayed, and you use the Back button to return to the previously displayed view.

The process doesn't initially appear to be particularly problematic if you stick to Landscape orientation (although take my word for it, it is), but when you switch to Portrait orientation, you soon realize that you're in a bit of a bind. You can see the outlines of that bind in the sequence in Figure 13-4. Again, in the current (unimproved) version of RoadTrip, when you're in Landscape orientation, tapping the Master button displays the Master view in a popover. If you then tap the Test Drive cell, the Test Drive view slides into place. (You also need to tap anywhere in the Test Drive view to dismiss the popover — you'll fix that so it's automatically dismissed when a new view is displayed.)

Figure 13-3:
Master view and Detail view using a Split view.

At that point, you see a Back button (Detail) that's designed to get you back to the original view. But what if you didn't want to go back to the Detail view and just wanted to tap another item (say, Weather) in the Master view? The way things are implemented now, you're out of luck. The only way you can get back to the Master view in Portrait orientation is to keep tapping the Back button until you're at the Detail view you see on the left side of Figure 13-4.

I'm not crazy about this user experience. If I had my druthers, whenever I wanted to go from one Detail view to another in Portrait orientation, the Master button would *always* be present and I would tap it to display the Master view in a popover, which would allow me to make another selection. In Landscape orientation, the Maser View would be present, so I could just make a selection and get to where I wanted to go, and there would be no Back button to get me back to a previous view; I'd just select what I wanted to see in the Master view. In other words, I don't want to *push* the next view controller when I select a cell in the Master view; I want to *replace* the Detail View controller with another view controller.

Using a Navigation Controller in the Master View

Before I explain how to replace one view controller with another, I want to make it clear that I am in no way saying I never want to do the traditional kind of Navigation controller navigation on the iPad. For example, I might want to use a Navigation controller in the Master view. I'll show you how to do that by creating a *segue* — a storyboard object that creates a transition from one view controller to another — so that when you select Test Drive in the Master view, the Test Drive view will slide into place, Back button and all, in the Master view (as opposed to the Detail view, which had been the case). Then, when you tap the Back button, you'll be back in the Master view.

I'm doing this just to show you how to do it. After I explain it, I'll have you go back to having the Test Drive view display in the Detail view.

Here is how to create a push segue that allows your Test Drive button to display the Test Drive controller.

1. **Select MainStoryboard_iPad in the Project navigator.**

   The storyboard will appear.

2. **Select the Test Drive cell, control-drag it to the Test Drive controller, as I have done in Figure 13-5, and then release the mouse button.**

   You'll see the pop-up menu that allows you to select the Storyboard Segues type, as shown in Figure 13-6.

3. **Choose Push from the Selection Segue menu items.**

   Let me remind you that I explained the difference between Selection Segues and Accessory Actions in Chapter 5. You'll notice that the Test Drive view resizes to the same size as the Master view.

   Select the segue in the Document Outline, as I have in Figure 13-7. The Attributes inspector shows you that the Destination is set to Current. (Current is in fact the default.) That means that the Destination view for this segue — the view that is displayed by the Test Drive controller — is the view that the segue is from, or the Master view.

Figure 13-5:
Control-drag
to create a
segue.

Figure 13-6:
Create a
push segue.

Figure 13-7:
The
Destination
is Current —
the Master
View.

4. **Enter** TestDrive **in the Identifier field, as I have in Figure 13-7.**

5. **Select the Table View cell and, in the Attributes inspector, change the Accessory field from Disclosure Indicator to None.**

   I'm of the opinion that a disclosure indicator isn't necessary here, but feel free to reject my opinion if you so desire.

If you click the Run button now and then tap Test Drive in the Master view, you get to test drive the 1959 Cadillac Eldorado Biarritz in the Master view; tapping the New York City button (as you recall, what appears in the Back button is the title of the previous view controller and you made that your destination in Chapter 12) in the Test Drive view takes you back to the Master view. This works even in Portrait orientation, as you can see in Figure 13-8.

If you tap Road Trip to return to the Master view, you may notice that the Test Drive cell stays highlighted; not to worry, you'll fix that soon.

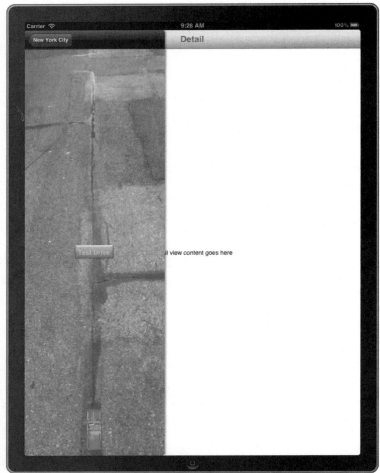

Figure 13-8:
Using a
Navigation
controller in
the Master
view.

Adding a Gesture Recognizer

If you want to truly understand the iOS user experience, you need to understand the importance of gestures, one of the features that make the use of any iOS device an intimate experience for the user, as I explain in Chapter 1.

`UIKit` includes gesture recognizers that you can use in your app to make it work the same way as all those fancy apps Apple has come up with. In this section, you'll use `UIKit` to add a gesture recognizer to the Main view so that the user can swipe to the left to make the Test Drive view appear.

Adding the gesture recognizer is easy for both the iPhone and iPad. In `RTMasterViewController.m`, add the bolded code in Listing 13-1 to `viewDidLoad`.

Listing 13-1:   Adding a Gesture Recognizer

```
- (void)viewDidLoad
{
  [super viewDidLoad];
  RTAppDelegate* appDelegate =
            [[UIApplication sharedApplication] delegate];
  self.title = appDelegate.trip.destinationName;
  UIImageView* imageView = [[UIImageView alloc]
      initWithImage:[appDelegate.trip destinationImage]];
  self.tableView.backgroundView = imageView;

  UISwipeGestureRecognizer *swipeGesture =
  [[UISwipeGestureRecognizer alloc] initWithTarget:self
                action:@selector(handleSwipeGesture:)];
  swipeGesture.direction =
                UISwipeGestureRecognizerDirectionLeft;
  [self.view addGestureRecognizer:swipeGesture];
}
```

`UISwipeGestureRecognizer` is a subclass of `UIGestureRecognizer` — the abstract base class for concrete gesture-recognizer classes. The gesture recognizer does the hard work of recognizing a specific gesture and then sends an action message (that you specify) to the target (that you also specify) to go ahead and do something.

In addition to `UISwipeGesture`, you have gesture recognizers for

- **Tap:** `UITapGestureRecognizer`
- **Pinch:** `UIPinchGestureRecognizer`
- **Rotate:** `UIRotationGestureRecognizer`
- **Pan:** `UIPanGestureRecognizer`
- **Touch and hold:** `UILongPressGestureRecognizer`

A window delivers touch events to a gesture recognizer before it delivers them to the *hit-tested view* — the view where it determined the user has touched — attached to the gesture recognizer. (Note that the gesture recognizer is attached to the view and isn't part of the responder chain.) Generally, if a gesture recognizer doesn't recognize its gesture, the touches are passed on to the view. If a gesture recognizer does recognize its gesture, the remaining touches for the view are canceled.

UISwipeGestureRecognizer is a concrete subclass of UIGesture Recognizer that looks for swiping gestures in one or more directions. Because a swipe is a discrete gesture, the action message is sent only once per gesture.

UISwipeGestureRecognizer recognizes a gesture as a swipe when the specified number of touches (numberOfTouchesRequired) have moved mostly in an allowable direction (direction) far enough to be considered a swipe. You can configure the UISwipeGestureRecognizer recognizer for the number of touches (the default is 1) and the direction (the default is right), as follows:

```
UISwipeGestureRecognizer *swipeGesture =
  [[UISwipeGestureRecognizer alloc] initWithTarget:self
                      action:@selector(handleSwipeGesture:)];
```

Here, you create a swipe gesture with a target of self and an action of handleSwipeGesture:. This means that when the gesture recognizer determines it is a swipe, it will send the handleSwipeGesture: to the RTMasterViewController (self in this case).

Next, because we want the user to swipe to the left to make the Test Drive view appear, you set the direction to left from the default right, as follows:

```
swipeGesture.direction =
                    UISwipeGestureRecognizerDirectionLeft;
```

To handle the swipe — in effect program the response you want to come up with when the swipe occurs — add the code in Listing 13-2 to RTMasterViewController.m.

Listing 13-2:   Adding handleSwipeGesture to RTMasterViewController.m

```
- (IBAction)handleSwipeGesture:(id)sender {

  UIStoryboard *storyboard =
  [UIStoryboard storyboardWithName:@"MainStoryboard_iPad"
                                     bundle:nil];
  UIViewController *viewController =
    [storyboard instantiateViewControllerWithIdentifier:
                                     @"TestDrive"];
  [[self navigationController]
        pushViewController:viewController animated:YES];
}
```

What you do here is first find the storyboard in the *bundle* — in iOS (and OS X) a bundle is a directory that appears to be a single file and contains the executable code, resources such as images and sound, and the nib (storyboard) files.

```
UIStoryboard *storyboard =
   [UIStoryboard storyboardWithName:
                            @"MainStoryboard_iPad"
            bundle:nil];
```

Then the code in Listing 13-2 creates `TestDriveController`. This is the same thing that the storyboard does (in the segue logic) when you tap the Test Drive button:

```
UIViewController *viewController =
   [storyboard instantiateViewControllerWithIdentifier:
                                @"TestDrive"];
```

Here's where that identifier I nagged you about entering comes in handy. It's the only way you can find the view controller that you've configured in the storyboard.

Next, you tell the Navigation controller to push the View controller onto the stack (note that this method also updates the Navigation bar) and have it slide its view into place. (If the `animated` parameter is `YES`, the view is animated into position; otherwise, the view is simply displayed in place.)

```
[[self navigationController] pushViewController:
                           viewController animated:YES];
```

This is what would've been done for you in the segue logic generated by the storyboard.

While this is all très cool — so cool, in fact, that it's how I implemented the Test Drive view in one of the (many) iterations of this book — it's really not a good idea to do it this way. Navigation like this works best when it allows a user to drill down into a data hierarchy (like albums to songs in the Music app). In that case, the views have a relationship to each other — the next view gives you more detail about what you selected in the previous view. In the case of RoadTrip, however, the Map view for example, is not a more detailed look at the Weather.

Oh, and by the way — you've only installed the Swipe gesture in the Master View controller. When you are in the Test Drive view, you can only go back by using the Back (New York City) button.

So, rather than push view controllers here, there, and everywhere, in the next few sections, you find out how to replace one view controller with another. And the place to start is with the Split View controller.

The Split View Controller

The UISplitViewController class is an iPad-only view controller that simply manages the presentation of two side-by-side view controllers in Landscape orientation — it is, in this respect, a container controller. It has no interface — its job is to coordinate the presentation of its two view controllers and to manage the transitions between different orientations.

Using this class, a view controller is created on the left which is referred to as the *Master view* (and is named that in the template), which presents a list of items, and another view controller on the right, which presents the details, or content, of the selected item and which is referred to as the *Detail view* (and is named that in the template).

After you create and initialize a UISplitViewController object, you assign two view controllers to it by using the viewControllers property — an array that contains the two (and only the two) controllers. The first view controller (index 0) is displayed on the left side (in the case of RoadTrip, the RTMasterViewController), and the second view controller (index 1) is displayed on the right side (the RTDetailViewController).

All of this is set up for you in the storyboard (see Figure 13-9). You'll notice that both of the view controllers managed by the Split View controllers are embedded in Navigation controllers, which is why when you select a cell in the RTMasterViewController view, a Navigation bar appears with a Back button (in either the Master or Detail view).

As you have seen, when the iPad is in Landscape orientation, you can see both view controllers' views side by side. When you rotate to Portrait orientation, however, the RTMasterViewController's view is hidden, and the RTDetailViewController displays a button *in the Navigation bar* that enables you to see the RTDetailViewController's view in a popover. Adding the button is done in the UISplitViewControllerDelegate protocol method. And if you look at the RTDetailViewController interface file, you see it has adopted the protocol — the popover sends its delegate messages at the right time so that the delegate can add and remove the button.

Figure 13-9:
The Master
and Detail
View
controllers
in the
storyboard.

I've made my preferences clear, however. I don't want a Navigation controller and its bar when I select Weather, for example, in RoadTrip. Admittedly, one *could* implement the popover button by placing it on the right side of the Navigation bar, but then you end up with a gaggle of Navigation controllers that really serve no purpose (and whose views have no relation to each other) because I can just as easily navigate to any view I'd like (including the last one) using the Master view.

The way to implement the user interface I want is to use a toolbar instead, and have the Display View controller be responsible for managing the toolbar. In fact, I'll show you how to implement the delegate to use either a toolbar or a Navigation bar when you choose a cell in the RTMasterViewController. I'm doing both because some of the features I want to implement (like the UIPageViewController page transitions in the EventsController) require a Navigation bar. In addition, at some point you may want to implement some functionality where a Navigation controller is the right way to go.

To start with, you'll add a toolbar to the TestDriveController and make TestDriveController a UISplitViewController delegate. But first I want to explain a little more about how the UISplitViewController delegate works.

The UISplitViewController delegate

The UISplitViewController does what you'd expect a class doing delegation to do: It sends its delegate messages at the appropriate times to add and remove the button that enables the user to display the Master View controller in the popover you see in Figure 13-10. The Master button is displayed in Portrait view until the user touches it. Then it is covered by the Master view, which slides in from the left.

If you look at the RTDetailViewController interface (RTDetailView Controller.h) in your project, you can see that this whole delegation business has already been done for you. Listing 13-3 gives the details:

Listing 13-3:   The RTDetailViewController Interface

```
#import <UIKit/UIKit.h>

@interface RTDetailViewController : UIViewController
                         <UISplitViewControllerDelegate>

@property (strong, nonatomic) id detailItem;
@property (strong, nonatomic)
                 IBOutlet UILabel *detailDescriptionLabel;

@end
```

You see that RTDetailViewController adopts the UISplitView ControllerDelegate protocol, and as you see in Figure 13-10, it already adds a button to the Navigation bar when the user moves into Portrait orientation. It also removes the button when the iPad is rotated back from Portrait to Landscape orientation.

All you'll need to do is modify what the UISplitViewControllerDelegate already does and have it place the button in a toolbar or a Navigation bar, depending on what you're using. You'll do all of that in the RTDetail ViewController, and then, if you end up deriving all your view controllers (including the TestDriveController you've already implemented) from RTDetailViewController, voilà, all your view controllers will be able to add a button to the toolbar or a Navigation bar when the iPad is in Landscape orientation, dutifully display the popover when the user selects the button, and then remove the button when the user rotates the iPad to Portrait orientation.

Figure 13-10:
The Road
Trip button
that displays
the Master
view in
Portrait ori-
entation.

To prepare for that occurrence, you'll start by getting rid of the "sample" code that was included by the template to display something in the Detail view — you won't use the Detail View controller to actually display anything; that will be done in the individual view controllers you'll create to display the Road Trip content (the weather, for example, or a map) as well as the Test Drive controller you've already created.

Start by pruning two properties used by the Master View controller that you definitely won't need. Delete the commented out bold, underline, and italic lines in Listing 13-4 in RTDetailViewController.h, and add the code in bold. (You'll add some properties that will be used in managing the popover.)

Listing 13-4:   Update RTDetailViewController.h Interface

```
#import <UIKit/UIKit.h>

@interface RTDetailViewController : UIViewController
                            <UISplitViewControllerDelegate>

//@property (strong, nonatomic) id detailItem;
//@property (strong, nonatomic)
              IBOutlet UILabel *detailDescriptionLabel;

@property (weak, nonatomic) IBOutlet UIToolbar *toolbar;
@property (weak, nonatomic)
                            UIBarButtonItem * popOverButton;
@property (strong, nonatomic)
          UIPopoverController *masterPopoverController;
@end
```

I'll explain these new properties as you use them, but it's worth noting here that you're adding a toolbar as a home for the button the user will use to display the Master View controller in Portrait orientation.

You have more things to prune in the `RTDetailViewController` implementation file. To do that, delete the commented out code in bold, underline, and italic in Listing 13-5 from the `RTDetailViewController.m` implementation file.

Listing 13-5:   Update the RTDetailViewController.m Implementation File

```
#import "RTDetailViewController.h"

//@interface RTDetailViewController ()
//@property (strong, nonatomic)
          UIPopoverController *masterPopoverController;
//- (void)configureView;
//@end

@implementation RTDetailViewController
```

Here you're mostly getting rid of the instance variables you no longer need. In Listing 13-4, you also moved the `masterPopoverController` property to the interface file from where it was to the implementation file. As you'll soon see, you had to do that because the Master View controller will need to access the `masterPopoverController` property in order to dismiss the popover after the user makes a selection in the Master View controller in the popover.

Finally you can delete the methods that display "content" in the Detail view — that means the two methods in bold, underline, and italic in Listing 13-6 in `RTDetailViewController.m`.

Listing 13-6: Delete the Unnecessary Methods

```
#pragma mark - Managing the detail item

- (void)setDetailItem:(id)newDetailItem
{
    if ( detailItem != newDetailItem) {
        detailItem = newDetailItem;

        // Update the view.
        [self configureView];
    }

    if (self.masterPopoverController != nil) {
        [self.masterPopoverController
                        dismissPopoverAnimated:YES];
    }
}

- (void)configureView
{
    // Update the user interface for the detail item.

    if (self.detailItem) {
        self.detailDescriptionLabel.text =
                        [self.detailItem description];
    }
}
```

You'll need to delete the message sent to configure the view. In `Detail ViewController.m`, delete the commented out code in bold, underline, and italic in `viewDidLoad`, as shown in Listing 13-7.

Listing 13-7: Delete the Unnecessary Code in viewDidLoad

```
- (void)viewDidLoad
{
    [super viewDidLoad];
// Do any additional setup after loading the view,
        typically from a nib.
//  [self configureView];
}
```

Now, I look at how the delegate mechanism works and how the button is added when the iPad is rotated from Landscape to Portrait orientation and then removed when it is rotated back. In `RTDetailViewController.m`, the code in this template already does what you need to do to display the kind of popover I just explained. It does so by implementing two `UISplitViewController` delegate methods:

```
splitViewController:willHideViewController:
                withBarButtonItem:forPopoverController:
```

and

```
splitViewController:willShowViewController:
                            invalidatingBarButtonItem:
```

The first of these methods is invoked when the Split View controller rotates from a Landscape to Portrait orientation and hides the Master View controller. When that happens, the Split View controller sends a message to add a button to the Navigation bar (or toolbar) of the Detail View controller. If you look in Listing 13-8, this is how it works in `RTDetailViewController.m`:

Listing 13-8: Adding the Button

```
- (void)splitViewController:
                (UISplitViewController *)splitController
    willHideViewController:
                    (UIViewController *)viewController
    withBarButtonItem:
                        (UIBarButtonItem *)barButtonItem
    forPopoverController:
                (UIPopoverController *)popoverController
{
    barButtonItem.title =
                NSLocalizedString(@"Master", @"Master");
    [self.navigationItem setLeftBarButtonItem:
                            barButtonItem animated:YES];
    self.masterPopoverController = popoverController;
}
```

In this method, you are passed a button that you can use to display the popover. This is no ordinary button, however; its target is a selector implemented for you that can display the popover. The way the app works now, only one view controller displays a popover — but in the final version of the RoadTrip app, all the view controllers will be able to display a popover, so you'll need to pass that button to the view controller that's replacing the current one.

You'll notice the presence of `NSLocalizedString` in Listing 13-9. `NSLocalizedString` is a macro that can be used to *localize* the text you display. And because I let the term *localize* drop here, I might as well explain about localization.

Localization

When you localize an app, you display the text the user sees on the screen in the user's preferred language (and even a language-specific image).

Localizing an application isn't difficult, just tedious. To localize your application, you create a folder in your application bundle (I'll get to that) for each language you want to support. Each folder has the application's translated resources.

For example, if the user's language is Spanish, available regions range from Spain to Argentina to the United States and lots of places in between. When a localized application needs to load a resource (such as an image, property list, or nib), the application checks the user's language and region and looks for a localization folder that corresponds to the selected language and region. If it finds one, it loads the localized version of the resource instead of the *base* version — the one you're working in.

Looking up such values in the table is handled by the NSLocalizedString macro in your code.

As you can see, the text "Master" button will change based on the user's preferred language.

```
barButtonItem.title =
            NSLocalizedString(@"Master", @"Master");
```

The macro has two inputs. The first is the string in your language, and the second is the general comment for the translator. At runtime, NSLocalized String looks for a strings file named localizable.strings in the language that has been set: Spanish, for example. (A user would've done that by going to Settings and selecting General⇨International⇨Language⇨ Español). If NSLocalizedString finds the strings file, it searches the file for a line that matches the first parameter. If the macro doesn't find the file or a specified string, it returns its first parameter — and the string will appear in the base language.

To create the localizable.strings file, you run a command-line program named genstrings, which searches your code files for the macro and places them all in a localizable.strings file (which it creates), ready for the (human) translator. genstrings is beyond the scope of this book, but it's well documented. When you're ready, I leave you to explore it on your own.

Back to the main feature

After absorbing that little localization detour, you then add the longed-for button to the Navigation bar:

```
[self.navigationItem setLeftBarButtonItem:
                        barButtonItem animated:YES];
```

Passing in YES to animated animates the adding of the button. Specifying NO sets the item immediately, without animating the change. In this case, it really makes no difference.

Finally, you save a reference to the popover controller that you'll dismiss when the user makes a selection:

```
self.masterPopoverController = popoverController;
```

As I said, when the user selects a new view in the popover, you'll need to pass this button on to the new view controller so it can display it as well. (You'll do that later in this chapter in a method called prepareForSegue: in Listing 13-16.) In addition, as I explained, you'll also use toolbars in addition to Navigation bars to display the button; adding the button to a toolbar is done differently than adding it to the Navigation bar. To do that, enter the code in bold in Listing 13-9 and delete the bold, underline, and italic code in RTDetailViewController.m.

Listing 13-9: **Extending the splitViewController: willHideViewController: withBarButtonItem:forPopoverController:**

```
- (void)splitViewController:
                (UISplitViewController *)splitController
    willHideViewController:
                (UIViewController *)viewController
    withBarButtonItem:
                (UIBarButtonItem *)barButtonItem
    forPopoverController:
                (UIPopoverController *)popoverController
{
// barButtonItem.title = NSLocalizedString(@"Master",
        @"Master");
  barButtonItem.title =
        NSLocalizedString(@"Road Trip", @"Road Trip");
  if ([[self.splitViewController.viewControllers
        lastObject] isKindOfClass:[UINavigationControl
        ler class]])
    [self.navigationItem
        setLeftBarButtonItem:barButtonItem animated:YES];
  else {
    NSMutableArray *itemsArray =
                [self.toolbar.items mutableCopy];
    [itemsArray insertObject:barButtonItem atIndex:0];
    [self.toolbar setItems:itemsArray animated:YES];
  }
  self.masterPopoverController = popoverController;
  self.popOverButton = barButtonItem;
}
```

Listing 13-9 starts off by changing the title of the button from *Master* to *Road Trip* — I think it's less ominous sounding and more descriptive — indicating the view controller that you'd see if you tap the button:

```
//barButtonItem.title =
                NSLocalizedString(@"Master", @"Master");
  barButtonItem.title =
            NSLocalizedString(@"Road trip", @"Road Trip");
```

You then check to see whether you're dealing with a Navigation bar or toolbar.

```
  if ([[[self.splitViewController.viewControllers
        lastObject] isKindOfClass:[UINavigationControl
        ler class]])
```

As I mention earlier, the Split View controller manages two view controllers, with the last one in its list of controllers corresponding to what's displayed in the Detail view. You check if the Detail View controller is embedded in a Navigation controller by sending it the isKindOfClass: message. This method returns a Boolean indicating whether it is, in this case, a UINavigationController.

As you know, classes in Objective-C are first-class objects in and of themselves, so you can use a class method to determine what class something is. This method is defined in the NSObject class, from which all your classes are (ultimately) derived.

If you're dealing with a Navigation controller, you do what you've already been doing and set the left bar button.

```
[self.navigationItem
        setLeftBarButtonItem:barButtonItem animated:YES];
```

If you're not dealing with a Navigation controller, you go through some similar logic to add the button to the toolbar.

```
NSMutableArray *itemsArray =
                        [self.toolbar.items mutableCopy];
[itemsArray insertObject:barButtonItem atIndex:0];
[self.toolbar setItems:itemsArray animated:NO];
```

On a toolbar, the buttons are specified in the items property as an array. So you make a copy of the array and add the button you're passed to the top of the array. The items — instances of UIBarButtonItem — are shown on the toolbar in the order they appear in this array. You then take that array and assign it as the items property.

You'll notice that you first make a copy of the toolbar items, insert the button, and then assign the items property. You do it this way because (as you'll see in Chapter 16) there may be other buttons on the toolbar that you'll want to keep there.

Then you save a reference to the button that you'll use later.

```
self.popOverButton = barButtonItem;
```

The second of the delegate methods is invoked when the view controller rotates from Portrait to Landscape orientation and the "hidden" Master View controller is displayed.

When the iPad is rotated back to Landscape orientation, the `splitViewCo ntroller:willShowViewController:invalidatingBarButtonItem:` message is sent.

If you added the button to your toolbar to allow the user to display the Master View controller in a popover, you remove the button in the `splitVi ewController:willShowViewController:invalidatingBarButtonI tem:` method. Listing 13-10 shows how `splitViewController:will ShowViewController:invalidatingBarButtonItem:` is currently implemented in `DetailViewController.m:`.

Listing 13-10:   **splitViewController:willShowViewController: invalidatingBarButtonItem:**

```
- (void)splitViewController:
                (UISplitViewController *)splitController
        willShowViewController:
                (UIViewController *)viewController
        invalidatingBarButtonItem:
                (UIBarButtonItem *)barButtonItem
{
 // Called when the view is shown again in the split view,
        invalidating the button and popover controller.
    [self.navigationItem
            setLeftBarButtonItem:nil animated:YES];
    self.masterPopoverController = nil;
}
```

This method as implemented sets the `leftBarButtonItem` and the `master PopoverController` (the reference to the popover controller) to `nil`.

Here you've simply reversed what you did earlier — you've removed the button from the toolbar and set the `self.popoverController` property to `nil`.

As with the `splitViewController:willHideViewController:withBa rButtonItem: forPopoverController:` method, you'll now have to deal with both a toolbar and a Navigation controller. So add the code in bold in Listing 13-11 to `splitViewController:willShowViewController:inva lidatingBarButtonItem:` in `DetailViewController.m`.

Listing 13-11:   Update splitViewController:willShowViewController: invalidatingBarButtonItem:

```
- (void)splitViewController:
                (UISplitViewController *)splitController
        willShowViewController:
                (UIViewController *)viewController
        invalidatingBarButtonItem:
                        (UIBarButtonItem *)barButtonItem
{
  if
   ([[self.splitViewController.viewControllers lastObject]
        isKindOfClass:[UINavigationController class]])
    [self.navigationItem setLeftBarButtonItem:nil
                                      animated:YES];
  else {
    NSMutableArray *itemsArray =
                        [self.toolbar.items mutableCopy];
    [itemsArray removeObject:barButtonItem];
    [self.toolbar setItems:itemsArray animated:YES];
  }
  self.popOverButton = nil;
  self.masterPopoverController = nil;
}
```

The logic here determines whether it's a Navigation controller or a toolbar, with managing the toolbar identical to what you did in Listing 13-9, when you extended the `splitViewController:willHideViewController:` with `BarButtonItem:forPopoverController:` method.

While you have the button saved, you still need to transfer the button — and have it displayed — when the user taps the Road Trip button and selects an entry (Weather, for example) that results in a new view controller being instantiated to display its view.

The display part will be done in the `viewDidLoad` method of the new controller.

Currently, the `viewDidLoad` method does nothing but send its superclass the same `viewDidLoad` message (you removed the `configureView` message in Listing 13-7).

```
- (void)viewDidLoad
{
    [super viewDidLoad];
// Do any additional setup after loading the view,
        typically from a nib.
}
```

Add the code in bold in Listing 13-12 to `viewDidLoad` in `RTDetailViewController.m`.

Listing 13-12:   Update viewDidLoad

```
- (void)viewDidLoad
{
  [super viewDidLoad];

  if (self.popOverButton) {
 if ([[self.splitViewController.viewControllers
                                   lastObject]
       isKindOfClass:[UINavigationController class]]) {
     [self.navigationItem setLeftBarButtonItem:self.
        popOverButton
                                     animated:YES];
    }
    else {
      NSMutableArray *itemsArray =
                        [self.toolbar.items mutableCopy];
      [itemsArray
             insertObject:self.popOverButton atIndex:0];
      [self.toolbar setItems:itemsArray animated:NO];
    }
  }
}
```

When the view is loaded, it's checked to see whether it contains a popover button. If it does, it simply uses the same logic you see in splitView Controller: willHideViewController:withBarButtonItem:for PopoverController: (Listing 13-9) using the button that you saved in spl itViewController:willHideViewController: withBarButtonItem :forPopoverController: in the popOverButton property.

Finally, you can add what you've done to the TestDriveController. Update the TestDriveController.h interface to make the TestDrive Controller a subclass of the RTDetailViewController by deleting the commented out bold, underline, and italic code and adding the bolded code in Listing 13-13.

Listing 13-13:   Update the TestDriveController.h Interface

```
#import <UIKit/UIKit.h>
#import "RTDetailViewController.h"

//@interface TestDriveController : UIViewController
@interface TestDriveController : RTDetailViewController

@end
```

Adding the Toolbar

Finally, to eliminate the Navigation controller in the Detail view and set it up so that you always see the button to display the Master view in a popover (Road Trip in this case), you'll need to add the toolbar to the `Test Drive controller` in the storyboard and create an outlet to the toolbar. The outlet is needed to be able to add and remove the Road Trip button (and other buttons you'll add along the way, in Chapter 16 for example).

Follow these steps to add the toolbar that supports the RoadTrip button (needed by the popover) to the Test Drive controller.

1. **In the Project navigator, select MainStoryboard_iPad, and in the View selector, display the Utility area.**

2. **Select the segue from the Master View controller (it is really from the Table View cell but you can't see that) to the Test Drive controller in the Canvas to display it in the Attributes inspector.**

   Optionally, you could select Push Segue from Table View Cell to TestDrive in the Master View Controller – Master Scene in the Document Outline.

   If the Attributes inspector isn't visible, select its icon in the Inspector selector.

3. **In the Attributes inspector, choose Replace from the Style drop-down menu, choose Detail Split from the Destination drop-down menu, and enter** TestDrive **in the Identifier field, as I have in Figure 13-11.**

   You'll notice that doing so resizes the view so it can display in the Detail view. That means Test Drive will no longer be displayed in the Master view. If you really want Test Drive to still display in the Master view, you can take that on as your personal exercise.

4. **In the Document Outline (or in the Canvas — as you can see you can use either) select the SeeTheUSA Image View in Test Drive Controller – TestDrive Scene.**

5. **In the Size inspector that appears, set the origin of the Image view to x = 0, y = 44 and the height to 704 to make room for the toolbar, as I have in Figure 13-12.**

6. **Drag in a toolbar from the Library in the Utility area and delete the Item button (it's included in the toolbar by default), as I have in Figure 13-13.**

   In the Library, the toolbar item is way down at the bottom of the gallery. Don't confuse the toolbar item with a Navigation bar.

Figure 13-11:
Update the segue.

Figure 13-12:
Make room for the toolbar.

Figure 13-13:
The new
toolbar.

Keep in mind that you'll also have to adjust the Sizing inspector's Autosizing parameters. Right now, the toolbar is configured based on the iPhone, where the toolbar is on the bottom. (While that may seem odd, the iPhone was the first kid on the block and toolbars on the iPhone were originally only on the bottom.)

7. **To keep the toolbar on top of the screen, click the bottom center strut in the inspector's Autosizing section to disable it, and click the top strut to enable it. (Again, Figure 13-13 shows you what I mean.)**

We're getting there, but now you'll need to connect the toolbar to the outlet in the `RTDetailViewController` base class.

8. **Select the Test Drive controller in the Document Outline and open the Connections inspector.**

You'd open the Connections inspector as you'd open any inspector: by clicking its icon in the Inspector selector.

9. **In the Connections inspector, drag from the Toolbar outlet to the toolbar proper, as I have in Figure 13-14.**

You may remember that you added the Toolbar outlet to the `RTDetailViewController` base class in Listing 13-4.

Figure 13-14:
Set the
toolbar
outlet.

Because you deleted the `RTDetailViewController`'s `detailDescription Label` outlet in Listing 13-4, you'll have to delete it in the storyboard as well. (If you don't, you get a runtime error that I explain in Chapter 15. Just Control-click the Detail View controller entry in the Document Outline to open the Connections window, as I have in Figure 13-15. You'll see a yellow warning triangle next to the `detailDescriptionLabel` line in the Outlets section of the window. Simply delete that outlet by clicking the x in front of the `Label - Detail view content goes here` line. (I explain this more in Chapter 15.)

Because you've added the toolbar, you'll have to change the math controlling the route your car takes in the `TestDriveController`.

Update the `TestDriveController`'s `testDrive:` method in `TestDriveController.m` with the code in bold in Listing 13-14.

Figure 13-15:
An unused
outlet.

Listing 13-14: Take the Toolbar into Account

```
- (IBAction)testDrive:(id)sender {

  AudioServicesPlaySystemSound(burnRubberSoundID);
  [self performSelector:@selector(playCarSound)
                          withObject:self afterDelay:.2];

  CGPoint center = CGPointMake(car.center.x, self.view.
          frame.origin.y + car.frame.size.height/2 +
          self.toolbar.frame.size.height);

  void (^animation)() = ^(){

    car.center = center;
  };

  void (^completion)(BOOL) = ^(BOOL finished){
    [self rotate];
  };

  [UIView animateWithDuration:3 animations:animation
                          completion:completion];

}
```

Adding the button when the view controller is replaced

While all of this gets you close to wrapping up the whole toolbar business, you still need to do one more important thing — and a couple of minor things. The first of these — the important one — I cover in this section. Because you're replacing the view controller with a new one — albeit one from the same base class — the new view controller has no access to the button it needs to display or the popover it needs to dismiss. Fortunately, the folks at Apple provide a perfect place to do that.

When a segue is triggered — which you do when you tap a Table entry — but before the new controller slides its view into place, the storyboard runtime calls the current view controller's method so that it can pass data to the view controller that's about to be displayed. That means that you can pass the button information on to the new view controller before it even gets launched. Then, prepareForSegue:sender:, the method you override in Listing 13-15, will both assign the button to be used in viewDidLoad (Listing 13-12) and (if necessary) dismiss the view controller as well.

prepareForSegue:sender: is a view controller method that notifies a view controller that a segue is about to be performed. segue is the UIStory boardSegue object, and it contains information about the view controllers involved in the segue.

While default implementation of this method does nothing, UIView Controller subclasses can override it and pass data to the view controller that's about to be displayed. The segue object has properties that point to the source view controller as well as the destination view controller (among other information).

sender is the object that caused the segue, but you won't need to use it here.

You add the code to the prepareForSegue:sender: method to make the DestinationController the UISplitViewController delegate and assign the popOverButton and masterPopoverController properties.

You'll also dismiss the popover when it's present so the user doesn't have to touch in the view to get rid of it.

To do all that, add the code in Listing 13-15 to RTMasterViewController.m.

Listing 13-15:   Overriding prepareForSegue:sender:

```
- (void)prepareForSegue:
             (UIStoryboardSegue *)segue sender:(id)sender {

  if ([[UIDevice currentDevice] userInterfaceIdiom] ==
                                UIUserInterfaceIdiomPad) {
    RTDetailViewController *currentDetailViewController;
    if ([[self.splitViewController.viewControllers
                                   lastObject] isKi
          ndOfClass:[UINavigationController class]])
      currentDetailViewController =
        (RTDetailViewController *)
          ((UINavigationController *)
            [self.splitViewController.viewControllers
                         lastObject]).topViewController;
    else
      currentDetailViewController = [self.
          splitViewController.viewControllers
                                    lastObject];
    if(currentDetailViewController.masterPopoverController
                                              != nil)
      [currentDetailViewController.masterPopoverController
                          dismissPopoverAnimated:YES];

    RTDetailViewController
                    *destinationDetailViewController;

    if ([segue.destinationViewController isKindOfClass:[UI
          NavigationController class]])
      destinationDetailViewController =
        (RTDetailViewController *)
          ((UINavigationController *)
        segue.destinationViewController).topViewController;
    else
      destinationDetailViewController =
                       segue.destinationViewController;
    self.splitViewController.delegate =
                       destinationDetailViewController;
    destinationDetailViewController.popOverButton =
            currentDetailViewController.popOverButton;
    destinationDetailViewController.
                            masterPopoverController =
    currentDetailViewController.masterPopoverController;
  }
}
```

You start by finding the current Detail View controller because it has the button and popover properties the new view controller needs.

This code appears more complicated than it is. You use the very same logic you used earlier (say, in Listing 13-8) to decide whether you're faced with a Navigation bar or toolbar. That means I first check to see whether I'm running on an iPad. If I am, I get the current Detail View controller by accessing the list of view controllers in the splitViewController's viewController array. Fortunately, the UIViewController class has a splitView Controller property to make that easy for me.

I then check to see whether a Navigation controller is in the view Controllers array and, if one is there, I get the Navigation controller's topViewController (the current view controller); if not, I simply use the controller in the array. (You'll notice a whole lot of casting going on here; I leave it to you to work your way through it.)

```
if ([[self.splitViewController.viewControllers lastObject]
        isKindOfClass:[UINavigationController class]])
    currentDetailViewController =
    (RTDetailViewController *)((UINavigationController *)
            [self.splitViewController.viewControllers
                        lastObject]).topViewController;
    else
        currentDetailViewController = [self.
            splitViewController.viewControllers
                                    lastObject];
```

Next, if I see a popover, I want to dismiss it. I check to see whether a popover controller (that's why you had to make the masterPopoverController property accessible by moving it into the header file in Listing 13-4) is currently there, and if I see one, I dismiss it.

```
if (currentDetailViewController.masterPopoverController
                                            != nil)
    [currentDetailViewController.masterPopoverController
                        dismissPopoverAnimated:YES];
```

Next, I find the new destination controller (the one being transitioned to) using logic similar to the logic I used to find the current Detail View controller.

```
if ([segue.destinationViewController isKindOfClass:[UINavi
        gationController class]])
destinationDetailViewController =
    (RTDetailViewController *)((UINavigationController *)
        segue.destinationViewController).topViewController;
else
    destinationDetailViewController =
                            segue.destinationViewController;
```

Then I simply set the Split View Controller delegate to the new view controller, so it will get the `splitViewController:willHideViewController:withBarButtonItem:forPopoverController:` and `splitViewController:willShowViewController:invalidatingBarButtonItem:` messages.

```
self.splitViewController.delegate =
                        destinationDetailViewController;
```

Finally, I assign the `popOverButton` and `masterPopoverController` properties in the new view controller.

```
destinationDetailViewController.popOverButton =
          currentDetailViewController.popOverButton;
destinationDetailViewController.masterPopoverController =
      currentDetailViewController.masterPopoverController;
```

Admittedly, this just dismisses the popover and assigns the properties, but doesn't do anything to display the button. That actually gets done in `viewDidLoad` — which you added earlier in Listing 13-12.

You also can specify the size of the popover window by assigning a value to the `contentSizeForViewInPopover` property. You should be aware that the actual size may be reduced so that the popover fits on the screen and that the popover does not overlap a keyboard when a keyboard is presented. You can see the code that does that in the `RTMasterViewController`'s `awakeFromNib` method.

```
- (void)awakeFromNib
{
  if ([[UIDevice currentDevice] userInterfaceIdiom] ==
                              UIUserInterfaceIdiomPad) {
    self.clearsSelectionOnViewWillAppear = NO;
    self.contentSizeForViewInPopover =
                          CGSizeMake(320.0, 600.0);
  }
    [super awakeFromNib];
}
```

The `awakeFromNib` message is sent to an object that has been instantiated from the storyboard after all the objects have been loaded and initialized. When the message is sent, all its outlet and action connections have been set.

If you decide to ignore the advice in this section and don't dismiss the popover controller, taps outside the popover window will cause the popover to be dismissed. You can, however, allow the user to interact with the specified views and not dismiss the popover, using the `passthroughViews` property (although you won't be doing that here). You'd then have to dismiss the popover yourself.

A Few More Tweaks to the RTMasterViewController

You're almost, but not quite, done. Right now, when you make a selection in the Table view, it stays highlighted. To fix that, you'll need to implement a Table view method `tableView:didSelectRowAtIndexPath:`. Add the method in Listing 13-16 to `RTMasterViewController.m` to unhighlight a selected cell.

Listing 13-16:   Deselect the Cell

```
- (void)tableView:(UITableView *)tableView
        didSelectRowAtIndexPath:(NSIndexPath *)indexPath   {

    [tableView deselectRowAtIndexPath:indexPath
                                        animated:YES];
}
```

This is a Table View Delegate method that is invoked when the user selects a cell. Normally, you'd launch a view controller here or do something else. (I explain more about this method and other Table View Delegate and Data Source methods in Chapter 20.) But because you're using a segue, the only thing you need to do is deselect the cell that was tapped, which will remove the highlight.

A partner in crime here is the `self.clearsSelectionOnViewWillAppear = NO;` statement you see in the `RTMasterViewController`'s `awakeFromNib` method I mention in the previous section. If that were set to `YES`, a highlighted selection wouldn't stay highlighted when a view appeared. I have you deselect it here so you begin to get a feel of how things are connected in a Table view — and that I explain in detail in Chapter 20.

And (a Little Extra) One More Thing

While tapping the Test Drive cell now replaces the Detail View controller with the Test Drive controller, the gesture recognizer still works. The only problem with it is that now you have both a Navigation bar and a toolbar.

To fix that, you'll need to duplicate the Test Drive controller in the storyboard (select it and then choose Edit⇨Duplicate from the main menu) and give it a different identifier (`TestDriveNavigation`, for example). Remove the toolbar and change the image view origin and size in the Size inspector back to where it was when you started this Chapter (origin of x = 0, y = 0, and height of 1004 — the change in height has to do with the fact that this is now just a view controller without any segues that influence the size). Then change `handleSwipeGesture` in Listing 13-2 to instantiate the new view controller in `RTMasterViewController.m`.

Delete

```
UIViewController *viewController =
    [storyboard instantiateViewControllerWithIdentifier:
                                      @"TestDrive"];
```

and replace it with

```
UIViewController *viewController =
    [storyboard instantiateViewControllerWithIdentifier:
                               @"TestDriveNavigation"];
```

You should also add the following to `TestDriveController` to keep the popover the right size in Portrait orientation:

```
- (void)awakeFromNib
{
  if ([[UIDevice currentDevice] userInterfaceIdiom] ==
                         UIUserInterfaceIdiomPad) {
    self.contentSizeForViewInPopover =
                         CGSizeMake(320.0, 600.0);
  }
  [super awakeFromNib];
}
```

Well, that concludes your long and winding tour of Split View controllers. While it may have been a bit arduous, at this point you have a firm understanding of how Split views and popovers work together — one that you can apply to whatever you want to do in your own app.

Before you do that, however, you'll want to complete the storyboard so you can start adding features and functionality to RoadTrip (besides the Test Drive functionality). You'll also want to change the Detail view that appears when you launch the RoadTrip application.

Don't Forget the iPhone

This chapter was primarily about how to handle the Split View controller used in the iPad user interface. The iPhone doesn't use a Split view, but it does use the `TestDriveController`. In the last section of this chapter, you added another `TestDriveController` scene to the iPad storyboard with a `TestDriveNaviagtion` identifier. This second scene does not need a toolbar, because it is launched with a swipe gesture.

Well, you need that same "toolbarless" scene for using swipe gestures on the iPhone. In fact, the `handleSwipeGesture:` method shown in Listing 13-2 still works fine on the iPhone, so you don't have to do any extra work. It's a bit odd, because it uses part of the iPad storyboard on the iPhone, but it works.

Chapter 14

Finishing the Basic Application Structure

In This Chapter

▶ Laying out the basic application structure in the storyboard

▶ Adding and formatting the rest of the view controllers for the RoadTrip app

▶ Creating the segues

▶ Adding a gesture recognizer to the Content controller

*I*n earlier chapters, I've waxed poetic about storyboards but I haven't really (completely) shown you why I find them so appealing. Now it's time for you to experience the reason yourself.

As I say earlier in the book, the storyboard is basically about working with view controllers. Normally, I would lay out the basic application flow at the very beginning of a project, but I deferred doing it until now when you have enough background so that it makes sense.

In this chapter, I show you how to extend your storyboard to lay out the flow, or the *user experience architecture,* of most of your application — or at least the big pieces of the app, such as the structure for the user to find out the weather forecast for the destination, find events that are happening at the destination, bring up a map, and find a location on a map.

I'll start by explaining the Weather view controller and then have you move on to complete most of the rest of the view controllers.

I'll also have you replace the Detail View controller that's now displayed at application launch with the Weather controller.

Extending the iPad Storyboard to Add More Functionality to Your App

You start the day's work by selecting MainStoryboard_iPad in the Project navigator and showing the Utility area by selecting its icon in the Xcode toolbar's View selector. Next, hide the Project navigator by deselecting it in the Xcode toolbar's View selector (remember, as I explain in Chapter 2, it's a toggle). Doing so gives you a little more real estate onscreen. (If you have an extra-large monitor, though, you can keep the Project navigator open.)

Continuing with your prep work, go ahead and select the Attributes inspector in the Inspector selector bar in the Utility area. Close all the disclosure triangles in the Document Outline to give you a little more room to work in.

Adding the Weather view controller

Here's where the rubber meets the road. To add the Weather view controller — complete with a web view for displaying the weather — you need to do the following:

1. **Select Objects in the Utility area's Library pane and then select a view controller from the pane and drag it onto your storyboard (see Figure 14-1).**

   A new scene is created. (If you're a bit hazy on how storyboards work, check out Chapter 5.)

2. **Select the new view controller on the storyboard.**

   Doing so reveals its attributes in the (already opened) Attributes inspector.

3. **In the View Controller section of the Attributes inspector, enter** Weather **in the Title field, as shown in Figure 14-2. Also enter** Weather **in the Storyboard ID field in the Identity inspector.**

   Be sure to press Return when entering text in a text field in the Attributes inspector.

   The field in the storyboard isn't updated until you press Return, or sometimes until you click in another field *in that inspector.*

   Adding an identifier isn't a requirement, but it's a good habit to get into. For example, you used an identifier in the handleSwipeGesture: method in Chapter 13, and you'll need the Weather identifier in prepare ForSegue later in this book to pass some data to the Destination Controller. As for the Title field, giving anything a title always makes it easier to figure out what's what in the storyboard.

Figure 14-1:
Drag in a
view
controller.

Figure 14-2:
Set the title
and
identifier.

4. **Drag a toolbar from the Utility area's Library pane and position it at the top of the view.**

5. **Delete the Item button (the button that comes by default with the toolbar when you drag it in from the Library) and, after opening the Size inspector by clicking its icon in the Inspector selector, set Autosizing to be a fixed indent from the top and variable from the bottom by selecting (the top strut) and deselecting (the bottom strut) the appropriate struts, as shown in Figure 14-3.**

   You did the very same thing for the toolbar you added to the `TestDriveController` in Chapter 13.

6. **Select the Weather cell in the Master View controller (it's there under the Table View heading) and Control-drag from there to View Controller – Weather, as shown in Figure 14-4.**

   I find doing this from the Document Outline is easier.

Figure 14-3:
The
Autoresizing
settings.

7. **Select Replace from the Selection Segue pop-up menu that appears, as shown in Figure 14-5.**

   As I explain in Chapter 5, you use a segue whenever you want to create a transition from one view controller to another. A segue performs the visual transition between two view controllers and supports push (navigation), modal, and custom transitions. All you have to do (as you just saw) is Control-drag from a button or Table View cell to the view controller you want to be displayed.

   A *push segue* causes the new view controller (with a Back button) to slide into place when the user taps a button; the Navigation bar items are updated appropriately. (See Chapter 5 for more about adding a Navigation controller.)

   In contrast to a push segue, a *modal segue* presents the view controller modally, with the transition style you specify, and requires the user to do something (tap Save or Cancel, for example) to get back to the previous view controller. (This requirement that the user *do* something is the modal part of a modal segue.) Segues support the standard visual transition styles, such as Cover Vertical, Flip Horizontal, Cross Dissolve, and Partial Curl.

In addition, segue objects are used to prepare for the transition from one view controller to another. Segue objects contain information about the view controllers involved in a transition. When a segue is triggered, but before the visual transition occurs, the storyboard runtime calls the current view controller's `prepareForSegue:sender:` method so that it can pass any needed data to the view controller that's about to be displayed.

A Replace segue causes the existing view controller to be replaced by a new one.

You'll notice that the view resizes itself. It defaults to a Destination that's the same as the originating view. You'll need to fix that. (The Destination here is the Master view.)

8. **Select the segue on the storyboard Canvas or in the Document Outline and, back in the Attributes inspector, make sure that *Replace* appears in the Style menu in the Attribute inspector; then enter** Weather **in the Identifier field and press Return.**

   Again, you won't always use the identifier, but it's good practice to name it so that you can identify it, as shown in Figure 14-6.

Figure 14-5:
Creating a Replace segue.

Figure 14-6:
Setting the Replace style for the Weather storyboard segue.

9. **Still in the Attributes inspector, choose Detail Split from the Destination drop-down menu, as I have in Figure 14-7.**

Notice that the segue is selected in the Document Outline as well as on the Canvas (it turns from grey to white), and the view controller has resized its view.

10. **Select the Table View cell containing the Weather label in either the Canvas or the Document Outline and, in the Attributes inspector's Accessory field, make sure that the Disclosure Indicator has been set to None.**

In the rest of this section, I show you how to add the rest of the scenes you need in your storyboard for the RoadTrip app. Some other view controllers in the storyboard aren't launched by segues, and you'll add those as needed.

Adding the Events controller

The next view controller I have you add is the Events controller, which will display events that you might be interested in at your destination. Interestingly enough, as you'll find in Chapter 16, for the Events controller to work properly, you'll need to have it embedded in a Navigation controller. Fortunately, you have that covered because the work you did in Chapter 13 enables you to handle either a Navigation controller or a toolbar in the Detail View controller's `UISplitViewControllerDelegate` delegate methods.

Figure 14-7:
Setting the
destination.

To add an Events controller, do the following:

1. **Select a new view controller from the Objects section of the Library pane and drag it onto your storyboard.**

2. **In the Attributes inspector, enter** Events **in the view controller's Title field, as well as in the Identity inspector's Storyboard ID field.**

3. **Choose Editor⇨Embed In⇨Navigation Controller from the main menu, as shown in Figure 14-8.**

   A navigation controller scene is added to your storyboard, along with something called a *Relationship* from UINavigationController to View Controller.

4. **Select the Navigation controller in the canvas, and in the Attributes inspector, enter** EventsNavigation **in the Title field as well as in the Identity inspector's Storyboard ID field for the Navigation controller so you can find it for the next step.**

   You can see in Figure 14-9 that, in the Document Outline and on the Canvas, the Navigation controller is now identified as EventsNavigation.

   Now you'll want to create a segue from the Events cell to the Navigation controller.

Figure 14-8:
Embedding the Events controller in a Navigation controller.

Figure 14-9:
Naming the Navigation controller.

5. **In the Document Outline, select the Events cell in the Master View controller (it's there under the TableView Section – At My Destination under the Table View heading) and Control-drag to the Navigation controller you just added — the one in which you embedded the Events controller and named in Step 4.**

You can see all the action in Figure 14-10.

I find it is easier to do this from the Document Outline.

6. **Select Replace from the Storyboard Segues pop-up menu that appears.**

7. **Select the segue on the Canvas and, in the Attributes inspector, enter** Events **in the Identifier field and choose Detail Split from the Destination drop-down menu.**

Your storyboard should look like Figure 14-11 when you're done. Figure 14-11 also shows the segue you created in the Attributes inspector.

8. **Select the Events Table View cell, and in the Attributes inspector's Accessory field, make sure the Disclosure Indicator has been set to None (just because I like it better without one, as I explain in Chapter 5).**

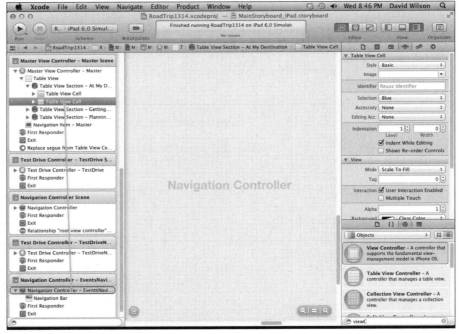

Figure 14-10: Drag from the Events cell to the Navigation controller within which the Events controller is embedded.

Figure 14-11:
The story-
board thus
far with a
Weather
controller,
an Events
control-
ler, and a
Navigation
controller.

Adding the remaining controllers

The remaining controllers will be added in pretty much the same way, with a
little twist when it comes to the Destination controller.

1. **Repeat the steps that you went through when you added the Weather
   controller to the storyboard in the earlier section "Adding the
   Weather view controller" to add the Map controller. Be sure to enter**
   Map **in the view controller's Title and Identifier fields. Enter** Map **in
   the segue Identifier as well.**

2. **Add the Find controller by repeating Steps 1–5 you followed to
   add the Weather controller to the storyboard in the earlier section
   "Adding the Weather view controller." Enter** Find **in the view
   controller's Title and Identifier fields, respectively.**

   You won't be using a segue for the Find controller. I'll show you a
   different way to launch a view controller in Chapter 20.

3. Add the Destination controller by repeating Steps 1, 2, 3, 6, 7, 8, 9, and 10 (don't add a toolbar) that you followed when adding the Weather controller to the storyboard in the earlier section "Adding the Weather view controller." Enter Destination in the view controller's Title and Identifier fields, respectively.

4. For the Destination controller, in Step 7, create a segue but make it modal. Select the segue and, in the Attributes inspector, enter Destination in the Identifier field and choose Presentation Form Sheet from the Presentation pop-up menu.

I explain this bit of business in Chapter 20.

Changing the Split View Controller to a Detail View Controller Relationship

At this point, because it really doesn't do anything, you can delete the `Detail View controller` object from the iPad storyboard (but be sure not to delete the RTDetailView controller class files in the Project navigator). You'll replace the relationship between the Split View controller and the `Detail View` controller with one to the Weather controller. I chose Weather controller arbitrarily here — you could just as easily have replaced it with any of the other view controllers. This is the Detail view the user will see when the application is launched.

The following steps show you how to replace the Detail View controller.

1. In the Document Outline, select the Navigation controller associated with the Detail View controller (see Figure 14-12) and press Delete.

2. Select the Detail View controller in the Document Outline (see Figure 14-13) and press Delete as well.

   You'll need to create a new relationship between the Split View controller and the Weather controller.

3. Select the Split View controller on the storyboard, Control-drag to the Weather controller and then select Relationship – Detail View Controller from the pop-up menu that appears (as I have in Figure 14-14).

   The final result of what has been added to the storyboard so far should look like Figure 14-15. I've rearranged things a bit for the sake of clarity.

Figure 14-12:
Select the Navigation controller in the Document Outline.

Figure 14-13:
Select the Detail View controller in the Document Outline.

Figure 14-14:
A new
Detail View
controller
relationship.

Figure 14-15:
The nearly
complete
storyboard.

You're also going to have to make some changes in `application:did FinishLaunchingWithOptions:`. Add the code in bold shown in Listing 14-1 to that method in `RTAppDelegate.m`.

Listing 14-1:   Updating application:didFinishLaunchingWithOptions:

```
- (BOOL)application:(UIApplication *)application
      didFinishLaunchingWithOptions:
                         (NSDictionary *)launchOptions
{
  UINavigationController *navigationController;
  if ([[UIDevice currentDevice] userInterfaceIdiom] ==
         UIUserInterfaceIdiomPad) {
    UISplitViewController *splitViewController =
         (UISplitViewController *)self.window.
         rootViewController;
    splitViewController.presentsWithGesture = NO;
    if ([splitViewController.viewControllers[1]
         isKindOfClass:[UINavigationController class]]) {
      UINavigationController *detailNavigationController =
         [splitViewController.viewControllers
                                    lastObject];
      splitViewController.delegate =
         (id)detailNavigationController.topViewController;
    }
    else
      splitViewController.delegate =
         [splitViewController.viewControllers lastObject];
    navigationController =
    splitViewController.viewControllers[0];
  }
  else {
    navigationController = (UINavigationController *)
                         self.window.rootViewController;

  }
... the rest of the method
}
```

The change you make here is in how you get the Detail View controller that you will assign as the Split View controller delegate.

As I mention earlier, the Split View controller manages two view controllers, with the last one in its list of controllers corresponding to what's displayed in the Detail view. You check the last view controller to see whether it's a Navigation controller (that contains the Detail View controller) by sending it the `isKindOfClass:` message. This method returns a Boolean indicating whether it is a `UINavigationController`.

```
    if ([splitViewController.viewControllers[1]
        isKindOfClass:[UINavigationController class]]) {
      UINavigationController *detailNavigationController =
        [splitViewController.viewControllers lastObject];
      splitViewController.delegate =
        (id)detailNavigationController.topViewController;
    }
```

If it is a Navigation controller, you need to find its view controller (it's the one that has adopted the `SplitViewControllerDelegate` protocol, implemented the protocol methods, and can become the Split View controller's delegate), which you get by accessing the Navigation controller's `top VewController` property. (It points to the first and only view controller on its stack.) Then you'll assign it as the delegate.

If it's a view controller, rather than a Navigation controller (which it will be because you just made the Weather controller the Detail View controller, and it has no Navigation controller), you just assign that view controller as the delegate.

```
else
  splitViewController.delegate =
      [splitViewController.viewControllers lastObject];
```

If you build and run your project now, it looks like you've taken a step backward; all you'll see is a blank screen — in Portrait orientation no less (unless you've kept the Test Drive controller as the initial Detail View controller). You'll fix that in the next chapter.

Repeat for iPhone

You now need to update the iPhone storyboard file with the same kind of view controllers you just added to the iPad storyboard file. They are as follows:

- ✔ `WeatherController` with a Push segue (instead of the iPad's Replace segue)
- ✔ `EventsController` with a Push segue (instead of the iPad's Replace segue)
- ✔ `MapController` with a Push segue (instead of the iPad's Replace segue)
- ✔ `FindController`
- ✔ `DestinationController` with a Modal segue

The iPhone storyboard uses Push segues because you are pushing a new view controller onto the stack when the user touches a cell such as "Weather" in the `tableView` in iPhone's Master View controller.

Part V

Adding the Application Content

The 5th Wave   By Rich Tennant

"Other than this little glitch with the landscape view, I really love my iPad."

In this part . . .

Now that you have the application foundation and the user experience architecture in place, Part V takes you into the world of applications that contain major functionality. You see how to display the weather using a web page right off the Internet, allow the user to page through local events as if he were reading a book, display a map of where the user is going and where he is right now, find a location that he has always wanted to visit and display it on a map, and even change where he is going (limited in the RoadTrip app to New York and San Francisco, but it's incredibly easy to add other destinations). You don't yet have to slog through every detail of every detail, but you see almost all the technology you need to master in order to create a compelling application like this on your own.

Chapter 15

How's the Weather? Working with Web Views

Getting the framework (no pun intended) in place for a new app is certainly a crucial part of the development process, but in the grand scheme of things, it's only the spadework that prepares the way for the really cool stuff. After all is said and done, you still need to add the content that the users see or interact with. Content (and functionality) is, after all, the reason they will buy the application.

Now that you have created the storyboard scenes by specifying the view controllers and have spiffed up the Master View controller, it's time to make those new view controllers earn their keep. As I've explained more than once, view controllers are the key elements here. They're the ones that get the content from the `Trip` model object and send it to the view to display. In this chapter, you create a view controller that lets the Weather view know where to get the weather information it needs.

The Plan

You will be adding a custom view controller for displaying the weather, which is actually pretty easy. But you will have to do the job twice — once for your iPad storyboard and again for your iPhone storyboard.

The iPad storyboard

The Weather-related part of the iPad storyboard is shown in Figure 15-1.

The control flow through the iPad storyboard goes like this:

1. The iPad user interface is controlled by an instance of Apple's `UISplitViewController`, which manages a Master View controller and a Detail View controller.

2. The Master View controller, displayed on the left in Landscape orientation, has a relationship to a `UINavigationController`. This relationship is shown as an object in the storyboard file.

3. The Detail View controller, which is always displayed, has a relationship with the custom `WeatherController` that you'll develop in this chapter.

4. You need a navigation controller as a wrapper around the Table view that is displayed in the Master View controller (there is another navigation controller used with the Events controller).

5. The first navigation controller has a relationship to your custom `RTMasterViewController`.

Relationship "detail view controller" to Weather

Relationship "master view controller" to Navigation

Replace segue

Figure 15-1:
Weather-related part of the iPad storyboard.

UISplitViewController "SplitView"

UINavigationController "Navigation"

RTMasterViewController "Weather"

WeatherController "Weather"

Relationship "root view controller" to Master

6. The `RTMasterViewController` manages the Table view that you provide to let the user decide what should be displayed in the Detail view.

7. You'll create a Replace segue to connect the first (Weather) item in the Table view to your weather scene.

8. You'll use a `UIWebView` to display the contents of a web page inside your custom `WeatherController`. Voilà — the user can see a weather forecast.

The iPhone storyboard

The Weather-related part of the iPhone storyboard is shown in Figure 15-2.

The control flow through the iPhone storyboard goes like this:

1. The iPhone user interface is controlled by an instance of Apple's `UINavigationController`. The Navigation controller is needed to allow the user to pop (for example, return from) any view controller that is pushed using the Push segue in Step 4.

2. Your `UINavigationController` has a relationship to your Master View controller.

3. The `RTMasterViewController` manages the Table view that you are using to let the user decide what should be displayed when a table element is selected.

Figure 15-2: Weather-related part of the iPhone storyboard.

Relationship "root view controller" to Master

Push Segue to Weather

UINavigationController "Navigation"

RTMasterViewController

WeatherController "Weather"

4. You'll connect the first item in your `RTMasterViewController` to your `WeatherController` using a Push segue.

5. You'll use a `UIWebView` to display the contents of a web page inside your custom `WeatherController`. Voilà — the user can see a weather forecast.

Setting Up the Weather Controller

If the user selects Weather from the Master view in the RoadTrip application, he comes face-to-face with an Internet site displaying weather information. (You'll start with the URL specified in the `Destination.plist`, but you can use any site that you'd like.)

In this section, you add the initial Objective-C code for `WeatherController` class, and then add the logic it needs to get the right URL for the weather from the `Trip` object and send it on to the Weather (Web) view to load.

You'll use the same `WeatherController` class in both the iPad and iPhone storyboard files. Add the `WeatherController` to the iPad storyboard first. After that, you can use the same class in the iPhone storyboard.

Adding the custom view controller

Although you have a view controller defined in the storyboard, it's a generic view controller — in this case, a `UIViewController` — and it's clueless about what you want to display in a view, much less the model it will need to get the data from. In this section, you create a custom controller that *does* know about its view and the model. So, let's replace the generic controller with a custom one. Follow these steps:

1. **In the Project navigator, select the ViewController Classes group and then right-click and choose New File from the contextual menu that appears.**

   Or choose File➪New➪New File from the main menu (or press ⌘+N).

   Whatever method you choose, the New File dialog appears.

2. **In the left column of the New File dialog, select Cocoa Touch under the iOS heading, select the Objective-C class template in the top-right pane, and then click Next.**

   You'll see a dialog that will enable you to choose the options for your file.

3. **In the Class field of the dialog, enter** WeatherController, **choose or enter** RTDetailViewController **in the Subclass Of field, make sure that the Target for iPad check box is selected and that the With XIB for User Interface is deselected, and then click Next.**

4. **In the Save sheet that appears, click Create.**

   You've got yourself a new a custom view controller.

Setting Up WeatherController in the MainStoryboard_iPad file

Adding a new custom view controller is a good start, but you still need to tell the storyboard that you want it to load the new custom view controller rather than a UIViewController. Follow these steps:

1. **In the Project navigator, select MainStoryboard_iPad and, in the Document Outline, select View Controller – Weather in the View Controller – Weather Scene.**

   The Weather View controller is selected on the canvas.

2. **Open the Utility area and then click the Identity Inspector icon in the Inspector selector bar to open the Identity inspector in the Utility area. Choose WeatherController from the Class drop-down menu (replacing UIViewController) in the Custom Class section, as I have in Figure 15-3.**

   Doing so means that, when Weather is selected in the Master View controller, WeatherController will now be instantiated and initialized and will receive events from the user and connect the view to the Trip model.

3. **Drag in a Web view from the Utility area's Library pane and position it in the Weather controller, just under the toolbar, as shown in Figure 15-4.**

   For the RoadTrip application, you want to use a UIWebView to display the weather information. This makes sense, because you'll be using a website to display the weather. (As you'll see in Chapter 16, it makes sense to display the events with the help of a UIWebView as well.)

   As I explain in Chapter 4, the UIWebView class provides a way to display HTML content. These views can be used as the Main view, or as a subview of another view; wherever they're used, they can access websites.

Because of constraints imposed by the fact that I'm presenting this material within the pages of a printed book rather than on a lovely display monitor, I find it easier to position and size the user interface elements in Interface Builder using the Size inspector, as you can see back in Figure 15-4. The origin (x, y) coordinate is $(0, 44)$ with a width of 704 and a height of 704.

4. **Click the Size inspector icon in the Inspector selector to open the Size inspector in the Utility area.**

   Just as you did with the toolbar in Chapter 13, and the car in Chapter 5, you are going to have to adjust the Autosizing settings.

   Figure 15-2 shows that the Web view is currently configured to be a fixed size. The springs — the two indicators, each with an arrowhead in the inner square — are both disabled (when they're enabled, they're solid and bright red, and when disabled, dim and dashed). Configured this way, the Web view will be sized correctly for the Detail view in Landscape orientation, but won't expand to fill the larger Detail view in Portrait orientation. You need to fix that.

5. **Select both springs, as I have in Figure 15-5, to enable them. Also select the bottom and right-side struts (the indicators with two perpendicular lines at each end) to enable them.**

Figure 15-4:
Adding the
Web view.

Interestingly enough, you may have noticed that you don't always have to adjust the Autosizing settings. For example, you didn't have to do it for the Image view in Chapter 5 — that's because Image views come out of the box automatically sized the way we need.

Finally, you need to set up two outlets: one to the Web view so that `WeatherController` can tell the Web view what website to load and a second one to the toolbar so it can place the button there.

6. **Close the Utility area and select the Assistant from the Editor selector in the Xcode toolbar.**

7. **If the `WeatherController.h` file isn't the one that's displayed in the Assistant editor, go up to the Assistant's Jump bar and select it, as I have done in Figure 15-6.**

8. **Control-drag from the Web view (either on the Canvas or in the Document Outline) to the `WeatherController` interface and create an `IBOutlet` (just as you do in Chapter 9) named *weatherView*.**

9. **Control-drag from the Web view in the storyboard Canvas (or in the Document Outline) to the `WeatherController` object in the Document Outline and then choose Delegate (see Figure 15-7) from the Outlets menu that appears.**

Figure 15-5:
The
corrected
Autosizing
settings.

Figure 15-6:
Displaying
the correct
file in the
Assistant.

Figure 15-7:
Make the
Weather
Con
troller
a Web view
delegate.

I'm showing you this to illustrate that you can do all this dragging either on the Canvas or in the Document Outline.

Because you have an outlet set up, you could make Weather Controller a delegate in your code. I actually prefer to do it that way because it's more obvious when it is there in your code; in fact, you get to do it that way in the next chapter. (It's up to you, though.)

You still need to connect the toolbar to the RTDetailViewController, the WeatherController's superclass. You take care of that in the next step.

10. **Select the Standard editor in the Editor selector on the toolbar, select Weather Controller in the Document Outline, and open the Connections inspector using the Inspector selector, as I have in Figure 15-8.**

    You could also right-click or Control-click WeatherController in the Document Outline to get a similar menu.

11. **Drag from the toolbar Outlet in the Connections inspector to the toolbar in the Weather Controller on the canvas. (See Figure 15-8.)**

    You didn't need to create the toolbar Outlet because it had already been created along with UIViewController. The idea here is that you can use the same click-and-drag technique you used to create an outlet to modify which object an existing outlet connects to.

Figure 15-8:
Connecting
the toolbar
to the RT
Detail
View
Con
troller
base class.

If you were to compile and run the RoadTrip project, you'd see the blank screen displayed at application launch, but with a functioning toolbar. You could select Weather or Test Drive in the Master View controller (in Portrait or Landscape orientation, mind you), but you'd just see a blank screen if you selected Weather. You'll fix that next.

But keep in mind this is a major step forward. You now have a fully functioning application structure that can, with equal aplomb, use a Navigation controller and its Navigation bar (as you'll see in the next chapter), or simply replace the controller in the Detail view and use a toolbar.

At this point, you have the `WeatherController` class set up and you've arranged for the storyboard to create a `UIWebView` object and set all the outlets (the `toolbar` and `weatherWebView`) for you when the user selects Weather for the view he or she wants to see.

Because the `Trip` object owns the data — in this case, the data is provided by the website you're using to display the weather information — you add the methods necessary to the `Trip` model to provide this to `Weather Controller`.

Select the Standard editor in the Editor selector on the toolbar and select `Trip.h` in the Project navigator. (If you managed to close the Project navigator at some point in your travels, select its icon in the View selector or choose View➪Navigators➪Show Project Navigator to open it again.)

Add the declaration for the `weather` method (the bolded code) to the Trip interface in `Trip.h`, as shown in Listing 15-1.

Listing 15-1: Updating the Trip.h Interface

```
#import <Foundation/Foundation.h>
#import <mapKit/MapKit.h>

@interface Trip : NSObject

- (id)initWithDestinationIndex:(int)destinationIndex;
- (UIImage *)destinationImage;
- (NSString *) destinationName;
- (CLLocationCoordinate2D) destinationCoordinate;
- (NSString *)weather;

@end
```

Add the `weather` method in Listing 15-2 to `Trip.m`.

Listing 15-2: Adding the weather Method

```
- (NSString *)weather {

    return destinationData[@"Weather"];
}
```

All the `Trip` object does here is return the URL that the Web view will use to download the weather HTML page for the site. It got the URL for that site from the dictionary you create in Chapter 11 when you load the `Destination` plist that provides the data for this destination.

The Weather Controller

Now that you have the `Trip` object set up to deliver the data you need, the `WeatherController` needs to pass on to the view to load the web page.

You need to add some `#import` compiler directives so that
`WeatherController` can access `RTAppDelegate` to get the `Trip` reference
and request the data it needs.

To do that, add the bolded code in Listing 15-3 to `WeatherController.m`.

Listing 15-3:   Updating the WeatherController Implementation

```
#import "RTDetailViewController.h"
#import "RTAppDelegate.h"
#import "Trip.h"
```

The template provides a `viewDidLoad` method stub when you create the
controller file. You may recall from previous chapters that this is where you
want to have the Web view (or any other view) load its data. Add the bolded
code in Listing 15-4.

Listing 15-4:   Adding to viewDidLoad

```
-  (void)viewDidLoad
{
   [super viewDidLoad];
   self.title = @"Weather";
   self.weatherView.scalesPageToFit = YES;
   RTAppDelegate *appDelegate =
                [[UIApplication sharedApplication] delegate];
   [self.weatherView loadRequest:
      [NSURLRequest requestWithURL:[NSURL
                URLWithString:[appDelegate.trip weather]]]];
}
```

The first thing you do in Listing 15-4 is set the title to `Weather`.

The title won't be showing up on the toolbar, however, because this just
sets the title in the Navigation bar. I'll use it when I add a Return to *Whatever*
button in the next section.

Because what gets loaded is going to be a website, you set `self.`
`weatherView.scalesPageToFit` to `YES`.

`scalesPageToFit` is a `UIWebView` property. If it's set to `YES`, the web page
is scaled to fit inside your view, and the user can zoom in and out. If it's set to
`NO`, the page is displayed in the view, and zooming is disabled.

I might set it to NO when I'm not displaying a web page and the HTML page I created fits just fine and I don't want it to be scalable. You may want to do something else here, of course; I did it this way to show you how (and where) you have control of web page properties.

You then create the NSURLRequest object that the Web view needs to load the data. To do that, you first create an NSURL object (an object that includes the utilities necessary for downloading files or other resources from web and FTP servers) using the URL you get from Trip. The code uses this NSURL and creates an NSURLRequest from it. The NSURLRequest is what the WeatherController needs to send to the Web view in the loadRequest: message, which tells it to load the data associated with that particular NSURL.

The NSURLRequest class encapsulates a URL and any protocol-specific properties, all the time keeping things protocol-independent. It also provides a number of other things that are beyond the scope of this book, but are part of the URL loading system — the set of classes and protocols that provide the underlying capability for an application to access the data specified by a URL. This is the preferred way to access files both locally and on the Internet.

The loadRequest message is sent to the Web view, and the Weather website is displayed in the window. This causes the Web view to load the data and display it in the window.

Managing links in a Web view

An interesting thing about the Weather view — or any other view that does (or can) load real web content into your application instead of using a browser — is that the links are live and users can follow those links from that view *if* you let them.

After the user is at the weather website, as you can see in Figure 15-9, the user might want to look at the NWS New York, NY link in the upper-left corner. If the user were to follow that link, though, he wouldn't have a way to get back to the originating page.

Figure 15-9:
You can select a link (left) to look at National Weather Service info for New York (right) — but you have no way to get back to the originating view.

Hmm.

To be able to navigate back to the originating view, you need to create another button and label it `Back to Weather` (or whatever the previous controller is) so that the user knows that she can use it to get back to the previous view. Creating this button is pretty easy to do, as you'll see in Listing 15-6.

Of course, I don't want to have that button pop up if the user is at the originating web page because, at that point, there's no going back. So, how do you keep track of who's where in the whole navigational link structure? Here, you're assisted by two Web view delegate methods, `webView:should StartLoadWithRequest:navigationType:` and `webViewDidFinishLoad:`.

`webView:shouldStartLoadWithRequest:navigationType:` is a `UIWebView` delegate method. It's called before a Web view begins loading content to see whether the user wants the load to proceed.

First, adopt the `UIWebViewDelegate` protocol by adding the bolded code in Listing 15-5 to `WeatherController.h`.

Listing 15-5: Updating the WeatherController Interface

```
#import "RTDetailViewController.h"

@interface WeatherController : RTDetailViewController
                            <UIWebViewDelegate>

@property (weak, nonatomic)
                    IBOutlet UIWebView *weatherView;

@end
```

Remember that when you adopt a delegate protocol, the compiler will then check to make sure that all required methods are in fact there and that all types are correct — so do it!

Next, add the code in Listing 15-6 to `WeatherController.m`.

Listing 15-6: Implementing the webView:shouldStartLoadWith Request:navigationType: Method

```
- (BOOL)webView:(UIWebView *)webView
        shouldStartLoadWithRequest:
        (NSURLRequest *)request navigationType:
            (UIWebViewNavigationType)navigationType {

    if (navigationType ==
            UIWebViewNavigationTypeLinkClicked){
    UIBarButtonItem *backButton = [[UIBarButtonItem alloc]
            initWithTitle:[NSString stringWithFormat:
                            @"Back to %@", self.title]
            style:UIBarButtonItemStyleBordered target:self
                            action:@selector(goBack:)];
        if ([[UIDevice currentDevice]
            userInterfaceIdiom] == UIUserInterfaceIdiomPad) {
        NSMutableArray *itemsArray =
                            [self.toolbar.items mutableCopy];
        UIBarButtonItem *flexibleSpace=
        [[UIBarButtonItem alloc]
            initWithBarButtonSystemItem:
            UIBarButtonSystemItemFlexibleSpace target:self
            action:@selector(goBack:)];
        flexibleSpace.width = 1.0;
        [itemsArray addObject:flexibleSpace];
        [itemsArray addObject:backButton ];
        [self.toolbar setItems:itemsArray animated:NO];
```

(continued)

Listing 15-6 *(continued)*

```
    }
    else {
       self.navigationItem.rightBarButtonItem = backButton;
    }
  }
  return YES;
}
```

Early on in Listing 15-6, you check to see whether the user has touched an embedded link. (You have to see whether a link is clicked because this message is sent to the delegate under several different circumstances.)

```
if (navigationType == UIWebViewNavigationTypeLinkClicked){
```

You create the Back to *Whatever* button, using the view controller `title`, and return `YES` to tell the Web view to load from the Internet. The `action:@ selector(goBack:)` argument is the standard way to specify Target-Action. It says that when the button is tapped, you need to send the `goBack:` message to the `target:self`, which is the `WeatherController`.

```
UIBarButtonItem *backButton = [[UIBarButtonItem alloc]
   initWithTitle:[NSString stringWithFormat:
                             @"Back to %@", self.title]
   style:UIBarButtonItemStylePlain target:self
   action:@selector(goBack:)];
self.navigationItem.rightBarButtonItem = backButton;
return YES;
```

I think it looks better if the button appears on the right side of the toolbar, especially in Portrait orientation when you have the Road Trip button as well.

To do that, you first add a *flexible space* — space that's distributed equally between the other Bar Button items in the toolbar — and *then* add the Back to *Whatever* button.

```
UIBarButtonItem *flexibleSpace= [[UIBarButtonItem alloc]
   initWithBarButtonSystemItem:
           UIBarButtonSystemItemFlexibleSpace target:self
   action:@selector(goBack:)];
flexibleSpace.width = 1.0;
[itemsArray addObject:flexibleSpace];
[itemsArray addObject:backButton];
[self.toolbar setItems:itemsArray animated:NO];
```

You're creating a `UIBarButtonItem` that's a flexible space. This adds a space that's distributed equally between the other Bar Button items on the toolbar (other properties are ignored).

Next, add the `goBack:` method in Listing 15-7 to the `WebViewController.m` file. This is the message sent when the Back to *Whatever* button is tapped.

Listing 15-7:   Adding the goBack: Method

```
- (void)goBack:(id)sender {
  [self.weatherView goBack];
}
```

Note that you don't need to declare this method in `WeatherController.h` because it's used only in the Target-Action, which is resolved at runtime, not compile time.

The `UIWebView` actually implements much of the behavior you need here. The Web view keeps a Backward *and* Forward list. When you send the `UIWebView` the message (`goBack:`), it reloads the previous page.

Finally, you want to get rid of the Back to *Whatever* button when you're displaying the original page. The code to do that is shown in Listing 15-8.

Listing 15-8:   Implementing webViewDidFinishLoad:

```
- (void)webViewDidFinishLoad:(UIWebView *) webView {

  if ([self.weatherView canGoBack] == NO ) {
    if (([[UIDevice currentDevice] userInterfaceIdiom] ==
           UIUserInterfaceIdiomPad) &&
                    ([self.toolbar.items count] >= 3)){
      NSMutableArray *itemsArray =
                      [self.toolbar.items mutableCopy];
      [itemsArray removeLastObject];
      [itemsArray removeLastObject];
      [self.toolbar setItems:itemsArray animated:NO];
    }
    else {
      self.navigationItem.rightBarButtonItem = nil;
    }
  }
}
```

The delegate is sent the `webViewDidFinishLoad:` message after the view has loaded. At this point, you check to see whether there's anything to go back to (the Web view keeps track of those sorts of things). If not, remove the button from the toolbar or Navigation bar.

That being said, the Apple Human Interface Guidelines say it's best to avoid creating an application that looks and behaves like a mini–web browser. As far as I'm concerned, making it possible to select links in a Web view doesn't do that.

But if you really don't want to enable the user to follow links (either because of Apple's suggestion that you not make your app act as a mini-browser or if you'd just prefer that your app users stick around for a bit and don't go gallivanting around the Internet), you have to disable the links that are available in the content. You can do that in the `shouldStartLoadWith Request:` method in the `WeatherController.m` file by replacing the code you added in Listing 15-6 with the code shown in Listing 15-9.

Listing 15-9:   Disabling Links

```
- (BOOL)webView:(UIWebView *)webView
  shouldStartLoadWithRequest:(NSURLRequest *)request
  navigationType:(UIWebViewNavigationType)navigationType {

  if (navigationType ==
     UIWebViewNavigationTypeLinkClicked){
   return NO;
  }
  else return YES;
}
```

You should add an alert to inform the user of the fact that no Internet gallivanting is to be had here.

More Opportunities to Use the Debugger

A couple of runtime errors are easy to get. Two that pop up frequently are `unrecognized selector sent to instance` and `NSUnknown KeyException`. Although the former error is pretty easy to track down if you actually read the error message, the latter can be a real mystery (it was to me), especially the first time you encounter it. So I want to explain both of them now.

Unrecognized selector sent to instance

The `unrecognized selector sent to instance` runtime error is probably the most common one I get e-mails about; it (understandably) throws many people for a loop. But if you take time to read the error message, you can make sense of it.

```
2011-12-07 19:34:07.166 RoadTrip[1202:12503] ***
Terminating app due to uncaught exception
'NSInvalidArgumentException', reason: '-[WeatherController
goBack]: unrecognized selector sent to instance 0xb7331f0'
```

This error occurs when you thought you created a selector in your code but it's not (really) there.

If, in the `webView shouldStartLoadWithRequest:navigationType:` method, you mistakenly typed `goBack` (without a colon, designating a method with no arguments) rather than `goBack:` (a method with a single argument) when you allocated and initialized the `backButton`:

```
UIBarButtonItem *backButton = [[UIBarButtonItem alloc]
   initWithTitle:[NSString stringWithFormat:
   @"Back to %@", self.title]
   style:UIBarButtonItemStylePlain target:self
   action:@selector(goBack)];
```

and then you ran the application, selected Weather, selected a link, and then tapped the Back to Weather button, what you will see in the Debugger Console pane is

```
2011-12-07 19:34:07.166 RoadTrip[1202:12503] ***
Terminating app due to uncaught exception
'NSInvalidArgumentException', reason: '-[WeatherController
goBack]: unrecognized selector sent to instance 0xb7331f0'
```

You get this error message because you're sending the `goBack` message (not the `goBack:` message) to the `target` — the `WeatherController`. The `WeatherController` *does* have a fully functional `goBack:` method implemented, but it *doesn't* have a `goBack` method implemented — as the debugger so clearly informs you.

Repeat for the iPhone Storyboard

The good news is that you can use the same custom `WeatherController` class in your iPhone storyboard as you used in the iPad storyboard file. You can also reuse the changes you made to the Trip model. You can update the iPhone Storyboard file the same way that you did in Chapter 12.

Adding the WeatherController to the iPhone storyboard file

The following steps show how to update the iPhone Storyboard file.

1. **Select the** `MainStoryboard_iPhone.storyboard` **file in the Project Navigator.**

2. **Select the generic** `UIViewController` **scene in your storyboard.**

3. **Open the Utility area, and select the Identity inspector.**

4. **Change the class name to** `WeatherController` **in the Class drop-down menu, just as you did in Figure 15-3.**

5. **With the** `WeatherController` **scene selected in the storyboard file, select the view in the document outline.**

6. **Change the class name of the view from** `UIView` **to** `UIWebView`.

7. **In the Document Outline, Control-drag from the** `WeatherController` **to the Web view and select** `weatherView` **from the pop-up menu.**

This step connects the `weatherView` outlet in the `WeatherController` class to the instance of `UIWebView` that you'll use to display the weather.

Test in the iPhone Simulator

Run the iPhone app in the Simulator. You should see the web page displayed in Figure 15-10.

Figure 15-10:
The
`Weather`
`Control`
`ler`
display on
the iPhone.

Chapter 16

Displaying Events Using a Page View Controller

● ●

In This Chapter

▶ Displaying HTML pages in a Web view

▶ Creating page transitions with a `UIPageViewController`

▶ Understanding how Page View controllers work and implementing page turns

● ●

*A*fter you have finished this chapter, when the user selects Events from the Master view in the RoadTrip application, he or she will come face-to-face with a series of pages that describes the latest activities happening at his destination. In this chapter, I'll show you how to use a feature, first introduced in iOS 5, that will allow you to create a view controller that enables a user to "turn event pages" in the same way as he or she can in an iBook.

You will also find out how to use a Web view again to display data, but this time you will download an HTML page stored on my website, rather than download a website itself.

The best part of what you discover in this chapter is page-turn transitions. These transitions are implemented by Apple's `UIPageViewController` class — a new container view controller (first provided in iOS 5) that creates page-turn transitions between view controllers. Just as a Navigation controller animates the transitions between, say, the Master View controller and the Test Drive controller in Chapter 5, the Page View controller does its thing between two view controllers — in this case, two `EventPageController`s.

You implement this functionality by adding a `UIPageViewController` to your view controller — `EventsController` — in your code and then creating a view controller (`EventPageController`) for each page.

As I mention in Chapter 13, the `UIPageViewController` needs a Navigation bar. You need it if you want to be able to display the Road Trip button. Because of the way the class is implemented, tapping a button on a toolbar is intercepted and interpreted by the `UIPageViewController` as a page turn. Fortunately, you made it possible for the delegate methods to deal with both Navigation bars and toolbars with equal aplomb.

The Plan

The Events feature actually requires that you add a number of interrelated components to each storyboard file. The components used in the iPad storyboard are shown in Figure 16-1.

UINavigation Controller
EventsNavigation

Replace segue from Table View
Cell to EventsNavigation.

Events

Embed segue from Container View to
EmbeddedPageViewController.

UIPageViewController
EmbeddedPageViewController

Figure 16-1:
Components
used in
the iPad
storyboard
file for the
Events
feature.

Relationship from root view
controller to Events

Events Controller
Events

EventPageController
EventPage

The key components for the Events feature include

✔ The "Events" Table view cell in the `RTMasterViewController`'s Table view.

✔ A Replace segue from the "Events" Table view cell to a Navigation controller that displays a Navigation bar-equipped view controller in the detail view. This bar contains a RoadTrip button used by the user to return from the Events display to the `RTMasterViewController`.

✔ A custom `EventsController` container.

✔ An instance of `UIPageViewController` embedded in the `Events Controller` container, responsible for managing transitions (such as page curls) between events pages, where each page is managed by an instance of `EventPageController`.

✔ A custom `EventPageController`, responsible for displaying event information in an HTML web page rendered by an instance of `UIWebView`.

Setting Up the EventsController

In this section, you need to do the same thing you did in Chapter 15 to create and connect the `EventsController` object. As I explain in Chapter 15, the way you develop a storyboard is rather formulaic. I review it here (and for the last time):

1. Lay out the view controllers you need for the user experience architecture.

2. Add the custom view controller to your app.

3. Tie the two together in your storyboard.

4. Add the code you need to the custom view controller.

After you get into the routine of how to do it, your life as a developer becomes much easier.

You'll also add another view controller to the storyboard (the aforementioned `EventPageController`) that will be used by the `UIPageViewController`.

Adding the custom view controller

To add the `EventsController` to the RoadTrip project, follow these steps:

1. **In the Project navigator, select the View Controller Classes group and then either right-click the selection and choose New File from the menu that appears or choose File⇨New⇨New File from the main menu (or press ⌘+N).**

   Whatever method you choose, you're greeted by the New File dialog.

2. **In the left column of the dialog, select Cocoa Touch under the iOS heading, select the Objective-C class template in the top-right pane, and then click Next.**

   You'll see a dialog that will enable you to choose the options for your file.

3. **Enter** EventsController **in the Class field, choose or enter** RTDetail ViewController **in the Subclass Of field, make sure that the Target for iPad check box is selected and that With XIB for User Interface is deselected, and then click Next.**

4. **In the Save sheet that appears, click Create.**

You'll also need to create a controller that manages each event page. Follow these steps:

1. **In the Project navigator, select the View Controller Classes group and then either right-click the selection and choose New File from the menu that appears or choose File⇨New⇨New File from the main menu (or press ⌘+N).**

   Say hello again to the New File dialog box.

2. **In the left column of the dialog, select Cocoa Touch under the iOS heading, select the Objective-C class template in the top-right pane, and then click Next.**

   You'll see a dialog that will enable you to choose the options for your file.

3. **Enter** EventPageController **in the Class field, choose or enter** UIView Controller **in the Subclass Of drop-down menu, and make sure that the Target for iPad check box is selected and that With XIB for User Interface is deselected. Click Next.**

4. **In the Save sheet that appears, click Create.**

Setting up the EventsController in the MainStoryboard

Just as you did in Chapter 15, you need to tell the storyboard to load your custom view controller rather than a `UIViewController`. Follow these steps:

1. **In the Project navigator, select MainStoryboard_iPad and, in the Document Outline, select View Controller – Events in the View Controller – Events Scene.**

   The Events view controller will be selected on the canvas.

2. **Open the Utility area and then click the Identity Inspector icon in the Inspector selector to open the Identity inspector in the Utility area.**

3. **Choose EventsController from the Class drop-down menu (replacing UIViewController) in the Custom Class section.**

While in `WeatherController`, you added a Web view, but you won't be doing that here. You also created an outlet, but you don't need that here, either. Instead, you'll use a Web view and create an outlet in the `EventPageController`. The `EventPageController` is what you'll need to add to implement a `UIPageViewController`. You do that in the next section.

Adding and setting up the EventPage Controller in the MainStoryboard

You need a view controller to manage each view within the Page View controller. Although you could've added this view controller when you extended the storyboard, I didn't have you do so because I didn't want my coverage of the topic to get lost among the discussion about segues.

To add the `EventPageController` to the storyboard, follow these steps:

1. **Add another view controller to the storyboard by dragging in a view controller from the Library pane and placing it next to the** `EventsController` **on the Canvas.**

   (You don't *have* to put it there, but doing so hints that a relationship exists.)

2. **Open the Identity inspector in the Utility area using the Inspector selector bar, and in the Class drop-down menu in the Custom Class section, choose EventPageController (replacing UIViewController).**

3. **Switch to the Attributes inspector and use its text fields to give the controller the Title of** EventPage. **Then add** EventPage **to the Identity inspector's Storyboard ID field.**

4. **Add a Web view to the** EventPageController **by dragging in a Web view from the Library pane and into the Event Page controller, just as you did in Chapter 15.**

   The Event Page view will be a Web view because you'll want it to download and then display an HTML page.

As you may recall from Chapter 15, the UIWebView class provides a way to display HTML content and has the built-in functionality to download HTML content from the web.

5. **Click the Size inspector icon in the Inspector selector to open the Size inspector in the Utility area.**

    Just as you did with the Web view in Chapter 14, you are going to have to adjust the Autosizing settings.

6. **Click on all the currently disabled springs (the two indicators, each with an arrowhead at each end in the inner square) and struts (the indicators with two perpendicular lines at each end) to enable them.**

    Note that when they're enabled, they're solid and bright red, and when disabled, dim and dashed.

    If you are unclear about why you are doing this, refer to Chapter 15.

7. **Drag in an Activity Indicator view from the Library pane and center it in the view.**

    Because these pages can be large and take some amount of time to download, you want to have some kind of Activity Indicator view to let the user know that the application is still running but busy, as opposed to frozen.

    As you can see by looking at the Document Outline in Figure 16-2, both the Web view and Activity Indicator view are siblings — and subviews of the view. It's important that both are siblings, and that the Activity Indicator view is below the Web view in order for it to display. (Remember the Last-One-In-Is-On-Top principle from Chapter 4 when it comes to subviews.) If that's not the case, rearrange the views in the Document Outline.

8. **Switch to the Size inspector in the Utility area using the Inspector selector, and then update the Autosizing values for the Activity indicator by simply deselecting all the struts and springs to keep it in the middle, as shown in Figure 16-2).**

9. **Close the Utility area and select the Assistant from the Editor selector in the toolbar. If the EventPageController.m implementation file isn't the one that's displayed, go up to the Assistant's Jump bar and select it.**

10. **Control-drag from the Web view in either the Canvas or the Document Outline to the EventPageController interface and create an IBOutlet (just as you do in Chapter 15) named eventDataView.**

Figure 16-2:
A Web
view with
an activity
indicator.

11. **Control-drag from the Activity Indicator view to the**
 `EventPageController` **interface and create an** `IBOutlet` **named**
 `activityIndicator`.

12. **Working within the Document Outline, control-drag from the Web**
 view to the Event Page controller, and then select Delegate from the
 Outlets menu that appears.

 This will make `EventPageController` the Web view delegate.

Extending the Trip Model

The `EventsController` will need two pieces of information from the `Trip`
model: the number of events and the URL for a specific event.

Add the declaration for the two `Events` methods (bolded) to the Trip
interface in `Trip.h`, as shown in Listing 16-1.

Listing 16-1:   Update the Trip Interface

```
@interface Trip : NSObject

- (id)initWithDestinationIndex:(int)destinationIndex;
- (UIImage *) destinationImage;
- (NSString *) destinationName;
- (CLLocationCoordinate2D) destinationCoordinate;
- (NSString *)weather;
- (NSUInteger)numberOfEvents;
- (NSString *)getEvent:(NSUInteger)index;
```

But `Trip` isn't going to go at this alone (as it did with `Weather`). It will use an `Events` object (which you'll create shortly). So that `Trip` can use the `Event` object, add the bolded code in Listing 16-2 to `Trip.m`.

Listing 16-2:   Updating the Trip Implementation

```
#import "Trip.h"
#import "Destination.h"
#import "Events.h"

@interface Trip () {
  NSDictionary *destinationData;
  Destination* destination;
  Events *events;
}
@end
```

Until you add the `Events` class in the next section, you'll see some Live Issues errors.

The `EventsController`, as you will see, will need to know the number of events and also get the event information.

Add the implementation of methods you need in Listings 16-3 and 16-4 to `Trip.m`.

Listing 16-3:   The Number of Events

```
- (NSUInteger)numberOfEvents {

  return [events numberOfEvents];
}
```

Listing 16-4:   Get an Event

```
- (NSString *)getEvent:(NSUInteger)index {

  return [events getEvent:index];
}
```

To have `Trip` create the required `Events` object, add the bolded code in Listing 16-5 to `initWithDestinationIndex:` in `Trip.m`.

Listing 16-5:   Updating initWithDestinationIndex:

```
- (id)initWithDestinationIndex:
                            (NSUInteger)destinationIndex {
  self = [super init];
  if (self) {

    NSString *filePath = [[NSBundle mainBundle]
        pathForResource:@"Destinations" ofType:@"plist"];
    NSDictionary *destinations = [NSDictionary
          dictionaryWithContentsOfFile: filePath];
    NSArray *destinationsArray =
          destinations[@"DestinationData"];
    destinationData = destinationsArray[destinationIndex];
    destination = [[Destination alloc] initWithDestination
          Index:destinationIndex];
    events = [[Events alloc]
            initWithDestinationIndex:destinationIndex];
  }
  return self;
}
```

As I mention in Chapter 12, `Trip` is a composite object that uses other objects to carry out its responsibilities. Whereas you put the `Weather` logic in the `Trip` object itself, in this case, you create a new model object to handle the events' responsibilities. That's because handling the events is a bit more complex and deserving of its own model object to encapsulate the logic. Hiding the `Events` object behind `Trip` makes things more loosely coupled — a very good thing, which you'll find as you extend and enhance your app. (See Chapter 12 for an explanation of loose coupling.)

Adding the Events Class

If `Trip` is to use an `Events` object, you had better create the class. Follow these steps:

1. **In the Project navigator, select the Model Classes group and then either right-click the selection and choose New File from the menu that appears or choose File➪New➪New File from the main menu (or press ⌘+N).**

    Whatever method you choose, you're greeted by the New File dialog.

2. **In the left column of the dialog, select Cocoa Touch under the iOS heading, select the Objective-C Class template in the top-right pane, and then click Next.**

You'll see a dialog that will enable you to choose the options for your file.

3. **Enter** Events **in the Class field.**

4. **Choose or enter** NSObject **in the Subclass Of field then click Next.**

The iPad and With XIB for User Interface check boxes are dimmed because they are not relevant here — Events is derived from NSObject, and not from any type of view controller.

5. **In the Save sheet that appears, click Create.**

The Events class is the model object that manages the events. Earlier, I said that I'm creating this model object to encapsulate the event logic, and although doing so may seem to be an overreaction here given that the logic isn't that complex, I mainly want to show you how to do that. And in reality, you can imagine that the Events class could be expanded to do a lot more — such as return the location, process events from multiple sources, or even allow a user to add her own events.

To start adding the Events class, add the bolded code in Listing 16-6 to Events.h.

Listing 16-6: Updating the Events Interface

```
@interface Events : NSObject

- (id)initWithDestinationIndex:
                          (NSUInteger)destinationIndex;
- (NSUInteger)numberOfEvents;
- (NSString *)getEvent:(NSUInteger)index;
@end
```

This code has three methods: an initialization method and two methods to process the Trip requests.

Next, you need to add an instance variable. Add the code in bold in Listing 16-7 to Events.m.

Listing 16-7: Updating the Events Implementation

```
#import "Events.h"

@interface Events() {
  NSMutableArray *events;
}
@end

@implementation Events
```

As you can see, Listing 16-6 has an initialization method (which is used by `Trip` when it creates the `Events` object). Add the code in Listing 16-8 to `Events.m` to implement the `initWithDestinationIndex:` initialization method.

Listing 16-8   Initializing the Events Object

```
- (id)initWithDestinationIndex:
                            (NSUInteger)destinationIndex {
  self = [super init];
  if (self) {

    NSString *filePath = [[NSBundle mainBundle]
        pathForResource:@"Destinations" ofType:@"plist"];
    NSDictionary *destinations = [NSDictionary
                dictionaryWithContentsOfFile: filePath];
    NSArray *destinationsArray =
        destinations[@"DestinationData"];
NSDictionary *data =
      destinationsArray[destinationIndex];
    events = [NSMutableArray arrayWithArray:
                            data[@"Events"]];
  }
  return self;
}
```

All this method does at this point is get the array of URLs for the HTML pages I created and you entered in the `Destinations` plist. It puts these URLs in an array that you create — for more efficient retrieval later. (I make this a mutable array because in the future you may want to allow a user to add his own events.)

The `EventsController`, as you will see, will need to know the number of events and the event information. You've added the methods to `Trip` in Listings 16-3 and 16-4, but `Trip` will actually be getting that information from `Events`. Add the code in Listing 16-9 to `Events.m` to implement the method that returns the number of events.

Listing 16-9:   The Number of Events

```
- (NSUInteger)numberOfEvents {

  return [events count];
}
```

To get the number of events, you return the `count` of the array.

The `EventsController` will also need to have a list of the event URLs. Add the code in Listing 16-10 to `Events.m` to implement that method.

Listing 16-10:   Getting an Event

```
- (NSString *)getEvent:(NSUInteger)index {

    return events[index];
}
```

To return an `Event`, you return the URL based on the index into the array. This will make more sense when you go through the `EventsController` and `EventPageController` code, which you do next.

The EventsController and Its PageViewController

At the start of this chapter, I promised to show you how to enable users to turn the page between one view controller and another. To implement this cool page-turning stuff, you need a `UIPageViewController`. You create that in the `EventsController` in its `viewDidLoad` method.

To start, though, you need to make the `EventsController` a `UIPageView Controller` data source and delegate. (Actually, in this implementation, you won't need to use any of the delegate methods, but it's good for you to know about them.) Add the bolded code in Listing 16-11 (which includes the declaration of another method that you'll use shortly) to `EventsController.h`.

Listing 16-11:   Updating the EventsController Interface

```
#import "RTDetailViewController.h"
@class EventPageController;

@interface EventsController : RTDetailViewController
                <UIPageViewControllerDelegate,
                            UIPageViewControllerDataSource>

- (EventPageController *)viewControllerAtIndex:
  (NSUInteger)index storyboard:(UIStoryboard *)storyboard;

@end
```

Now read on to find out about the data source and delegate.

Data sources and delegates

You've used delegates a few times already, such as when you add the code to the app delegate in Chapter 8. A data source is really just another kind of delegate that supplies the data that a framework object needs. In Chapter 20, when you implement a dynamic Table view, you do that as well, and data sources are also used in many other places in the framework — in picker views, for example, when you select a time or date in the Calendar application.

Data source

The `UIPageViewController` is a new Container View controller for creating page-turn transitions between view controllers first implemented in iOS 5. This means that for every page, you create a new view controller.

The `UIPageViewControllerDataSource` protocol is adopted by an object that provides view controllers (you'll be using the `PageDataController`) to the Page View controller as needed, in response to navigation gestures.

`UIPageViewControllerDataSource` has two required methods:

✔ `pageViewController:viewControllerAfterViewController:` returns the view controller after the current view controller.

✔ `pageViewController:viewControllerBeforeViewController:` returns the view controller before the current view controller.

Delegate

The delegate of a Page View controller must adopt the `UIPageView ControllerDelegate` protocol. The methods in this protocol allow you to receive a notification when the device orientation changes or when the user navigates to a new page. In the implementation in this book, you don't need to be concerned with either of those two situations.

The EventsController

Before you add any code, update `EventsController.m` with the bolded code in Listing 16-12.

Listing 16-12:   Updating the EventsController Implementation

```
#import "EventsController.h"
#import "RTAppDelegate.h"
#import "Trip.h"
```

(continued)

Listing 16-12 *(continued)*

```
#import "EventPageController.h"

@interface EventsController () {
  NSUInteger pageCount;
  UIPageViewController *pageViewController;
  NSUInteger currentPage;
}
@end

@implementation EventsController
```

The `viewDidLoad` method is where most of the work is done. Add the bolded code in Listing 16-13 to `viewDidLoad` in `EventsController.m`.

Listing 16-13:   Updating viewDidLoad

```
- (void)viewDidLoad
{
  [super viewDidLoad];
  self.navigationController.navigationBar.tintColor =
                                    [UIColor blackColor];
  RTAppDelegate *delegate =
            [[UIApplication sharedApplication] delegate];
  pageCount = [delegate.trip numberOfEvents];
  pageViewController = [[UIPageViewController alloc]
    initWithTransitionStyle:
              UIPageViewControllerTransitionStylePageCurl
    navigationOrientation:
      UIPageViewControllerNavigationOrientationHorizontal
    options:nil];
  pageViewController.dataSource = self;
//pageViewController.delegate = self;
  EventPageController *startingViewController =
    [self viewControllerAtIndex:0
                      storyboard:self.storyboard];
  NSArray *viewControllers = @[startingViewController];
[pageViewController setViewControllers:viewControllers
    direction:
            UIPageViewControllerNavigationDirectionForward
    animated:NO completion:NULL];
  [self addChildViewController:pageViewController];
  [pageViewController didMoveToParentViewController:self];
  [self.view addSubview:pageViewController.view];
  self.view.gestureRecognizers =
                    pageViewController.gestureRecognizers;
}
```

In the bolded code added here, you start out by setting the Navigation bar color to black. (You could've also done this in Interface Builder in the Events Controller Attributes inspector, where you set the title and identifier.)

Next, you get the number of events from the `Trip` model so that you know how many pages you'll have:

```
RTAppDelegate *delegate = [[UIApplication
                        sharedApplication] delegate];
pageCount = [delegate.trip numberOfEvents];
```

Then you allocate and initialize the `PageViewController` and make yourself the data source. I have commented out the delegate assignment because you aren't implementing any of the delegate methods, but here's where you would do it:

```
pageViewController = [[UIPageViewController alloc]
   initWithTransitionStyle:
            UIPageViewControllerTransitionStylePageCurl
   navigationOrientation:
      UIPageViewControllerNavigationOrientationHorizontal
      options:nil];
   pageViewController.dataSource = self;
//pageViewController.delegate = self
```

You're using a `UIPageViewControllerTransitionStylePageCurl` (which gives the appearance of turning a page) and you use a Navigation orientation of `horizontal`, which gives you left-to-right page turning (`UIPageViewControllerNavigationOrientationVertical` gives you pages turning up and down.)

You then request the first view controller (I show this method in Listing 16-14 and explain it there), create an array, add the first view controller to the array, and pass that array to the `pageViewController`:

```
EventPageController *startingViewController = [self
      viewControllerAtIndex:0 storyboard:self.storyboard];
NSArray *viewControllers =
         [@startingViewController];
[pageViewController setViewControllers:viewControllers
   direction:UIPageViewControllerNavigationDirectionForward
   animated:NO completion:NULL];
```

This array will hold the view controllers that the `UIPageController` manages. You specify the direction as `Forward`. You set animated to `NO` for this transition (setting the view controller array, not the page turning) and you specify no completion block.

Although this approach is pretty simple, you can get way more sophisticated and include features such as double pages and even two-sided pages, and so on. You won't be doing that here.

Next, you add the `pageViewController` as a child view controller, inform the `pageViewController` that it's now the child of another view controller, and make its view a subview so that it's displayed. The idea behind a Container View controller (which the `UIPageViewContainer` and `UINavigationController` both are) is that it manages the presentation of the content from its child view controllers (contained view controllers).

```
[self addChildViewController:pageViewController];
[pageViewController didMoveToParentViewController:self];
[self.view addSubview:pageViewController.view];
```

Finally, add the Page View controller's gesture recognizers to the `EventsController` view so that the gestures are started further up the chain. (I explain gesture recognizers in Chapter 13.)

```
self.view.gestureRecognizers =
                    pageViewController.gestureRecognizers;
```

As a supplier of view controllers, you'll be responsible for creating, managing, and returning the right view controller for a page. You'll do that in the `view ControllerAtIndex:storyboard:` method.

Add the `viewControllerAtIndex:storyboard:` method in Listing 16-14 to `EventsController.m`.

You'll see some Live Issues errors until you add the page property in the next section.

Listing 16-14:   Adding the viewControllerAtIndex:storyboard: Method

```
- (EventPageController *)viewControllerAtIndex:
    (NSUInteger)index
                    storyboard:(UIStoryboard *)storyboard {

  if ((pageCount == 0) || (index >= pageCount)) {
    return nil;
  }
  EventPageController *eventPageController = [storyboard
    instantiateViewControllerWithIdentifier:@"EventPage"];
  eventPageController.page = index;
  return eventPageController;
}
```

With Listing 16-14, you're simply doing some error checking to make sure that both pages are available and that the page for the view controller you're supposed to return is available:

```
if ((pageCount == 0) || (index >= pageCount)) {
  return nil;
}
```

You then allocate and initialize the view controller for that page, setting its page (relative number of the URL to display) so that it knows which event URL to load:

```
EventPageController *eventPageController = [storyboard
    instantiateViewControllerWithIdentifier:@"EventPage"];
eventPageController.page = index;
```

 You have more efficient ways to do this. You could create a cache of controllers that you've created and reuse them as needed. (As you'll see in Chapter 19, that's how I do it with Table View cells.) I'll leave you to explore that topic on your own.

You also need to add the required data source methods in Listing 16-15 to EventsController.m.

Listing 16-15: **Implementing pageViewController:viewControllerAfter ViewController: and pageViewController:viewController BeforeViewController:**

```
- (UIViewController *)pageViewController:
              (UIPageViewController *)pageViewController
              viewControllerBeforeViewController:
                    (UIViewController *)viewController {

    NSUInteger index =
              ((EventPageController *)viewController).page;
    if (index == 0)
      return nil;
    index--;
    currentPage = index;
return [self viewControllerAtIndex:index
                  storyboard:viewController.storyboard];

    }

- (UIViewController *)pageViewController:
              (UIPageViewController *)pageViewController
              viewControllerAfterViewController:
                    (UIViewController *)viewController {
    NSUInteger index =
              ((EventPageController *)viewController).page;
    index++;
    if (index == pageCount)
      return nil;
    currentPage = index;
return [self viewControllerAtIndex:index
                  storyboard:viewController.storyboard];

    }
```

Both of these methods return an EventDisplayController initialized with the right page (relative event number) to display. They use the view

`ControllerAtIndex:storyboard:` method that you add in Listing 16-14 and indicate which view controller is required by taking the current view controller's page number and then either incrementing or decrementing it appropriately. It then does some error checking to be sure that the page requested is within bounds. If it's not, the method returns `nil`, and the `UIPageViewController` inhibits the page turn.

These data source methods are used by the `UIPageViewController` to get the view controllers that can display the next or previous page, depending on the way the user is turning the page. As mentioned previously, the `UIPageViewController` just manages controllers and the transitions between them. The view controllers that you return operate like the run-of-the-mill view controller you've been using, such as the Weather controller that displays a website.

The next section gives you a look at how these controllers work.

The EventPageController

The `EventPageController` is almost identical to the `WeatherController` that you implemented in Chapter 15.

To follow along in this section, you need to close the Assistant, display the Project navigator, and select `EventPageController.m`.

I have you add the same functionality to this controller as you did to the `Weather Controller` so that you can select a link and navigate back from it. You could've created an abstract class — a `WebViewController`, for example — that both `WeatherController` and `EventPageController` were derived from, but because the `EventPageController` is contained by the `UIPageViewController`, having an abstract class gets to be a bit more complex.

The `EventPageController` is what actually displays the event and works exactly the same as the `WeatherController`.

First, add the `page` property, which is set by the `viewController AtIndex:storyboard:` method, by adding the bolded code to the `EventPageController.h` interface in Listing 16-16.

Listing 16-16: Updating the EventPageController Interface

```
#import <UIKit/UIKit.h>

@interface EventPageController : UIViewController
                                    <UIWebViewDelegate>

@property (readwrite, nonatomic) NSUInteger page;
@end
```

Here's where you make the page (number) a property to enable you to determine which URL to load. You also have the EventPageController adopt the UIWebViewDelegate protocol.

Add the bolded code to the EventPageController.m implementation in Listing 16-17.

Listing 16-17:   Updating the EventPageController Implementation

```
#import "EventPageController.h"
#import "RTAppDelegate.h"
#import "Trip.h"

@interface EventPageController ()
@property (weak, nonatomic) IBOutlet UIWebView
          *eventDataView;
@property (weak, nonatomic) IBOutlet
          UIActivityIndicatorView *activityIndicator;

@end


@implementation EventPageController
```

All the work is done in viewDidLoad and the other methods you add. These methods are the same as the code and methods you added to create the WeatherController. If you are hazy on what each does, refer to Chapter 15.

Add the bolded code in Listing 16-18 to EventPageController.m.

Listing 16-18:   Updating viewDidLoad

```
- (void)viewDidLoad
{
  [super viewDidLoad];
  self.eventDataView.delegate = self;
  [self.activityIndicator startAnimating];
  self.activityIndicator.hidesWhenStopped = YES;
  [self.eventDataView setScalesPageToFit:YES];
  RTAppDelegate *appDelegate =
            [[UIApplication sharedApplication] delegate];
  [self.eventDataView loadRequest:
    [NSURLRequest requestWithURL:
        [NSURL URLWithString:
            [appDelegate.trip getEvent:self.page]]]];
}
```

Next, add the rest of the Web View Delegate methods in Listing 16-19, just as you do in Chapter 15.

Listing 16-19: Implementing webView:shouldStartLoadWithRequest: navigationType:, webViewDidFinishLoad:, and add goBack

```objc
- (BOOL)webView:(UIWebView *)webView
    shouldStartLoadWithRequest:(NSURLRequest *)request
  navigationType:(UIWebViewNavigationType)navigationType {

  if (navigationType ==
                    UIWebViewNavigationTypeLinkClicked) {
    UIBarButtonItem *backButton = [[UIBarButtonItem alloc]
      initWithTitle:[NSString stringWithFormat:
        @"Back to %@", self.parentViewController.
                            parentViewController.title]
      style:UIBarButtonItemStylePlain target:self
                            action:@selector(goBack:)];
    self.parentViewController.parentViewController.
          navigationItem.rightBarButtonItem = backButton;

    return YES;
  }
  else return YES;
}

- (void)goBack:(id)sender {

  [self.eventDataView goBack];
}

- (void)webViewDidFinishLoad:(UIWebView *)webView {

  [self.activityIndicator stopAnimating];
  if ([self.eventDataView canGoBack] == NO ) {
    self.parentViewController.parentViewController.
                navigationItem.rightBarButtonItem = nil;
  }
}
```

This code enables you to click a link in an event and then return to the original event page. This is similar to the WeatherController functionality, but here you're adding a button to the Navigation bar rather than to a toolbar.

And Then There's the Bar Button Item

If you build and run the app now, all is well and good except for one thing — because you're now using a Navigation controller, the text color of the Road Trip button is yellow. (If you remember, you set the default in application :DidFinishLaunchingWithOptions: in Chapter 8.)

Not to worry. In `RTDetailViewController splitViewController: willHideViewController:withBarButtonItem: forPopover Controller:`, you just need to add one line of code to make the Road Trip button text green. Add the code in bold in Listing 16-20 to `splitView Controller:willHideViewController:withBarButtonItem:for PopoverController:` in `RTDetailViewController.m`.

Listing 16-20:   Keeping the Road Trip Button Color Green

```
- (void)splitViewController:
               (UISplitViewController *)splitController
         willHideViewController:
                    (UIViewController *)viewController
         withBarButtonItem:
                    (UIBarButtonItem *)barButtonItem
         forPopoverController:
               (UIPopoverController *)popoverController
{
  barButtonItem.title =
         NSLocalizedString(@"Road Trip", @"Road Trip");
  [barButtonItem setTitleTextAttributes:
   [NSDictionary dictionaryWithObject:[UIColor
         greenColor] forKey:UITextAttributeTextColor]
     forState:UIControlStateNormal];
  if ([[self.splitViewController.viewControllers
         lastObject] isKindOfClass:[UINavigationControl
         ler class]])
    [self.navigationItem setLeftBarButtonItem:barButtonI
         tem animated:YES];
  else {
    NSMutableArray *itemsArray =
                    [self.toolbar.items mutableCopy];
    [itemsArray insertObject:barButtonItem atIndex:0];
    [self.toolbar setItems:itemsArray animated:YES];
  }
  self.masterPopoverController = popoverController;
  self.popOverButton = barButtonItem;
}
```

Adding Events Support to the iPhone Storyboard

The Events-related parts of storyboard file for the iPhone is simpler than the one you just did for the iPad, because you don't start with a Navigation controller. The necessary components for the iPhone are shown in Figure 16-3. This figure includes both a Push segue and an Embed segue.

Embed segue from Container View to
EmbeddedPageViewController

Events Controller
Events

UIPageViewController
EmbeddedPageViewController

Push segue from Cell to Events

EventPageController
EventPage

Events

Figure 16-3:
Components
used in
the iPhone
storyboard
file for the
Events
feature.

Your Objective-C code doesn't have to change at all. The key components
for the Events feature on the iPhone only require that you add components
to the iPhone Storyboard file, connect them to the appropriate Objective-C
classes, and connect them to work together. Your small task is summarized
in the following. See Figure 16-3 for a diagram of how these components fit
together.

✔ You must add a new Events controller to the iPhone Storyboard. This
Events controller must be set to use the custom EventsController class.

✔ The "Events" Table view cell in the RTMasterViewController's Table
view must be connected with a push segue to the new Events controller.

✔ An instance of UIPageViewController must be embedded in the
EventsController container. This UIPageViewController is
responsible for managing transitions (such as page curls) between
events pages.

✔ A custom Event Page controller must be added to the iPhone
Storyboard. It is responsible for displaying event information in an
HTML web page rendered by an instance of UIWebView. This Event
Page controller must be set to use the custom EventPageController
class.

You can assemble this the same way that you added the Events-related
component to your iPad storyboard earlier in this chapter, except that you
can skip the Navigation controller and connect a Push segue directly to your
Events controller scene.

Chapter 17

Finding Your Way

In This Chapter

▶ Using the `MapKit` framework

▶ Specifying and changing the type, location, and zoom level of a map

▶ Identifying the iPad's current location

▶ Annotating significant locations on the map

*O*ne of the things that makes an iOS app compelling is the ability you have as a developer to incorporate the user's location into the application functionality. One of the more compelling ways to do that is through the use of maps.

Including the capability to display a map in an application became important as people began to realize the kinds of solutions that can be delivered on the iPad or iPhone. To many travelers, nothing brands you as a tourist like unfolding a large paper map (except, of course, looking through a thick guidebook). In this chapter, I show you how to take advantage of the device's built-in capability to display a map of virtually anywhere in the world, as well as its capability to quickly determine the device location and then indicate it on the map. As I mention way back in Chapter 1, this awareness of your location is one of the things that enables you to develop a totally new kind of application.

In this chapter, I show you how to center your map on an area you want to display (New York, for example), add *annotations* (those cute pins in the map that display a callout to describe that location when you touch them), and even show the user's current location.

The Plan

Your tasks in this chapter are summarized in the following list:

1. First, you define a new custom view controller class, `MapController`, which will be used to display an instance of Apple's `MKMapView`. `MKMapView` is a very useful class, because it does most of the hard work involved in displaying maps, and allowing users to find their way. You will, however, have to add some code to your `MapController` class, so that users can control exactly what map data is displayed. In later chapters, you will even allow users to find specific locations — or themselves — on the map.

2. You will add the `MapController` scene to your iPad storyboard.

3. In your iPad storyboard, you'll use a Replace segue to connect the Map table cell in your `RTMasterViewController` to your new `MapController`. The result will be as shown in Figure 17-1.

4. You will also need to add Apple's `MapKit` framework to your project, so that the `MKMapView` actually can work.

5. Then you add a `MapController` scene to your iPhone storyboard file.

6. In your iPhone storyboard, you'll use a Push segue to connect the Map table cell in your `RTMasterViewController` to the `MapController`. The result is shown in Figure 17-2.

Map   Replace segue from Table View Cell to Map.

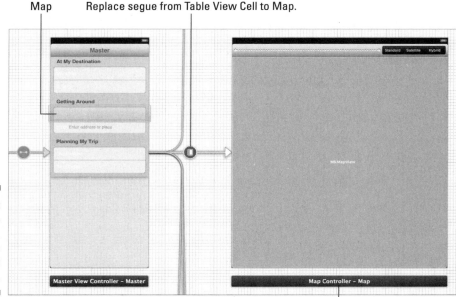

Figure 17-1:
The `Map Controller` scene in your iPad storyboard.

MapController (Map)

Push segue from Cell to Map.

Figure 17-2:
The Map
Control
ler scene
in your
iPhone
storyboard.

Map

MapController (Map)

Setting Up the Map Controller

In this section, you will use the same approach for adding a new view controller that you did in Chapter 16. In this chapter, you will create a new `MapController` class, and use it with a new Map controller scene that you will add to your storyboard. Here we go again!

Adding the custom view controller

To add the `MapController` to the RoadTrip project, follow these steps:

1. **In the Project navigator, select the View Controller Classes group and then either right-click the selection and choose New File from the menu that appears or choose File⇨New⇨New File from the main menu (or press ⌘+N).**

   Whatever method you choose, you're greeted by the New File dialog.

2. **In the left column of the dialog, select Cocoa Touch under the iOS heading, select the Objective-C class template in the top-right pane, and then click Next.**

You'll see a dialog that will enable you to choose the options for your file.

3. **Enter** MapController **in the Class field, choose or enter** RTDetailViewController **in the Subclass Of field, make sure that the Target for iPad check box is selected and that With XIB User Interface is deselected, and then click Next.**

4. **In the Save sheet that appears, click Create.**

Setting up the MapController in the MainStoryboard_iPad

Now that you have a custom view controller, you need to tell the iPad storyboard to load your custom view controller rather than a UIViewController. Follow these steps:

1. **In the Project navigator, select MainStoryboard_iPad and then select View Controller in the View Controller – Map Scene in the Document Outline.**

 2. **Using the Inspector selector, open the Identity inspector in the Utility area and then choose MapController from the Custom Class section's Class drop-down menu, as you did in Chapters 15 and 16.**

Now when Map is selected in the Master View controller, MapController will be instantiated and initialized and will receive events from the user and connect the view to the Trip model.

3. **In the Library pane, scroll back up and drag a Map view onto the Map controller in the Canvas, right below the toolbar.**

The MKMapView class provides a way to display maps and has a lot of functionality that I describe later in this chapter.

4. **Open the main disclosure triangle next to Map Controller in the Document Outline (notice that the name changed from View Controller to Map Controller) and then open the sub-disclosure triangle next to View (see Figure 17-3).**

Notice in Figure 17-3 how the name of the view in the Document Outline is now Map View.

 5. **After selecting the Size inspector in the Inspector selector, update the Autosizing values as I have in Figure 17-3 — selecting all the struts and springs.**

This setting will result in the map being resized to fill the view as the iPad is rotated.

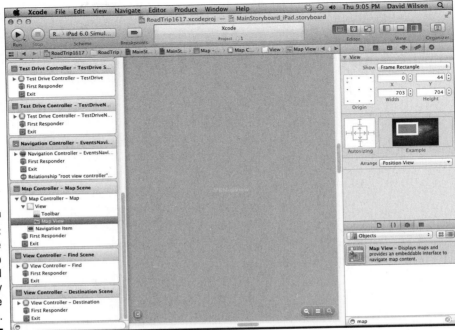

Figure 17-3:
Making sure
the Web
view is sized
correctly
for the
orientation.

You still need to connect the toolbar to the view controller in `RTDetail
ViewController`, the `MapController`'s superclass. You do that just
as you did it in Chapter 15.

6. **Select Map Controller on the Canvas, click the Connections icon in the
   Inspector selector bar to open the Connections inspector, and then
   just drag from the toolbar Outlet in the inspector to the toolbar in the
   `MapController` in the Canvas or the Document Outline.**

   You could also right- or Control-click the Map controller in the
   Document Outline to open the Connections window and then click and
   drag from there.

I want to have a nice segmented control in the toolbar to allow the user
to select a particular Map type — standard, satellite, hybrid, whatever.
Fortunately, the code that implements the Split View Delegate methods that
add the Road Trip button won't get in the way of that. It will just insert the
Road Trip button on the extreme left of the toolbar.

But what if I want the Type selector to be aligned right (and I do)? All I
have to do is add in Interface Builder (or in the code itself, which you did
in Chapter 15) a Flexible Space Bar button item — space that's distributed
equally between the other Bar Button items on the toolbar and the
segmented control. (This is shown in Figure 17-4.)

Figure 17-4:
A Flexible
Space Bar
button item
is added.

To do that, do the following:

1. **To set up a segmented control (the Map Type selector on the toolbar), drag a Flexible Space Bar button item onto the toolbar in the** `MapController`, **as I have in Figure 17-4.**

   This item will expand appropriately to make your segmented control aligned right (along with any other button you may add subsequently — look ahead to Figure 17-8).

2. **Drag a Segmented Control from the Library onto the toolbar and place it to the right of the Flexible Space Bar button item (see Figure 17-5).**

3. **Click the Attributes Inspector icon in the Inspector selector bar to open the Attributes inspector; in the Segmented Control section, change the number of segments to 3.**

4. **Still in the Segmented Control section, make sure that Segment – 0 is selected in the Segment menu, enter** Standard **in the Title field, and then press Return.**

   The Segment menu should change to Segment – 0 Standard.

5. **Now select Segment – 1 in the Segment menu and enter** Satellite **in the Title field; then select Segment – 2 and enter** Hybrid **in the Title field.**

   Be sure to press Return after each change.

6. **Finally, select Black Color from the Segmented Control section's Tint drop-down menu.**

Your Map controller should now look like Figure 17-5.

With your Map selector taken care of, it's time to create an outlet so that `MapController` has access to the Map view to center the map and have the annotations display. Follow these steps:

1. **Close the Utility area and select the Assistant from the Editor selector on the Xcode toolbar.**

   If the `MapController.m` file isn't the one that's displayed, go up to the Assistant's Jump bar and select it.

2. **Control-drag from the Map view in the Canvas or the Document Outline to the** `MapController` **private interface and create an** `IBOutlet` **named** `mapView`**.**

   You'll notice a compiler (Live Issue) error (see Figure 17-6) — `Unknown type name 'MKMapView'`.

3. **Because you'll be using the** `MapKit` **framework that you add in Chapter 11, and have a property of type** `MKMapView`**, you need to update the** `MapController` **public interface (in the MapController.h file) with the bolded code in Listing 17-1 that follows. (You have it adopt the** `MKMapViewDelegate` **protocol as well.)**

Figure 17-5: A segmented control on the right side of the toolbar.

Figure 17-6:
Whoops!

4. **Select and then Control-drag from the segmented control (in this case, it is easier to select and drag from the Document Outline) to the** `MapController` **private interface between the** `@interface` **and** `@end` **statements.**

5. **In the dialog that appears, choose Action from the Connection drop-down menu.**

6. **In the same dialog, leave Value Changed as the selection in the Event drop-down menu.**

   Value Changed is the event that is generated when the user touches a segment to change the selection.

7. **Still in the same dialog, name this action *mapType* by entering** `mapType` **in the Name field, as shown in Figure 17-7; then click Connect.**

   This action will be provided to your code the type of map selected by the user making a choice using the segmented control.

   Because you now have an outlet set up, you'll make the Map controller a delegate in your code as opposed to doing it in Interface Builder as you have been doing previously. I prefer to do it that way because it's more visible when I can see it in the code (it's up to you, though). You'll do this delegating business a bit later — in Listing 17-2, to be precise.

Figure 17-7:
Connecting
the seg-
mented
control.

Listing 17-1:   Updating the MapController Interface

```
#import "RTDetailViewController.h"
#import <MapKit/MapKit.h>

@interface MapController : RTDetailViewController
                                        <MKMapViewDelegate>

@end
```

Adding the MapKit framework

Since you are using an MKMapView, you need to add the MapKit framework
to your project, in the same way that you added other frameworks to the
project. The process is:

1. **Select the project file in the Project Navigator.**

2. **Select the RoadTrip target.**

3. **Select the Build Phases tab.**

4. **Open the Link Binaries with Libraries section.**

5. **Click on the + button to add a new framework.**

6. **Select MapKit.framework.**

7. **In the Project Navigator Drag, drag your new framework into the Frameworks folder.**

Test

Go ahead and run the project.

Presto change-o! If you select the Map entry in the Content controller, you'll see a map centered in the United States as shown in Figure 17-8 (at least you will if you're in the United States). It's as easy as that.

Cute — and pretty impressive given how little work you've done. (The segmented control doesn't count because you still have to implement it.) You need to do some more work to make the map really useful, though.

This is the general approach that you follow when you add more functionality to your application — add the new controller classes, update the storyboard, and so on.

But you — and your users — want and deserve more than a map centered on the United States. Figure 17-9 shows what you'd like to see on your road trip, rather than the standard Map view you get right out of the box.

Figure 17-8:
Your first map.

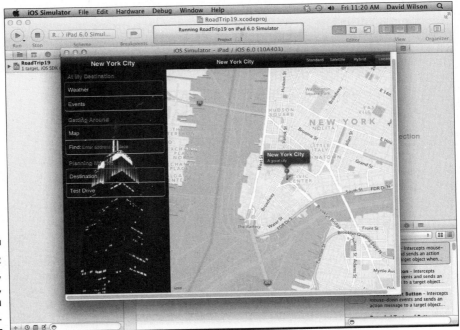

Figure 17-9:
New York,
New York,
a helluva
town.

Putting MapKit through Its Paces

You've done the groundwork for some great map functionality, and now it's time to put the code in place to get that done. Apple's `MapKit.framework` provides all the heavy lifting to make this actually function. `MapKit` enables you to bring up a simple map and also do things with your map without having to do much work at all.

The map looks like the maps in the iOS's built-in apps and creates a seamless mapping experience across multiple applications.

MKMapView

The essence of mapping in iOS is the `MKMapView`. It's a `UIView` subclass, and as you saw in the previous section, you can use it out of the box to create a map. You use this class as is to display map information and to manipulate the map contents from your application. It enables you to center the map on a given coordinate, specify the size of the area you want to display, and annotate the map with custom information (by becoming a Map View delegate).

When you initialize a Map view, you can specify the initial region for that map to display. You do this by setting the *region* property of the map. A region is defined by a center point and a horizontal and vertical distance, referred to as the *span*. The span defines how much of the map will be visible and also determines the zoom level. The smaller the span, the greater the zoom.

The Map view supports these standard map gestures:

- ✔ **Scroll**
- ✔ **Pinch** (to zoom)
- ✔ **Double-tap** (to zoom in)
- ✔ **Two-finger tap** (to zoom out)

You can also specify the Map type — regular, satellite, or hybrid — by changing a single property.

Because `MapKit.framework` was written from scratch, it was developed with the limitations of the iPhone (and later the iPad) in mind. As a result, it optimizes performance on iOS 6 devices by caching data as well as managing memory and seamlessly handling connectivity changes (such as moving from a cellular network to Wi-Fi, for example).

The map data itself is network-hosted, so network connectivity is required.

Although you shouldn't subclass the `MKMapView` class itself, you can tailor a Map view's behavior by providing a delegate object. The delegate object can be any object in your application, as long as it conforms to the `MKMapViewDelegate` protocol.

Enhancing the map

Having this nice global map centered on the United States is kind of interesting but not very useful if you're planning to go to New York. The following sections show you what you would have to do to make the map more useful.

To get things started, you need to close the Assistant, show the Project navigator, and select `MapController.m`.

The current location

What about showing the user's location on the map? That's almost as easy!

In the `MapController.m` file, add the code in bold shown in Listing 17-2 to `viewDidLoad` in `MapController.m`.

Listing 17-2:   Updating viewDidLoad

```
- (void)viewDidLoad
{
  [super viewDidLoad];
  self.mapView.delegate = self;
  self.mapView.showsUserLocation = YES;
}
```

Your additions in Listing 17-2 start by making the `MapController` the Map View delegate. `showsUserLocation` is a `MKMapView` property that tells the Map view whether to show the user location. If `YES`, you get that same blue pulsing dot you see displayed in the iPad's built-in Map application.

If you were to compile and run the application as it stands now on your iPad, you'd be asked if it were okay to use your current location, and if you tapped OK, you'd get what you see in Figure 17-10 — a U.S. map in Landscape orientation with a blue dot that represents the iPad's current location. (You may have to pan the map to see it; a lag may occur while the iPad determines that location, but you should see it eventually.) Of course, to see it in Landscape orientation, you have to turn the iPad, or choose Hardware⇨Rotate Right (or Rotate Left) from the Simulator menu.

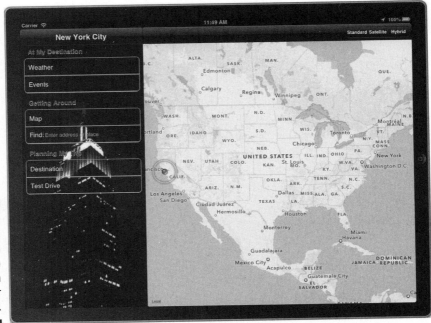

Figure 17-10: Displaying a map in Landscape orientation with a user location.

If you don't see the current location, you might want to check to make sure that you've created the `mapView` outlet to the Map view in the storyboard.

You get your current location if you're running your app *on the iPad.* If you're running it on the Simulator, you get to choose a simulated location.

After launching the application in the Simulator (see Figure 17-11), I've chosen San Francisco by showing the Debug area in the View selector on the toolbar, clicking the Simulate Location icon (it looks like the standard Location icon) in the Debug bar in the Workspace window, and then selecting San Francisco from the menu that appears. I didn't choose New York because later you're going to add some code to shift your map back and forth from the current location to your destination. You can also add more locations (but you don't do that in this book).

You also can simulate the location (with some interesting choices) on the Simulator Debug menu — choose Debug➪*Location.* Check out City Run for example, or even enter the GPS coordinates for any location (choose Custom Location).

Touching the blue dot also displays what's called an *annotation,* and I tell you how to customize the text to display whatever you cleverly devise — including, as you discover in Chapter 18, the address of the current location.

Figure 17-11:
Simulating a location.

It's about the region

Okay, now you've got a blue dot on a map. Cute, but still not that useful for the purposes of the app.

As I mention at the beginning of this chapter, ideally, when you get to New York (or wherever), you should see a map that centers on New York as opposed to the entire United States. To get there from here, however, is also pretty easy. First, you need to look at how you center the map. To do that, you need to add the method declaration `setInitialRegion` to `MapController.m`.

First, update the private interface by adding the bolded code in Listing 17-3 to the class extension in `MapController.m`.

Listing 17-3: Updating the MapController's Private Interface

```
@interface MapController ()
- (IBAction)mapType:(id)sender;
- (void)setInitialRegion;
@end
```

Because the Map controller will get its data from the `Trip` object, as it should, you have to update the implementation to import the `Trip` class as well. Add the bolded code in Listing 17-4 to `MapController.m`.

Listing 17-4: Updating the MapController Implementation

```
#import "MapController.h"
#import "RTAppDelegate.h"
#import "Trip.h"
```

Finally, add the `setInitialRegion` method in Listing 17-5 to `MapController.m`.

Listing 17-5: Add setInitialRegion

```
- (void) setInitialRegion {

  RTAppDelegate* appDelegate =
            [[UIApplication sharedApplication] delegate];
  MKCoordinateRegion region;
  CLLocationCoordinate2D  initialCoordinate =
            [appDelegate.trip destinationCoordinate];
  region.center.latitude = initialCoordinate.latitude;
  region.center.longitude = initialCoordinate.longitude;
  region.span.latitudeDelta = .05;
  region.span.longitudeDelta = .05;
  [self.mapView setRegion:region animated:NO];
}
```

You then need to update `viewDidLoad` to use this method. Add the code in bold in Listing 17-6 to `viewDidLoad` in `MapController.m` to send this message.

Listing 17-6:   Updating viewDidLoad

```
- (void)viewDidLoad
{
    [super viewDidLoad];
    self.mapView.delegate = self;
    self.mapView.showsUserLocation = YES;
    [self setInitialRegion];
}
```

If you run this now, you see more or less the region you see back in Figure 17-9 (but not the annotations . . . at least not yet).

Setting the *region* is how you center the map and set the zoom level. You accomplish all this with the following statement:

```
[self.mapView setRegion:region animated:NO];
```

A region is a Map view property that specifies four pieces of information (as illustrated in Figure 17-12):

- ✔ `region.center.latitude`: Specifies the latitude of the center of the map.

- ✔ `region.center.longitude`: Specifies the longitude of the center of the map.

  For example, the center of the map would be New York if I were to set those values as

  ```
  region.center.latitude = 40.712756;
  region.center.longitude = -74.006047;
  ```

- ✔ `region.span.latitudeDelta`: Specifies the north-to-south distance (in latitudinal degrees) to display on the map. One degree of latitude is approximately 111 kilometers (69 miles). A `region.span.latitudeDelta` of 0.0036 would specify a north-to-south distance on the map of about a quarter of a mile. Latitudes north of the equator have positive values, whereas latitudes south of the equator have negative values.

- ✔ `region.span.longitudeDelta`: Specifies the east-to-west distance (in longitudinal degrees) to display on the map. Unfortunately, the number of miles in one degree of longitude varies based on the latitude. For example, one degree of longitude is approximately 69 miles at the equator, but shrinks to 0 miles at the poles. Longitudes east of the zero meridian (by international convention, the zero or prime meridian passes through the Royal Observatory, Greenwich, in east London) have positive values, and longitudes west of the zero meridian have negative values.

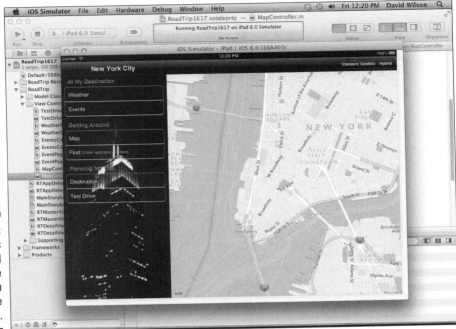

Figure 17-12:
How regions
work and
determine
what you
see on the
map.

Although the span values provide an implicit zoom value for the map, the actual region you see displayed may not equal the span you specify because the map will go to the zoom level that best fits the region that's set. This also means that even if you just change the center coordinate in the map, the zoom level may change because distances represented by a particular span may change at different latitudes and longitudes. To account for that, those smart developers at Apple included a property you can set that changes the center coordinate without changing the zoom level:

```
@property (nonatomic)
                CLLocationCoordinate2D centerCoordinate
```

When you change the value of this property with a new CLLocation Coordinate2D, the map is centered on the new coordinate, and the span values are updated to maintain the current zoom level.

That CLLocationCoordinate2D type is something you'll be using a lot, so I'd like to explain that before I take you any further. The CLLocation Coordinate2D type is a structure that contains a geographical coordinate using the WGS 84 reference frame (the reference coordinate system used by the Global Positioning System):

```
typedef struct {
CLLocationDegrees latitude;
CLLocationDegrees longitude;
} CLLocationCoordinate2D;
```

Here's a little explanation:

- ✔ `latitude`: The latitude in degrees. This is the value you set in the code you just entered (`region.center.latitude = latitude;`). Positive values indicate latitudes north of the equator. Negative values indicate latitudes south of the equator.

- ✔ `longitude`: The longitude in degrees. This is the value you set in the code you just entered (`region.center.longitude = longitude;`). Measurements are relative to the zero meridian, with positive values extending east of the meridian and negative values extending west of the meridian.

`CLLocationDegrees` represents a latitude or longitude value specified in degrees and is a `double`.

To center the map display on New York, you send the `setInitialRegion` message (the code you just entered) when the view is loaded in the `viewDidLoad:` method.

Dealing with network failure

But what if the Internet isn't available? The Apple Human Interface Guidelines (and common sense) say that you should keep the user informed of what's going on. By virtue of the fact that you've made the `MapController` an `MKMapView` delegate, your app is in the position to send a message in the event of a load failure, because if a failure occurs, you're notified if you implement the `mapViewDidFailLoadingMap:` method. You can respond to a load failure by adding the code in Listing 17-7 to `MapController.m`.

Listing 17-7:   Implementing mapViewDidFailLoadingMap:

```
- (void)mapViewDidFailLoadingMap:(MKMapView *)mapView
                        withError:(NSError *)error {

  NSLog(@"Unresolved error %@, %@", error,
                            [error userInfo]);

  UIAlertView *alert = [[UIAlertView alloc]
     initWithTitle:@"Unable to load the map"
     message:@"Check to see if you have internet access"
     delegate:self cancelButtonTitle: @"Thanks"
     otherButtonTitles:nil];
  [alert show];
}
```

Testing this failure business requires disconnecting from the Internet after you have launched RoadTrip. And because of map caching, you might have to pan the map to get the warning.

Changing the Map Type

`MapKit` supports three Map types — standard, satellite, and hybrid.

The Map type is a Map View property and is represented as an enumerated type, which I have cleverly made the segment numbers in the segmented control correspond to:

```
enum {
   MKMapTypeStandard,
   MKMapTypeSatellite,
   MKMapTypeHybrid
};
```

Add the code in bold in Listing 17-8 to the `mapType:` method stub that was created when you added the action in Interface Builder. The code ensures that, when the user selects a new value in the segmented control, it will change the Map type based on the selection.

Listing 17-8:   Updating mapType:

```
- (IBAction)mapType:(id)sender {

    self.mapView.mapType =
        ((UISegmentedControl *)sender).selectedSegmentIndex;
}
```

Avoiding the cast

Because I know that the sender in the `mapType:` method is a `UISegmentedControl`, I could have been clever and instead changed the Sender type in the method declaration:

```
- (IBAction)mapType:(UISegmentedControl *)sender {

    self.mapView.mapType = sender.selectedSegmentIndex;
}
```

I could've changed the Sender type because you have the option to specify the Sender type when you create the action. (Just be sure you've got the right type.) In fact, I could've changed it by changing the type in the dialog back in Step 6 in the "Setting up the MapController in the MainStoryboard_iPad" section earlier in this chapter, where I first created the action.

When the user selects a segment in the segmented control, a *value-changed* event is generated. This is the event (Value Changed) that you specified when you created the action in Step 4 in the "Setting up the MapController in the MainStoryboard_iPad" section, earlier in this chapter.

The segmented control has a `selectedSegmentIndex` property, which contains the value of the selected segment.

I had to do a cast here because the sender is of type `id` — a pointer to an object — which doesn't have a `selectedSegmentIndex` property.

Notice that the text is white — pretty plain vanilla, if you know what I mean. To change the text to something more spring-like — a nice green, in other words — add the code in bold in Listing 17-9 to `application:didFinishLaunchingWithOptions:` in `RTAppDelegate.m`.

Listing 17-9: Making the Segmented Control Text Green

```
- (BOOL)application:(UIApplication *)application
  didFinishLaunchingWithOptions:
                          (NSDictionary *)launchOptions
{
… // other code here
  [[UIApplication sharedApplication] setStatusBarStyle:UIS
        tatusBarStyleBlackOpaque
                                      animated:NO];
  navigationController.navigationBar.barStyle =
                                      UIBarStyleBlack;
  [navigationController.navigationBar setTitleTextAttribu
        tes:[NSDictionary dictionaryWithObject:[UIColor
        yellowColor] forKey:UITextAttributeTextColor]];
  [[UIButton appearance] setTitleColor:
     [UIColor greenColor] forState:UIControlStateNormal];
  [[UIBarButtonItem appearanceWhenContainedIn:
     [UINavigationBar class], nil] setTitleTextAttributes:
        [NSDictionary dictionaryWithObject:
                              [UIColor yellowColor]
     forKey:UITextAttributeTextColor]
     forState:UIControlStateNormal];
  [[UIButton appearanceWhenContainedIn:
              [UIAlertView class], nil] setTitleColor:
     [UIColor whiteColor] forState:UIControlStateNormal];
  [[UIToolbar appearance] setBarStyle:UIBarStyleBlack];
  [[UISegmentedControl appearance]
     setTitleTextAttributes:[NSDictionary
        dictionaryWithObject:[UIColor greenColor]
        forKey:UITextAttributeTextColor]
        forState:UIControlStateNormal];
  [self createDestinationModel:0];
  return YES;
}
```

This will set the text in every segmented control to green.

Adding Annotations

The MKMapView class supports the capability to annotate the map with custom information. The annotation has two parts: the annotation itself, which contains the data for the annotation, and the Annotation view, which displays the data.

Creating the annotation

Any object that conforms to the MKAnnotation protocol is an Annotation object; typically, Annotation objects are existing classes in your application's model. The job of an Annotation object is to know its location (coordinates) on the map along with the text to be displayed in the callout. The MKAnnotation protocol requires a class that adopts that protocol to implement the coordinate property. It can also optionally implement title and subtitle properties. In that case, that text will be displayed in the annotation callout when the user taps the annotation.

Actually, you already have one class that meets that criteria — Destination.

And that's why, when you create the Destination class in Chapter 11 (I told you that I would explain this), I have you add the property with the attributes in the way I do. Annotations are required by the protocol to have the properties I have bolded in the following code:

```
@property (nonatomic, readwrite)
                        CLLocationCoordinate2D coordinate;
@property (nonatomic, readwrite, copy) NSString *title;
@property (nonatomic, readwrite, copy) NSString *subtitle;
```

That's it. You already have the properties in place and initialized (see Chapter 12 if you need to review why that's the case).

Also, in Chapter 11, you include some point-of-interest data in your plist. Although in this example, you only have one point of interest (annotation), you can imagine that in a complete RoadTrip app, you'd have quite a few. You want your points of interest to be annotations as well.

You're going to need to go back to the Trip object to create the annotations, but first you have to add an Annotation class to the Model Classes group by following these steps:

1. **In the Project navigator, select the Model Classes group, and then either right-click the selection and choose New File from the menu that appears or choose File➪New➪New File from the main menu (or press ⌘+N) to open the New File dialog.**

2. **In the left column of the dialog, select Cocoa Touch under the iOS heading, select the Objective-C Class template in the top-right pane, and then click Next.**

   You'll see a dialog that will enable you to choose the options for your file.

3. **Enter** Annotation **in the Class field.**

4. **Choose or enter** NSObject **in the Subclass Of field and then click Next.**

   Note that the Target for iPad and With XIB for User Interface check boxes are dimmed because they are not relevant here — Events is derived from NSObject, and not any type of view controller.

5. **In the Save sheet that appears, click Create.**

Next, you need to add the code necessary for an annotation.

Add the code in bold in Listing 17-10 to Annotation.h.

Listing 17-10: Updating the Annotation Interface

```
#import <Foundation/Foundation.h>
#import <MapKit/MapKit.h>

@interface Annotation: NSObject <MKAnnotation>

@property (nonatomic, readwrite)
                        CLLocationCoordinate2D coordinate;
@property (nonatomic, readwrite, copy) NSString *title;
@property (nonatomic, readwrite, copy) NSString *subtitle;

@end
```

I'm using a generic Annotation class to display the points of interest. As you build out the app, you could also include more information about the points of interest and other information, and create a PointOfInterest class. Then you could make it and Destination subclasses of Annotation. In an annotation, you can also have a right and left Callout Accessory view, which display on the right and left side of the standard callout bubble, respectively.

The Callout view is typically used to link to more detailed information about the annotation. Also, you could link to something such as the EventController to display information about a PointOfInterest. Just food for thought.

You need to update the `Trip` initialization method to create the annotation, but first you have to import the headers you need. Add the bolded code in Listing 17-11 to `Trip.m`.

Listing 17-11:   Updating the Trip Implementation

```
#import "Trip.h"
#import "Destination.h"
#import "Events.h"
#import "Annotation.h"

@interface Trip () {
  NSDictionary *destinationData;
  Destination* destination;
  Events *events;
  NSMutableArray *pois;
}
@end
```

Now you can add the bolded code in Listing 17-12 to `initWithDestination Index:` in `Trip.m`. This will turn the point-of-interest data in the plist (the POIs) into annotations (okay, just one) and add the destination as an annotation to boot.

Listing 17-12:   Updating initWithDestinationIndex:

```
- (id)initWithDestinationIndex:(int)destinationIndex {
  self = [super init];
  if (self)) {

    NSString *filePath = [[NSBundle mainBundle]
        pathForResource:@"Destinations"   ofType:@"plist"];
    NSDictionary *destinations =
      [NSDictionary dictionaryWithContentsOfFile:filePath];
    NSArray *destinationsArray =
        [destinations objectForKey:@"DestinationData"];
    destinationData =
        [destinationsArray objectAtIndex:destinationIndex];
    destination = [[Destination alloc]
          initWithDestinationIndex:destinationIndex];
    events = [[Events alloc] initWithDestinationIndex:dest
        inationIndex];
    NSArray *poiData = destinationData[@"POIs"];
    pois = [[NSMutableArray alloc]
              initWithCapacity:[ poiData count]+1];

    [pois addObject:destination];

    for (NSDictionary *aPOI in poiData) {
```

(continued)

Listing 17-12 *(continued)*

```
        Annotation *annotation = [[Annotation alloc] init];
        CLLocationCoordinate2D coordinate;
        coordinate.latitude =
             [aPOI[@"Latitude"] doubleValue];
        coordinate.longitude =
             [aPOI[@"Longitude"] doubleValue];

        annotation.coordinate = coordinate;
        annotation.title = aPOI[@"Title"];
        annotation.subtitle = aPOI[@"Subtitle"];
        [pois addObject:annotation];
    }
  }
 return self;
}
```

As you can see, you're creating an `Annotation` for each point of interest (`aPOI`) in the `poiData` array and adding it to a `pois` array you create — an array that will hold all the annotations I want to display on the map. `poiData` is the `POIs` array in the `Destination.plist` you created in Chapter 11. Note that instead of adding an initialization method to `Annotation`, you're simply assigning the properties directly rather than sending them as parameters in an initialization method.

If you look closely, you can see that I'm adding `Destination` to the `pois` array as well. That way, it, too, will display on the map.

You have to add some new methods to the interface so that `Trip` can return the annotations (and a map title). You also need to update the `Trip` interface. To do that, add the bolded code in Listing 17-13 to `Trip.h`.

Listing 17-13:   Updating the Trip Interface

```
@interface Trip : NSObject

- (UIImage *) destinationImage;
- (NSString *) destinationName;
- (CLLocationCoordinate2D) destinationCoordinate;

- (id)initWithDestinationIndex:(int)destinationIndex;
- (NSString *)weather;
- (NSUInteger)numberOfEvents;
- (NSString *)getEvent:(NSUInteger)index;
- (NSArray *)createAnnotations;
- (NSString *)mapTitle;
@end
```

Now you get to add all the `Trip` methods that will be used by the `MapController`. Start by adding the `createAnnotations` method shown in Listing 17-14 to `Trip.m`.

Listing 17-14: Adding createAnnotations

```
- (NSArray *)createAnnotations {

    return pois;
}
```

Even though `pois` is a mutable array, I return it as a basic array because that's all that is needed. `MapController` won't be adding any annotations to it.

You also need to add a method to return the map title. Add the `mapTitle` method in Listing 17-15 to `Trip.m`.

Listing 17-15: Add mapTitle

```
- (NSString *)mapTitle {

    return destination.destinationName;
}
```

All that's really left at this point is to add the code to `MapController` to get the annotations and send them to the Map view. The next section walks you through that.

Displaying the map title and annotations

Start by adding the bolded code in Listing 17-16 to update the private interface in `MapController.m`. As you can see, you'll be adding two methods — one to add the annotations, and another to provide the map title. I explain both as you go along.

Listing 17-16: Updating the MapController Private Interface

```
@interface MapController ()
- (IBAction)mapType:(id)sender;
- (void)setInitialRegion;
- (void)addAnnotations;
- (NSString *)mapTitle;
@end
```

With these code additions, you'll display the annotations by sending yourself the `addAnnotations` message in `viewDidLoad`. But another thing I would like to do is display the title of the destination either on the Navigation bar or the toolbar, and I'll do that in `viewDidLoad` as well.

Displaying a title in the Navigation bar is really easy, as you can see in Listing 17-17 — all you need to do is assign whatever you want it to be to the view controller's `title` property. But if you have a toolbar, your task isn't quite as easy, but it does give me a chance to show you a little more about how to work with toolbar items, so in a sense that's a good thing.

Update `viewDidLoad` by adding the bolded code in Listing 17-17 to `viewDidLoad` in `MapController.m`.

Listing 17-17: Update viewDidLoad

```
- (void)viewDidLoad
{
  [super viewDidLoad];
  self.mapView.delegate = self;
  self.mapView.showsUserLocation = YES;
  [self setInitialRegion];
  RTAppDelegate* appDelegate = [[UIApplication
                                sharedApplication] delegate];
  if ([[UIDevice currentDevice] userInterfaceIdiom] ==
                                UIUserInterfaceIdiomPad) {
    UILabel * titleLabel = [[UILabel alloc]
                    initWithFrame:CGRectMake (0,0,250,44)];
    titleLabel.textColor = [UIColor yellowColor];
    titleLabel.font = [UIFont boldSystemFontOfSize:17];
    titleLabel.textAlignment = NSTextAlignmentCenter;
    titleLabel.backgroundColor = [UIColor clearColor];
    titleLabel.text = [self mapTitle];
    UIBarButtonItem *titleView = [[UIBarButtonItem alloc]
                    initWithCustomView:titleLabel];
    UIBarButtonItem *flexibleSpace=
    [[UIBarButtonItem alloc] initWithBarButtonSystemItem:
        UIBarButtonSystemItemFlexibleSpace
                                target:nil action:nil];
    flexibleSpace.width = 1.0;
    NSMutableArray *itemsArray =
                        [self.toolbar.items mutableCopy];
    [itemsArray insertObject:flexibleSpace atIndex:
                                [itemsArray count]-2];
    [itemsArray insertObject:titleView atIndex:
                                [itemsArray count]-2];
    [self.toolbar setItems:itemsArray animated:NO];
  }
  else
    self.title = [appDelegate.trip mapTitle];
[self addAnnotations];
}
```

You begin by determining whether you're on the iPad or the iPhone. If you're on the iPad, I make the assumption that you have a toolbar. (You could add the logic to see whether it is a toolbar or a Navigation bar on the iPad if you need to, just as you do in Chapter 8).

If you're on an iPad, you create a `Label` object with a clear background, a bold system font of size `17`, aligned center and with a width of `250`. (You could determine the actual size you need by using a number of methods in `NSString`, but that's pretty complicated and outside the scope of this book.) You also send the `mapTitle` message to get the title, which I get to next.

```
UILabel * titleLabel = [[UILabel alloc]
                    initWithFrame:CGRectMake (0,0,250,44)];
    titleLabel.textColor = [UIColor yellowColor];
    titleLabel.font = [UIFont boldSystemFontOfSize:17];
    titleLabel.textAlignment = NSTextAlignmentCenter;
    titleLabel.backgroundColor = [UIColor clearColor];
    titleLabel.text = [self mapTitle];
```

You then create a `UIBarButtonItem` by initializing it with the view (`UILabel`) you just created. This enables you to add virtually whatever you want to the toolbar, as long as it's a view.

```
UIBarButtonItem *titleView = [[UIBarButtonItem alloc]
                    initWithCustomView:titleLabel];
```

Then you create a flexible space of the kind you did in Chapter 15 — doing so adds a space that's distributed equally between the other Bar Button items on the toolbar — so the title will be centered between the Map-type segmented control on the right (which already has a flexible space item in front of it) and the Road Trip button (if there is one) or the left side of the toolbar (if there isn't).

```
UIBarButtonItem *flexibleSpace=
  [[UIBarButtonItem alloc] initWithBarButtonSystemItem:
        UIBarButtonSystemItemFlexibleSpace
                            target:nil action:nil];
flexibleSpace.width = 1.0;
```

You then add the items to the toolbar's `items` array just as you do in Chapter 13.

```
[itemsArray insertObject:flexibleSpace atIndex:
                            [itemsArray count]-2];
[itemsArray insertObject:titleView atIndex:
                            [itemsArray count]-2];
[self.toolbar setItems:itemsArray animated:NO];
```

The `[itemsArray count]-2` index means that you'll add this item before the two existing items (the existing flexible space and the segmented control).

If you are not on the iPad, you just assign whatever you want the title to be to the `title` property of the view controller and it is displayed on the Navigation bar.

```
else
  self.title = [appDelegate.trip mapTitle];
```

With the title taken care of, you send yourself the `addAnnotations` message.

```
[self addAnnotations];
```

Before I get to the `addAnnotations` method you'll need to add, I'll have you finish up the title by adding the `mapTitle` method in Listing 17-18 to `MapController.m`.

Listing 17-18:   Add mapTitle

```
- (NSString *)mapTitle {

  RTAppDelegate* appDelegate = [[UIApplication
                                sharedApplication] delegate];

  return [appDelegate.trip mapTitle];
}
```

`mapTitle` gets the map title by sending the `mapTitle` message to the `Trip` object — another model responsibility. (This also gives you a chance, as you'll see in Chapter 19, to title the map based on whatever criteria you would like, such as the current location.)

With your title taken care of, it's time to add the annotations. Start by adding the `addAnnotations` method in Listing 17-19 to `MapController.m`.

Listing 17-19:   Add addAnnotations

```
- (void)addAnnotations {

  RTAppDelegate* appDelegate =
              [[UIApplication sharedApplication] delegate];
  [self.mapView addAnnotations:
                  [appDelegate.trip createAnnotations]];
}
```

I make this a separate method because I want to be able to add more annotations after the view is loaded. Although you won't be adding additional annotations here, you take advantage of this method when you implement the `FindController` in Chapter 19 to display locations the user wants to see on a map.

To add an annotation to a Map view, just send the `addAnnotations` message with an array of annotations that have adopted the `MKAnnotation` protocol; that is, each one has a `coordinate` property and an optional `title` (and `subtitle`) method — if it turns out you want to actually display something in the annotation callout.

The Map view places annotations on the screen by sending its delegate the `mapView:viewForAnnotation:` message. This message is sent for each annotation object in the array. Here you can create a custom view or return `nil` to use the default view. (If you don't implement this delegate method — which you won't, in this case — the default view is also used.)

Creating your own (customized) Annotation views is beyond the scope of this book (although I can tell you that the most efficient way to provide the content for an Annotation view is to set its `image` property). Fortunately, the default Annotation view is fine for your purposes. It displays a pin in the location specified in the coordinate property of the Annotation delegate. When the user touches the pin, the optional title and subtitle text will display if the `title` and `subtitle` methods are implemented in the Annotation delegate.

You can also add callouts to the Annotation view, such as a Detail Disclosure button (the one that looks like a white chevron in a blue button in a Table View cell) or the Info button (like the one you see in many of the utility apps), by using the built-in `MKPinAnnotationView` — you don't have to create your own Annotation view, in other words.

If you compile and build your project, your map is going to proudly display the annotations you added, as shown in Figure 17-13. (You'll have to pan a bit to see both annotations). Notice the Map view is beginning to look more and more like our gal back in Figure 17-9.

Figure 17-13:
Displaying
an annota-
tion and its
callout.

Going to the Current Location

Although you require the user to pan to the user location on the map if he or
she wants to see it, it's kind of annoying in this particular case unless you're
actually coding this in or around New York City. To remove at least that
annoyance from your life, I show you how easy it is to add a button to the
Navigation bar to zoom in to the current location and then back to the map
region and span you're currently displaying.

Add the bolded code in Listing 17-20 to add the button in the
`MapController` method `viewDidLoad`.

Listing 17-20:   Updating viewDidLoad

```
- (void)viewDidLoad
{
  [super viewDidLoad];
  self.mapView.delegate = self;
  self.mapView.showsUserLocation = YES;

  [self setInitialRegion];
  RTAppDelegate* appDelegate = [[UIApplication
```

```
                            sharedApplication] delegate];
 if ([[UIDevice currentDevice] userInterfaceIdiom] ==
                            UIUserInterfaceIdiomPad) {
   UILabel * titleLabel = [[UILabel alloc]
                 initWithFrame:CGRectMake (0,0,250,44)];
   titleLabel.textColor = [UIColor yellowColor];
   titleLabel.font = [UIFont boldSystemFontOfSize:17];
   titleLabel.textAlignment = NSTextAlignmentCenter;
   titleLabel.backgroundColor = [UIColor clearColor];
   titleLabel.text = [self mapTitle];
   UIBarButtonItem *titleView = [[UIBarButtonItem alloc]
                 initWithCustomView:titleLabel];
   UIBarButtonItem *flexibleSpace=
   [[UIBarButtonItem alloc] initWithBarButtonSystemItem:
       UIBarButtonSystemItemFlexibleSpace
                            target:nil action:nil];

   flexibleSpace.width = 1.0;
   NSMutableArray *itemsArray =
                 [self.toolbar.items mutableCopy];
   [itemsArray insertObject:flexibleSpace atIndex:
                            [itemsArray count]-2];
   [itemsArray insertObject:titleView atIndex:
                            [itemsArray count]-2];
   [self.toolbar setItems:itemsArray animated:NO];
 }
 else {
   self.title = [appDelegate.trip mapTitle];
 }
[self addAnnotations];
 UIBarButtonItem *locateButton = [[UIBarButtonItem
         alloc] initWithTitle:@"Locate" style:UIBarB
         uttonItemStyleBordered target:self action:@
         selector(goToLocation:)];;
 if ([[UIDevice currentDevice] userInterfaceIdiom] ==
         UIUserInterfaceIdiomPad) {
   NSMutableArray *itemsArray =
                 [self.toolbar.items mutableCopy];
   [itemsArray insertObject:locateButton
                 atIndex:[itemsArray count]];
   [self.toolbar setItems:itemsArray animated:NO];
 }
 else {
   self.navigationItem.rightBarButtonItem = locateButton;
 }
}
```

This may look familiar because it's what you did to add the Back button in
Chapter 15. When the user taps the Locate button you create here, you've
specified that the goToLocation: message is to be sent [action:@
selector(goToLocation:)] to the MapController (target:self).

```
UIBarButtonItem *locateButton =
    [[UIBarButtonItem alloc] initWithTitle: @"Locate"
    style:UIBarButtonItemStylePlain target:self
    action:@selector(goToLocation:)];
self.navigationItem.rightBarButtonItem = locateButton;
```

Notice that I don't check to see whether this is a Navigation bar or a toolbar. I'm assuming a toolbar, but if you think you may want to someday, for some reason, make this a Navigation bar, I leave this as an exercise for the reader.

Don't forget, to go back to a location you need to choose a simulated location if you are using the Simulator, as you did in the earlier section "Enhancing the map."

Next, add the `goToLocation:` method in Listing 17-21 to `MapController.m`.

Listing 17-21: Adding goToLocation:

```
- (void)goToLocation:(id)sender {

  MKUserLocation *annotation = self.mapView.userLocation;
  CLLocation *location = annotation.location;
  if (nil == location)
    return;
  CLLocationDistance distance = MAX(4*location.
        horizontalAccuracy,500);
  MKCoordinateRegion region =
        MKCoordinateRegionMakeWithDistance
            (location.coordinate, distance, distance);
  [self.mapView setRegion:region animated:NO];

  if ([[UIDevice currentDevice] userInterfaceIdiom] ==
                              UIUserInterfaceIdiomPad) {
    NSArray *itemsArray = self.toolbar.items;

    UIBarButtonItem *locateButton = [itemsArray
                objectAtIndex:[itemsArray count]-1];
    locateButton.action = @selector(goToDestination:);
    locateButton.title = @"Destination";
  }
  else {
    self.navigationItem.rightBarButtonItem.action =
                          @selector(goToDestination:);
    self.navigationItem.rightBarButtonItem.title =
                                        @"Destination";
  }
}
```

When the user taps the Locate button, your app first checks to see whether the location is available. (It may take a few seconds after the application starts for the location to become available.) If not, you simply return from the method without changing the region. (You could, of course, show an alert informing the user what's happening and to try again in 10 seconds or so — I leave that up to you.)

If the location is available, your app computes the span for the region the user is moving to. In this case, the following code

```
CLLocationDistance distance =
            MAX(4*location.horizontalAccuracy,500);
```

computes the span to be four times the `horizontalAccuracy` of the device (but no less than 1,000 meters). `horizontalAccuracy` is a radius of uncertainty given the accuracy of the device; that is, the user is somewhere within that circle.

You then call the `MKCoordinateRegionMakeWithDistance` function that creates a new `MKCoordinateRegion` from the specified coordinate and distance values. `distance` and `distance` correspond to `latitudinalMeters` and `longitudinalMeters`, respectively. (I'm using the same value for both parameters here.)

If you didn't want to change the span, you could've simply set the Map view's `centerCoordinate` property to `userLocation`, and as I said earlier in the "It's about the region" section, that would've centered the region at the `userLocation` coordinate without changing the span.

When the user taps the Location button, you change the title on the button to the Map title and change the `@selector` to `(goToDestination:)`. You access the button on the iPad in the toolbar `itemsArray` and on the iPhone via the `navigationItem`.

This means that the next time the user touches the button, the `goToDestination:` message will be sent, so you'd better add the code in Listing 17-22 to `MapController.m`. This sets the region back to the Destination region and toggles the button title back to Locate.

Listing 17-22:   Adding goToDestination:

```
- (void)goToDestination:(id)sender {

  [self setInitialRegion];
  if ([[UIDevice currentDevice] userInterfaceIdiom] ==
        UIUserInterfaceIdiomPad) {
```

(continued)

Listing 17-22 *(continued)*

```
    NSArray *itemsArray = self.toolbar.items;
    UIBarButtonItem *locateButton = [itemsArray
            objectAtIndex:[itemsArray count]-1];
    locateButton.action = @selector(goToLocation:);
    locateButton.title = @"Locate";
  }
  else {
    self.navigationItem.rightBarButtonItem.action =
                              @selector(goToLocation:);
    self.navigationItem.rightBarButtonItem.title =
                                        @"Locate";
  }
}
```

Now run your app (and if you're running on the Simulator, choose your default location as explained in the section "Enhancing the map," earlier in this chapter).

By the way, look at the button style. Because you use an appearance proxy in Chapter 8, all your buttons will be customized in the way you specified.

You can see the result of touching the Locate button in Figure 17-14.

Figure 17-14:
Go to the current location.

Because you have the user location, you might be tempted to use that to center the map, and that would work fine, as long as you start the location-finding mechanism stuff as soon as the program launches. The problem is that the hardware may take a while to find the current location, and if you don't wait long enough, you get an error. You can add the code to center the map to a method that executes later, such as

```
-(void)observeValueForKeyPath:(NSString *)keyPath
    ofObject:(id)object change:(NSDictionary *)change
                              context:(void *)context {
```

This message is sent as soon as the map starts getting location information, but you'll see an initial view and then a redisplay of the centered view. For aesthetic reasons, you really need to initialize MapController and MapView at program startup — an exercise for the reader.

Update the iPhone Storyboard

The iPhone storyboard for maps is very similar to the iPad storyboard. In fact, the quick and easy way to update your iPhone storyboard is as follows:

1. **Select the iPad storyboard file in the Project Navigator.**

2. **Click the mouse on the Map Controller – Map Scene to select it. Make sure that the whole Map Scene is selected and highlighted.**

3. **Copy the Map Controller Scene by choosing Edit⇨Copy.**

4. **Select your iPhone storyboard file in the Project Navigator.**

5. **Paste the Map Controller Scene into the iPhone storyboard file.**

6. **Control-drag from the Map item in the Master View controller over to the Map Controller Scene, and choose the Push segue from the pop-up menu.**

7. **Test your new map capabilities in the iPhone simulator.**

8. **Congratulate yourself on a job well done.**

Chapter 18

Geocoding

*B*eing able to see where I am on an iPad map has visual appeal — that dot is a real nice shade of blue — but I'm an exacting kind of guy who'd like to know *exactly* where I am in the scheme of things. I'd like to know the street address of where I'm standing, in other words. Geocoding makes that possible. (If I have the address, I can also write some code to turn the iPad's current address into an Address Book contact.)

In this chapter, I explain geocoding and have you write the code that will take the user's current location and turn it into an address that you display in the Current Location annotation. (In the next chapter, I show you how to take an address or point of interest and display it as an annotation on a map.)

Understanding Geocoding on the iPad

Converting an address to a set of map coordinates is called *forward geocoding*, while converting from a set of coordinates to an address is called *reverse geocoding*. Both forward and reverse geocoding are supported in Apple's CLGeocoder class — which is part of Apple's CoreLocation framework. I showed you how to add the CoreLocation framework to the RoadTrip project way back in Chapter 11.

The CLGeocoder class provides services for converting between a coordinate (specified as a latitude and longitude) and the user-friendly representation of that coordinate. *User-friendly representation of the coordinate* means the street, city, state, and country information of a given location or a relevant point of interest, landmark, or other identifying information. The CLGeocoder class also provides services for the reverse: returning the coordinate value for a text string that is the user-friendly representation of that coordinate.

To use a `CLGeocoder` object, first create it and then send it a forward- or reverse-geocoding message.

- ✓ **Reverse-geocoding:** These requests take a latitude and longitude value and find a user-readable address.

- ✓ **Forward-geocoding:** These requests take a user-readable address and find the corresponding latitude and longitude value. Forward-geocoding requests may also return additional information about the specified location, such as a point of interest or building at that location.

For both types of request, the results are returned as an array of `CLPlacemark` objects to a completion handler block. In the case of forward-geocoding requests, multiple `placemark` objects may be returned if the provided information yields multiple possible locations.

A `CLPlacemark` object contains, among other things, the following properties:

- ✓ `location`: Very useful for forward geocoding, which I explain in Chapter 19

- ✓ `name`: The name of the placemark

- ✓ `addressDictionary`: A dictionary containing the Address Book keys and values for the placemark

- ✓ `ISOcountryCode`: The abbreviated country name

- ✓ `country`: The name of the country

- ✓ `postalCode`: The postal code

- ✓ `administrativeArea`: The state or province

- ✓ `subAdministrativeArea`: Additional administrative area information (such as county)

- ✓ `locality`: The city

- ✓ `subLocality`: Additional city-level information such as neighborhood or a common name for the location

- ✓ `thoroughfare`: The street

- ✓ `subThoroughfare`: Additional street-level information, such as the building number

- ✓ `region`: The `CLRegion`

Landmark and geographic information may also be available in the `CLPlacemark` object in the following properties:

✔ `areasOfInterest`: The relevant areas of interest associated with the placemark

✔ `inlandWater`: The name of the inland water body associated with the placemark

✔ `ocean`: The name of the ocean associated with the placemark

To make smart decisions about what types of information to return, the geocoder server uses all the information provided to it when processing the request. For example, if the user is moving quickly along a highway, the geocoder might return the name of the overall region rather than the name of a small park that the user is passing through.

Here are some rather loose rules (Apple's) for using the `CLGeocoder` object:

✔ Send at most one geocoding request for any single user action. That is, don't start another request until the first one has completed.

✔ If the app needs the geocoded location in more than one map location, save and then reuse the results from the initial geocoding request instead of doing another one.

✔ When you want to update the user's current location automatically (such as when the user is moving), issue new geocoding requests only when the user has moved a significant distance, a reasonable amount of time has passed, or both. For example, in a typical situation, you should not send more than one geocoding request per minute.

✔ Do not start a geocoding request if your application is inactive or in the background.

✔ An iOS-based device must have access to the network in order for the `CLGeocoder` object to return detailed placemark information. Although iOS stores enough information locally to report the localized country name and ISO country code for many locations, if country information is not available for a specific location, the `CLGeocoder` object may still report an error.

You can use a `CLGeocoder` object either in conjunction with, or independent of, the classes of the `MapKit` framework.

In this chapter, I show you how to add the code to do a reverse geocode. Essentially, you are going to update the `goToLocation:` method to use reverse geocoding to display the address of the current location in the annotation. In the next chapter, you get to do pretty much the same thing in order to set up a forward geocode, although you send a different message and process the placemark differently.

Reverse Geocoding

You'll begin the process of implementing reverse geocoding by adding a new instance variable to `MapController.m` to store a reference to the `CLGeocoder` object. You do all this by adding the bolded code in Listing 18-1 to `MapController.m`. As you'll see later, you'll need that reference to cancel a request.

Listing 18-1: Updating the MapController Implementation

```
#import "MapController.h"
#import "RTAppDelegate.h"
#import "Trip.h"

@interface MapController () {
  CLGeocoder* geocoder;
}
- (IBAction)mapType:(id)sender;
- (void)setInitialRegion;
- (NSString *)mapTitle;
- (void)addAnnotations;
@end
```

Next, you allocate and initialize the `CLGeocoder` and send it a message to return the information for the current location. Adding the bolded code in Listing 18-2 to `goToLocation` in `MapController.m` does that for you.

Listing 18-2: Updating goToLocation

```
- (void)goToLocation:(id)sender {

void (^clGeocodeCompletionHandler)(NSArray *, NSError *) =
  ^(NSArray *placemarks, NSError *error){


    CLPlacemark *placemark = [placemarks objectAtIndex:0];
    if (error!= nil || placemark == nil) {
      NSLog(@"Geocoder failure! Error code: %u,
        description: %@, and reason: %@", error.code,
          [error localizedDescription],
                          [error localizedFailureReason]);
    }
    else {
      self.mapView.userLocation.subtitle =
          [NSString stringWithFormat: @" lat:%f lon:%f",
            placemark.location.coordinate.latitude,
                  placemark.location.coordinate.longitude];
```

```
      if ([placemark.areasOfInterest objectAtIndex:0]) {
        self.mapView.userLocation.title =
              [placemark.areasOfInterest objectAtIndex:0];
      }
      else {
        if (placemark.thoroughfare) {
          if (placemark.subThoroughfare)
            self.mapView.userLocation.title =
             [NSString stringWithFormat:@"%@ %@",
                          placemark.subThoroughfare,
                                placemark.thoroughfare];

        else
           self.mapView.userLocation.title =
             [NSString stringWithFormat:@"%@",
                                placemark.thoroughfare];
        }
        else {
          if (placemark.locality) {
            self.mapView.userLocation.title =
                                      placemark.locality;

          }
          else
            self.mapView.userLocation.title = @"Your
          location";
        }
      }
    }
};

MKUserLocation *annotation = self.mapView.userLocation;
CLLocation *location = annotation.location;
if (nil == location)
  return;
CLLocationDistance distance = MAX(4*location.
        horizontalAccuracy,500);
MKCoordinateRegion region =
        MKCoordinateRegionMakeWithDistance
              (location.coordinate, distance, distance);
[self.mapView setRegion:region animated:NO];

if ([[UIDevice currentDevice] userInterfaceIdiom] ==
                              UIUserInterfaceIdiomPad) {
  NSArray *itemsArray = self.toolbar.items];
  UIBarButtonItem *locateButton = [itemsArray
                objectAtIndex:[itemsArray count]-1];
  locateButton.action = @selector(goToDestination:);
  locateButton.title = @"Destination";
}
else {
```

(continued)

Listing 18-2 *(continued)*

```
    self.navigationItem.rightBarButtonItem.action =
                          @selector(goToDestination:);
    self.navigationItem.rightBarButtonItem.title =
                          @"Destination";
}
geocoder = [[CLGeocoder alloc]init];
[geocoder reverseGeocodeLocation:location completionHand
       ler:clGeocodeCompletionHandler];

}
```

The code you've added allocates and initializes the CLGeocoder, sends it the message to reverse geocode, and provides it with a completion handler block (just as you did with the animation you did in Chapter 10).

```
geocoder = [[CLGeocoder alloc]init];
[geocoder reverseGeocodeLocation:location completionHand
       ler:clGeocodeCompletionHandler];
```

Sending the reverseGeocodeLocation:completionHandler: message is how you make a reverse-geocoding request for the specified location.

This method submits the location data to the geocoding server asynchronously and returns. Your completion handler block will be executed on the main thread. (As I explain in Chapter 8, the main thread encompasses the application's main run loop — applications can add [spawn] additional threads, which is beyond the scope of this book).

After initiating a reverse-geocoding request, you shouldn't make another reverse- or forward-geocoding request until the first request is completed.

For both types of requests, the results are returned to the completion block in a CLPlacemark object. In the case of forward-geocoding requests, multiple placemark objects may be returned if what you submitted results in more than one possible location.

Note that the block is called *whether or not the request is successful.* It's invoked when the CLGeocoder either finds placemark information for its coordinate or receives an error. The CLPlacemark object, as you previously saw in the "Understanding Geocoding on the iPad" section, earlier in this chapter, will contain placemark data for a given latitude and longitude. Placemark data includes the properties that hold the country, state, city, and so on.

The completion handler is a block that appears in the following form:

```
void (^CLGeocodeCompletionHandler)
                    (NSArray *placemark, NSError *error);
```

As you can see, `placemark` contains an array of `CLPlacemark` objects. For most geocoding requests, this array should contain only one entry. However, forward-geocoding requests may return multiple placemark objects in situations in which the specified address couldn't be resolved to a single location.

If the request was canceled or an error in obtaining the placemark information occurred, `placemark` is `nil`.

`error` contains a pointer to an `error` object (if any) indicating why the placemark data wasn't returned.

```
if (error!= nil || placemark == nil) {
  NSLog(@"Geocoder failure! Error code:%u, description:
    %@, and reason: %@", error.code,
        [error localizedDescription],
                    [error localizedFailureReason]);
    }
```

The `CLGeocoder` can fail for a variety of reasons, such as the service is down or it can't find an address for the coordinate. If the `CLGeocoder` fails, you get back an `error` object that can have some useful information. I'll leave it to you to explore the details of the error information on your own.

Although I simply log a message here, you may want to expand the user interface to inform the user what's happening. Doing so isn't important in this case because you can always just leave the annotation as Current Location, but when you start dragging annotations (which you can do, but won't in this book), you might want to develop a plan for what to display in the annotation if the `CLGeocoder` fails.

If the `CLGeocoder` is successful, you update the `userLocation` annotation — provided, as always by the Map view (if you set the `showsUserLocation` property to `YES` as you did in Chapter 17) — in the completion handler. `userLocation`, as I explain in Chapter 17, is a Map View property representing the user's current location.

As I explain earlier, the `CLPlacemark` object returned when the block is invoked stores placemark data for a given latitude and longitude. To update what's displayed in the annotation using the information you get back from the geocoder, you start by setting the subtitle using the `coordinate` in the Placemark Location property:

```
self.mapView.userLocation.subtitle =
  [NSString stringWithFormat: @" lat:%f lon:%f",
     placemark.location.coordinate.latitude,
              placemark.location.coordinate.longitude];
```

If an `areasOfInterest` exists in the placemark, you set the `title` to that:

```
if ([placemark.areasOfInterest objectAtIndex:0]) {
  self.mapView.userLocation.title =
            [placemark.areasOfInterest objectAtIndex:0];
}
```

Otherwise, you see whether you have a `thoroughfare` and use that for the `title` (along with a `subthoroughfare`; together they provide the "street address"). Occasionally, however, you may find that a thoroughfare (street) exists, but no sub-thoroughfare (street number). When that's the case, you just display the thoroughfare.

```
if (placemark.thoroughfare) {
  if (placemark.subThoroughfare)
    self.mapView.userLocation.title =
      [NSString stringWithFormat:@"%@ %@",
        placemark.subThoroughfare, placemark.thoroughfare];
  else
    self.mapView.userLocation.title =
            [NSString stringWithFormat:@"%@",
                                placemark.thoroughfare];
}
```

If no `thoroughfare` exists, you try for a `locality`, and if all else fails, you use a general-purpose location string.

```
if (placemark.locality ) {
  self.mapView.userLocation.title = placemark.locality;
}
else
  self.mapView.userLocation.title = @"Your location";
```

Because the `CLGeocoder` operates asynchronously, the user might tap the button to return to the Destination map before the `CLGeocoder` has completed the request. If that's the case, you'll want to cancel the `CLGeocoder` request. To do so, add the bolded code in Listing 18-3 to `goToDestination:` in `MapController.m`.

Listing 18-3: **Updating goToDestination:**

```
- (void)goToDestination:(id)sender {

   [geocoder cancelGeocode];
   geocoder = nil;

   [self setInitialRegion];
   self.navigationItem.rightBarButtonItem.title =
   @"Locate";
   self.navigationItem.rightBarButtonItem.action =
   @selector(goToLocation:);
}
```

The `cancelGeocode` message cancels a pending geocoding request, which causes the completion handler block to be called.

You cancel the `CLGeocoder` request in this method because although you start the `CLGeocoder` in the `goToLocation:` method, it actually doesn't return the information in that method. It operates asynchronously when it constructs the placemark, gives up, or sends an error. You also set the instance variable to `nil` so that ARC will release the `CLGeocoder`.

But not only might the user return to the Destination map before the geocoder request completes, he or she might also leave the Map view entirely and return to the Content controller. This means that you'll want to cancel the request when the view disappears as well, and the logical place to do that is in `viewWillDisappear:`, which notifies the view controller that its view is about to be dismissed, covered, or otherwise hidden from view. In the Map controller, that will happen only if the user taps the Back button to return to the Main view.

Add `viewWillDisappear:` to `MapController.m` with the code in Listing 18-4. (If you added the capability to track user location changes in Chapter 17, `viewWillDisappear` will already be there.)

Listing 18-4: **Overriding viewWillDisappear:**

```
- (void) viewWillDisappear:(BOOL)animated {

   [geocoder cancelGeocode];
   geocoder = nil;
   [super viewWillDisappear:animated];
}
```

After initiating a forward-geocoding request, don't make another forward- or reverse-geocoding request until the first one completes or you cancel it.

Figure 18-1 shows the result of your adventures in reverse geocoding.

Figure 18-1:
Reverse
geocoding.

Chapter 19

Finding a Location

*I*t's pretty useful when traveling to be able to enter a location and have that display on a map. Although you can do that in many of the map applications currently available, it does take you out of the app you are in. What's more, you can't take that information and then do something with it in your own app, such as display it with all your other annotations.

As I explain in the previous chapter, geocoding allows you to take an address and turn it into a map coordinate. This enables you to add a feature to RoadTrip that allows the user to enter an address, or even just the name of a well-known landmark, and display it on the map. (Reverse geocoding, demonstrated in the previous chapter, allows you to take a map coordinate — your current location, for example — and turn it into an address.) In this chapter, you find out how to enter a location (an address or point of interest) and display it on a map as an annotation.

Setting Up the Find Controller

You already have one piece of the geocoding puzzle in place on your storyboard; I'm talking about the appropriately named Find controller. The trick now is to add the custom controller that will implement the Find features you want.

Adding the custom view controller

To add the `FindController` to the RoadTrip project, follow the same steps you have several times before:

1. **In the Project navigator, select the View Controller Classes group and then either right-click the selection and choose New File from the menu that appears or choose File⇨New⇨New File from the main menu (or press ⌘+N).**

   Whatever method you choose, you're greeted by the New File dialog.

2. **In the left column of the dialog, select Cocoa Touch under the iOS heading, select the Objective-C class template in the top-right pane, and then click Next.**

   You'll see a dialog that will enable you to choose the options for your file.

3. **Enter** FindController **in the Class field, choose MapController from the Subclass Of drop-down menu (**FindController **is a subclass of** MapController **with a little more functionality), and make sure that the Target for iPad check box is selected and that With XIB for User Interface is deselected. Click Next.**

4. **In the Save sheet that appears, click Create.**

Setting up FindController in the MainStoryboard_iPad

Because Find Controller's user interface is identical to the Map Controller's, setting up the Find controller in the storyboard is virtually the same as setting up the Map controller in Chapter 17. You do, however, have two choices here. First, you can simply duplicate what you did in Chapter 17 to create the Map Controller user interface, or you can duplicate Map Controller in the storyboard and adjust a few values in the Identity and Attribute inspectors.

Personally, I vote for the latter, but feel free to go with the former if you feel the need. Follow these steps to do the latter — for example, duplicate the Map Controller and convert the copy to a Find Controller.

1. **In the Project navigator, select the iPad's MainStoryboard file and then select Map Controller in the Map Controller – Map Scene in the Document Outline. Then select the Find Controller scene in the actual Storyboard canvas.**

2. **Chose Edit⇨Duplicate from the main menu (or press ⌘+D).**

   Doing so adds a copy of the selected element. Duplicate puts the duplicate Map controller *directly* on top of the original Map controller and partially on top of the Find controller you added to the storyboard in Chapter 12. In Figure 19-1, I've moved the duplicate a bit off to the side so you can see it. I've also highlighted the entry for it in the Document Outline.

The error you see in the Interface Builder Jump bar and in the Activity Viewer informs you that you now have "Multiple view controllers with the identifier "Map" — duplicate really does mean duplicate. You'll fix this as you go along.

3. **Delete the old Find Controller (I know I had you add it, but it really was just a placeholder) by selecting it either on the Canvas or in the Document Outline and then dragging the duplicated Map to the old Find Controller's place on the Canvas (see Figure 19-2).**

4. **Select the duplicated Map controller on the Canvas or in the Document Outline, open the Identity inspector by clicking its icon in the Inspector selector bar, and then select FindController from the Inspector Class drop-down menu, as I have in Figure 19-3.**

5. **Move to the Attributes inspector by clicking its icon in the Inspector selector bar and then enter** Find **in the inspector's Title field, as well as in the Identity inspector's Storyboard ID field.**

The errors that I mention back in Step 2 go away, as you can see in Figure 19-4.

Figure 19-1:
The duplicate Map controller.

Figure 19-2: Delete the `Find Controller` and move the duplicated `Map Controller` to its place on the Canvas.

Figure 19-3: Make this use the `Find Controller` class.

Figure 19-4:
The new
`Find
Control
ler` in the
storyboard.

You'll find that all the required connections to the `MapView` and `toolbar` outlets as well as the `mapType` action are (fortunately, or maybe even miraculously) in place.

Implementing the Find Controller

For your geocoding functionality to work, you're going to need to do several things in the Find controller. Most of what you need to do revolves around getting the text the user enters. You'll also have to have the text geocoded and have the geocoded location implemented as an `Annotation` by the `Trip` model object, which the Find controller will then add to the map.

Getting the text

In Chapter 14, you format the Find cell with a label and a Text field. In this chapter, you set things up so that the Master View controller can get the text a user enters and pass it on to the Find controller to, well, find that location.

To access the text, you first need to create an outlet for the Text field. Follow these steps:

1. **Select MainStoryboard in the Project navigator.**

2. **Select the Master View controller in the Document Outline.**

3. **Select the Assistant in the Editor selector, and if the** `RTMasterViewController.h` **file doesn't appear, navigate to it using the Jump bar.**

4. **In the Document Outline, open the disclosure triangle for the second Table View section in the Master View Controller – Master Scene — to get to the Table View cell holding the Find label and text.**

5. **Open that cell's disclosure triangle to display the Text field, and then control-drag from the Text field to the Master View controller interface (in the Assistant editor) between the** `@interface` **and** `@end` **compiler directives, and add an outlet named** findText.

   You can see it in Figure 19-5.

Yes, you could have dragged from the Text field in the cell on the Canvas, but in case you can't find it, this is another way to create the outlet.

Figure 19-5: Creating a text Field outlet.

A `UITextField` object is a control that displays editable text and sends a message to its delegate when the user presses the Return key. You typically use a `UITextField` object to enable the user to enter small amounts of text and then do something with it — like search for something or add a new contact.

Select the Text field, select the Standard editor in the Editor selector on the Xcode toolbar, and then open the Utility area. You can set a number of Text field properties in the Attributes inspector, as you see in Figure 19-6. Here, I've selected the Appears While Editing option from the Clear Button drop-down menu, I've selected the Clear When Editing Begins check box, and I've selected Go from the Return Key drop-down menu to change what's displayed in the Return key. Go will provide a visual clue to the user on how to get RoadTrip to go find that location.

You may be thinking that, for all this to work, you'd need some kind of Target-Action design pattern that would make sure that some event gets triggered when text gets entered. Otherwise, how would you know when the user has entered some text? Also, how do you get the keyboard to show, and then hide? To answer that, I explain what happens with a `UITextField`.

Figure 19-6:
Change the
Return key
to Go.

Scrolling a view

The way to be notified that the keyboard is about to appear is to register for the `UIKeyboardWillShowNotification`. That notification is posted by the `UIWindow` class. You pass a block object to the Notification Center and tell it to execute the block when the notification is posted. In that block, you determine the amount you'll need to scroll the view, and you scroll the view by assigning a new frame in an animation block.

When a user taps in a `UITextField`, it becomes the first responder (explained in Chapter 4), and the keyboard automatically rises to allow the user to enter text — you don't have to do a thing to make that happen. Although normally you're responsible for scrolling the view if the keyboard will cover the text field — which in this case will only happen when running the app on the iPhone — because the text field is in a Table View cell, scrolling the view is done by the Table view.

When the user is done entering text, he taps the Return key — the Return key whose label you managed to change to Go.

When the Go key (née Return key) is tapped, the text field determines whether it has a delegate and whether the delegate has implemented a `textFieldShouldReturn:` method — one of the optional `UITextField Delegate` protocol methods. If the delegate has done so, it sends the delegate the `textFieldShouldReturn:` message. So `textFieldShould Return:` is the place to capture the text.

Long story short: To capture the text and send it on to the `FindController`, you need to become the text field's delegate and implement the `textField ShouldReturn:` method. But before you do that, you need to do one more thing in Interface Builder.

You start by making the `RTMasterViewController` a `UITextField Delegate`. Update `RTMasterViewController.h` with the bolded code in Listing 19-1 to have it adopt the `UITextFieldDelegate` protocol.

Listing 19-1: Updating the RTMasterViewController Interface

```
#import <UIKit/UIKit.h>

@interface RTMasterViewController : UITableViewController
                              <UITextFieldDelegate>

@property (strong, nonatomic)
        RTDetailViewController *detailViewController;
```

```
@property (weak, nonatomic)
                            IBOutlet UITextField *findText;

@end
```

The heavy lifting will be done in the `TextField`'s `textFieldShould Return:` delegate method. The delegate will be passed the Text field being edited as an argument, and the Master View controller (the delegate) will pass that on to the Find controller.

First, you have to update the `RTMasterViewController` implementation by adding the bolded code in Listing 19-2 to `RTMasterViewController.m`.

Listing 19-2:   Updating the RTMasterViewController Implementation

```
#import "RTMasterViewController.h"
#import "RTDetailViewController.h"
#import "RTAppDelegate.h"
#import "Trip.h"
#import "FindController.h"

@implementation RTMasterViewController
```

You'll need to make `RTMasterViewController` the `textField` delegate. To do that, add the code in bold in Listing 19-3 to `viewDidLoad` in `RTMasterViewController.m`.

Listing 19-3:   Make the RTMasterViewController the textField Delegate

```
- (void)viewDidLoad
{
  [super viewDidLoad];
  RTAppDelegate* appDelegate =
            [[UIApplication sharedApplication] delegate];
  self.title = appDelegate.trip.destinationName;
  UIImageView* imageView = [[UIImageView alloc]
      initWithImage:[appDelegate.trip destinationImage]];
  self.tableView.backgroundView = imageView;

  UISwipeGestureRecognizer *swipeGesture =
  [[UISwipeGestureRecognizer alloc] initWithTarget:self
          action:@selector(handleSwipeGesture:)];
  swipeGesture.direction =
          UISwipeGestureRecognizerDirectionLeft;
  [self.view addGestureRecognizer:swipeGesture];
  self.findText.delegate = self;
}
```

Now you can implement the `textFieldShouldReturn:` delegate method by adding the code in Listing 19-4 to `RTMasterViewController.m`.

Listing 19-4: Implementing textFieldShouldReturn:

```
- (BOOL)textFieldShouldReturn:(UITextField *)textField {

  [textField resignFirstResponder];

  if ([[[UIDevice currentDevice] userInterfaceIdiom] ==
          UIUserInterfaceIdiomPad){
    FindController * findController =
    [[UIStoryboard
      storyboardWithName:@"MainStoryboard_iPad" bundle:nil]
        instantiateViewControllerWithIdentifier:@"Find"];
    findController.findLocation = textField.text;

    RTDetailViewController *currentDetailViewController;
    currentDetailViewController =
    [self.splitViewController.viewControllers lastObject];
    if (
      currentDetailViewController.masterPopoverController
          != nil)
        [currentDetailViewController.
                masterPopoverController
                        dismissPopoverAnimated:YES];

    self.splitViewController.delegate = findController;
    findController.popOverButton =
                currentDetailViewController.popOverButton;
    findController.masterPopoverController =
      currentDetailViewController.
                                masterPopoverController;

    NSMutableArray* controllers =
      [NSMutableArray arrayWithObjects:
        (self.splitViewController.viewControllers)[0],
          findController, nil];
    self.splitViewController.viewControllers =
                                        controllers;

  }
  else {
    FindController *findController =
    [[UIStoryboard
      storyboardWithName:@"MainStoryboard_iPhone"
                                        bundle:nil]
        instantiateViewControllerWithIdentifier:@"Find"];
    findController.findLocation = textField.text;
    [self.navigationController
        pushViewController:findController animated:YES];
  }
  return YES;
}
```

The first thing Listing 19-4 does for you is to send a message to the Text field asking it to resign as first responder:

```
[textField resignFirstResponder];
```

This has the side effect of dismissing the keyboard.

What you do next is another case where what happens depends on whether your app is running on an iPad or iPhone.

If you're running on an iPad, you instantiate `FindController` from `MainStoryboard_iPad`, just as you instantiate the Event Page controller in Chapter 16.

```
FindController * findController =
  [[UIStoryboard storyboardWithName:
     @"MainStoryboard_iPad" bundle:nil]
       instantiateViewControllerWithIdentifier:@"Find"];
```

You then assign the text from `textField` to the `FindController` `findLocation` property (which you'll add shortly to the `FindController`).

```
findController.findLocation = textField.text;
```

You then dismiss the popover if it's present.

```
RTDetailViewController *currentDetailViewController;
    currentDetailViewController =
      [self.splitViewController.viewControllers lastObject];
 if (currentDetailViewController.masterPopoverController
                                                != nil)
   [currentDetailViewController.
               masterPopoverController
                          dismissPopoverAnimated:YES];
```

Then you assign the `popOverButton` and `masterPopoverController` properties and make `FindController` the Split View controller delegate.

```
self.splitViewController.delegate = findController;
    findController.popOverButton =
                currentDetailViewController.popOverButton;
    findController.masterPopoverController =
       currentDetailViewController.
                                masterPopoverController;
```

Then you simply make `FindController` the new Detail View controller in the Split View controller's `viewControllers` property.

```
NSMutableArray* controllers =
    [NSMutableArray arrayWithObjects:
        (self.splitViewController.viewControllers)[0],
                    findController, nil];
self.splitViewController.viewControllers = controllers;
```

Note that, if it's an iPhone you're dealing with, you instantiate the `FindController`, assign the `findLocation` property, and push it on the Navigation controller stack, which causes the view to slide into place.

```
FindController *findController =
  [[UIStoryboardstoryboardWithName:
      @"MainStoryboard_iPhone" bundle:nil]
        instantiateViewControllerWithIdentifier:@"Find"];
    findController.findLocation = textField.text;
    [self.navigationController
        pushViewController:findController animated:YES];
```

You finally return `YES` to have the Text field implement its default behavior for the Go-Key-Formerly-Known-As-Return.

If you look back to Chapter 13, this is pretty much the same logic you added to `prepareForSegue:sender:`. As an exercise, you might want to create a new method that includes the common code.

By the way, you'll notice some Live Issue errors here. You'll need to add the `findLocation` property to the `FindController`, which you will do in the "Finding the Location" section, later in the chapter.

Disabling cell highlighting

You do have a problem, though. If the user touches outside the label, the cell is automatically highlighted when selected, and it stays selected. The solution is to disable the blue highlight when a cell is selected. To do that, you'll need to do the following:

1. **Select the MainStoryboard in the Project navigator.**

2. **Select the Master View controller in the Document Outline, open all the disclosure triangles, and select the Table View Cell for Find.**

3. **In the Table View Cell section of the Attributes inspector, choose None from the Selection pop-up menu.**

Now you're ready to add the `FindController` methods.

Finding the Location

In Listing 19-3, you assigned the text that the user entered into the Text field to a `FindController` property. Now you need to update the `FindController` interface to declare the property by adding the bolded code in Listing 19-5.

Listing 19-5: Updating the FindController Interface

```
#import "MapController.h"

@interface FindController : MapController

@property (strong, nonatomic) NSString *findLocation;

@end
```

Next, add the bolded code in Listing 19-6 to the `FindController.m` file to synthesize it and import the header files of the classes you'll use.

Listing 19-6: Updating the FindController Implementation

```
#import "FindController.h"
#import "RTAppDelegate.h"
#import "Trip.h"
#import "Annotation.h"


@implementation FindController
```

In my discussion of geocoding in Chapter 18, I point out that `Map Controller` sends the `CLGeocoder` the `reverseGeocodeLocation:` message to convert a coordinate to an address. The idea now is for you to send the `geocodeAddressString:` message to convert an address or point of interest into a coordinate.

This time, however, you go about it in a very interesting way. When the user enters a location he or she wants to find, you want to create an annotation for that found location and display it on the map. The problem here is that you really don't want the `FindController` (or any other controller) to start creating annotations — that's the `Trip` model's job.

Instead, based on the principles of encapsulation and loose coupling, you'll have the `Trip` object add the found location as additional model data.

Therefore, you want the `Trip` object to create the `Annotation` object and send it to the `FindController` to add as a Map annotation.

Although you could create view controller methods to be used by the `Trip` object to add the annotation, a more interesting (and better) way is to use the block design pattern. As I say when I introduce you to blocks in Chapter 10, blocks actually could make your code less complex, and here's an opportunity for you to see why.

Add the code in bold in Listing 19-7 to `viewDidLoad` in `FindController.m`.

Listing 19-7:   Updating viewDidLoad

```
-  (void)viewDidLoad
{
   [super viewDidLoad];
   self.title = self.findLocation;

   void (^addFindLocationCompletionHandler)
    (Annotation *, NSError *) = ^(Annotation *annotation,
                                            NSError *error){
      if (error!= nil || annotation == nil) {
         NSLog(@"Geocoder Failure! Error code: %u,
            description: %@, and reason: %@", error.code,
               [error localizedDescription],
                              [error localizedFailureReason]);
      }
      else {
         MKCoordinateRegion region;
         region.center.latitude =
                              annotation.coordinate.latitude;
         region.center.longitude =
                              annotation.coordinate.longitude;
         region.span.latitudeDelta = .05;
         region.span.longitudeDelta = .05;
         [self.mapView setRegion:region animated:NO];
         [self.mapView addAnnotation:annotation];
      }
   };
   RTAppDelegate *appDelegate =
               [[UIApplication sharedApplication] delegate];
   [appDelegate.trip addLocation:self.findLocation
      completionHandler:addFindLocationCompletionHandler];
}
```

You get a compiler error when adding this code, but you fix that by declaring the completion handler method in the Trip interface, which is covered in the following section.

You set the title to the string the user entered:

```
self.title = self.findLocation;
```

You then send the `Trip` object the `addLocation:completionHandler:` message. The completion handler is the block you declared. It's defined in `Trip`, as you'll see, as

```
(void (^)(Annotation *annotation, NSError* error))
```

That's a block that has no return value and two parameters, an `Annotation` and an `NSError`. The block's logic is actually quite straightforward. First, you check for an error, as you do in Chapter 18:

```
if (error!= nil || annotation == nil) {

  NSLog(@"Geocoder Failure! Error code: %u, description:
    %@, and reason: %@", error.code,
        [error localizedDescription],
                        [error localizedFailureReason]);
}
```

You're passed in an `Annotation` (which will be created in the `Trip` method `addLocation:completionHandler:`), which conforms to the `MKAnnotation` protocol, and you set the region based on the annotation's coordinates:

```
MKCoordinateRegion region;
region.center.latitude = annotation.coordinate.latitude;
region.center.longitude = annotation.coordinate.longitude;
region.span.latitudeDelta = .05;
region.span.longitudeDelta = .05;
[mapView setRegion:region animated:NO];
```

Next, you add the annotation to the map:

```
[mapView addAnnotation:annotation];
```

`addAnnotation:` is an `MKMapView` method that adds an object that conforms to the `MKAnnotation` protocol to the map. This is similar to what you did in `MapController` when you sent the `addAnnotations:` message to add an array of annotations. Doing this, as you see on the map, is additive; that is, adding a new annotation doesn't replace the array you added in `MapController`.

Next, you add the `addLocation:completionHandler:` method (the one that will create the `Annotation`) to `Trip.m`. But first, you need to update the `Trip.m` implementation, so add the bolded code in Listing 19-8 to `Trip.h`.

Listing 19-8: Updating the Trip Interface

```
#import <Foundation/Foundation.h>
#import <MapKit/MapKit.h>
@class Annotation;

@interface Trip : NSObject

- (UIImage *) destinationImage;
- (NSString *) destinationName;
- (CLLocationCoordinate2D) destinationCoordinate;
- (id)initWithDestinationIndex:(int)destinationIndex;
- (NSString *)weather;
- (int)numberOfEvents;
- (NSString *)getEvent:(int)index;
- (NSArray *)createAnnotations;
- (NSString *)mapTitle;
- (void)addLocation:(NSString *)findLocation
    completionHandler:
      (void (^)(Annotation *annotation, NSError* error))
                                            completion;

;
@end
```

This code adds the `addLocation:completionHandler:` method declaration, and because one of its parameters is an `Annotation`, you need to add the `@ class` statement as well.

`void (^foundLocationCompletionHandler) (Annotation *annotation, NSError* error);` is a type just like `int` or `Find Controller`. It's a block object with the name of `foundLocation CompletionHandler` that has no return value and two parameters: `Annotation` and `NSError`.

I'm going to save `FindController`'s completion block in the `foundLocation CompletionHandler` instance variable. I really don't need to, because, as you'll see, the `addLocation:completionHandler:` has access to it as a parameter. I did it this way to show you how to do that. It took me some time to really get my head around blocks and passing them as parameters, and I wanted to show you how easy it is after you see how it's done. You can use this example as a model for your own apps. I know that it may seem a bit overwhelming now, but I promise you that you'll find yourself using blocks in this way (as I do) as you gain more experience in your own application development.

Add the `foundLocationCompletionHandler` instance variable to `Trip.m` by adding the code in bold in Listing 19-9.

Listing 19-9:   Updating the Trip Implementation

```objc
#import "Trip.h"
#import "Destination.h"
#import "Events.h"
#import "Annotation.h"


@interface Trip () {
  NSDictionary *destinationData;
  NSMutableArray *pois;
  Destination* destination;
  Events *events;
  void (^foundLocationCompletionHandler)
                (Annotation *annotation, NSError* error);
}
```

Next, add the `addLocation:completionHandler:` in Listing 19-10 to
`Trip.m`.

Listing 19-10:   Adding the addLocation:completionHandler: Method

```objc
- (void)addLocation:(NSString *)findLocation
                                  completionHandler:
    (void (^)(Annotation *annotation, NSError* error))
                                     completion {

  void (^clGeocodeCompletionHandler)(NSArray *, NSError *)
        = ^(NSArray *placemarks, NSError *error){
CLPlacemark *placemark = placemarks[0];
    Annotation *foundAnnotation;
    if (error!= nil || placemark == nil) {
      NSLog(@"Geocoder Failure! Error code: %u",
        error.code);
    }
    else {
      foundAnnotation = [[Annotation alloc]init];
      foundAnnotation.coordinate =
                          placemark.location.coordinate;
      foundAnnotation.subtitle =
        [NSString stringWithFormat:@" Lat:%f Lon:%f",
          placemark.location.coordinate.latitude,
              placemark.location.coordinate.longitude];
if (placemark.areasOfInterest[0]) {
        foundAnnotation.title =
            placemark.areasOfInterest[0];
      }
      else {
```

(continued)

Listing 19-10 *(continued)*

```
        if (placemark.thoroughfare) {
          foundAnnotation.title =
            [NSString stringWithFormat:@"%@ %@",
              placemark.subThoroughfare,
                                placemark.thoroughfare];
        }
        else {
          if (placemark.locality  ) {
            foundAnnotation.title = placemark.locality;
          }
          else
            foundAnnotation.title =
                                    @"Your location";
        }
      }

    }
    foundLocationCompletionHandler(
                              foundAnnotation, error);
  };

  foundLocationCompletionHandler = completion;
  CLGeocoder* geocoder = [[CLGeocoder alloc] init];
    [geocoder geocodeAddressString:findLocation
          completionHandler:clGeocodeCompletionHandler];
}
```

First (skipping past the block declarations for a moment), you save a reference to the block that was sent as a parameter:

```
foundLocationCompletionHandler = completion;
```

You really don't need to save a reference to the block here, but I want to illustrate that blocks are treated like any other variable.

Then you allocate and initialize CLGeocoder just as you do in Chapter 18:

```
CLGeocoder* geocoder = [[CLGeocoder alloc] init];
  [geocoder geocodeAddressString:findLocation completionHa
          ndler:clGeocodeCompletionHandler];
```

This time, however, you send the geocodeAddressString:completionHandler: message after you initialize the CLGeocoder (rather than the reverseGeocodeLocation:location completionHandler: message you sent in Chapter 18).

This message submits a forward-geocoding request using the text the user entered and describes the location you want to look up. For example, you could specify the string "1 Infinite Loop, Cupertino, CA" to locate Apple headquarters.

In the completion block, you check for a successful completion and then create a new `Annotation`. When you're done, you call the completion block that the `FindController` sent you, using the block you had assigned to the `foundLocationCompletionHandler` variable earlier:

```
foundLocationCompletionHandler(foundAnnotation, error);
```

Finally, if you decide that you don't want the destination and the point of interest annotations you display in the `MapController` displayed, just override the method that adds the annotations in the `MapController` superclass:

```
- (void) addAnnotations {
}
```

Making the Map Title the Found Location

In Chapter 17, I show you how to add the map title to the toolbar. In that discussion, I add a method named `mapTitle`, which in the case of the `MapController`, sends a message to the `Trip` object to get the map's title. In the case of the `FindController`, I want to use the text the user entered as the title, so all I do is override `mapTitle`. Add the code in Listing 19-11 to `FindController.m` to display the title as the found location.

Listing 19-11:   Override mapTitle

```
- (NSString *)mapTitle {

  return  self.findLocation;
}
```

If you build and run RoadTrip, and enter **Radio City Music Hall** in the Find field in the Master view and tap the annotation, you should see the screen displayed in Figure 19-7. (Notice I did not go down the road of displaying the Destination and the Point of Interest annotations, but even if you did, you'd still see the Radio City Music Hall annotation.)

If you wanted to, you could even create a `typedef` for the `addLocation: completionHandler:`. The purpose of `typedef` is to assign another name to a type whose declaration is unwieldy. You'd want to use a `typedef` if you were going to have to type `void (^foundLocationCompletionHandler) (Annotation *annotation, NSError* error);` more than once. And while that is not true for RoadTrip, I wanted to show you how to create a `typedef` for a block that you could use in your own projects. Type the following code:

Figure 19-7:
Skippy
loves the
Rockettes.

```
typedef void (^addLocationCompletionHandler)
                (Annotation *annotation, NSError* error);
```

Add the instance variable as

```
addLocationCompletionHandler
                        addFindLocationCompletionHandler;
```

and then save the block in the new instance variable

```
addFindLocationCompletionHandler = completion;
```

and (finally) call the block in this way instead:

```
addFindLocationCompletionHandler(foundAnnotation, error);
```

Adding the FindController to the iPhone Storyboard

The iPhone storyboard, fortunately, uses the same Objective-C `Find Controller` class that you just defined for the iPad storyboard. But you still have some work to do, because you need to add a `FindController` scene to your iPhone storyboard.

One approach is to copy the Find scene from the iPad storyboard file and paste it into the iPhone storyboard file. This will work, but the iPad version has the Toolbar at the top of the view, which is the right answer for the iPad, but not for the iPhone.

You should rearrange the view elements in the iPhone version by dragging the toolbar to the bottom of the view and moving the Map view to the top of the enclosing view. Be sure to adjust the location of the iPhone toolbar in the Size inspector, as shown in Figure 19-8.

Figure 19-8: Adjusting the toolbar in the `Find Controller` scene in the iPhone storyboard.

The Find operation in the iPhone looks as shown in Figure 19-9.

Figure 19-9:
The Find
function on
the iPhone.

Chapter 20

Selecting a Destination

In This Chapter

▶ Finding an address for a map coordinate and displaying it on the map

▶ Finding the map coordinate from an address and displaying it on the map

*I*n this chapter, you are down to the final parts needed for the RoadTrip app to be complete. Back in Chapter 11, you add multiple destinations to the Destinations.plist, and now it would be nice if the user could select any of the ones you added.

Providing the user with the ability to select a destination is what you implement in this chapter. You also discover more about Table views along the way. I also show you how to work with modal controllers (which present views that require the user to do something) by creating your own protocol.

The Plan

You're going to add a new view controller that manages a modal Table view that allows the user to select a destination — such as New York or San Francisco. Figure 20-1 shows the results for both the iPad and iPhone.

Figure 20-1:
The
Destinations
modal Table
view on
both the
iPad and
iPhone.

iPad   iPhone

Setting Up the DestinationController for the iPad Storyboard

If you've followed along throughout this book, by now you should know the drill. As you might expect, you need a view controller to implement the Selecting a Destination interface.

Adding the custom view controller

Follow these steps to add a new Objective-C DestinationController class to the RoadTrip project.

1. **In the Project navigator, select the View Controller Classes group and then either right-click the selection and choose New File from the menu that appears or choose File⇨New⇨New File from the main menu (or press ⌘+N).**

   Whatever method you choose, you're greeted by the New File dialog.

2. **In the left column of the dialog, select Cocoa Touch under the iOS heading, select the Objective-C class template in the top-right pane, and then click Next.**

   You'll see a dialog that will enable you to choose the options for your file.

3. **Enter** DestinationController **in the Class field, enter or choose UIViewController from the Subclass Of drop-down menu, make sure that the Target for iPad check box is selected and that With XIB for User Interface is deselected, and then click Next.**

4. **In the Save sheet that appears, click Create.**

The Destination controller will be using a Table view, but it won't actually use a Table View Controller class. That's because I show you how to use a Table view with dynamically generated cells (as well as cell selection handled by the controller) as only one element in the view. This is a handy thing to know if you want to take advantage of the power of a Table view without letting a Table view take over the entire screen.

Setting up the DestinationController in the MainStoryboard_iPad

Now that you have a custom view controller, you need to tell the storyboard to load your custom view controller rather than a `UIViewController`. Follow these steps:

1. **In the Project navigator, select the MainStoryboard_iPad file, and in the Document Outline, select View Controller in the View Controller – Destination Scene.**

2. **Open the Identity inspector in the Utility area using the Inspector selector bar and then choose DestinationController from the Custom Class section's Class drop-down menu, as you did in Chapters 15, 16, 17, and 19.**

   Now when Destination is selected in the Master View controller, `DestinationController` will be instantiated and initialized and will receive events from the user and connect the view to the `Trip` model.

   In Chapter 14, you left this segue style as modal, and I said I would explain a little more about that in Chapter 20. Well, here we are.

3. **Select the segue to the Destination controller on the Canvas.**

4. **Select the Attributes inspector for the Inspector selector bar.**

   As I explain in Chapter 4, a modal dialog requires the user to do something (tap a Table View cell or the Cancel button, for example) before returning to the application.

   When you have a modal segue, you can choose a transition style.

5. **Choose Flip Horizontal in the Transition pop-up menu in the Attributes inspector for the segue.**

Actually, you can select whatever transition you'd like, but I'd go for Flip Horizontal.

Make sure that Form Sheet is selected in the Presentation pop-up menus. The Presentation choices include:

- ✔ **Full Screen:** The modal view covers the screen.

- ✔ **Page Sheet:** The height and width are set to the height and width of the screen in Portrait orientation, with the background view dimmed.

- ✔ **Form Sheet:** The width and height of the modal view are smaller than those of the screen, with the modal view centered on the screen and the background view dimmed.

- ✔ **Current Context:** The modal view is the same style as its presenting view controller. But if the presenting view controller is in a popover, you can use this presentation style only when the transition style is `UIModalTransitionStyleCoverVertical`. If not, you'll get an exception.

After you have the Presentation and the Transition selected in the Attributes inspector, you can get on with formatting the Destination Controller view, which will have a Table view, a Label view, and a very spiffy image as well after you follow these steps:

1. **Select the Destination controller in the storyboard Canvas and then drag in a Navigation bar from the Library.**

   You're going to need someplace to put the Cancel button.

2. **Select the Navigation bar you just added (either in the Destination controller on the Canvas or in the Document Outline) and then choose Black Opaque from the Style drop-down menu in the Attributes inspector.**

3. **In the Navigation bar on the Canvas, select the Title (field). Still in the Attributes inspector, enter** Destinations **in the Title field for the selected element (Navigation bar, in this case).**

4. **Drag a Bar Button item from the Library and place it on the left side of the Navigation bar on the Canvas.**

5. **Choose Cancel from the Identifier drop-down menu in the Bar Button section of the Attributes Inspector.**

   You'll use this button to cancel selecting a new destination.

You don't have to select a tint for the button in the Bar Button Tint section of the Attributes inspector. When you selected Black Opaque, you gave all the Bar Button items the right tint as well. (You will, by the way, get yellow text because of how you set the Bar Button appearance in Chapter 9.)

6. **Drag an Image view from the Library in the Utility area and place it in the Destination controller on the Canvas so that it takes up the rest of the view.**

7. **In the Image View section of the Attributes inspector, select DestinationImage_iPad.png from the Image drop-down menu.**

   The `.png` file should be in the Resources file you downloaded in Chapter 3.

8. **Drag a Label from the Library and add it to the view toward the top of the Image view.**

9. **With the Label selected, enter** Pick a place, any place **in the Text field in the Label section of the Attributes inspector.**

10. **Still in the Attributes inspector, change the font size to System 24 by selecting the Text icon in the Font field (which opens a window in which you can change the font size) or by using the stepper control.**

11. **Select the label and then choose Editor➪Size Fit to Content from the Xcode main menu.**

    The label will expand to fit the text.

12. **Position the *Pick a place, any place* label, as shown in Figure 20-2.**

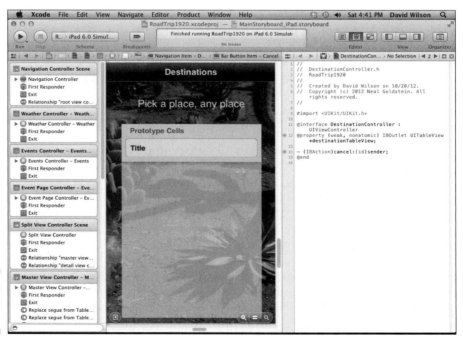

Figure 20-2:
Ready to code.

13. **Looking nice, but change the text color to white in the Text Color drop-down menu.**

    A word of warning: You need to follow the next set of steps exactly. You can get the look you want in other ways, but this is the most straightforward. A bit of a bug exists in Interface Builder, and the Table view won't be transparent; you'll fix that in `viewDidLoad` in the "Creating the Table View" section, later in the chapter.

14. **Drag a Table view (not Table View controller) from the Library onto the Image view and position it as shown in Figure 20-2.**

    This is the area in which the Table view will display. If you have more selections than can fit in the visible area, the user will be able to scroll the Table view.

15. **With the Table view selected, scroll down the Attributes inspector to reach the View section and then select Clear Color from the Background drop-down menu.**

16. **Still in the Attributes inspector, scroll back up to the Table View section and choose Grouped from the Style menu.**

17. **Enter 1 in the Prototype Cells field (or just use the stepper control to get to 1).**

    Leave these as prototype cells because you'll provide the content for the cells programmatically.

18. **Select the prototype cell, either on the Canvas or in the Document Outline, and then choose Basic from the inspector's Style menu and enter DestinationCell in the Identifier field.**

    You will need to have a reuse identifier (which I explain in the section "Displaying the cell," later in this chapter).

19. **Still in the Attributes inspector, scroll down to the View section and select Clear Color from the Background drop-down menu.**

20. **Select the Table View cell in the Document Outline, open the disclosure triangle, and select the label.**

21. **In the Attributes inspector, scroll down and then choose Clear Color from the Background drop-down menu.**

22. **Close the Utility area and select the Assistant in the Editor selector.**

23. **If the** `DestinationController.h` **file doesn't appear, select it in the Jump bar.**

24. **Control-drag from the Table view in Document Outline or on the Canvas to the** `DestinationController.h` **Interface. Release the mouse button, and in the dialog that pops up, enter** destination TableView.

25. Control-drag from the Cancel button in Document Outline or in the Navigation bar on the Canvas to the DestinationController.h **Interface. Release the mouse button, and in the dialog that pops up, select Action in the Connection drop-down menu and enter** cancel **in the Name field.**

When all is said and done, you should see a screen that looks like Figure 20-2.

Adding a Modal View

Modal views are great for those situations when you want the user (or the user wants) to do something outside the application flow. Rather than use a Navigation controller with a Back button, you display a Modal view with controls that allow the user to either select an action or cancel the procedure. (Much of the work in adding the Destination controller to the storyboard spelled out in the steps list in the previous section has to do with enabling the user to either select a destination in the Table view or to press Cancel to leave things as they are.)

The usual way to manage Modal views is by creating an Objective-C *protocol* that's adopted by the controller presenting the Modal view. The Modal view, when the user has selected an action or Cancel, calls the presenting controller's delegate method. The requesting controller then dismisses the Modal controller. Using this approach means that, before it dismisses the Modal controller, the presenting controller can get any data it needs.

You start implementing the Modal view by declaring the protocol and a few other properties you'll need, as well as the protocols the Destination Controller needs to adopt.

To get things started, add the bolded code in Listing 20-1 to Destination Controller.h.

Listing 20-1:   Updating the Destination Interface

```
#import <UIKit/UIKit.h>
@protocol DestinationControllerDelegate;

@interface DestinationController : UIViewController
             <UITableViewDelegate, UITableViewDataSource>

@property (weak, nonatomic) IBOutlet UITableView
          *destinationTableView;
@property (strong, nonatomic) id
```

(continued)

Listing 20-1 *(continued)*

```
                    <DestinationControllerDelegate> delegate;
@property (nonatomic) NSUInteger selectedDestination;
- (IBAction)cancel:(id)sender;
@end

@protocol DestinationControllerDelegate
- (void)destinationController:
     (DestinationController *)controller
                    didFinishWithSave:(BOOL)save;
@end
```

The Objective-C language provides a way to formally declare a list of methods (including declared properties) as a protocol. You've used framework-supplied protocols extensively in this book, and now you're defining your own protocol.

You declare formal protocols with the `@protocol` directive. In Listing 20-1, you declared a `DestinationControllerDelegate` protocol with one method, `destinationController:didFinishWithSave:`, which is *required*. Required is the default; if you wanted to declare optional methods, you would use the keyword `@optional`, and all methods following that keyword would be optional. For example, consider this:

```
@protocol SimpleDelegate
@optional
- (void)doNothing;
@end
```

The `@protocol DestinationControllerDelegate:` statement (at the top) tells the compiler that a protocol is on the way. Like the `@class` statement, it says, "Trust me, you'll find the protocol." You need this here only because you added this:

```
@property (strong, nonatomic) id
                <DestinationControllerDelegate> delegate;
```

This statement tells the compiler to type check whatever it is you assign to `delegate` to make sure that it implements the `DestinationController Delegate` protocol.

You also added the `selectedDestination` property, which you'll use in the `ViewController` to determine which destination the user selected. Notice that you have made it read-only because there is no reason for any other object to be able to set it.

You also adopted two protocols, `UITableViewDelegate` and `UITableViewDataSource`, which you'll use to manage the Table view.

Next, you're going to need to update the `DestinationController` implementation in Listing 20-2 with the bolded code for some header files you'll need to use later.

Listing 20-2: Updating the DestinationController Implementation

```
#import "DestinationController.h"
#import "RTDetailViewController.h"
#import "RTAppDelegate.h"

@interface DestinationController ()
@end

@implementation DestinationController
```

Now that you have the plumbing in, you can look at what will go on in the `DestinationController`.

Implementing a Table View

The functionality in the `DestinationController` is in the Table view. You've worked with Table views before — but those used *static* cells, and all the work was done for you by the storyboard. Now it's time to branch out on your own and understand what the storyboard was doing for you behind the scenes, as it were.

It's a good thing to know how Table views work, because Table views are front and center in several applications that come with the iOS devices out of the box; they play a major role in many of the more complex applications that you can download from the App Store. (Obvious examples: Almost all the views in the Mail, Music, and Contacts applications are Table views.) Table views take on such a significant role because, in addition to displaying data, they can also serve as a way to navigate a hierarchy.

If you take a look at an application such as Mail or Music, you find that Table views present a scrollable list of *items* (or *rows* or *entries* — I use all three terms interchangeably) that may be divided into *sections*. A row can display text or images, so when you select a row, you may be presented with another Table view or with some other view that may display a web page or even controls such as buttons and Text fields. (You can see an illustration of this diversity back in Chapter 4, where Figure 4-6 shows how selecting Map leads to a Map view displaying a map of New York, which is very handy when you roll into town.)

It's worth noting that iOS Table views only provide a single column of data — not the two-dimensional tables that you might build in a Microsoft Excel spreadsheet. The Macintosh OS X frameworks do provide a multi-column `NSTableView` class, but the IOS `UITableView` only supports a single column. There are open-source grid views available for iOS, such as the `DTGridView` found on GitHub (`http://github.com/danielctull/DTGridView`).

To kick off the Table view creation process, you first need to decide what you want to have happen when the user selects a particular row in the Table view of your app. As you saw with static cells, you can have virtually anything happen. You can display a Web view as you do in Weather or even display another Table view.

In this case, however, the Destination View controller will be dismissed, and the user will find herself in the Main view, ready to make another selection.

A Table view is an instance of the class `UITableView`, where each visible row of the table uses a `UITableViewCell` to draw its contents. Think of a *Table view* as the object that creates and manages the table structure, and the *Table View cell* as being responsible for displaying the content of a single row of the table.

Creating the Table View

Although powerful, Table views are surprisingly easy to work with. To create a Table view, you follow only four — count 'em, four — steps, in the following order:

1. **Create and format the view itself.**

   This includes specifying the Table style and a few other parameters, most of which you do in Interface Builder.

2. **Specify the Table view configuration.**

   Not too complicated, actually. You let `UITableView` know how many sections you want, how many rows you want in each section, and what you want to call your section headers. You do that with the help of the `numberOfSectionsInTableView:`, `tableView:numberOfRowsInSection:`, and `tableView:titleForHeaderInSection:` methods, respectively.

3. **Supply the text (or graphic) for each row.**

   You return that from the implementation of the `tableView:cellForRowAtIndexPath:` method. This message is sent for each visible row in the Table view, and you return a Table View cell to display the text or graphic.

4. **Respond to a user selection of the row.**

   You use the `tableView:didSelectRowAtIndexPath:` method to take care of this task. In this method, you can create a view controller and push it onto the stack (as the storyboard does in a segue), or you can even send a message to the controller that presented a Modal View controller (or any other object).

A `UITableView` object must have a data source and a delegate:

- ✔ The **data source** supplies the content for the Table view.
- ✔ The **delegate** manages the appearance and behavior of the Table view.

The data source adopts the `UITableViewDataSource` protocol, and the delegate adopts the `UITableViewDelegate` protocol — no surprises there. Of the preceding methods, only `tableView:didSelectRowAtIndexPath:` is included in the `UITableViewDelegate` protocol. All the other methods that I list earlier are included in the `UITableViewDataSource` protocol.

The data source and the delegate are often (but not necessarily) implemented in the same object, which is often a subclass of `UITableViewController`. `UITableViewController` adopts the necessary protocols and even furnishes some method stubs for you. In this case, the Table view is just another object in the `DestinationController` view. I had you do that when creating `DestinationController` earlier in the chapter so I could explain the real guts of Table views and because I wanted you to be able to display that Pick a Destination label, which you couldn't have done if you had made this a `UITableView` subclass.

Implementing these five (count 'em, five) methods (in the four steps earlier) is all you need to do to implement a Table view.

Not bad.

I already had you adopt the Table View delegate and Data Source protocols in Listing 20-1, so you are already partway there.

Add the bolded code in Listing 20-3 to the `DestinationController.m` file's `viewDidLoad` method.

Listing 20-3: Updating viewDidLoad

```
- (void)viewDidLoad
{
  [super viewDidLoad];
  self.destinationTableView.delegate = self;
  self.destinationTableView.dataSource = self;
}
```

As you might surmise, this makes the `DestinationController` both the delegate and the data source.

You'll remember back in Chapter 8 I had you make the title in the Navigation bar yellow. But in that case it was just for that specific Navigation bar because I wanted to show you how to customize control appearance on a control-by-control basis. Here is an example of why I would want to set the appearance for all controls of a certain type. To set the title color to yellow for all Navigation bars, go back into `application:didFinishLaunchingWithOptions:` in `RTAppDelegate.m` and replace

```
[navigationController.navigationBar
                             setTitleTextAttributes:
   [NSDictionary dictionaryWithObject:[UIColor yellowColor]
                        forKey:UITextAttributeTextColor]];
```

with

```
[[UINavigationBar appearance] setTitleTextAttributes:
   @{UITextAttributeTextColor: [UIColor yellowColor]}];
```

Adding sections

In a grouped Table view, each group is referred to as a *section*.

The two methods you need to implement to start things off are as follows:

```
numberOfSectionsInTableView:(UITableView *)tableView

tableView:(UITableView *)tableView
              numberOfRowsInSection:(NSInteger)section
```

Each of these methods returns an integer, and that integer tells the Table view something — the number of sections and the number of rows in a given section, respectively.

Add the methods in Listing 20-4 to `DestinationController.m` to create a Table view that has one section with the number of rows equal to the number of destinations you have in your `Destinations.plist`. You will get compiler errors that you will fix with code in the next Listing.

Listing 20-4: Implementing numberOfSectionsInTableView: and tableView:numberOfRowsInSection:

```
- (NSInteger)numberOfSectionsInTableView:
                            (UITableView *)tableView {

  return 1;
}

- (NSInteger)tableView:(UITableView *)tableView
            numberOfRowsInSection:(NSInteger)section {

  NSString *filePath = [[NSBundle mainBundle]
        pathForResource:@"Destinations" ofType:@"plist"];
NSDictionary *destinations =
    [NSDictionary dictionaryWithContentsOfFile: filePath];
  destinationsArray = destinations[@"DestinationData"];
  return [destinationsArray count];
}
```

The numberOfSectionsInTableView: method is obvious. In the tableV
iew:numberOfRowsInSection: method, you do what you did in both the
Trip and Events classes — you access Destination.plist to extract
what you need. In this case, it's the DestinationData array, which, to
refresh your memory, is an array of dictionaries that have the data for each
destination and return the count.

Keep in mind that the first section is zero, as is the first row. This means, of
course, that whenever you want to use an index to get to the first row or
section, you need to use 0, not 1 — and an index of 1 for the second row and
so on.

You'll get an Xcode Live Issue warning here because you need to add the new
destinationsArray instance variable (you'll use this same array later in
tableView:cellForRowAtIndexPath:). To do that, add the bolded code
in Listing 20-5 to DestinationController.m.

Listing 20-5: Updating the DestinationController Implementation

```
#import "DestinationController.h"

@interface DestinationController () {
  NSArray *destinationsArray;
}
@end
```

Displaying the cell

To display the cell content, your delegate is sent the `tableView:cel`
`lForRowAtIndexPath:` message. Add this method in Listing 20-6 to
`DestinationController.m`.

Listing 20-6:   Implementing tableView:cellForRowAtIndexPath:

```
- (UITableViewCell *)tableView:(UITableView *)tableView
         cellForRowAtIndexPath:(NSIndexPath *)indexPath {

  static NSString *CellIdentifier = @"DestinationCell";
  UITableViewCell *cell = [tableView dequeueReusableCellWi
         thIdentifier:CellIdentifier];
  NSDictionary * destinationData =
         destinationsArray[indexPath.row];

  NSAttributedString *attributedString =
         [[NSAttributedString alloc]
                           initWithString:destinationData[
         @"DestinationName"]

         attributes:@{ NSFontAttributeName : [UIFont
         systemFontOfSize:17.0f],
                           NSForegroundColorAttributeName:
         [UIColor whiteColor]}];
  cell.textLabel.attributedText = attributedString;
  return cell;
}
```

Walking through Listing 20-6, you see that one of the first things you do is
determine whether any cells that you can use are lying around. You may
remember that, although a Table view can display quite a few rows at a time
on the iPad's screen, the table itself can conceivably hold a lot more. A large
table can eat up a lot of memory, however, if you create cells for every row.
Fortunately, Table views are designed to *reuse* cells. As a Table view's cells
scroll off the screen, they're placed in a queue of cells available to be reused.

If the system runs low on memory, the Table view gets rid of the cells in the
queue, but as long as it has some available memory for them, it holds on to
them in case you want to use them again.

You create a string to use as a *cell identifier* to indicate what cell type you're
using:

```
static NSString *CellIdentifier = @"DestinationCell";
```

You recall that this is what you entered in the Identifier field of the
Prototype cell in Step 18 in the "Setting up the DestinationController in the
MainStoryboard_iPad" section, earlier in this chapter.

It is critical that the `CellIdentifier` and the `Identifier` field of the Prototype cell in Step 18 are the same. If they are not, you won't get a transparent cell you specified in the storyboard. (It's happened to me more than once.)

Table views support multiple cell types, which makes the identifier necessary. In this case, you need only one cell type, but sometimes you may want more than one.

You ask the Table view for a specific reusable cell object by sending it a `dequeueReusableCellWithIdentifier:` message:

```
UITableViewCell *cell = [tableView
        dequeueReusableCellWithIdentifier:CellIdentifier];
```

This determines whether any cells of the type you want are available. If no cells are lying around, this method will create a cell using the cell identifier that you specified. You now have a Table View cell that you can return to the Table view.

You have several choices on how to format the Table View cell. Although you're going to be using `UITableViewCellStyleDefault`, you can choose from a number of different styles, listed as follows:

- `UITableViewCellStyleDefault`: Gives you a simple cell with a Text label (black and left-aligned) and an optional Image view.

- `UITableViewCellStyleValue1`: Gives you a cell with a left-aligned black Text label on the left side of the cell and a right-aligned Text label with smaller blue text on the right side. (The Settings application uses this style of cell.)

- `UITableViewCellStyleValue2`: Gives you a cell with a right-aligned blue Text label on the left side of the cell and a left-aligned black Text label on the right side of the cell.

- `UITableViewCellStyleSubtitle`: Gives you a cell with a left-aligned Text label across the top and a left-aligned Text label below it in smaller gray text. (The Music application uses cells in this style.)

With the formatting out of the way, you then set the Label properties that you're interested in.

You pluck out the name for each destination you've stored by accessing the `DestinationName` in each Destination dictionary. You do that by accessing the dictionary in the (saved) `destinationsArray` corresponding to the sections and row in `indexPath`, which contains the section and row information in a single object. To get the row or the section out of an `NSIndexPath`, you just have to invoke its section method (`indexPath.section`) or its row method (`indexPath.row`), either of which returns an `int`:

```
NSDictionary * destinationData =
        destinationsArray[indexPath.row];
```

Next, create an attributed string, which can manage both the character strings and attributes such as fonts, colors, and even kerning:

```
NSAttributedString *attributedString =
        [[NSAttributedString alloc]
                            initWithString:destinationData[
        @"DestinationName"]
                            attributes:@
        { NSFontAttributeName : [UIFont
        systemFontOfSize:17.0f],
                            NSForegroundColorAttributeName:
        [UIColor whiteColor]}];
```

Now, use this attributed string to format the cell's text label:

```
cell.textLabel.attributedText = attributedString;
```

Finally, return the formatted cell with the text it needs to display in that row:

```
return cell;
```

Working with user selections

Now you can look at what happens when the user selects a row with a destination displayed.

When the user taps a Table View entry, what happens next depends on what you want your Table view to do for you.

If you're using the Table view to display data (as the Albums view in the Music application does, for example), you want a user's tap to show the next level in the hierarchy, such as a list of songs or a detail view of an item (such as information about a song).

In the case of the RoadTrip app, you want a user's tap to take you back to the Master view and, behind the scenes, create the correct model so that when you tap the Travel button, the right data is there.

To do that, add the final delegate method you need to implement, `tableView:didSelectRowAtIndexPath:`. Add the code in Listing 20-7 to `DestinationController.m`.

Listing 20-7:   Implementing tableView:didSelectRowAtIndexPath:

```
- (void)tableView:(UITableView *)tableView
        didSelectRowAtIndexPath:(NSIndexPath *)indexPath
{
  [tableView deselectRowAtIndexPath:
                              indexPath animated:YES];
  self.selectedDestination = indexPath.row;
  [self.delegate destinationController:self
        didFinishWithSave:YES];
}
```

You set the `selectedDestination` property to the selected row. Notice that you access the instance variable here instead of using the setter because you made the property `readonly`.

Then you send the delegate the `destinationController:didFinish WithSave:` message with a value of `YES`.

Before I explain the `destinationController:didFinishWithSave:` method, implement the last part of the `DestinationController`. Add the bolded code in Listing 20-8 to the `cancel` method (generated when you created the action) in `DestinationController.m`.

Listing 20-8:   Adding cancel:

```
- (IBAction)cancel:(id)sender {

  [self.delegate destinationController:self
                              didFinishWithSave:NO];

}
```

When the user taps Cancel, the `DestinationController` sends the `desti nationController:didFinishWithSave:` message with a value of `NO` to its delegate — which will be the `RTMasterViewController`. Now you'll go back to the `RTMasterViewController` and implement the `destinationC ontroller:didFinishWithSave:` message.

You also need to have the `RTMasterViewController` adopt the `DestinationControllerDelegate` protocol and declare the `destinati onController:didFinishWithSave:` method. To do that, add the bolded code in Listing 20-9 to `RTMasterViewController.h`.

Listing 20-9: Updating the RTMasterViewController Interface

```
#import <UIKit/UIKit.h>
#import "DestinationController.h"
@class RTDetailViewController;

@interface RTMasterViewController : UITableViewController
    <UITextFieldDelegate, DestinationControllerDelegate>

@property (strong, nonatomic) RTDetailViewController
        *detailViewController;
@property (weak, nonatomic) IBOutlet UITextField
        *findText;
- (void)destinationController:(DestinationController *)
            controller didFinishWithSave:(BOOL)save;
```

Next, add the destinationController:didFinishWithSave: method in
Listing 20-10 to RTMasterViewController.m.

Listing 20-10: Adding destinationController:didFinishWithSave:

```
- (void)destinationController:(DestinationController *)
            controller didFinishWithSave:(BOOL)save {

  RTAppDelegate *appDelegate =
            [[UIApplication sharedApplication] delegate];

  if (save) {
    [appDelegate createDestinationModel:
                    controller.selectedDestination];
    [self viewDidLoad];
    RTDetailViewController* currentDetailViewController;
    if ([[self.splitViewController.viewControllers
                                      lastObject]
        isKindOfClass:[UINavigationController class]]) {
      UINavigationController *navigationController =
          [self.splitViewController.viewControllers
                                      lastObject];
      currentDetailViewController =
          (RTDetailViewController *)
                navigationController.topViewController;
    }
    else
      currentDetailViewController = [self.
          splitViewController.viewControllers
                                      lastObject];
    [currentDetailViewController viewDidLoad];

    if (currentDetailViewController.popOverButton) {
```

```
        if (![[[self.splitViewController.viewControllers
                                        lastObject]
            isKindOfClass:[UINavigationController class]]) {
          NSMutableArray *itemsArray =
            [currentDetailViewController.toolbar.items
                                        mutableCopy];

          [itemsArray removeObjectAtIndex:0];
          [currentDetailViewController.toolbar
                        setItems:itemsArray animated:NO];

        }
      }
      if ([currentDetailViewController
            isKindOfClass:[MapController class]]) {
        NSMutableArray *itemsArray =
          [currentDetailViewController.toolbar.items
                                        mutableCopy];

        [itemsArray removeLastObject];
        [currentDetailViewController.toolbar
                        setItems:itemsArray animated:NO];

      }
    }
    if (appDelegate.trip == nil)
      [appDelegate createDestinationModel:0];
    [self dismissModalViewControllerAnimated:YES];
  }
```

If the user has chosen a new destination, you send the app delegate a message to create that model:

```
[appDelegate
    createDestinationModel:controller.selectedDestination];
```

It determines the selection the user made by accessing the selected Destination property you set in the tableView:didSelectRowAtIndex Path: method.

As you may recall, createDestinationModel: is an already existing method in the app delegate. As I say back in Chapter 11, the create DestinationModel: method will actually be creating the model, and I made this a separate method because you'll have to be able to send the RTAppDelegate a message to create a new Trip when the user chooses a new destination in Chapter 20. Well, here it is Chapter 20, and that's exactly what you're doing.

You reload the Master view based on the new destination so you can change the Background image.

```
[self viewDidLoad];
```

You'll also need to update the Detail view.

```
RTDetailViewController* currentDetailViewController;
if ([[self.splitViewController.viewControllers lastObject]
          isKindOfClass:[UINavigationController class]]) {
  UINavigationController *navigationController =
     [self.splitViewController.viewControllers lastObject];
  currentDetailViewController = (RTDetailViewController *)
                  navigationController.topViewController;
}
else
  currentDetailViewController =
     [self.splitViewController.viewControllers lastObject];
[currentDetailViewController viewDidLoad];

}
```

You'll need to determine whether the current Detail view is embedded in a Navigation controller. Then you get the current Detail view and simply send it the viewDidLoad message, which will cause it to reload all its data.

You also need to take a nuance here into account. If the current view controller isn't embedded in a Navigation controller, that means it has a toolbar. If it already has a Road Trip button, to keep things in sync, you'll need to remove the Road Trip button, which will then be added back in when the view reloads.

```
if (currentDetailViewController.popOverButton) {
  if (![[self.splitViewController.viewControllers
     lastObject] isKindOfClass:
                     [UINavigationController class]]) {
    NSMutableArray *itemsArray =
     [currentDetailViewController.toolbar.items
                                       mutableCopy];
    [itemsArray removeObjectAtIndex:0];
    [currentDetailViewController.toolbar
                  setItems:itemsArray animated:NO];
  }
}
```

And yet another thing: If the current Detail view is a Map view, you'll also need to remove the Locate button if it's on the toolbar:

```
if ([currentDetailViewController
          isKindOfClass:[MapController class]]) {
  NSMutableArray *itemsArray =
     [currentDetailViewController.toolbar.items
                                       mutableCopy];
  [itemsArray removeLastObject];
  [currentDetailViewController.toolbar
                  setItems:itemsArray animated:NO];
  }
```

If the user hasn't chosen a new destination but no model exists yet (when the user first launches the program, for example, no model exists yet — you'll see how that works in a second), you'll have the app delegate create a model using a default destination. I have arbitrarily chosen the first one.

You then send the `dismissModalViewControllerAnimated:` message, which, as you might expect, dismisses the view controller using the transition you specified in the "Setting up the DestinationController in the MainStoryboard_iPad" section, earlier in this chapter.

If the user has canceled, you simply send the `dismissModalViewController Animated:` message, and the user finds herself back in the Main view.

But you still have some more work to do.

Previously, you added a `delegate` property to the `Destination Controller`, which it uses when it sends the `destinationController: didFinishWithSave:` message when the user selects a cell or taps Cancel.

The problem is, how do you set that property? Because you use a segue to take care of creating and initializing the controller, how do you assign the delegate property? If you recall from Chapter 19, when setting up `FindController`, you didn't use a segue, so you could assign any property you wanted after you created (but before you added) the `FindController` to the Split View controller `viewControllers` in `textFieldShouldReturn:` (I've bolded where you do that in the `RTMasterViewController.m` code).

```
- (BOOL)textFieldShouldReturn:(UITextField *)textField {

    [textField resignFirstResponder];

    if ([[UIDevice currentDevice] userInterfaceIdiom] ==
                                UIUserInterfaceIdiomPad){
        FindController * findController =
        [[UIStoryboard storyboardWithName:@"MainStoryboard_
            iPad"
                                        bundle:nil]
            instantiateViewControllerWithIdentifier:@"Find"];
        findController.findLocation = textField.text;
    ...
)
```

Fortunately, you have a way to use a segue and still be able to pass some data on to the view controller that's being instituted by the segue.

`prepareForSegue:sender:` is a view controller method used to notify the view controller that a segue is about to be performed. `segue` is the `UIStory boardSegue` object that contains information about the view controllers involved in the segue. You've already used `prepareForSegue:sender:` to dismiss the popover and assign the `popOverButton` and `masterPop overController` properties.

Now you need to add the code in bold in Listing 20-11 to `prepareFor Segue:sender:` in `RTMasterViewController.m`. (I've omitted the code that was already there.)

Listing 20-11:   Update prepareForSegue:sender:

```
- (void)prepareForSegue:(UIStoryboardSegue *)segue
         sender:(id)sender {

  if ([segue.identifier isEqualToString:@"Destination"]) {

    if ([[UIDevice currentDevice] userInterfaceIdiom] ==
                              UIUserInterfaceIdiomPad) {
      RTDetailViewController *currentDetailViewController;

      DestinationController *destinationController =
          (DestinationController *)
            segue.destinationViewController;
      destinationController.delegate = self;

      if ([[self.splitViewController.viewControllers
                                          lastObject]
          isKindOfClass:[UINavigationController class]]) {
      UINavigationController *navigationController =
          [self.splitViewController.viewControllers
                                          lastObject];
      currentDetailViewController =
          (RTDetailViewController *)
                  navigationController.topViewController;
      }
      else
        currentDetailViewController = [self.
            splitViewController.viewControllers
                                          lastObject];
      if (currentDetailViewController.
                          masterPopoverController != nil)

        [currentDetailViewController.
                      masterPopoverController
                              dismissPopoverAnimated:YES];
      }
      else {
        DestinationController *destinationController =
            (DestinationController *)
                          segue.destinationViewController;
        destinationController.delegate = self;
      }
      return;
  }
... // previous code here
}
```

You first check to see whether the segue is the `Destination` segue (see, those identifiers are really useful):

```
if ([destinationSegue.identifier
                      isEqualToString:@"Destination"])
```

If it's the `Destination` segue, you check to see whether the device is an iPad. If it is, you go through the usual logic to find the Detail View (Destination) controller and assign its delegate to `self`.

```
RTDetailViewController *currentDetailViewController;

DestinationController *destinationController =
                                (DestinationController *)
  [segue.destinationViewController topViewController];
                      destinationController.delegate = self;
```

You then go through the usual logic and find the current Detail View controller and dismiss the popover, if one exists.

```
if ([[self.splitViewController.viewControllers lastObject]
          isKindOfClass:[UINavigationController class]]) {
UINavigationController *navigationController =
      [self.splitViewController.viewControllers lastObject];
  currentDetailViewController = (RTDetailViewController *)
                      navigationController.topViewController;
}
else
   currentDetailViewController =
      [self.splitViewController.viewControllers lastObject];
  if (currentDetailViewController.
                              masterPopoverController != nil)

    [currentDetailViewController.masterPopoverController
                              dismissPopoverAnimated:YES];
```

If you're on the iPhone, you simply assign the delegate to the segue's `destinationViewController`.

```
DestinationController *destinationController =
              destinationSegue.destinationViewController;
destinationController.delegate = self;
```

Saving the Destination Choice and Selecting a Destination

At this point, if you were to run your project, you would be able to tap the Destination button, choose a destination, and see the data for either New York or San Francisco.

But you're not done yet.

First, if the application is terminated (and I mean terminated, not running in the background and relaunched), the user will find that the destination she selected has reverted to being the default one. You would like RoadTrip to be in position to save, and then restore, the user's destination preference. (In Chapter 11, you see how to default to the *first* destination in the plist. I mention in that chapter that I show you how to allow the user to *select* a destination in Chapter 20, and here you are.)

Start by adding the destinationPreference property to RTAppDelegate by adding the bolded code in Listing 20-12 to RTAppDelegate.h.

Listing 20-12:   Updating the RTAppDelegate Interface

```
#import <UIKit/UIKit.h>
@class Trip;

@interface AppDelegate : UIResponder
                          <UIApplicationDelegate>

@property (strong, nonatomic) UIWindow *window;
@property (nonatomic, strong) Trip *trip;
@property (nonatomic, strong) NSString *
                          destinationPreference;

- (void) createDestinationModel:(int)destinationIndex;

@end
```

Apple provides NSUserDefaults object — available to any app — that you can use to store user preferences, or any small data values that should be saved by your app. In this section, you use the NSUserDefaults object to save the destination preference, so if the user chooses "San Francisco" the first time they use the app, "San Francisco" will be the location used when the app is next launched.

Data is stored in the user defaults object as a key-value pair. The value will be the destinationPreference string (which will be @"0" or @"1". The key will be the static DestinationPreferenceKey that you should now add to RTAppDelegate.m, as shown by the bolded code in Listing 20-13.

Listing 20-13:   Updating the RTAppDelegate Implementation

```
#import "RTAppDelegate.h"
#import "Reachability.h"
#import "Trip.h"

static NSString *DestinationPreferenceKey =
                              @"DestinationPreferenceKey";

@implementation RTAppDelegate
```

You're adding a key (string) that you'll need to use when you save the preference.

What you would like to do is direct the user to select a destination rather than using the default one. I'll have you post an alert to the users that they need to do that. More elegant ways are available to get the users to select the initial destination, but I'll leave that as an exercise for the reader.

Start by adding the bolded code in Listing 20-14 to `viewDidLoad` in `RTMasterViewController.m`.

Listing 20-14:   Adding to viewDidLoad

```
- (void)viewDidLoad
{
  [super viewDidLoad];
  RTAppDelegate* appDelegate = [[UIApplication
            sharedApplication] delegate];
  self.title = appDelegate.trip.destinationName;
  UIImageView* imageView = [[UIImageView alloc]
      initWithImage:[appDelegate.trip destinationImage]];
  self.tableView.backgroundView = imageView;

  UISwipeGestureRecognizer *swipeGesture =
    [[UISwipeGestureRecognizer alloc] initWithTarget:self
                    action:@selector(handleSwipeGesture:)];
  swipeGesture.direction =
          UISwipeGestureRecognizerDirectionLeft;
  [self.view addGestureRecognizer:swipeGesture];
  self.findText.delegate = self;

  if(appDelegate.destinationPreference == nil) {
    UIAlertView *alert = [[UIAlertView alloc]
        initWithTitle:@"Welcome to Road Trip"
        message:@"Please select a Destination from the
                                      Road Trip Menu"

        delegate:nil
        cancelButtonTitle:@"OK"
        otherButtonTitles:nil];
    [alert show];
  }
}
```

As you can see, if the `appDelegate.destinationPreference` property is `nil`, you'll post the `Please select a destination from the Road Trip` menu alert.

Unfortunately, every time you compile and run your app (or launch it), you'll see the alert because you will never have anything other than `nil` in the `appDelegate.destinationPreference` property.

In Listing 20-15, you fix that problem. At application launch, you'll check to see whether a user preference is saved. If one is, you assign it to `destination Preference`. If no preference is saved, you leave that preference as `nil`, and the alert to the user to select a destination will be posted by the `RTMasterViewController`.

Add the bolded code in Listing 20-15 to `application:didFinishLaunc hingWithOptions:` in `RTAppDelegate.m` and delete the one line of code that's commented out in, bold, italic, and underline.

Listing 20-15: Updating application:didFinishLaunchingWithOptions:

```objc
- (BOOL)application:(UIApplication *)application
    didFinishLaunchingWithOptions:
                             (NSDictionary *)launchOptions
{
    … // previous code here
    self.destinationPreference = [[NSUserDefaults
            standardUserDefaults] objectForKey:Destination
            PreferenceKey];
    if ( self.destinationPreference == nil) {
        NSDictionary *currentDestinationDict = @
            {DestinationPreferenceKey: @"0"};
        [[NSUserDefaults standardUserDefaults]
                registerDefaults:currentDestinationDict];
    }
    else
        [self createDestinationModel:
                    [self.destinationPreference intValue]];
//[self createDestinationModel:0];

    return YES;
}
```

At application launch, you check an `NSUserDefaults` object to see whether an entry exists with a key of `DestinationPreferenceKey` (you added this previously in Listing 20-13):

```objc
self.destinationPreference =
    [[NSUserDefaults standardUserDefaults]
            objectForKey:DestinationPreferenceKey];
```

You use NSUserDefaults to read and store preference data to a defaults database, using a key value, just as you access keyed data from an NSDictionary. In this case, the preference is the destination.

NSUserDefaults is implemented as a *singleton,* meaning that only one instance of NSUserDefaults is running in your application. To get access to that one instance, I invoke the class method standardUserDefaults:

```
[NSUserDefaults standardUserDefaults]
```

standardUserDefaults returns the NSUserDefaults object. As soon as you have access to the standard user defaults, you can store data there and then get it back when you need it.

objectForKey: is an NSUserDefaults method that returns the object associated with the specified key, or nil if the key wasn't found.

Obviously, the first time the app is launched, no data is there, so you create a dictionary with the default value:

```
NSDictionary *currentDestinationDict =
  @{DestinationPreferenceKey: @"0"};
```

Note that you save the value as an NSString. That's because the NSUserDefaults requires a property list object.

You then send the NSUserDefaults object the registerDefaults message. This creates a new entry in the NSUserDefaults database that you can later access and update using the key you provided in the dictionary.

Because destinationPreference is still nil, when viewDidLoad executes, it will launch the Destination controller.

If a value exists in NSUserDefaults, you create the Destination model by sending the createDestinationModel: message with the value you had stored — which will be, as you will see, the index of the destination in the Destinations plist:

```
[self createDestinationModel:
                [self.destinationPreference intValue]];
```

Note that you use an NSString method intValue. This method returns the value in a string as an int, which is handy because that's what the createDestinationModel: method expects.

You also could've made the currentDestinationIndex an NSNumber. It's an object wrapper for any C scalar (numeric) type. It defines a set of methods that allow you to set and access the value in many different ways, including as a signed or unsigned int, double, float, BOOL, and others. Also,

NSNumber defines a compare: method to determine the ordering of two NSNumber objects.

If no destinationPreference exists, the user will see a blank Detail view with a default Master view (it looks a little different on the iPhone) and the alert asking her to select a destination. As I said, you have more elegant ways of doing this.

The last step in saving the Destination preference is actually storing destinationPreference itself, and you do that in createDestination Model:. Add the bolded code in Listing 20-16 to createDestination Model: in RTAppDelegate.m.

Listing 20-16:   Updating createDestinationModel:

```
- (void) createDestinationModel:(int)destinationIndex {

  NSString *selectedDestinationIndex =
      [NSString stringWithFormat: @"%i",destinationIndex];
  if(![selectedDestinationIndex
          isEqualToString:self.destinationPreference]) {
    self.destinationPreference = selectedDestinationIndex;
    [[NSUserDefaults standardUserDefaults]
         setObject:self.destinationPreference
         forKey:DestinationPreferenceKey];
  }
self.trip = [[Trip alloc] initWithDestinationIndex:destina
          tionIndex];
}
```

You start out in Listing 20-16 by converting the destinationIndex parameter to a string and comparing it to see whether the Destination preference is the same as the one just selected by the user. (The user may have chosen the same destination again in the Destination controller):

```
NSString *selectedDestinationIndex =
      [NSString stringWithFormat: @"%i",destinationIndex];
if(![selectedDestinationIndex
          isEqualToString:self.destinationPreference]) {
```

If the destination isn't the same, you assign the new value to the destinationPreference:

```
self.destinationPreference = selectedDestinationIndex;
```

and then you save the new value in NSUserDefaults:

```
[[NSUserDefaults standardUserDefaults]
    setObject:self.destinationPreference
                   forKey:DestinationPreferenceKey];
```

To store data, you use the `setObject:forKey:` method. The first argument, `setObject:`, is the object I want `NSUserDefaults` to save. This object must be `NSData`, `NSString`, `NSNumber`, `NSDate`, `NSArray`, or `NSDictionary`. In this case, `savedData` is an `NSString`, so you're in good shape.

The second argument is `forKey:`. To get the data back (and for `NSUser Defaults` to know where to save it), you have to be able to identify it to `NSUserDefaults`. You can, after all, have a number of preferences stored in the `NSUserDefaults` database, and the key tells `NSUserDefaults` which one you're interested in.

Next, you create the model passing in the destination index:

```
self.trip = [[Trip alloc]
            initWithDestinationIndex:destinationIndex];
```

Displaying the Destination Table

One remaining problem is that the Destination table should appear automatically when the user dismisses the `UIAlertView` — the one that displays the "Welcome to Road Trip" message the first time the app is launched. The best way to handle this is to provide a method that will be called when the Alert is dismissed by the user, and then display the Destination table in that method. Here are the steps to do that:

1. Add `UIAlertViewDelegate` to the `RTMasterViewController`'s comma-separated list of delegates in `RTMasterViewController.h`.

2. Designate the `RTMasterViewController` as the `UIAlertViewDelegate` by adding the line of code shown in Listing 20-17 to the `viewDidLoad` method in `RTMasterViewController.m`.

3. Add the `alertView:clickedButtonAtIndex:` method to `RTMasterViewController.m`. The simple code shown in Listing 20-18 displays the Destination table as desired.

Listing 20-17: Designating the Master View Controller as the Alert Delegate

```
- (void) createDestinationModel:(int)destinationIndex {
… // previous code
if(appDelegate.destinationPreference == nil) {
    UIAlertView *alert = [[UIAlertView alloc]
        initWithTitle:@"Welcome to Road Trip"
        message:@"Please select a Destination from the
                            Road Trip Menu"

        delegate:nil
```

(continued)

Listing 20-17 *(continued)*

```
        cancelButtonTitle:@"OK"
        otherButtonTitles:nil];
    alert.delegate = self;
    [alert show];
}
```

Listing 20-18:   Displaying the Destination Table

```
- (void)alertView:(UIAlertView *)alertView
        clickedButtonAtIndex:(NSInteger)buttonIndex {
[self performSegueWithIdentifier:@"Destination"
        sender:self];
}
```

Testing

You're done. Run your app and test your work.

To test this part of your app, you need to first stop it in the Simulator (or device) by clicking the Stop button on the Xcode toolbar. Then remove RoadTrip from the background by following these steps:

1. **Double-click the Home button to display the applications running in the background.**

2. **Select the RoadTrip icon and hold down the mouse button until the icon starts to wiggle.**

3. **Click the Remove button, the red circle with the X that appears in the upper-left corner of the icon.**

4. **Run your app.**

To test this part of your app again later, you need to first stop it in the Simulator (or device) by clicking the Stop button on the Xcode toolbar. Then remove RoadTrip and its user defaults from the device by following these steps:

1. **Press and hold the RoadTrip icon until it wiggles.**

2. **Click the app Delete icon, the circle with the X that appears in the upper-left corner of the icon.**

3. **Press the Delete button when asked if you should delete the app and all of its data.**

4. **Build and run your app again, with the default** `destination Preference` **again set to nil. This gives you a fresh start.**

Adding Destination Support to the iPhone Storyboard

Your goal is to add a Destination scene to your iPhone storyboard in the same way that you added one to your iPad storyboard file. Follow the same directions for creating the Destination Controller scene for iPad storyboard. Steps include the following:

1. **Drag a** `UIViewController` **into the iPhone storyboard.**

2. **Use the Inspector to change the class name to** `DestinationController`, **and the Storyboard ID to Destination.**

3. **Drag a Model segue from the Destination table cell in the** `RTMasterViewController` **to the** `DestinationController`. **Set the segue ID to Destination.**

4. **Add the Navigation bar, and then place a Cancel button in it.**

5. **Choose the** `DestinationController`**'s cancel action for the Cancel button.**

6. **Add a** `UIImageView` **with an image.**

7. **Add a Label "Pick a Place, Anyplace."**

8. **Add a Table view.**

9. **Set the Table view's delegate and** `dataSource` **to be the** `DestinationController`.

10. **Format the Table View cell as described earlier in the chapter.**

The resulting layout is shown in Figure 20-3.

The good news is that you don't have to change your Objective-C code at all — the same `DestinationController` code works fine.

A Word about Adding Settings

Although space doesn't allow me to show you how to implement settings — for example, letting the user choose whether she wants to hear the car sound when she taps the Test Drive button, or to change the speed of the car — you implement such settings in exactly the same way that you just implemented the Destination preference. You add a setting to `NSUserDefaults` and create an `RTAppDelegate` property that you check in the car animation messages, for example, before you play the sound. To get even more sophisticated, you could create a `Preferences` class, in the same way you create a `Trip` class, that manages all preferences and uses that rather than the `RTAppDelegate` to provide Preference data to the rest of your app.

Figure 20-3:
The Destination scene in the iPhone storyboard.

What's Next?

Although this point marks the end of your guided tour of iOS app development, it should also be the start — if you haven't started already — of your own development work.

Developing for the iPad is one of the most exciting opportunities I've come across in a long time. I'm hoping that it ends up being as exciting for you.

Do keep in touch, though. Check out my website, www.nealgoldstein.com, on a regular basis. There you can find the completed RoadTrip Xcode project.

Finally, keep having fun. I hope I have the opportunity to download one of your applications from the App Store someday.

Part VI
The Part of Tens

In this part . . .

Neal once had a boss who liked to hire smart-but-lazy people. He figured that if he gave them a hard job, they'd find an easy way to do it.

In this part, you see some ways to (first) avoid doing more work than you have to and (second) avoid redoing things because you outsmarted yourself. You also see how to take the RoadTrip app further and create an app that you can really sell (and people will want to buy) in the App Store.

Chapter 21

Ten Ways to Extend the RoadTrip App

In This Chapter

▶ Discovering some additional features for the RoadTrip app

▶ Making structural improvements to the app

▶ Creating an application ecosystem

Although the example app developed in this book — the RoadTrip app — has the basic structure and features that you would include in a commercial app of this type, you would have some additional tasks to take care of if you intended to make it a true, viable commercial application.

Of course, you would have to add more content to the app. You would also need to add more features, as well as strengthen the basic structure a bit.

In this chapter, I suggest some additions you would need to give RoadTrip to make it a commercial success.

Add Preferences

If you go international, roaming charges could make your app prohibitively expensive to use, and the user may want to turn off those features that use the Internet in your app. The app also has some features (see an example in the upcoming section, "Monitor the Current Location's Distance from the Destination") that the user may want to use only under certain circumstances, such as tracking and notifying you of how far away your are from your final destination or a specified location (or even the wonderful car sound). To make for happy users, you want to program any optional features to be present based on a preference setting — and enable setting preferences both through the Settings application as well as in the RoadTrip app.

Cache Data

If you allow users to turn off Internet access, or if the user is someplace where Internet service isn't available, you need to add the logic to RoadTrip to cache data (such as events). Then, when Internet access isn't available or the user doesn't want to use the Internet, RoadTrip will use the cached data.

Monitor the Current Location's Distance from the Destination

In other books and in my classes, I show developers how to add a fun feature to the RoadTrip app. When the user shakes the device, a semitransparent window drops from the top of the screen and displays the distance for either a found location or the final destination. You add this feature by using the accelerometer and core location frameworks.

If the user finds this feature annoying — and because this added feature can chew up the battery life — you want to offer the user the option to toggle it on and off. See the earlier section "Add Preferences."

Post to Facebook and Twitter

Unless you're living under a rock, you know that social networking apps are all the rage. Apple added Twitter support in iOS 5 and has expanded social network support even further with the Social Framework in iOS 6. The Social Framework includes support for Facebook.

Send Postcards from the Road

In some of my applications, I have a postcard feature. It would be nice in RoadTrip to allow the user to take a photo and attach it to an e-mail to make all her friends jealous.

Add Hotels and Reservations

A great feature to include in the RoadTrip app is to allow the user to add hotel reservations. You keep track of them in the app by enabling the user to add a reservation to her calendar, a hotel to the address book, and so on.

Create an Itinerary

You can build in a feature in the app that helps the user plan his trip. Enable the user to add his own points of interest and create an itinerary. You should be able to see the itinerary both as a list view and plotted on the map.

Make the App Part of an Application Ecosystem

As I mention in Chapter 1, you want to do the right task on the right device. Although the iPad is the perfect device for both planning and going on your trip, the iPhone is great to use when you're actually traveling. That's why it's always a good idea to consider creating a universal app, as you have done with the Road Trip example app.

It's Never Early Enough to Start Speaking a Foreign Language

With the world growing even flatter and the iPhone and iPad available worldwide, the potential market for your app is considerably larger than just among people who speak English. Localizing an application isn't difficult, just tedious. While you obviously can't implement all the features in your app all at once (that is, some have to be done later than others), when it comes to localizing the strings you use in your application, you had better build them right — and build them in from the start. The painless way is to use the `NSLocalizedString` macro from the very start (the one I explain in Chapter 13), and you'll still be a happy camper at the end.

Provide Some Implementation Enhancements

You could definitely tighten up some of the implementation code in the RoadTrip app. Some of the things I did (or didn't do) in the book were intentional to make the initial app building easier for you to follow. To remedy the less-than-stellar structure that came about as a result, here are a few things you could add on your own:

- ✓ Because both the Event Page controller and the Weather controller use a Web view, you could create a Web view superclass that implements all the Web view functionality.

- ✓ Because `Trip` is designed to be a singleton, you could add a class method to `Trip` that returns a reference to itself so that you don't have to go through the App Delegate every time.

- ✓ I also recommend putting all your constants into a single file and replacing all hard-coded values with constants as well. As you change, or experiment with, those values during the development process, having *one* place to find constants makes life much easier.

Chapter 22

Ten Ways to Be a Happy Developer

Think of all the things you know you're supposed to do but don't because you think they'll never catch up with you. Not that many people probably enjoy balancing the checkbook or cleaning out gutters, and after all, not flossing won't cause you problems until your teeth fall out years from now (right?).

But in iOS app development, those *mañana* gotchas will catch up with you early and often, so I want to tell you about what I've learned to pay attention to from the very start in app development, as well as give you a few tips and tricks that lead to happy and healthy users.

Keep Things Loosely Coupled

A *loosely coupled* system is one in which each of its components has little or no knowledge (or makes no use of any knowledge it may have) of other components. And because loose coupling refers to the degree of direct knowledge that one class has of another, it's not about encapsulation or to one class's knowledge of another class's attributes or implementation, just knowledge of that other class itself.

I explain loose coupling more in Chapter 11.

Remember Memory

iOS does not store "changeable" memory (such as object data) on disk to free space and then read it back in later when needed. This means that running out of memory is easy, and you should use automatic reference counting (ARC) to make the most of the memory available to you. All you have to do is follow the rules:

- ✔ **Rule 1:** Follow the naming conventions. This is really important. Good naming conventions help your code to be self-documenting. Sloppy, lazy, lethargic, sluggish, careless programmers who don't take the time to follow the naming conventions will be dealt with harshly!

- ✔ **Rule 2:** Do not send `retain`, `release`, or `autorelease` messages.

- ✔ **Rule 3:** Do not store object pointers in C structures.

- ✔ **Rule 4:** Inform the compiler about ownership when using Core Foundation–style objects.

- ✔ **Rule 5:** Use the `@autoreleasepool` keyword to mark the start of an autorelease block.

If you follow the rules, all you have to worry about is the retain cycle. This cycle occurs when one object has a back pointer to the object that creates it, either directly or through a chain of other objects, each with a strong reference to the next leading back to the first. Use the `weak` lifetime qualifiers for objects and the `weak` property attribute.

But even if you do everything correctly, in a large application, you may simply run out of memory and need to implement the methods that `UIKit` provides to respond to low-memory conditions, as follows:

- ✔ Override the `viewDidUnload` and `didReceiveMemoryWarning` methods in your custom `UIViewController` subclass.

- ✔ Implement the `applicationDidReceiveMemoryWarning:` method of your application delegate.

- ✔ Register to receive the `UIApplicationDidReceiveMemoryWarning Notification:` notification.

Don't Reinvent the Wheel

The iPhone and iPad are cutting-edge enough that opportunities to expand their capabilities are plentiful, and many of them are (relatively) easy to implement. You're also working with a very mature framework. So if you think that something you want your app to do is going to be really difficult, check the framework; somewhere there you may find an easy way to do what you have in mind.

For example, I once needed to compute the distance between two points on a map. So I got out my trusty trig books, only to find out later that the `distanceFromLocation:` method did exactly what I needed.

Understand State Transitions

The `UIApplication` object provides the application-wide control and coordination for an iOS application. It is responsible for handling the initial routing of incoming user events (touches, for example) as well as dispatching action messages from control objects (such as buttons) to the appropriate target objects. The application object sends messages to its Application Delegate to allow you to respond, in an application-unique way, when your application is executing, to things such as application launch, low-memory warnings, and state transitions, such as moving into background and back into foreground.

You should implement the following `UIAppDelegate` methods in your application. Most of these methods are already basically implemented in the code provided by Apple's templates, complete with comments explaining their purposes.

Method	What You Do with It
`application:didFinish LaunchingWithOptions:`	In this method, do what you need to do to initialize your application after it's launched.
`applicationWill ResignActive:`	This message is sent when the application is about to move from the active to inactive state. Use this method to do things such as pause ongoing tasks and anything based on a timer (such as a game). Using this method doesn't mean that you will be entering background, but it does mean that your application won't be executing.

Method	What You Do with It
`applicationDidEnter Background:`	This message is sent when your application is going to be entering background. At this point, you need to assume that your application may eventually be terminated without warning, so save user data, invalidate timers, and store enough application state information.
`applicationWillEnter Foreground:`	This message is sent when your application has been rescued from background. In this method, reverse what you did in `applicationDidEnterBackground:`.
`applicationDidBecome Active:`	Your application is now active. You should reverse whatever you did in `application WillResignActive:`. You also might want to refresh the user interface.

Do the Right Thing at the Right Time

When it comes to the view controller, you need to be aware of two methods, and you need to know what to do in each method.

The `viewDidLoad` message is sent to a view controller when the view has been loaded and initialized by the system. It is sent only when the view is created — and not, for example, when your app returns from background or when a view controller is returned to after another view controller has been "dismissed."

The `viewWillAppear:` message, on the other hand, is sent whenever the view appears, including when the view reappears after another view controller is "dismissed."

Do view initialization in `viewDidLoad`, but make sure that anything you do to refresh a view whenever it appears is done in `viewWillAppear:`.

Avoid Mistakes in Error Handling

Opportunities for errors abound; use common sense in figuring out which ones you should spend time on. For example, don't panic over handling a missing bundle resource in your code. If you included it in your project, it's supposed to be there; if it's not, look for a bug in your program. If it's *really* not there, the user has big problems, and you probably won't be able to do anything to avert the oncoming catastrophe.

Having said that, here are two big potential pitfalls you do have to pay attention to:

- ✔ Your app goes out to load something off the Internet, and (for a variety of reasons) the item isn't there, or the app can't get to it. You especially need to pay attention to Internet availability and what you're going to do when the Internet isn't available.

- ✔ A geocoder may fail for any number of reasons. For example, the service may be down, a certain GPS coordinate may not have a street address, or the user may access the data before the geocoder has returned.

Use Storyboards

Storyboards are a great way to examine the flow of the application as a whole. In addition, they require you to use less code. They are one of my favorite parts of Xcode 4.3 and iOS 5.0 and above, and I use them in all my apps.

Remember the User

I've been singing this song since Chapter 1, and I'm still singing it now: Keep your app simple and easy to use. Don't build long pages that take lots of scrolling to get through, and don't create really deep hierarchies. Focus on what the user wants to accomplish, and be mindful of the device limitations, especially battery life. And don't forget international roaming charges.

In other words, try to follow the Apple iOS Human Interface Guidelines, found with all the other documentation in the iOS Dev Center website at `http://developer.apple.com/devcenter/ios` in the iOS Developer Library section. Don't even *think* about bending those rules until you really, *really* understand them.

Keep in Mind That the Software Isn't Finished Until the Last User Is Dead

One thing that I can guarantee about app development is that nobody gets it right the first time. The design for RoadTrip (the example app in this book) evolved over time as I learned the capabilities and intricacies of the platform and the impact of my design changes. Object orientation makes extending your application (not to mention fixing bugs) easier, so pay attention to the principles.

Keep It Fun

When I started programming for the iPhone and iPad, it was the most fun I'd had in years. Keep things in perspective: Except for a few tedious tasks (such as provisioning and getting your application into the Apple Store), expect that developing iOS apps will be fun for you, too. So don't take it *too* seriously.

Especially remember the *fun* part at 4 a.m., when you've spent the last five hours looking for a bug.

Index

Notes